The ASHES

A CELEBRATION

ALSO BY ROLAND PERRY

Cricket
Bradman's Best
Bradman's Best Ashes Teams
The Don
Miller's Luck: The Life and Loves of Keith Miller, Australia's
Greatest All-rounder
Captain Australia: A History of the Celebrated Captains of
Australian Test Cricket
Bold Warnie
Waugh's Way
Shane Warne: Master Spinner

Others
Monash: The Outsider Who Won a War
Last of the Cold War Spies
The Fifth Man
The Programming of the President
Elections Sur Ordinateur
Mel Gibson, Actor, Director, Producer
The Exile: Wilfred Burchett, Reporter of Conflict
Lethal Hero
Programme for a Puppet (*fiction*)
Blood is a Stranger (*fiction*)
Faces in the Rain (*fiction*)

Documentary films
The Programming of the President
The Raising of Galleon's Ghost
Strike Swiftly
Ted Kennedy and the Pollsters
The Force

The ASHES

A CELEBRATION

ROLAND PERRY

RANDOM HOUSE AUSTRALIA

Chapters 4 and 9 based on material published in *Captain Australia* (RHA 2000)
Chapters 5, 7, 17 and 22 based on material published in *Bradman's Best Ashes Teams*
(RHA 2002)
Chapters 11, 12 and 13 based on material published in *Miller's Luck* (RHA 2005)

Random House Australia Pty Ltd
20 Alfred Street, Milsons Point, NSW 2061
http://www.randomhouse.com.au

Sydney New York Toronto
London Auckland Johannesburg

First published by Random House Australia 2006

National Library of Australia
Cataloguing-in-Publication Entry

Perry, Roland, 1946–.
The Ashes: a celebration.

Includes index.
ISBN 978 1 74166 490 4.
ISBN 1 74166 490 X.

1. Cricket – Australia – History. 2. Cricket – England –
History. 3. Test matches (Cricket) – Australia – History.
4. Test matches (Cricket) – England – History. I. Title.

796.35865

Cover design by Darian Causby/www.highway51.com.au
Front cover photos courtesy Getty Images
Typeset by Midland Typesetters, Australia
Printed and bound by Griffin Press, Netley, South Australia

10 9 8 7 6 5 4 3 2 1

To the memory of my grandfather, George Dutch, a Scot, who introduced me to the game, and who supported another Scot, Douglas Jardine, in the Bodyline furore.

CONTENTS

INTRODUCTION

There have been innumerable highlights and plenty of lowlights from which to celebrate the Ashes contest, the longest-running international sporting competition. A factor that has kept it as a fascinating event for 130 years is the number of sensational occurrences that have captivated public interest in the UK and Australia. So much so that an April 2006 survey by Newspoll Market Research found that a whopping 63 per cent of Australians considered the Ashes urn to be the nation's most valued team trophy. The soccer World Cup was second with 8 per cent, while cricket's World Cup (for one-day cricket) was third with 7 per cent.

The battle – and that is what the Ashes is – on the pitch had its roots in two vastly different countries and cultures in the late 1800s. The game had its beginnings in England after the Norman conquests. It was played in a primitive form by the wilder, younger members of society as early as the 13th century, when the nobility went in for more chivalrous activity such as hunting or jousting. It was transported with the convicts and prostitutes to Sydney in the late 1700s.

When England touring sides began coming to Australia, the colonialists were very keen to beat the centre of Empire to prove themselves better. It was a tolerated inferiority complex that the British did not take too seriously, until they were beaten. When the first Australian team toured in 1868, the novelty of an Aboriginal team (led by Englishman Charles Lawrence) attracted crowds everywhere they played. At Lord's there was nearly a major embarrassment when the team should have beaten the much-vaunted Marylebone Cricket Club. It was only prevented by some inexperience in a tight finish.

That wonderful, gruelling tour of mixed standard and high drama, which captured public imagination, was the precursor to international cricket, and the Ashes.

In March 1877 an Australian team beat England at the MCG in the first ever international cricket match (although officially Australia was still a loose collection of colonies, not federated until 1901). It only raised eyebrows from those reading the account of the game in England. Seeing was believing. When Australia beat England by 7 runs in a thriller at the Oval in 1882, the international contest definitely had a life, at least until the Colonialists were again well and truly belted regularly. That never happened. All the colonies celebrated the 1882 victory against the seat of Empire inside its own bastion. For those wishing to break from the mother country and see a nation formed, it was a huge inspiration. Even a young John Monash, who went on to be the finest battle commander of World War I, celebrated that seminal victory by Will Murdoch and his team, despite not being a great cricket fan.

The Ashes competition was born.

From the beginning, it was a more or less even competition, which drew out the best and worst of each side. And while it was not dominated by either nation, it was tolerated by the British ruling class through several decades in which Australia was formed and came of age as a nation that produced the most effective Army on the Western Front in the 1914–1918 World War.

England had produced the finest cricketer in Dr W. G. Grace. He dominated the nineteenth century and never allowed the challengers from Australia to get on top of England regularly. But by 1930 all that changed with the emergence of Donald George Bradman. His complete domination of England in the 1930 Ashes summer superseded all that had come and gone before in 700 years, including the good Dr Grace. It was a humiliation too far for an Empire that had controlled every opponent in every area of life for 400 years.

Bradman had to be stopped. The Bodyline method of bowling was developed to cut him down to size, which it did. His batting average was reduced to about 57, which placed him for one series in Australia (1932–33) with the rest of the best bats in history. Bodyline was a one-Ashes wonder. It was banned and this allowed Bradman to dominate the game until 1948.

Post–World War II, post-Bradman, two players stood out for the second half of the 20th century. One was England's fine all-rounder Ian Botham. The other was Shane Warne, Australia's outstanding leg-spinner. They brought crowds back to the sport after the biggest threat ever to the Ashes – World Series Cricket – looked likely to usurp the game as it was previously constituted.

There have been numerous Tests that have captivated fans. The most celebrated in the first 100 years of England–Australia contests was the Centenary Test of 1977. It had everything in a titanic five day contest.

But one complete Ashes series ranks above all others in history – in England in 2005. It included four evenly fought games – three of them tight to the last ball. There were also amazing individual performances, notably by all-rounder Andrew Flintoff and Warne. After eight straight Ashes wins for Australia, the wheel turned.

My selection of the ten biggest impacts – events and individuals – in the history of the competition are:

1: The 2005 Ashes
2: The Lawrence-led Aborigine tour of England in 1868
3: W.G. Grace
4: The 1882 win by Australia at the Oval
5: Bodyline
6: Don Bradman
7: The 1977 Centenary Test
8: The Packer Revolution – World Series Cricket
9: Ian Botham
10: Shane Warne

The book also covers the four cricketing characters on whom I've written biographies: Don Bradman, Shane Warne, Steve Waugh and Keith Miller. Bradman figures strongly, partly because of our six-year association and partly because he had so much influence over Australian cricket for more than half a century. His decision to stop an all-white cricket team from touring Australia was one of the most momentous in sporting history, and this untold story is included. So is analysis of his selections of the best Ashes teams, and a world team, along with reactions from the media and public to Bradman's choices.

I believe Bradman may one day be remembered for his letter output nearly as much as for his performances as a cricketer. The book includes a story on our correspondence, discussions and meetings, which gives added insights to the man and his character.

Also featured is Steve Waugh, and the trouble his twin, Mark, and Warne had during the bribery and corruption period of the turbulent 1990s. Steve Waugh's thoughts are included in an exclusive interview. Profiles are added on other cricket greats: England's finest ever bowler, S. F. Barnes, and Australia's leading all-rounder, Keith Miller. An innings by the latter at Lord's in 1945 is one of the best played by an Australian in an international match. It deserved a chapter of its own.

Featured also is the unheralded but brilliant Victory Tests of 1945, in which Miller became a superstar of the game.

Warne is also a subject from the perspective of his life as a TV mini-series or movie. This was inspired by Warne's own life-imitates-art throwaway line when he said he thought his life was 'like a soap opera'. In fact, no film, mini-series or soapie could ever do justice to Warne's headline-grabbing life on and off the sporting arena. But I give clues to future dramatists.

Roland Perry, 2006

TITANIC STRUGGLE

Impact One: The Greatest Ashes and Beyond

It was the most hyped Ashes in history. Early in 2005, England was coming off a winning series in South Africa. Australia was firmly entrenched as the most successful cricket team in the world over at least a decade. All Britain knew that the big test was the Ashes for the summer of 2005. The England team had the form but a sizeable doubt about its real capacities. The British media began building the five Test contest as the battle of the heavyweights. Jingoism, and not just from the tabloids, was rife. Every paper had its commentators speculating and engaged in unabashed psychological warfare. Each Australia player was singled out and his abilities analysed. Real and imaged weaknesses were scrutinised in what seemed like an orchestrated campaign.

The British were looking to the team representing the national game to assert itself and bestow pride and reaffirmation of international supremacy. It was fervently hoped that this team would put the Great back into Britain. Belting the Aussies was a rare and wonderful event. England had last won the Ashes in 1986–87 when Mike Gatting led his team to victory down-under. England itself had not witnessed slaughter of the Aussies since 1985. A generation of British fans had grown up seeing, or choosing to turn their backs on, the national team being thrashed by Australia. Eight Ashes series in succession at home and away had seen that magnificent yet silly little urn of burnt bails – symbolically at least – in Australian hands.

On the other hand, Aussie supporters were over-confident. It was hard for them to be otherwise after such a long run of supremacy against all comers. They had read the propaganda many times before from their own media and that of opposition nations.

Cricket in the UK had slipped into obscurity and out of the national consciousness. Soccer had swamped everything – front page, back page and centre supplements too. Summer sports news on TV or radio rarely began with a cricket story. The Test team was associated with losing, especially to Australia, and no nation on the planet wished to be branded that way. Cricket fell away in the schools, especially the public (state) schools – the breeding ground for half the national team at its best in 1932–33, 1953, 1956, and 1981, remembered for Ian Botham's dominance. In the 1990s, the playing areas of 97 public schools around the country had been taken over for property development. There was no room for playing cricket, no incentive, and little support from the media for attempts at restoration. But by the late 1990s solutions to cricket's national malaise were being sought. Facts were faced. The British cricket hierarchy had to look to Australia's successful methods and copy them.

Two prime factors emerged. First, England needed a cricket academy run on Australian lines. Test players had to be isolated and supported to break the traditions of a debilitating county system. The best and brightest were put on fat contracts. Their county seasons were to take a distant second place. No longer would a player arrive drained at a Test arena having performed for his county until a couple of days before an international contest. A potentially fine all-rounder such as Andrew Flintoff could arrive fit and ready for a Test.

The second factor was former Australian wicket-keeper Rod Marsh, one of the toughest and best coaches and cricket motivators ever. He took over the fledgling Academy in 2000 on a A$250,000 annual contract. He was worth every cent and more. Marsh weeded out the uncommitted, did some straight talking to the half-hearted, and showed the way to become truly professional and fit enough to take on the Aussies. Marsh reckoned it would take five years to make a concerted challenge.

With these two developments, England began to improve. By early summer 2005, the Test team was as ready as it had ever been since 1953 to defeat Australia. Media hype and hysteria accompanied the build-up, yet there was substance in the record. England's coach, Duncan Fletcher – the optimist who looked like a grump – grabbed at England's win against Australia in the 2004 ICC Trophy semi-final at Edgbaston as proof that his team could topple the Aussies. Fletcher saw it differently from most other observers who wrote off the win – a one-day victory in September 2004 – as irrelevant to the coming 2005 Ashes. He thought the easy and even-handed win was a pointer to his team being capable. A more solid indicator was England's form throughout 2004. It did not lose a Test in 11 outings for 10 wins and a draw. It had also just come off a series win against South Africa away. Only Australia had done this (twice) since South Africa had come back into international cricket in the early 1990s.

Less convincing – even concerning – was the two Test series against weak Bangladesh before the 2005 Ashes summer. If anything, this was match-softening rather than Test match-hardening. Easy wins could precipitate complacency.

Australia's early form seemed to reinforce British hope. The tourists lost to England in a 20-over competition; a county (Somerset) beat them; and so did Bangladesh at Cardiff – all in limited overs games. This inspired the home team and the nation, as did the pre-match performance of Australia's Andrew Symonds. He was still affected by alcohol from a big night out. Ponting noticed his condition. Symonds was dumped from the team. Australia tried to cover up by saying the offender had 'a cold' but the media discovered his true condition. Was this careless indiscretion indicative of an attitude in the visitors' camp? Perhaps the Aussies were on the decline. Perhaps England, on the up, could actually defeat them. The media waded in even more feverishly than it had before the season began. The tabloids showed doctored shots of the Australians wearing handbags. London's *Daily Mirror*, whose editors had been gunning for Shane Warne for five years, pursued him relentlessly over some off-field sexploits, which caused his wife Simone to pack up in Southampton and take their three children back to Australia. England had long recognised him as the finest spinner in living memory. Warne, like actor Harrison Ford, had three off-field looks for the TV cameras – blank, happy and befuddled. The last was coming up more often on British screens with the news of his split with his wife. It was possible, every paper speculated, that he might be put off his game. But unlike the *Mirror*, no other press tried to smear him further. Warne took a couple of weeks off to sort out his troubles and vowed to be back for the Ashes.

In the meantime, the one-day triangular series between England, Australia and Bangladesh continued. Despite the poor start, Australia lined up against England in the final at Lord's on Saturday 2 July, and had the home team on the ropes at 5 for 33 in pursuit of Australia's modest 196. England's big four – Trescothick, Vaughan, Pietersen and Flintoff – had been shoved back in the hatch for very little on the scoreboard. Yet England recovered with grit and determination to squeeze a tie. Lord's reached a pitch of excitement unmatched in recent years, which indicated that the Ashes was going to be a hard fought affair. Neither heavyweight was going to go down for the count.

Then came the Natwest Challenge: three one-dayers between England and Australia. The 'supersub' was introduced for a trial, in which a 12th man could be played as an extra bowler or batsman. England won the first game with ease at Headingley. This would have been front page news but for an event that would sour the summer: during London's morning rush hour on 7 July, four bomb attacks struck the underground and a bus. Fifty-six people were killed, including the four suicide bombers, and another 700 were injured. It was the deadliest single act of terrorism in the UK since the 1988 bombing of Pan Am Flight 103, where 270 were killed. It was the worst bombing in London since World War II.

The nation was in shock trying to assess the impact, and whether there would be further attacks. There was speculation that the next one-dayer – at Lord's three days later – might not go on. The London underground was operating on most lines on 8 July, with a certain amount of tension amongst travellers, who were sobered by the thought that any one of them could have been victims the day before. Moving around beneath London's streets had a more than irksome extra dimension. Yet the great capital's life went on. Both teams said they would play at Lord's.

There was a precedent here. During World War II, not even the worst waves of bombing stopped cricket, especially at Lord's. It was then Government and MCC policy to keep playing in the face of Luftwaffe bombing and missile attacks. [In 1944, Keith Miller, playing for the RAAF at Lord's against the RAF, managed a dashing century while 'flying bombs' – missiles – were dropping close to the ground.] The Germans could not stop cricket, which was a propaganda victory for the British. Sixty-one years later, similar stoicism was needed, and indeed shown, in the wake of the suicide bombings.

At Lord's on 10 July, Australia came back in a fashion typical of the team over the past decade. They wiped England in the final two matches to take the trophy. Despite the propaganda, media ridicule and a retarded start, Australia had not been beaten in the two series played to that point in the summer. The thrashing of the home team had given the tourists momentum in the build-up to the Ashes contest.

The UK media went into a few weeks of self-doubt, introspection and shaky analysis. The Australian camp was still number one, and it still held the Ashes. The press was not yet ready to hand the handbags to the home team, but the tourists' gradual build to form was ominous.

Glenn McGrath proffered that he expected a 5-0 Australian

victory. It was the most telling remark in the spin stakes. The sound bite seemed arrogant and cocky, but he expressed a shrewd logic by saying he went into every Test believing he and his team would win. Coming from a man then one short of 500 wickets in Tests, the remarks had credibility. It followed that with this approach Australia should win with a clean sweep. Only McGrath or Warne amongst the players of both sides could make such a bold prediction with relative impunity. The comment brought British players out with defensive remarks about Warne being too old, and the Australians being bullies.

Kevin Pietersen recalled how, when playing grade cricket in Australia in 2002–2003, the English tourists 'copped it [put-downs, abuse, sledging] all day, every day, on chat shows, on adverts, on everything'. Now that he was playing for England (after leaving South Africa) he urged the British media and press 'to do the same to them'.

But the local media didn't need any encouragement. It had never been so one-eyed, with a passion bordering on hysteria. This season represented the best chance in two decades to win at home. No newspaper editor or journalist would die wondering if his or her efforts could assist the home team.

First Test: Lord's

By 21 July, the speculation, over-blown build-up and predictive opinion was silenced. It was the first day of the First Test at Lord's. The ground was packed, there was no breathing space in the Long-Room and emotions were high as a nervous England filed out to field after Ricky Ponting had won the toss and decided to bat under cloudy skies. It was a blessing for England to release its tensions and much-vaunted new aggression through their four-pronged bowling line-up in useful conditions for them. Tall Steve Harmison, who had been urged by all and sundry to 'give it to the Aussies', came out bowling with skill and fire. In the space of the first 45 minutes he hit

Justin Langer a painful blow on the elbow, Matty Hayden on the helmet and Ponting on the helmet grille. The England crowd and media had been baying for blood and now they had it. Ponting's dented grille lacerated his cheek. In the past, fielding teams would crowd around a struck batsman and offer sympathy, even if it were out of politeness rather than true feeling. Not this time. An over-pumped England was making a point it had never made before, except in the Bodyline series in Australia in 1932–33. In the Adelaide Test of that series, Douglas Jardine made the infamous remark to his top paceman, Harold Larwood: 'Well bowled, Harold!' after he had struck Australian skipper Bill Woodfull under the heart with a brutal short ball. It was again in 2005 the nearest thing to war on the pitch.

Meanwhile, at noon, Muslim terrorists were intending to do deliberate damage in their continuing real, if amorphous, war against Western society. Four attempted attacks hit underground stations and a bus: the same pattern of the atrocities committed two weeks earlier. London was again in near-chaos as many underground lines were closed and evacuated. Fortunately, this time the intended large-scale loss of life and injury did not eventuate. Only the detonators of bombs exploded and no one was injured.

Mobile phones ran hot at Lord's as the cricket continued. Management considered evacuating the ground, but decided against it when it was learned that there were no immediate threats to patrons. On the pitch, England stunned Australia by dismissing it for 190 before the end of the second session. The plan to throw everything possible at Australia had come off. Harmison had delivered the best spell of his career and had set a tone. He was well supported by Andrew Flintoff, Simon Jones and Matthew Hoggard. Almost all the plans for specific key batsmen had come off. England could not have wished for a better start to the Ashes.

The fans were delirious. Few, if any, observers would have expected such a startling beginning for England. The terrorists could do their worst outside, but all England supporters were staying in the confines of this arena in North London. Almost nothing could prevent them from seeing the national team performing beyond expectations.

McGrath, as if forced to back his 5-0 destruction of England claim, tempered England's premature celebrations by taking 5 wickets for 2 in the space of 32 balls of masterful bowling. England stumbled to 155. Australia's middle order then responded with enough runs to crush England by 239 runs.

Truths were driven home. Australia still held a psychological advantage against its ancient rival. England would struggle to win a Test if McGrath and Warne remained fit and in the touch they demonstrated at Lord's. Yet there were good signs for England. Its speed quartet dominated Australia's bats in the first innings and fought well in the second. Flintoff's dismissal of Adam Gilchrist cheaply, twice, would be significant if it registered a pattern. For the first time in decades, England's fielding was superior, although Geraint Jones behind the stumps left much to be desired. Perhaps the most telling factor was the unity of the home team. They were clearly all for one and one for all. This had been Australia's province for decades. Now England was a mirror image of their opponents. This was partly by training – the English management set out to copy the Aussie approach – and partly because the elite group was above the county system and not dependent on it. There was a greater sense of purpose and focus. Training together for years had bonded players with a common goal. They wanted to be judged the best in the world, which meant beating every team at home and abroad inside a space of three years.

***

What happened between the finish at Lord's and the Second Test at Edgbaston was indicative of the teams' attitudes and mindsets. A chastened, deflated yet far from defeated England spent a lot of time in the nets.

Perhaps Andrew Flintoff took the most instructive action. He had a little holiday in Devon with his wife Rachael and daughter Holly.

After that, he faced a bowling machine at Old Trafford under coaching from his manager and old-Lancashire team-mate, Neil Harvey Fairbrother. Finally, he had a consultation with sports psychologist Jamie Edwards. Flintoff was self-critical and down on himself after Lord's. He felt he let himself, the team and the nation down, especially with his batting, after being bowled for a duck by McGrath in the first innings and caught behind off Warne in the second for 3.

Edwards gave his usual advice: Flintoff should concentrate on the things he did when he was playing well. Edwards felt that Flintoff had put too much pressure on himself at Lord's.

According to Flintoff and Edwards in *Ashes Victory* (the team's book rendering of the series), at one point their consultation went like this:

Edwards: '[If you were the batsman facing] what would you learn about a bowler walking back to his mark with his head down?'

Flintoff: 'That I've got him.'

Edwards: 'What message would the bowler get if you were standing at the crease with your shoulders back and head held high?'

Flintoff: 'That I've got him.'

Edwards remarked that he had never met anyone of Flintoff's standing who was as humble. The psychologist reckoned that the Lancashire all-rounder would go on to be a legend because he was skilled at the game played between his ears.

Flintoff went away refreshed, physically and mentally.

The Australians preferred to play little cricket. They had every reason to believe that it was business as usual: they had taken control in the First Test. They thought that with continued pressure England would roll over as it had on every other occasion they could remember. There was no Steve Waugh in the team to recall the bad old days of the mid-1980s and an Ashes defeat. Each member of the Australian squad in 2005 had only ever known dominance and superiority over England, and every other nation. There was little or no room for self-doubt and only space for a justified optimism.

Second Test: Edgbaston

The press had held back after England's collapse in the one-dayers, but now it found scapegoats. Ex-players – that frustrated, ever growing group – with columns to fill with weighty headlines and lightweight opinions, hoed into the home team, calling for the chopping of young batsman Ian Bell (who managed scores of 6 and 8 in his first Ashes Test), and left arm spinner Ashley Giles, who didn't take a wicket at Lord's. Bell's reality check was predictable after coming to Lord's with a batting average of 297 following big innings against Bangladesh. But it would have been folly to dump the capable 23-year-old after just one game against the two best bowlers in the world. There had been precedents of such panic. In 1928–29 in Australia, selectors decided to drop 20-year-old Don Bradman after he scored just 18 and 1 at Brisbane in a losing First Test of the Ashes. That decision goes down as one of the least inspired in sport.

Yet England selectors did not lose their nerve. Giles, a whipping boy if things went even slightly off plan, had taken 22 wickets at 23.13 runs each in the previous summer against the West Indies. More significant was his taking Brian Lara, arguably the world's best batsman, three times in the series. Australia's preponderance of left-handers meant he had to be persevered with, especially as more spin-conducive pitches would come his way through the series.

***

Just before the game began, McGrath stood on a cricket ball while playing touch-rugby in a warm-up. He twisted his ankle and could not take part in the match.

One English journalist dubbed it 'the best ball of the match'. His prescience was remarkable. The England camp was relieved that one of their two tormentors would not be coming at them with that nagging, metronomic line and length, spiced with the unplayable delivery every over or so.

Before the England team had time to fully digest its good luck, it was given an even lovelier surprise: Ponting won the toss and decided to bowl. W. G. Grace's dictum, paraphrased, was always to bat, and if you had doubts about the pitch and conditions, think hard about it, and still bat. (A recent classic instance of this was Mark Taylor's courageous decision to bat on a heavily grassed, damp pitch after winning the toss at Old Trafford in 1997. Taylor's gamble paid off in a low-scoring affair and Warne wrapped up the game on the last day.)

Ponting did not ponder hard enough. When he canvassed opinion about what to do before the toss at Edgbaston, naturally the bowlers were happy to do their job, except for Warne. He was firmly for batting first. His attitude, which should have been his skipper's too, was to bat England out of the game and later in the game knock over the opposition on a wearing pitch. It was one of his specialties in Test cricket. But for reasons known only to the leader, England was sent in to bat to face an under-done Michael Kasprowicz, an out-of-form Jason Gillespie and an unpredictable Brett Lee – all on a perfect batting wicket under sunny skies that would provide no conditions for swing or movement. The fact that Ponting was without the finest strike bowler in history should have deterred him from such folly.

McGrath's injury was unavoidable. Ponting's decision was not.

It was as if he were giving England a helping hand back into the series. Some observers speculated that plonking England in against expectations was arrogance, especially without McGrath, but that has never been the Tasmanian's style. Others wondered if it was complacency, which was probably closer to the mark, especially after the easy win at Lord's.

Marcus Trescothick and Andrew Strauss took advantage of the wonderful strip and the wayward bowling, which was in stark contrast to McGrath's nagging accuracy. The Australians kept banging the ball in when the wicket was not speedy enough and they paid full toll. Within half an hour, the expectations for the series were turned on their head. The openers reached full confidence, as batsmen tend to do when nearly every stroke pierces the field. It was a terrific start to the Test for the home team as a big first innings score beckoned. Flintoff joined Pietersen in the middle of the innings and began to flay the already struggling bowlers in a century partnership that assured 400.

England finally reached 407 in just 79.2 overs, which represented a one-day pace of 5 an over. But this was a Test against the world's best. England had once more surprised itself, this time winning the first day's three sessions, rather than just two. Team confidence that soared until tea at Lord's, and was never restored, was now high again. The Australian camp was shell-shocked to a point, but that inner belief remained. On day two, this was shaken as the visitors struggled to 308 against steady contributions from all England's bowlers. Much maligned Giles snaffled key wickets in Ponting and Michael Clarke when they were set, thus justifying his selection.

The England batsmen, except for rollicking Freddie Flintoff (73), could not repeat their first innings spree and the side was rolled in the second dig for 182. Warne, in career-high form, was the destroyer. He out-thought his opponents, taking 6 for 46, giving him 10 for 162 for the match.

His dismissal of opener Andrew Strauss twice – for 48 and 6 – was typical of the Australian's attempt at mind-games. After bowling him in the first innings, Warne tormented Strauss when he padded up in the second innings.

'Hey, you're my new Daryll,' Warne called. This was in reference to South Africa's Daryll Cullinan, the former South African Test batsman who averaged 44 overall but just 12 against Australia. Warne had tied him up in Test and one-day cricket to the point that his technique deserted him whenever he faced Warne. He was invariably dismissed cheaply whether he defended, attacked or charged the leg-spinner. How Strauss reacted to this taunt was going to be a key to the Ashes outcome.

Lee was still more wayward than he would have liked in the

second innings, yet he showed fire and backed up the spinner, removing the other four batsmen.

This left Australia 282 to chase for victory.

Australia's openers began the chase well, but the middle order fumbled, then collapsed under serious pressure from all England's bowlers – especially the irrepressible Flintoff. He had looked fair with the ball at Lord's. Now he was menacing, accurate and difficult to keep out with his sleight-of-hand reverse swing, or the normal variety. His first over of hypnotic deliveries removed Langer and Ponting. After his disappointments at Lord's, his performance with bat and ball lived up to all expectations and more. Psychologist Edwards' words had hit the right note. Whatever beguiled Flintoff at Lord's was now forgotten.

Giles recalled his dismissals of Lara in 2004 and reckoned if he could remove the finest batsman – let alone left-hander – on the planet, then he had a good chance of dismissing any others. He again justified his place by removing under-rated Simon Katich and the magnificent Adam Gilchrist, the latter being the Australian England just had to remove in the middle order. In the past six years, Gilchrist had been the back-breaker for opposition bowlers. No matter what the score when he arrived at the wicket, he had more often than not performed the coup de grace with a quickfire innings ranging from 40 to the quickest (at the time) double hundred ever in Test cricket.

There were many aspects to Gilchrist's destructive nature with the bat. He was the fastest run-scorer in Test cricket. An hour of his mayhem left opposition sides demoralised; two hours would mean a win for Australia.

His average of around 50, along with his consistent pulverising of the opposition, made him a batsman of great impact. England had so far subdued him, thanks to Flintoff working to a plan in the First Test, and Giles in the Second. In the first innings at Edgbaston, Gilchrist had spent two hours – equivalent to a complete session – at the wicket to score a creditable 49 not out off 69 balls. Yet it was not Gilchrist the master-blaster, but a more cautious version of him, brought about by England's impressive scheming. They hemmed him in and didn't allow him to cut loose. And he ran out of partners. They were unsure of themselves, seeing the skill of England's combinations against them and the suppression of the world's number one striker.

In the second dig, Australia reached 7 for 137. The game seemed all over with the tourists still 144 short of England. Warne was at the wicket with Clarke. Australia was left at 8 for 175 at stumps after Harmison had bowled Clarke for a battling 30. Warne remained 20 not out at stumps on day three. The press and media from Australia and England wrote the tourists off as beaten.

***

Apart from being the most brilliant leg-spinner in half a century, Warne was also a player unfamiliar with capitulation and defeat. Without Warne saying it, there was a sense that he was lifting his rating, if that were possible, to compete with Flintoff, England's new superstar with bat and ball. Warne wished to demonstrate his prowess with the blade. He always had a natural technique, an excellent eye, timing and power but his cavalier attitude, fatigue or impatience often defeated him. Warne had a defence but he seemed to disdain it, much in the manner of a park cricketer. He had rarely played a rearguard innings, even if it were called for. He loved the up-and-under shot, even the hook against the quicks. More than anything, he loved to belt the spinners. And more often than not, he got himself out the way he loved to remove batsmen – with the jump down the wicket that would lead to a catch in the deep or even a stumping. Warne had never played for his batting average, which hovered around a far too modest 17 for much of his career. Now, in this 2005 series, he seemed intent on a fraction more control over the big shot as if he were mimicking his new best friend, Pietersen, and Flintoff – and of course, Gilchrist, who had blazed a trail for a new 21st century style of middle order batting. These three had a measured, intelligent brutality about them. They would settle in and then pick the right balls to smash. Once a bowler was rattled and submitting, they would step up the rate of big hits. Warne, in this second innings at Edgbaston, looked focused yet still belligerent. The situation was suitable for his bash and grab mentality, but with a more finely tuned concentration than was normally expected from him. With only three wickets left, defence against this strong attack was next to pointless. Warne hit four fours and two sixes in reaching 42 in 59 balls. There were fewer attempts to dominate Giles before it was feasible to do so. Warne still went for his shots but with better calibration.

His dismissal was as bizarre as it was disappointing. He stepped back on his stumps to an unthreatening Flintoff ball down leg-side. The sudden thrust back of Warne's leg was like the action of a player worried about stumping from a keeper standing up, when Jones was well back to the bowler, who was delivering at a top pace of 145 kph.

Warne trudged back to the pavilion looking more disappointed than usual. Being a consummate team player, he felt he was on the verge of greatness for the team – with the bat. He was getting on top of the strong five-pronged England attack, which few Australians would be able to claim for the series.

He left at 9 for 220. He and Lee had put on 45 in a pulsating link that had England's faint-hearted supporters, and even some of its hardier ones, concerned.

Kasprowicz strode out, his broad chest prominent and his bat seemingly ephemeral. He would never be called a complete bunny, but he had few pretensions to being a capable batsman. Yet still, he was someone who had had his moments with the bat, more than a MacGill or a Harmison. He came out to partner Lee, who had shown – in one-day cricket particularly – that he was capable of some demolition batting. Strike bowler Lee, despite scores in this series of 3, 8 and 6, would also have been inspired to show that he could bat. He was doing just that in this knock.

Australia was still 62 runs shy of victory. Not impossible, but in terms of cricket history and statistics, almost so. But then again, every so often, players, moments, and a little luck conspired to defy the inevitable. It was this possibility that kept fans glued to every delivery, both at the ground and through TV and radio broadcasts.

Lee toned down his tendency to thump the bowlers, but still played shots. Harmison looked to have Kasprowicz LBW, but Billy Bowden turned down a pleading, vociferous appeal. Was it the little bit of luck needed? The Australians certainly batted as if they were going for victory.

Vaughan had Harmison and Flintoff bowling. They were his two most potent strikers, although Jones could be bracketed with them. But they couldn't penetrate this last, desperate pair. The Edgbaston crowd grew quieter and quieter as the score mounted at a pace which suggested the game would be over after this pair had been together for an hour or less, one way or another.

It developed into one of the most nail-biting hours in the history of Test cricket. The justified strutting of the England players changed in this time as everyone became concerned. Then Kasprowicz sliced a Harmison delivery towards Jones at third man. Half the England players ran towards the bowler to congratulate him. But Jones misjudged the ball and missed the chance.

Several of the England players felt that this was it. They had lost the match, and the Ashes, near enough. Australia needed 15 runs for victory: they had wiped 47 off the target. The batsmen, in their own streaky way, were stretching for a win.

Vaughan, whose emotions had moved from his sleeve to his face, looked more than nervous after every ball. This was heart attack time for the England skipper. Still he clapped hands, urged concentration every delivery and prayed the ball would not come near him, airborne at least. He was the least reliable fielder on either side.

Fans at the ground reached for drinks, ruffled their hair, held their heads and looked increasingly edgy, even defeated.

Now it was 10 runs to win. British heads were dropping. Australian players remained in their seats in the dressing room, stuck in position because of a dodgy tradition about 'bad luck if you moved', which for silliness was somewhere near the myth of number

87 or 111 meaning misfortune. Yet as emotions grew and adrenalin pumped, rational behaviour slipped away. Only the batsmen, who would have to be more on edge than anyone, seemed somewhere near in control of themselves and the match's destiny.

At this point Harmison summed England's feeling and apparent plight in *Ashes Victory*:

'When they got down to 10, I believed that we had gone, and soon after I had gone. I was bowling OK but when I was standing in the field I was shaking. We'd already won the game in our minds. We'd put so much into it. I was thinking that if they won, from here it might be 5-0.'

Andrew Strauss told *The Times* (in December 2005):

'As they got closer, I was petrified of a catch coming, in case I dropped it. There is no doubt that we would not have come back from another defeat. To be frank, when they got within five runs or so I thought that was it.'

In other words, a few touches of Aussie fortune now might see McGrath's prediction come true: there would no way back from 2-0 down. Not against this team, with its brilliance, bullying, and cock-of-the-walk demeanour, which had been backed by performance against all comers from England for so long.

Australia edged to 3 runs from victory. Despite his acute worry and fatigue, Harmison managed to get a delivery to kick off a good length. Kasprowicz fended it off. The ball deflected from his right glove, which was off the bat. Geraint Jones took the catch down leg side. England went up and Bowden gave it out. Had there been a third umpire to turn to, it would have been given not out: the offending glove had to be on the bat to effect a catch. But it all happened too quickly for the naked eye and the euphoria of the England players swamped any doubt that the umpire may have had.

England had won by 2 runs, the smallest margin in Ashes history. It had been one of the most thrilling finishes ever.

A telling moment occurred when Flintoff approached a crouching Lee, who remained 43 not out after giving full commitment to winning, and shook his hand. The Englishman, showing unusual sportsmanship and character in a moment where he could have been forgiven for jigging with his team-mates, put his left hand on Lee's shoulder, and said, 'Well played, mate, bad luck.'

The photograph of this moment would become the symbol of the 2005 Ashes.

Andrew Strauss summed up the mood in the England dressing room after the closest of shaves:

'There wasn't a great feeling of joy . . . We were not so much deflated but still in shock. There was a "thank God we haven't mucked it up" kind of mood. People were just staring into space, emotionally drained and just not knowing what to say. It really took a few hours to sink in.'

***

What penetrated those stunned England minds was the fact that the series was 1-all and they were well in the fight. McGrath's prediction of a clean sweep, much to the joy of all the UK, had been washed away. England was back in the series with three Tests to play. What's more, the momentum was with the home side. Its bats were finding form; its bowlers had been steady and had improved as a group force since Lord's, with less reliance on devastation from Harmison. By contrast, Australia's bowlers, except for Warne, struggled in England's first innings, and could not stop the onslaught. The fielding of both sides had been ordinary with poor catching. Vaughan had led well under pressure, but Ponting's decision to bowl first, coupled with McGrath's injury, had cost Australia the Test.

The two stand-out players for the game were Flintoff and Warne. Flintoff was more effective with the bat, but Warne took the honours with the ball. England's win gave the Englishman a well-deserved man-of-the-match. Flintoff would not need to see the team psychol-ogist again. His head was in the right place, his confidence was up and the lapse at Lord's was all but history.

Those searching for some clues, other than in chicken entrails, for how the series might now unfold could well have detected a special attitude from Strauss. He felt Warne had made him look a fool when he padded up to him and was bowled. He did not appreciate the 'Daryll' comment either, which was meant to engender Steve Waugh's infamous 'mental disintegration'. Instead, it was a spur for Strauss. 'I had to change', he told *The Times*.

His method of adjustment was to face a bowling machine – 'Merlyn' – for hours during which he refused to pad up or use his pads to defend.

'Because of his line,' Strauss noted, 'and the way he uses the crease, Warne gets so much spin and drift. I couldn't just leave balls. If he has a hold on you, he will try his variations and put you under pressure.'

Easier said than done. Many batsmen had decided something similar rather than get caught in Warne's web of intrigue where he 'managed' batsmen and mentally undermined them in the process.

Around nine million viewers in England and Australia, not to mention the countless 'neutral' viewers in Asia and elsewhere, had witnessed the titanic struggle and finish. Fans in England and Australia – even those who had only a passing interest in the game – now looked forward to the next encounter just four days away.

FIGHT TO THE END

Third Test: Old Trafford

Australia surprised by bringing back McGrath, who replaced Kasprowizc. The lean superstar had torn two ligaments in his ankle, but was judged fit to play. England, looking for some spin on this inclusion, reckoned that Australia was desperate if it was bringing back an injured player, no matter how great he was.

Michael Vaughan won the toss for the first time and was delighted to bat. Then he led from the front with a superb innings of 166 off 215 balls in a 281 minute stay at the crease in England's good 444 tally. There were other contributors, but a pleasing effort for the home team came from Bell with a patient, stylish half century. England's judgment on McGrath's playing was accurate. His rhythm was upset and his stride was impeded. His figures of 0 for 86 were indicative of his reduction to an ordinary performer, at least in the first innings.

Australia's mediocre response of 302 was brought about by some fine bowling by Jones (6 for 53) and some brutal hitting by Warne, who continued to impress with the bat in the manner of Pietersen and Flintoff. They would always rely on force over finesse, and Warne matched them in this performance. His 90 was off 122 balls with 11 fours and a six. In England's second innings, Andrew Strauss (106) found his true touch after six attempts to register a century, while Bell compiled another confidence-gathering 50. Strauss had been bowled by Lee for just 6 in the first innings and the batsman did not get a chance to see if his hard work with the bowling machine against leg-breaks and variations of the art had paid off. But in the second innings he had to face Warne, who sent down the most overs – 25. For the first time in the series, Warne could not secure a wicket or a breakthrough. Strauss' hard work and diligence had brought exceptional dividends for his team, and his personal confidence.

The opener's effort allowed Vaughan to declare before the end of day four at 6 for 280, thus setting Australia the massive task of scoring 423 for victory. No Ashes team had ever managed such a target in the last innings of a match in 128 years of competition. But Ponting and his team would go for a win, if the chance arose. The openers survived the evening to be 0 for 24, and Australia faced the huge challenge of scoring at more than 4 an over for three sessions to snatch it.

England expected a win, if not a huge battle. The public responded. Fans started queuing up at 3 am. The 'house full' sign – indicating nearly 24,000 people at Old Trafford – was put out at 8.30 am. Perhaps another 15,000 – even 20,000 – swirled around the ground, unable to get tickets. The match had attracted more than 100,000 for the first time at this ground.

Ponting, in a brilliant captain's knock, provided the innings' mainstay with a performance that lasted just under seven hours. All his partners (except for Gilchrist with 4 runs in 30 balls) managed some sort of start in the face of masterful bowling from Flintoff and Harmison, with tenacious support from Hoggard and Jones.

With Ponting and Clarke travelling well and only five wickets down, Australia seemed to have a real chance. But the Clarke (39) dismissal at 6 for 263 meant Australia was 160 short of victory with just four wickets in hand. It was time to play for a draw.

In walked Gillespie, a consummate blocker. One run later, he returned to the pavilion after Hoggard had trapped him LBW for a duck. Warne, who would normally have preceded Gillespie, arrived at the crease unable to consider a defensive innings, not with 27 overs still to be bowled. In the back of Warne's mind was a rate of 5.5 runs an over for victory. With Ponting up the other end, he reckoned Australia could still pinch the game. Warne played sensibly, restraining his desire to slog. At one point in the partnership, Australia looked to have a chance of pulling off a sensational, history-making win. But Flintoff, Australia's main antagonist, removed Warne caught behind for 34 at 340, still 83 short. Ponting, already tired from nearly seven hours at the crease, had to change gear with just two wickets left. When Harmison removed him for 156 at 354, last man in McGrath joined Lee.

Australia was 68 short of England with just 24 balls left. That ruled out any chance of an Australian win. The only options left were an England victory or survival for Australia – and a draw. This was once more a nail-biter as England threw everything at the last pair. Again, the home team needed just one wicket to win, but found it tough to secure. The last batting pair showed grit as the number of deliveries ticked down on the scoreboard.

Lee once more proved to have nerve and skill in a tight finish. He stuck it out for 25 deliveries to be 18 not out, while McGrath faced 9 nerve-tingling balls to see out a draw.

Australia was left on 9 for 371 – 41 short.

***

Fans at the ground and around the world had now experienced a second successive thriller. This one lasted all day, compared to the one session on the last day at Edgbaston. Each Test seemed to be a step up in excitement. The importance to the attraction of cricket could not be measured, especially in England. Fans had fallen off because of the national team's failures until recent years. In Australia, too, lopsided series were not always attracting the numbers administrators would have wished at Tests.

Lee and McGrath were all smiles as they left the field after surviving a torrid finish, as were the rest of the Australians in the dressing room. Vaughan gathered his men before they departed the pitch in an attempt to lift morale. He pointed out the joy in the opposition camp at managing a draw, not a win. He added that England was on top for most of the game and would take further momentum into the next Test.

After three matches in this enthralling Ashes battle, patterns were emerging. All England's top six batsmen had found some form. Each member of its speed attack was contributing and keeping constant pressure on the opposition. The most telling individual battle was proving to be Flintoff versus Gilchrist. The Englishman had now removed him three times in six innings, and the great Australian striker had been nullified for the first time in his all too short, illustrious career.

In general, the home combination was proving a strong, unified group. Australia, on the other hand, had problems in its top batting six. Langer was solid and Ponting was in touch. But Hayden, Martyn, Katich and Gilchrist were not doing enough. Warne was bowling as well as ever, and was the only consistent menace to England. McGrath had taken five of England's six wickets to fall in its second dig. But there was not the penetration he managed at Lord's, especially early in a batsman's knock. His ankle injury had brought him back from the best performer in the competition to 'good and competitive'. Lee was battling well but also loose and expensive. The required pressure had not been exerted on the England bats, especially with the fourth bowler Gillespie out of touch. The three Tests had provided enough information to suggest a trend.

England was now a better-than-even-money bet to take the Ashes.

Fourth Test: Trent Bridge

The chances of England winning its first Ashes in nine attempts were lifted significantly in the hour before play commenced on 25 August at Trent Bridge, in a replica of the build to the start of play at Edgbaston. McGrath had an injured elbow that ruled him out of the game at the last moment, and England was able to bat first for the third successive time after Vaughan won the toss.

England batted steadily despite rain interruptions, but it wasn't until Flintoff and Geraint Jones (a solid 85 that helped balance his horrid time behind the stumps) came together on day two that it climbed on top. Flintoff seemed to be building to something and this was the innings to remember. Here was a superlative example of power over technique from a man who did not lack the latter. His 102 took 132 balls and included 14 fours and one six. Most important was the impact. Australia was stunned and deflated by seeing England's score balloon to 477 – the highest of the series. Ponting could not stop the onslaught and Australia was reduced to defence with out-riders patrolling the boundaries, and few in catching positions. The captain seemed an option short all innings and even brought himself on for six overs in which he removed his opposite number, Vaughan. Warne always maintained some pressure, but without McGrath at the other end, he too was vulnerable at times.

Flintoff had done to the Australians what Gilchrist had been doing to all opposition for six years. The result was a score that meant there was almost certainly no chance of Australia winning the game from that situation. This was confirmed in the last session of the second day when the tourists slumped at stumps to 5 for 99 and were on their knees. Four batsmen were dismissed LBW. There were two bad decisions, including one for the hapless Martyn, the victim of a second piece of unfortunate umpiring, and a run-out in the second innings. With the tourists' batting form in a slump, the luck went against them, a common occurrence for the cricket team not making the running.

Australia did not have a regular sports psychologist, but it could have done with one at that moment.

It seemed to have a glimmer of hope on the third morning as Gilchrist and Katich struck hard, but it was a momentary flash of competitiveness. Flintoff, using reverse swing, removed Gilchrist caught (brilliantly by Strauss, who couldn't believe replays of his airborne snaffle) for the fourth time in seven innings. Jones, in another inspired spell (5 for 44), bamboozled the batsmen and finished off the innings.

Warne was caught by Bell in the covers for a duck after catching a leading edge off Jones. A shapely blonde would later allege that she kept Warne up all night cavorting in his hotel room, and that this fatigued him. She claimed, in the *Mirror*, that she had 'done her bit for England' by helping Jones to get rid of the Australian for a duck. This was a stretch. Warne was often caught off a leading edge early in an innings, but no doubt England would be happy with any off field assistance it could get.

Lee, unencumbered by any allegations of nocturnal distractions, thumped 47, including three massive sixes, and managed to delay last rites. But the one-day futility about the knock seemed to exacerbate Australia's plight. This was a Test when one or two batsmen had to show grit and application over at least two sessions against a deviating ball.

Australia tallied just 218 – leaving it with the biggest gap in the series at 259.

Vaughan consulted his team and decided to ask Australia to follow on, which was a demand it had not faced in 191 Tests over the past 17 years. Jones limped off injured after a few overs, which was bad luck for him and England. It went some way to reducing his team's effectiveness with the ball. The relentless thrust of the four-pronged speed attack, which meant that England could rotate its bowlers and keep pressure from both ends, was now diminished.

It helped Australia towards its highest score of the series.

Ponting seemed in his Edgbaston mood and touch, but was run out for 48 by the sub, Garry Pratt from Durham, after Martyn had called for what seemed a suicidal single. Before the ground's video screen announced Ponting's dismissal, he was furious. He mouthed off at the England players and protested to the umpire about the use of the sub. Ponting felt that England was using subs – players not chosen in the 12 – to rest their bowlers. His tirade continued all the way back to the pavilion where he directed it to a surprised Duncan Fletcher, who was on the dressing room balcony. England may or may not have been playing at the margins 'outside the spirit of the game' as it was later alleged. But this had been a point of contention ever since the ground staff substitute fielder, Syd Copley, took a terrific catch to dismiss Stan McCabe off Maurice Tate for 49 in the 1930 Nottingham Test. In that innings, Bradman and McCabe had been powering along in a strong partnership of 77 and seemed to be on a victory course in the last innings of the match when the catch was taken. (England won by 93, promoting disquiet in the Australian ranks over the dubious point that, had McCabe been missed at that critical juncture, it may well have won that 1930 Ashes opener.)

Yet the issue of a specialist fielder being used as a sub would not have been the real reason for Ponting's outburst. He knew that his removal from the crease meant Australia was in big trouble in the series. England was likely to go 2-1 up, which would put the Australian captain under enormous pressure to win in the final Test at the Oval. His run-out meant that the odds were strongly in England's favour to take the Ashes. Ponting did not wish to be the skipper remembered for losing a series, especially to England, after such a long spell of Australian dominance. This situation, with negative emotion washing over him as he trudged off the field, precipitated his reaction.

On reflection, the England camp would have been pleased about it. This was acknowledgment that Australia knew it was in serious trouble.

The tourists had plenty of good contributors, but once more Gilchrist – a man who could turn a game in half a session – did not deliver. He had not scored a 50 in eight innings. Warne once more batted with force, as if he were attempting to 'do a Flintoff'. But there was not quite the calibration from the Australian. There was also a sense when Warne batted that a rush of blood would get him before he reached 50. He had managed to clear this barrier many times previously, yet such occurrences were more the exception than the norm. He was stumped off Giles for 45 off just 42 balls with five fours and two sixes – 32 in boundaries. This was wonderful entertainment. But for such a talent – and Warne could claim all-rounder status after this series – it seemed a waste, especially with Lee (26 not out off 39 balls in a 77 minute stay at the wicket) proving that he, too, could lay claims to fair batsmanship. Another 50 for Australia would have been useful. Yet it had to be content with 387 and a lead of 128.

England began its run chase after tea, and its fans at Trent Bridge rested easy, believing that there could not be the same gripping finish to this game, especially with the way Trescothick and Strauss began. After five overs, England – sailing at speed – was 0 for 32, with just 97 to get. Ponting threw the ball to Warne. He dismissed Trescothick (27) with his first ball, then out-thought Vaughan (0) in his next over. Suddenly, England was 2 for 36. Strauss and Bell struggled on but were both removed with the score at 57.

That 129 target now appeared a long way off. An England crowd, and the cricket world, was caught in the enthral of a Test for the third successive time. Few Ashes or any series could match this for knife-edge drama. Even one a series was not common. Two was freakish. Three was the work of *Boy's Own Annual* fiction. That most dangerous of couplings, Flintoff and Pietersen, moved hastily towards victory. Now it was England supporters' turn to count the runs down as Australia's had at Edgbaston.

Lee was showing as much determination with the ball as he had with the bat. He was a fighter. At 103, he had Pietersen (23) caught behind. Eight runs later Lee, now delivering at close to 150 kph, produced a ball that could be defined as a match-winner, nearly. It cut back from the off and hit the top of Flintoff's off-stump.

The crowd had expected Flintoff to win it for England. His abrupt removal was met with a silence from everywhere except the pockets of excited Australian supporters.

Soon afterwards, Geraint Jones tried to advance on Warne and was caught. England was 7 for 116. It was still 13 runs short of victory when Hoggard joined Giles. The English dressing room was in turmoil and down to two men if another wicket fell. One of them was a nervous wreck. The other was injured. Both were easy targets for Lee and Warne. But those unwell bunnies were not needed. Hoggard and Giles managed by faith and good luck to collect the runs and give England victory.

***

Ponting was fined 75 per cent of his match fee for his on-field misbehaviour. Katich was also fined half his fee when he showed his disappointment after another woeful LBW decision when on 59 and defying the England attack in Australia's second innings.

Ponting reckoned Australia would fight back at Brit Oval with a win and retain the Ashes. Yet at that moment England held them with a 2-1 lead. It had fought so hard and had been superior to Australia in the last three Tests. It was not going to relinquish them easily.

Fifth Test: Oval

Australia brought back McGrath, retained Shaun Tait after he showed promise at Trent Bridge, and dropped Gillespie. He had just not delivered in four Tests. England lost Simon Jones and selected all-rounder Paul Collingwood. The hype for this match surpassed everything else for the season as the UK adjusted to the strong possibility that England would win or draw the match and so take the Ashes.

Vaughan won his third toss in a row and batted. England's beginning could not have been better as Trescothick and Strauss rattled off 82 in 17 overs – a rate of nearly 5 an over. Again, McGrath was not the match-winner he had been at Lord's. Lee was wayward. Tait lacked penetration. Ponting had little choice but to throw the ball to Warne. He changed the game, taking the first four wickets (a remarkable feat for a spinner, and the first time he had done this in his 128 Test career) and reducing England to 4 for 131. Strauss and Flintoff then reclaimed the upper hand in a two-and-a-half-hour stand that put on 143. Its first innings tally of 373 was good but not quite the coup de grace that the nation wanted. The problem for England was Shane Keith Warne, as he had been all series, and all his career. He took 6 for 122, and reached 34 wickets for the series – the same number he collected in his first ever Ashes in 1993.

Hayden and Langer responded with their best stand for the series – reaching 112 unbroken when the umpires offered them the light just after tea on day two. They accepted. England was surprised. Its fans were joyous. The more time the Aussies were off the field, the less likely it was that they would win the game. Spectators who had paid a lot for their seats were very happy to see no play. Perhaps only in the game of cricket is such a contradiction possible. It appeared to be a wrong move by Australia, at least psychologically. Not batting sent a signal that the team might have a little caution, or indecision, about its approach to the outcome. Ponting had decided to treat the game just like any other Test. But this was not just any Test: the Ashes depended on it.

Langer and Hayden sailed on to 183 before Harmison broke through, removing Langer (105). Then the irrepressible Flintoff struck, sending back Ponting (35), leaving Australia 2 for 277 at stumps on day three, which had been rain interrupted. On day four, Flintoff took out Martyn (10) and Hayden (138) to nearly match Warne's penetration, and also turn the game once more. Flintoff's fifth victim, much to the crowd's enjoyment, was Warne for a duck, made this time without any claims he had been worn out by a sexual encounter.

Hoggard was a strong support, taking four wickets. Australia slid from 4 for 323 to all out 367.

The weather continued to be an issue on the afternoon of day four. Ponting opened the bowling with Warne to avoid the umpires offering the batsmen the light and he struck, having Strauss caught for 1. Then McGrath bowled a bouncer and the umpires had no choice but to offer the light to England's skipper. He took it. Then the fun and games began during umpire inspections: England fans put up their umbrellas to ward off non-existent rain; Australians took off their shirts to absorb non-existent sunshine. When the umpires finally went back on, all the Australian players joined in the fun by wearing sunglasses. But it didn't work. The players were off again at 3.42 pm. The day was abandoned two-and-a-half hours later. England was on 1 for 34, just 40 runs ahead. The home team now was not looking for a win. It wished to put enough runs on the board and see out enough overs to make it impossible for the Australians to win. Ponting and his men, on the other hand, would be looking for a breakthrough and an England collapse on the morning of day five. The Australian skipper would turn to the world's finest spinner and paceman to give the visitors a slim chance of pulling off a miracle win. In the UK, England fans were praying for a big innings from somebody to pull the home team clear of any chance of an Australian win.

This did not seem a tough demand on the many gods being appealed to in multicultural Britain. With a fine line-up of players in touch – Trescothick, Strauss, Vaughan, Bell, Pietersen and Flintoff – it seemed a fair request that just one out of six perform at his best, given that in an average Test (or any game), three would succeed and three would fail out of a team's top six batsmen. All except Bell and Pietersen had delivered brilliantly at some stage in the series. Even then, these two had performed well with three 50s from Pietersen and two from Bell. Of the two Pietersen had seemed likely to cut loose as he had in the one-dayers. But a question mark hung over his capacity to bat with controlled mayhem in a Test for a big score. There was no doubting his ability or technique, or even his capacity for a lucky 80, given that he would sky the ball often. Rod Marsh had adjudged him the best batsmen next to Ponting to pass through his hands at either the Australian or British cricket academies. Higher praise from such an astute coach/observer would be placing a batsman near Bradman himself.

Pietersen could be placed alongside the other top four England batsmen as a player who could deliver a match-saving innings. But such a performance would have to be on his terms. At age 25 years, he was not a man to deliver a Len Hutton-like rearguard action based on a sound defence. Pietersen at this age knew only one way, and that was to attack or counter-attack. Nuances of style and approach might or might not come by the time he was in his early 30s and peaking as a batsman. But for now, he would refuse to be bogged down and defending against any bowler in any situation in any game. His attitude was modern: very fast food, instant consumption.

'What happened 10 seconds ago in a cricket match, is the same as what happened 100 years ago: it's history.' This attitude had some merit, especially for a player who had dropped six catches in the series. If he reflected on it, and it let him undermine his confidence, he would not perform at his peak in the field or with the bat. The demerit in this existing-only-for-the-moment philosophy was the old saying that 'those who ignore history, would be condemned to repeat it'.

Pietersen's approach would probably not be tested again as a fielder. He was a very good one, who had a more than momentary case of the butter fingers under pressure. He would recover and take many screamers at the top level. More fascinating would be the application of this philosophy in the way he batted, not just in this match but over a period of say, five years, which would either establish him as an extraordinary Test batsman, or something else.

***

Pietersen had one advantage over all his fellow English batsmen. And it was a more than useful one: he was a good friend of Warne's. The Australian held no fears for him. Warne would not sledge or verbal his 'mate' from the Hampshire county club. This did not mean that Warne would not try to snare his wicket. He would treat him like any other world-class opposition bat: he was there to be scalped. But the mere fact that Pietersen felt a warm kinship with the spinner made it just that much easier to bat against him. It was an important factor in a tight Test. It lessened the nerves at the wicket knowing that the bloke bowling to you – in his heart – wished you well, and that he smiled with a wink and a nod after some deliveries. It was better than the experience of the other English bats who would feel frozen out by all the Australians, especially Warne with his scowls, frowns, glares, stares, cocky grins and verbal sprays.

England's openers travelled without problems for the first 45 minutes of the final day in front of a packed Oval. Vaughan, particularly, looked in touch and was batting as well as he did in the first innings at Old Trafford. Then McGrath caused him to edge one behind. Gilchrist, whose form with the bat had caused him to be less than at his best behind the stumps, hurled himself to his right to take a sensational catch. The acrobatics lifted all the Australians, especially McGrath. Next ball, he used his lanky frame to fire in a delivery with extra pace moving away from the right-hander, Bell. He edged it to Warne in slips. All Britain groaned. England was 3 for 67 – a lead of just 73. Already three of the team's top six batsmen had not delivered. Three were left. Pietersen, who had a shaky start, joined the steady Trescothick. Pietersen was missed in slips off Warne. First-slip Hayden's response to the nick was thrown in the one-third of a second he had to react to a deflection off Gilchrist's glove. Soon after this, Warne was convinced he had Trescothick LBW, which was supported by TV replays. Umpire Rudi Koertzen rejected his plea. Warne squeezed another through the batsman's defences and this time received a nod from the umpire and that familiar slow raise of his left arm. Warne now had a record 168 England wickets: one more than Dennis Lillee.

England had the wobbles at 4 for 109 and a lead of 115.

The team all but toppled over when Pietersen (on 15) drove at Lee. His edge presented a regulation slips catch to Warne, who spilled it. No one reproached him for it. He had bowled and batted his heart out for Australia to tremendous effect. But it was a 'dolly' that went to grass.

Australia had dropped Pietersen twice and would put another one down later. His luck was very much in. It was Pietersen's opportunity to seize the day, live out his philosophy and live very much for the moment. He must have sensed it. Not so with Flintoff, whom Warne caught and bowled for just 8. Pietersen looked on as the fifth of the top six England bats headed disconsolately back to the pavilion with the score at 5 for 126 after 38 overs.

At first, in this disorientating period of turmoil, dropped catches and falling wickets, Pietersen was defensive. He was hit a glancing blow on the shoulder by Lee and acted as if he had been struck by lightning. He feigned serious injury, calling for the team physio and wasting as much time as possible. He made the most of a performance worthy of a BAFTA award nomination and later boasted that his thespian skills had allowed him to last until lunch. One imagines the reaction from Ponting and even Pietersen's mate, Warne, if he ever tried such an act again. Even if he had a broken limb next time, the Australians would not believe him until shown the X-rays.

But on this occasion, crying wolf worked.

After lunch he cut loose against Lee, who Ponting had on because the speedster had looked like blasting through before the long break. Pietersen, showing a remarkable bat speed, lashed hard but with control, hitting fours and sixes with amazing precision. One slip with such batting and a catch was in the offing. But he was providing no more chances. He demonstrated a very good eye, and capacity similar to Garry Sobers in the use of strength over technical skills that are peculiar to cricket. Any American baseball team could well do with a hitter such as Pietersen, or Flintoff for that matter. This does not mean that either player was without technique. On the contrary, Pietersen showed that with such supple wrists, all ground shots were open to him. These two were leading the way in meeting the demands of modern markets in the 21st century. With 20-over games, and Tests played at a one-day pace, along with the penchant – displayed also by Warne and Lee for Australia – for the 'home run' hit over the fence, the attraction of cricket was edging closer to baseball in many ways.

At tea on this riveting last afternoon of the series, England was 7 for 199, a lead of 205. There were still 50 overs left. Everyone did his or her arithmetic. Australia batting at 4 an over – not a huge ask – could still win the Test. It was not until towards the end of the first hour after tea that Vaughan began to stop sweating. The lead of around 250 with 40 overs left meant that Australia would be forced to score at 6 an over. That would be feasible in a one-day game, but less so in the last session of a Test. Vaughan knew he could shut the game down with a mix of accurate bowling and defensive field settings.

In the second hour, with Pietersen motoring on, and Giles giving solid back-up, it was all over. The England dressing room relaxed. The crowd began to sing in comfort.

It even chanted to Warne: 'We wish you were English', which was a far cry from abuse he had received at Somerset in a game against the county some years before. In recent times, Warne may have had the same wish, preparing more and more to call Southampton home.

The generosity from the Oval crowd came from knowing that at last England was going to win the Ashes. Dreams and hopes would be realised. This mighty series had been a knife-edge affair right down to the last session of the last Test. It had kept fans riveted the entire time.

Pietersen went on to one of the great power innings of Ashes or any other Test history, hitting a record seven sixes and 15 fours – 102 – in boundaries in his match-saving, series-winning 158 off 187 balls in five minutes under four-and-a-half hours. He was aided and abetted by Collingwood, who made just 10, but in a valuable

72 minutes, and Giles – in the innings of his life – 59 in a 159 minute stay.

Vaughan let England bat to the end, making a point that he never considered giving Australia an unsporting chance, let alone a sporting one. The object was to force a draw and win the Ashes. This had been done. England reached 335 – an academic lead of 341. Australia could bat for 18 overs, which meant a risible 19 runs an over for victory. Bad light stopped play after four Harmison deliveries.

The most exciting, brilliant and watchable series in Test history was over.

FLINTOFF FACTORS AND FUTURE TRENDS

Afterglow

The analysis of events in the afterglow of this once-in-a-century competition showed instructive trends. England had three bats who averaged more than 40: Pietersen (52.55); Trescothick (43.10); and Flintoff (40.20). It also had Strauss, the only player from either side to score two centuries. Australia had one player with a 40 plus average: Langer (43.77). England batsmen managed five scores of a century or more; Australia had three. England batsmen Vaughan and Pietersen hit big hundreds – 150 or more. Only Ponting did this once. England reached 400 or more, thrice. Australia's highest score was 387. A feature of Australia's dominance over the last decade or more was its capacity for making scores of 400 or more a regular feature.

England's bowlers produced more intense, relentless, and tighter performances over the five Tests. Jones, who delivered the least number of overs of the top seven of both sides (102 overs), had the best figures for England (18 wickets at 21 runs each). Flintoff (24 at 27.29) was England's best bowler for the series, delivering more devastating spells than anyone for his team. Hoggard (16 at 29.56) was dogged and effective when conditions of swing suited him. He provided good support and did not offer relief to Australia's batsmen. Harmison (17 at 32.29) did not repeat his brilliant, bruising opening spell at Lord's. But he set a psychological tone for England's intent. Australia's 190 was the worst start for it in a long time.

None of the England or fellow Australian bowlers came near Warne, who was the stand-out with the ball, taking a terrific 40 wickets at 19.92. He delivered a whopping 252.5 overs. The figures showed that McGrath – on paper – was very much himself, taking 19 at 23.15. But he only played in three Tests. Even at that rate, he would have taken 30 wickets over five Tests. If he had been fully fit after Lord's, he may well have been closer to Warne's numbers. His injuries had a profound effect on the Ashes outcome, especially as Australia came so close at Edgbaston. The problem for Australia was that it had only one-and-a-half top line bowlers (given McGrath's problems), whereas England had four strong contributors over three-and-a-half Tests. Lee's 20 wickets were too costly at 40.10. He was too often belted out of the attack. Kasprowicz (4 at 62.50) could not sustain his good form of recent years, while Gillespie (3 wickets at 100.00) was the most out-of-touch Australian. Tait (5 at 42.00) showed promise. Yet it was tough for him stepping into Test cricket in the fiercest fought series ever seen against a strong batting contingent.

The keeping standard was low, especially from Geraint Jones, whose performances behind the stumps prompted the series' most demeaning joke: 'What does Jones have in common with Michael Jackson? Answer: Both wear gloves for no apparent reason'. Yet his batting (229 runs at 25.54) kept him afloat and his keeping improved to the point where he became the fastest England glove-man to reach 100 dismissals. This was achieved in May 2006 in the First Test versus Sri Lanka.

Gilchrist had uneven patches – sometimes brilliant, other times ordinary – in taking 18 catches and effecting one stumping, compared with Jones' 15 catches and one stumping. But Gilchrist suffered. His performance with the blade was well less than half his normal standard (181 runs at 22.62).

Fred-led recovery

In one way, the 2005 Ashes was a super-heavyweight contest between true all-rounder Flintoff and Warne, who could in recent years call himself a bowling all-rounder. His batting average in recent series had leapt to around 26 after hovering before at about 17. Flintoff was England's most consistent batsman and its most explosive bowler. Warne dominated the bowling scene, and ran sixth in Australia's batting (249 at 27.66). Flintoff's suppression of Gilchrist was the most telling tactical win for England and went a long way towards it taking the series. Warne's victories over all comers – no England bat played him with confidence all the time – represented a single-handed performance unmatched in history. This was because of the array of top-class bats he tackled and brought down, often without any telling support at the other end.

***

Duncan Fletcher named Warne Australia's player of the series, and John Buchanan had the easy job of picking Flintoff as England's player of the series. Flintoff was also given the inaugural Compton/ Miller medal for the Man of the Series from both sides. This award was named after England's Denis Charles Compton and Australia's Keith Ross Miller. Both were great players, and mates, but the reason they had been honoured by their names going on this prestigious trophy was more to do with their spirit in playing the game. Like Miller and Compton, Flintoff played the game very hard, but fairly, and with a fine sense of enjoyment. Both Compton and Miller would have approved of Andrew 'Freddie' Flintoff being the inaugural winner.

Ever since Ian Botham carved up Australia in the 1981 Ashes in England, the nation had been yearning for someone to do the same again. It has taken a generation for Flintoff to emerge, and there is no question he is in Botham's class. He has many similar characteristics, and one above all others that makes a player great: the killer instinct.

When he was 15 and in Lancashire's 2nd X1, Flintoff was

nicknamed 'Freddie' after the Neanderthal TV cartoon character, Fred Flintstone – presumably because of his height (193 centimetres) and weight (100 kilograms plus). The name stuck. It seemed to suit his laidback approach to how he used his amazing talent. He never really had to work hard to succeed with either bat or ball. He was a natural who never concerned himself with eating well despite being much heavier than he should have been for an athlete on his way up. But at one stage, the light-hearted appreciation of fat 'Freddie' turned to ridicule in a cup match against Surrey in 2000, soon after England had dumped him for being so bloated.

'Who ate all the pies?' and other less savoury cries came at him all day. It was the same abuse that Warne had endured in the 1990s in England at times when he was struggling with his weight – or more precisely, when he also could not resist junk food in excess. It upset both these champions. Former Australian Test captain, Bob Simpson, was the character who upbraided them both at different times. He suggested in no uncertain terms and ripe language that they had better shape up or ship out. Warne was tubby when he first made the Test team in 1991–92, but took several seasons to establish himself as a regular. Simpson told him he would not stay in the Test side if he did not make himself much fitter. Warne understood the message and transformed himself with Rocky-like application. Apart from one lapse in the West Indies when coming back after injury, Warne has never looked like being dropped. His weight has varied, but he has generally kept it under control, despite an ongoing penchant for junk food. Flintoff, similarly, heeded Simpson's hard advice, which was reinforced in a more gentle manner by Fairbrother. He cut back on the booze, at least until he had re-established himself as an England player.

Flintoff's new-found commitment was exemplified when he went to Rod Marsh's cricket academy at the age of 24 in the winter of 2001–02. His improved attitude and condition caused him to be drafted late into England's tour of India. But the new, lean machine was creaky. He had an awful time with the bat, and was in despair over his career, especially after such rigorous application. Yet he excelled with the ball. This kept his place in the team. In the next few years he changed from an imprecise blaster into a more patient player – one prepared to wait until his eye was in before going after the best balls to hit hard.

Once used to his new-found energy from greater fitness, Flintoff lifted his speed. This transformed him from a stock bowler delivering at 135 kph to a serious paceman consistently delivering at around 145 kph. His pleasant demeanour to umpires, team-mates and the opposition (when not straining to remove them from the batting or bowling crease) was a surprise for Australian fans. Flintoff clearly enjoyed his cricket. There was a menace about his bowling and batting which was not sustained between deliveries. This was in contrast to Warne, who also enjoyed himself, but who when bowling was animated with a variety of facial expressions and chat for everyone.

Flintoff has captured the imagination of British fans in much the same as Botham once did, and Warne has done with Australian fans. When they move onto a cricket field, or prepare to bowl or bat, something is bound to happen. Their mere presence electrifies crowds. They are box office. In the 2005 Ashes, even people who had never been cricket fans were glued to the game in the centre or on TV, especially when Flintoff and Warne were in the action, which was more often than not.

Future Ashes

Leadership
Much criticism was heaped on Ricky Ponting when Australia lost the Ashes. Ian Chappell reminded everyone that he had suggested Warne as successor to Mark Taylor, which was a scathing denigration of Steve Waugh and his outstanding leadership and Ponting. Dennis Lillee, always good for a headline, said Warne should be given the leadership now. This was a most unlikely option, given Warne's controversial personal life and Gilchrist's excellent credentials after

leading Australia to a series win in India when Ponting was absent due to injury.

It all seemed a bit hasty. Ponting made just one major error in the 2005 Ashes. The decision to bowl at Edgbaston was a shocker and did, as it turned out, cost Australia the Ashes. But if his team had found three runs, he would have been a hero. Equally, the skipper would have been let out of jail had his star paceman, McGrath, not stood on a cricket ball before the game began. His team would have been two up, with three Tests to play. England's players, on their own admission, would have capitulated. Even two runs would have been enough. A tie would have kept England from winning back the Ashes. No doubt for some decades to come, Ponting, Kasprowicz and Lee would have nightmares about combing through scorecards, shots and catches dropped, while searching, in vain, for a couple more runs from the Second Test.

Ponting was criticised for a mechanical aspect to his leadership, and an apparent lack of consultation. The latter alleged deficiency was worse than it looked. But he liked to get the views of others, just like Don Bradman, the most consultative captain in Australian history, and no-one criticised him for it. This was part of Ponting's generous character rather than a weakness. It gave the appearance – especially on the all-seeing eye of TV – of uncertainty. A habit of chewing his nails and frowning didn't help. His apparent perpetual concern was matched only by Vaughan's.

Towards the end of the series and in the Australian summer of 2005–06, Ponting consulted less in public and developed less trans-parent facial expressions. He could never copy Steve Waugh's ice-man look in a crisis, but he would do well to try. With TV in every dressing room, it would send signals to the opposition that were useful to Australia. Unfortunately for Vaughan, his image of tension would never be alleviated in the field because of his fear that the ball might come near him. His deficiencies as a catcher and fielder were his main causes for alarm, a problem that the agile Ponting would never have.

Ponting claimed to have learned much from the Ashes loss, and said that it may have been a good thing. It sharpened him and the team up, he said. It was a comment he would no doubt wish to rephrase if he pondered the plight of Gillespie, Martyn and Kasprowicz who had been dropped from the Test team, or even Hayden, who had lost his one-day place. But everyone understood what Ponting meant. Only time would tell if his blunt yet honestly-held opinion proved to be prescient. There was a certain resolve about his batting and leadership over 2005–06. He gave the very clear impression of a man on a mission and captained superbly in twelve Tests for eleven wins and one draw. Ponting also led brilliantly from the front, scoring 1383 runs at 72.79 with eight centuries. He was well-supported by Matthew Hayden (1387 runs at 63.05 with five centuries) and Michael Hussey (1139 runs at 75.93 with four centuries).

Australia proved near enough to unbeatable in the post-Ashes period over 2005–06 in the international matches against a World XI, the West Indies, South Africa (at home and away) and Bangladesh away. Ponting was a tougher character, which was saying something, for this nuggety Taswegian was anything but weak by look, nature or performance. Sometimes he even seemed to push umpires by querying decisions (against New Zealand and Bangladesh) in a way that Duncan Fletcher complained was intimidating during the Ashes. Ponting was fined another 25 per cent of his match fee for 'dissent' in the final Test in Bangladesh, yet this charge was not brought by the umpires themselves, but the opposition. Ponting had complained, accurately, that the umpires had blundered in their decision making during a third umpire referral. He was correct, but his manner, his body language, could have been less 'square on'. In his defence, the breakdown between umpires – the third umpire in the stand and the match referee – was pathetic for a televised international game, and he was frustrated after a very long season. Cricket Australia's James Sutherland called for a 'please explain'. Ponting is a quick learner in the behaviour stakes, and all he has to do is think of how the Queen of England would complain to the umpires in a similar circumstance, and he will meet with the approval of everyone, including Fletcher.

***

The 2006–07 season could not come around fast enough for Ponting. He would be under unusual pressure too. Another loss in an Ashes series would call his leadership into question. This possibility would add to Ponting's incentive to crush England and silence his critics.

Michael Vaughan, or his successor, Flintoff, on the other hand, could afford to lose in 2006–07and still lead England in the 2009 Ashes.

Coaching

John Buchanan came under heavy criticism too after 2005, whereas Duncan Fletcher was lauded. Yet Buchanan's record had been praised before the England debacle, so it was inevitable that his contract would be renewed.

The major issue to come out of the 2005 Ashes series was the need or otherwise for specialist coaches. England had them in each department of the game – batting, bowling and fielding. Would Australia be forced to keep up with the Jones' or at least those who coached them? Perhaps the classic example of this issue was the decline of Gillespie's form. Could Lillee, regarded as one of the best bowling coaches in the world, have aided the ailing South Australian, who improved in the 2005–06 season? His form was critical to Australia's performance, especially with injury to McGrath. The way Terry Jenner helped tune up Shane Warne, even when he was only marginally off his best form, indicates that personalised coaching is positive for any bowler at the top level. Brett Lee commented that it would be 'terrific' to have an individual coach. This was the point exemplified by the Warne/ Jenner combination. The instructor knew his 'pupil' well, and they have a fine rapport. The same applied to batting, and to fielding (where Australia was less than inspiring).

Cricket Australia's chief executive, James Sutherland, announced in December 2005 that CA had acquired Troy Cooley as a bowling coach. Cooley, a former Tasmanian player, had improved the skills of Harmison, Flintoff and Jones for England in the 2005 Ashes. He was poached by CA to help the Australian squad from May 2006 after his contract in England expired. Cooley had half a year to impart his knowledge on reverse swing – which had been so deadly for England in 2005 – and other bowling tips.

'Troy was our first choice', Sutherland told the media. 'The players from the captain down rated him highly, and his work in England spoke for itself.' That left England with a fascinating option. Lillee, most pundits' first choice, could be available to replace Cooley as England's coach. If this happened, it could be a big win for the Ashes holders in the psychological stakes.

Psychologist

As with coaching, England set a trend by using a team psychologist. Jamie Edwards did not travel with the team, yet was on tap for all players. Some, including Flintoff, used him at critical times during the Ashes. Australia also has a psychologist attached to Cricket Australia, but he has not been used at critical times for players. Certainly, he was not on tap in England when several players were down on form, including Gillespie, Martyn and Hayden. They may well have benefited from a consultation similar to the one Flintoff had with Edwards.

The teams

Soon after the 2005 Ashes season finished, many hotels in Sydney and Melbourne were booked out over Christmas 2006 and into the 2007 New Year. More than 50,000 England fans, revelling in the win, wanted to be at the defence of the little old urn. The build and hype until 23 November 2006 – the first day of the First Test at Brisbane – would surpass even that before the 2005 series. Whether 2006–07 could match the freakishly brilliant nature of 2005 would be debatable. Yet with such a short time between the two series, the themes of 2005 would be similar, and the strengths and weaknesses of both sides would be more or less the same.

Barring injury, England would retain its main bowlers and batsmen. Changes in the line-up would be at the margins. Its main dangers surfaced in a three Test series in November 2005 in Pakistan, which was lost 2-0. First, England was vulnerable against spin through the series and never looked comfortable on turning pitches, suggesting Warne and MacGill in combination would be a threat. But at least it received plenty of experience with spin between the Ashes, with a drawn series in India and especially in its home summer of 2006 with seven Tests: three against Sri Lanka and four against Pakistan.

Second, with Simon Jones injured, England's three-pronged pace attack was not as penetrating. The fitness of a strong four-man attack (whatever its composition) would be crucial in Australia. Third, Flintoff was not as effective with the bat on tour in Pakistan and India as he had been in the 2005 Ashes. Fatigue became evident as the main threat to his all-round dominance. If England was missing one of its four pacemen, then he would be called on to do too much. Flintoff being Flintoff would never deny his captain; never shirk a challenge. But this admirable competitive streak with the ball could cause problems with his batting. Flintoff applied himself in Pakistan, but concentration lapses reduced his efficiency. It was always the way. Keith Miller, an all-rounder of similar make-up and skill, was called on to do too much with the ball for his country. His batting suffered. When he first came onto the international scene, he was compared favourably to Wally Hammond. After a few seasons of international competition he was always capable with the bat, but never again reached the heights expected after his brilliant performances in the Victory Tests of 1945.

This issue would be crucial concerning Flintoff during a demanding 2006–07 tour of Australia.

***

Australia's team composition would be more problematic. Twelve Tests – seven at home over 2005–06, three in South Africa and two in Bangladesh – helped sort out the batting and bowling departments.

Australia has only five near-certainties for the 2006–07 series: Ponting, Gilchrist, Hayden, Warne and Hussey, who blossomed brilliantly in the long 2005–06 season. Justin Langer's injuries held him back. He will be another starter if fit. But astute (former) chairman of selectors Trevor Hohns put pressure on the 35-year-old Langer by saying that the older players would have to maintain strong form *not* to make way for younger men. With this in mind, NSW opener Phil Jacques was knocking at the door with two Test chances in 2005–06.

Ponting favoured Lee for his shock and blast-out capabilities with the ball. This was understandable if other bowlers were firing. But if Lee was called on to carry too much of the burden, as he was in England, then England's bats would feel confident that they could overcome him. Australia's selectors (and Ponting, too), influenced by Flintoff's success, wanted to develop an all-rounder. Shane Watson's injuries didn't allow him opportunities, but Andrew Symonds had plenty and he struggled at Test level. He was not quite there as a top six batsman, not penetrating enough as a bowler and could not complement his grand performances in one-day cricket.

Yet the all-rounder 'problem' could be solved by the consistent application of Lee with the bat, coming in at 7, with Gilchrist at 6. This would leave four places (8, 9, 10 and 11) for specialist bowlers and allow selectors to put both Warne and MacGill in the side for the five Tests. Spin was England's biggest weakness in the 2005 Ashes, and will be again. This would allow Lee to be joined by two other pacemen and give Australia a strong five-pronged attack, which will be needed to take on a powerful England batting line-up.

Ashes 2009

The outcome of the next Ashes series in England in 2009 appeared more predictable than 2006–07. Australia's biggest problem would be presented by Warne and McGrath. They would both be 39 years old. Would they be prepared and fit enough to face the demands of another tour and five Test series? In McGrath's case, probably not.

In late 2005, Richie Benaud suggested to Warne that he should play on until 2009. Warne's response was to give a non-committal 'thanks'. The media followed up on Benaud's comment, and Warne responded in typical fashion: 'It will depend on if I'm playing good (sic) and enjoying it'.

Later, he said that because Benaud wanted him to go on to 40, he would make a serious effort to do it.

If Warne played, along with Hayden (39), Langer (39), Gilchrist (37) and Ponting (34) for starters, then the Australians would have a 'Dad's Army' rather than 'Lad's Army' feel about its backbone of players. If Warne and McGrath were to retire by the 2006–07 Ashes, they would be the nearest thing to irreplaceable that human beings could be – in sport, at least. They have proved the best wicket-taking combination in history – the finest spinner and arguably top paceman ever seen.

An in-form Stuart MacGill, if he were to wait for Warne to retire, would solve the problem in the spin department. McGrath's absence due to his wife's illness allowed Stuart Clark to step up. He performed admirably in South Africa in March/April 2006, winning the player-of-the-series award, taking 20 wickets at 15.85. He demonstrated that McGrath's giant shoes might be well-filled after all. Gilchrist would be another player difficult to replace. He has proved a very good keeper. He has also been the best middle-order, match-winning batsman in history. No one has changed as many games so rapidly by a quick-fire innings ranging from 40 to 200 that took the team score beyond the opposition's reach, and also demoralised them in the process. Gilchrist's retirement will leave a hole equal to the size of that created by Warne and McGrath. This, along with the disappearance of Langer and Hayden, will create some serious challenges for new chairman of selectors Andrew Hilditch and his co-selectors in maintaining Australia's new Golden Age of world dominance (1995 to 2006).

Another problem has been the trend for players to play on for a lot longer, simply because they were paid enough to do so. This has created a new issue of a generation of players not being allowed the chance to force their way into the team. Perhaps this will result in massive gaps in winning ability in the wake of a long-serving successful squad, such as the current one. Trevor Hohns doubled well as both executioner of older players, and midwife to new ones. But not even these god-like capacities and inclinations mean much when you have a great band of superstars who will play on as long as they keep doing well. And the fact that they have teamed well means that they may well be retired within a few years of each other.

Australia might have to wait five or six years for a third wave of players to mature to Test standard after 2006–07. Yet batsman Mike Hussey, and Stuart Clark, proved that, even at 30 years of age, experienced players can step straight into the breach, if they are good enough.

THE ABORIGINES AND THE FIRST ENGLAND TOUR

Impact Two: Lawrence of Australia

The first foreign team ever to challenge England at its summer game, which had been around for 700 years, was a truly Australian side, made up entirely of Aborigines except for their enterprising leader, Charles Lawrence. The team's admirable performances half a world away from its members' homeland on the gruelling 1868 tour led to others that quickly secured international competition between England and Australia. So great was the impact of this squad of indigenous Australians that England supporters were disappointed when future tours did not include the skilled, entertaining Aboriginal players.

***

Charles Lawrence, a 40-year-old Sydney publican and professional cricketer, arrived at Lake Wallace in Victoria's Western District in mid-July 1867, intent on gathering a squad of Aborigines for a tour of his home country, England. He was a mild 'John Bull' type, with handsome aquiline features and a goatee beard, and he had a quasi-missionary zeal. Like many pioneers of the 19th century, he wanted to make his fortune in an acceptably 'Christian' way: rather than 'using' the Aborigines, he wanted to be seen as 'bettering' them along the road to his own goals. Lawrence regarded and dealt with the Aborigines as equals.

He could be both shrewd and single-minded. Lawrence knew from contact with the Aborigines, on their first trip earlier in 1867 through Victoria and NSW, that they loved alcohol. In order to get their attention, he drank with them. In the first week, this had unfortunate consequences: three ended up in the Edenhope town jail. Lawrence had not set out to get them drunk, but their excitement over his plans led to over-exuberance.

Lawrence met with the local policeman – Mounted Constable Thomas Kennedy – at the lock-up to bail out his prospective charges. Kennedy was unhappy with Lawrence's approach, complaining that 'a glass of grog was a potent reasoner with a blackfellow'. Lawrence explained that he would be imposing a moderation-with-booze rule, but Kennedy remained unconvinced. He wrote to his superior at Portland on the south-western Victorian coast and requested that the Central Board for the Protection of the Aborigines stop Lawrence's proposed tour. In this letter, Kennedy complained about the earlier tour of Australia in 1867 (that Lawrence had not organised, although he did once captain the team at Wollongong). The Aboriginal team had been allowed to drink too much. This led to the deaths of three players: Watty (his real, traditional name, Bilayarrimin), who died on the team cart just short of Edenhope; Jellicoe (Unamurramin); and Paddy (Pappinjuru-mun). The causes for their demise were said to be 'stress, city life, alcohol and lung disease'. Their 'captain' or manager was Tom Wills, an alcoholic, who was blamed for the problems. Kennedy also noted the fact that several of the new team had 'chest ailments'.

This police complaint, together with a supporting letter from local medico, Dr Molloy, who said that a change of climate would be fatal to many of the team, was posted to the Protection Board.

Lawrence continued on with his quest, making sure to ease the individuals into drinking less. He knew that his main hope of preventing their roistering would be to give them a full program of games and to keep them away from bars. Lawrence set about explaining the tour and providing incentives to each player. Some prize money, for events such as running, was promised. All expenses for the entire trip to England and back, lasting 18 months, would be paid. Lodgings and food would be 'good'.

This was enticing enough for each member of the prospective 14-strong group. The deal was portrayed and seen as better than another year of hard labour on pastoral properties.

Lawrence didn't 'boss' his charges. His open, genial, polite manner endeared him to the Aborigines and he gained their trust. Lawrence told them he would organise the tour. He led in most of the games and coached them in cricket, which was not always easy. The Aborigines were not enthusiastic about training. But when he organised them to practise their natural athletic gifts, and their traditional skills with spear and boomerang, he received a better response. Lawrence encouraged one of the players to perfect his ball-dodging ability, where three others threw cricket balls at him from 10 paces. He explained that in Australia and England they would be required to exhibit all their abilities during and after cricket matches. None was forced into the tour. All were prepared to go willingly. They were going to be exploited but in a way acceptable to them.

Confident he had a team that would stand up against all comers, Lawrence began to beat up publicity by issuing a challenge in the Hamilton *Advertiser* to any team in the Western District which could field sides of 16 or 18 players. They played three games, the last on 28 August 1867, winning two and drawing one. It gave Lawrence a chance to select the best Aboriginal players.

At the end of the training period, he presented each man chosen with a distinctive, warm uniform. It had white flannel trousers, a red Garibaldi shirt, diagonal blue sashes, hatbands, belts and neckties. Then, in a ceremony at Edenhope cricket ground, he handed each man a peaked cap of a different colour, which would be theirs for the entire tour and would distinguish them. It was an important moment for the Aborigines. One by one, the well-whiskered players stepped forward to receive their equivalent of the (later) 'baggy green': the brilliant all-rounder Johnny Mullagh (Unaarrimin);

classy stroke-player Bullocky (Bullchanach); hard-hitting, 'amusing' Dick-a-Dick (Jumgumjenanuke); fast-running, steady-bowling Twopenny (Jarrawuk from Bathurst in NSW); fragile King Cole (Bripumyarrimin); multi-talented all-rounder Johnny Cuzens (Yellanach); Charley Dumas (Pripumuarraman, from Wollongong, the only other player from NSW); accurate-bowling Tommy Red Cap (Brimbunyah, who was handed a black cap); Harry Tiger (Bonnibarngeet); Peter (Arrahmunyarrimun); Mosquito (Grongarrong); Jim Crow (Lytejerbillijun); Sundown (Ballrinjarrimin); Billy Officer (Cungewarrimin); Harry Rose (Hingingairah); and Tarpot (Murrumgunarrimin). (Later, Harry Rose, Tarpot and Billy Officer would drop out.) This event gave them a sense of being part of a special mission.

After a solid two months preparation, Lawrence and a local pastoralist, William Hayman, 26, who had begun the Edenhope Cricket Club, had moulded the squad into a well-knit group. On 16 September 1867, they and the Aborigines piled into an American-style covered wagon and a cart and set off from Edenhope on their adventure. Lawrence planned to escort his cricket team most of the way from Victoria's Western District to Melbourne and other major towns before a boat trip to Sydney. After touring NSW and playing several matches over two months, they were scheduled to be on a boat to England where they would play nearly 50 matches. Lawrence hoped the England tour, set to begin early in February 1868, would be the first ever by an Australian team. Every cricketer except him was an Aboriginal.

Bush and Board trouble

They endured a tough wagon trip and were once bogged in the wet. Later, a wagon overturned and the four horses bolted. Johnny Cuzens, one of the Aboriginal drivers, fell on his head but recovered after mild concussion. Despite these minor mishaps, the camping out as an ensemble drew them closer over the eight-day journey to

Warrnambool. Along the way, they took time off for hunting and traditional dancing.

Lawrence used the nights round the campfire to begin his proselytising, beginning with the concept of 'Our Saviour' as depicted by the child in the manger. Dick-a-Dick had become confused and distressed, thinking that 'the baby Jesus' had been killed. He wanted Lawrence to explain it. Lawrence didn't want them to be distracted. He wished 'to have them inclined to a belief in the after-life'.

It was not easy. The Aborigines had powerful spiritual beliefs based on big concepts including mountains, the earth and the sky. The idea of worshipping a baby in a stable didn't grip them.

'When one of your tribe beats the other in a fight', Lawrence asked them, 'who did you believe in?'

'Our king', they replied.

'Well, that's right. Now suppose we beat Warrnambool [in cricket]. Who will you believe in?'

'You, of course.'

'Why?'

'Because you are our captain.'

Lawrence went on to tell them how the baby wasn't killed but that he grew into 'the son of God', who went to heaven. If they were good and kind to each other they would end up there too. Lawrence was not too sure if they accepted these ideas. But he often worked these themes and promised to take them to church in Warrnambool.

One evening, an Aboriginal wandered into their camp and said he wanted to join them and play cricket. The other blacks were suspicious of him and suggested that he may have mates ready to ambush them. Lawrence said he could stay the night and he would test his playing ability in the morning. If he was good, Lawrence told the new man, he might stay with them. Lawrence then ordered all of his men to load their guns. Should anyone come near the camp, he would give the order 'to fire up in the air'. The Aborigines made a bed for Lawrence in a huge gum tree, so that he could be the lookout but Lawrence didn't think he could sleep.

'I was too anxious', he said.

Not long after he had bedded down, he heard 'a terrible noise, like the galloping of cattle'. In fact, it was six horsemen. Lawrence called for his men: 'Be ready!'

The invaders yelled they would smash the camp and kill everyone.

'Fire!' Lawrence ordered.

He and the Aborigines aimed their weapons above the heads of the would-be attackers and let go a volley of shots. It sent 'the brave men away quicker than they came', Lawrence noted in his memoirs. The new black in the camp claimed that they were Aborigines from his station. They had come after him to stop him leaving the station and joining the team. The Aboriginal cricketers were still unsure about the stranger. Lawrence bowled to him the next day, and gave him a bowl. The interloper wasn't good enough.

'I gave him some money,' Lawrence recorded, 'and told him to go back to his station.'

The incident caused Lawrence to ride shotgun on the wagon for half the day. He could not be sure whether they had been set up or the outsider had been telling the truth.

Lawrence was relieved when the eight-day trek was over.

***

They rested for a week in the Warrnambool hotel and relaxed by playing billiards and at night dancing waltzes and polkas. A big crowd filled the bar and dance area each night where local young women enjoyed themselves in the convivial atmosphere. Lawrence and Hayman mingled with the Aboriginal team members, making sure they didn't drink too much. They wanted the lads to make an impression in their first game, which they did, thrashing Warrnambool in front of a crowd of more than a thousand. It was a fine start to a tour. The Aborigines certainly believed in their captain.

On the Sunday after the game, he took them to Church, as promised.

'They seemed to like it [Church]', Lawrence noted.

They were attentive and put money in the collection plate.

Lawrence asked them about the experience. They replied: 'Music very nice and him [the minister] talk a lot and get a lot of money.'

'And what do you think he does with it?' Lawrence asked.

'Keep it, don't he?'

'No. He gives it to the poor people.'

They were 'astounded' and commented: 'Does he then? Well when we go to church again I will always put my money in the plate.'

Lawrence was pleased to report that they did.

Morale was high. But disaster was never far away from the squad. One member of the team arrived home late and wanted to light his pipe using a chandelier in a dormitory where the rest were asleep. He had to jump for it. In attempting to pull it down he brought it crashing to the floor. Kerosene spilt. Fire engulfed the room but was extinguished before anyone was hurt. The damage was paid for out of Lawrence's contingency funds.

The team was set to play exhibition games around Victoria, but a major problem developed that threatened the trip. The letters of complaint about the tour from Constable Kennedy and Dr Molloy arrived at the Protection Board early in October 1867. While no law prevented Lawrence from taking his men to other colonies and England, public pressure could see the government prevent it. The Board was then drafting the notorious Aborigine Protection Act (which became law in 1868), that would force Aborigines to relocate to missions and reserves. It was, in part, in response to the disaster of the early 1867 tour and to rightly attempt to 'protect' Aborigines from exploitation. But the proposed Act would have its own sinister ramifications: no black would be able to travel without the Board's permission. It would create a police state for Aborigines and a form of 'apartheid'. Had the Act been law then, Lawrence would have had no hope of getting his men out of Victoria, let alone Australia. (This law was still on state statute books in the 1930s. Then, the outstanding Aboriginal fast bowler, Eddie Gilbert, had to obtain written permission from the Queensland Board in order to travel interstate to play in Shield matches.)

The Victorian Board, frustrated in the knowledge that it would be a toothless tiger until mid-1868 when the Act was expected to become law, began a press campaign against Lawrence. It was to the point. Appeals were made to put an end to the 'heartless proceedings of the speculators who unscrupulously endanger the lives of the blacks for the sake of sordid gain . . .'

Lawrence received support from *The Age*, the most influential paper in the state. It reported a game at Corio and complimented the way the team behaved. They were not being 'used up' as Dr Molloy had told the Board. On the contrary, in *The Age*'s view, the players seemed as 'temperate as anchorites, as jolly as sandboys and as supple as deer'. In other words, they were mentally and physically alert.

In another game at Corio, there was a deal of ill feeling between Tom Wills and Lawrence. They had been friends since meeting in Ireland in 1854 during a cricket match between the Phoenix Club – where Lawrence had a coaching appointment – and a Liverpool team. Wills, a hero in Victoria for founding and playing Australian Rules Football, was bitterly disappointed about not being involved in the 1868 England cricket tour. He was aware of his former companion's concern about the Aborigines' drinking. Wills assumed that this was the reason he had not been invited to join the squad. He was right.

He bowled with anger that day at Corio and took four Aboriginal wickets in his first eight overs. But he couldn't remove Lawrence. When Corio batted, Lawrence brought himself on to bowl immediately Wills came to the wicket. When Wills was 6, Lawrence trapped him LBW. It didn't bring them any closer. Rain killed the game, which was drawn.

Backers of Lawrence's squad lobbied for a fixture at the MCG in November to coincide with a visit by the Duke of Edinburgh, but the Melbourne Cricket Club rejected them. The impact of the Protection Board's press push to stop the tour was having an effect.

Wills, a 'ground staff' coach at the MCC, influenced the decision not to stage a game.

Lawrence was aware of the building pressure to stop the Aborigines leaving Melbourne. There were strong rumours that the Victorian Government would order the police to intervene at the Melbourne port from which they were due to leave. He planned a return match at Corio and was reported in the press as scheduling further games. Lawrence instructed all the players to talk about upcoming matches. Secretly, he made arrangements for the team to leave by boat for Sydney, not from Melbourne but Queenscliff, close to Corio. Players were told they were going on a 'fishing trip' from Queenscliff. They boarded the *Rangatira* off Port Phillip heads late in October and it sailed to Sydney with its happy extra cargo.

***

Most of the press now supported the 'fugitives'. It was more attractive to readers than backing the Protection Board. *The Age* suggested the Board had been 'check-mated by the speculators' and sent a reporter to cover the team's exploits in NSW. These began with a win at Wollongong against Illawarra, followed by an athletics exhibition. The crowd was unruly. It surged near the track when Dick-a-Dick and Cuzens raced over 100 yards (91.5 metres). The two runners careered into spectators. Cuzens was concussed. Dick-a-Dick knocked over a horse and its rider. This kind of incident brought more headlines than the cricket, but the team continued to perform well, with wins over West Maitland, Singleton and Newcastle.

It went on to Sydney where it was based at Lawrence's Pier Hotel on the Esplanade at Manly Beach. Lawrence had sold the hotel and planned to be out of it by the time he caught the boat to England.

He continued to monitor the team's drinking. Lawrence was protecting his players and doing everything to ensure a successful mission. His management methods helped their performances, although a strong combined Sydney team beat them at the Albert Ground in Redfern. They also lost to Bathurst on Boxing Day, 1867.

On a return game at the Albert Ground in early February 1868, this time against a combined Army and Navy team, the Aborigines played brilliantly in front of big crowds – 4000 and 9000 – on two days. Each day, the Duke of Edinburgh was among the spectators. On the first, he was introduced to and mingled with them, much to their delight. On the second, enchanted by their cheerful, polite manner, he mixed with them again. The Aborigines were inspired. They rolled the Army and Navy team for 64, thanks to Cuzens, who took 8 for 23. The Aborigines replied with 237, with Cuzens smashing a top score of 86, Mullagh 64 and Bullocky 39. Mullagh had a correct defence, and a fine, wristy style that allowed him to play all round the wicket. Bullocky was aptly named. He liked to hit hard and often. The Army and Navy Combine was 2 for 51 in its second innings when the game ended in a draw.

It was followed by an athletics show. The strong 180 centimetre, 80 kilogram Mullagh jumped 5 foot 7 inches (170 centimetres) in the high jump. Then there was a mock battle of six men a side. Each had a spear and some were hurled as far as 85 metres, causing the human target to dodge or else be struck. The Aborigines appeared in a new costume of colourful dress and headgear featuring lyrebird plumage. The bigger second day crowd loved it.

Lawrence was satisfied. His troupe, he felt, would more than pay its way and maybe even return profit for the main investor, George W. Graham, a Sydney solicitor, who was making the trip. William Hayman left two weeks earlier to smooth the squad's entry into England.

England ho!

The first Australian cricket team to tour England sailed from Sydney on 8 February 1868 on the *Parramatta*, a wool ship, almost the same day as the last convict ship was leaving England for Australia after 81 years of transportation. The Aborigines were given a big cabin just below the first class area and were treated well. Lawrence continued his religious instruction and it helped calm them on the voyage. The man in charge of the ship, Captain Williams, they were told, had prayed to Jesus in heaven for their safe journey. Lawrence made an effort to teach them to read and write, but gave up when the team members lost concentration and began drawing animals and birds. During the day they shaped wooden needles, hair clips, bracelets and other items that made them a hit with the ladies and children on board. At night, after dinner, the team played draughts and various card games. They joined in dancing, again to the pleasure of the women passengers. Their agility and graceful movement made them naturals on the dance floor. Captain Williams occasionally joined them for the evening meal and even tried his hand at cards.

Return to green fields

Lawrence was thrilled to be travelling to his former homeland after seven years in Australia. He had come out with H. H. Stephenson's first All-England XI in 1861 for a tour of Victoria. Born in Surrey, Lawrence told his team how, as an 11-year-old, he hitched a ride on a cart from his home that took him 50 miles (80.5 kilometres) to London, where he walked a few more kilometres to Lord's to see his hero, batsman Fuller Pilch. Lawrence remembered settling in at a place near the boundary only to see Pilch caught first ball. At 18, after he had played for Surrey a few times, he hitched his way to Scotland to stay with a relative in Edinburgh where he found a job as an assistant stationmaster at a railway station. While there, Lawrence played as much cricket as possible and established himself as a capable all-rounder.

In 1849, at the age of 19, he was selected to play for Scotland against William Clarke's All-England XI. Lawrence made a name for himself by taking 10 for 53 in one innings. He bowled four batsmen.

In 1850, he met and married Ann Elizabeth Watts. (They were to have four children: Elizabeth in 1856, Anne in 1858, Charles in 1860 and Maud, who died at birth in 1866.) William Clarke was impressed by Lawrence's cricketing abilities and obtained a professional appointment for him in Ireland in 1851 as a coach at Dublin's Phoenix Club. (He also worked as a tennis coach, but that business did not develop and Lawrence lost money for investors.) He had returned to England to play for Surrey again when he was invited to join the All-England team to tour Australia in 1861. The new land was enticing. He brought out his family. Sydney, rough and rustic as it was, offered opportunities, especially for a professional sportsperson who knew much about outdoor games. Cricket was the boom sport in Australia, with clubs springing up like mushrooms. Lawrence opened a cricket goods shop and cafe at 353 George Street, played five games for NSW v Victoria and coached the cream of Sydney between 1862 and 1864.

A fellow Surrey man, William Caffyn, also coaching in Sydney, said of Lawrence in 1864: 'By his perseverance, energy and ability, he did a great deal toward the raising of the game to its present high standard'.

In that year, George Parr brought out his All-England team. Lawrence played in the NSW 22 and scored 25 out of the first innings of 135. In another game against England, bowling fast-round-arm, and experimenting with the new, legal over-arm ('Windmill'), he took 6 for 29 in one innings.

In 1866, Lawrence bought the Pier Hotel at Manly. Now, in 1868, he had sold that to pursue the biggest adventure and gamble of his opportunistic career so far.

Happy landing

Even before the team landed, there was a mini-crisis when those on board learned that the Duke of Edinburgh had been shot and wounded in Sydney. The Aborigines were distraught. They vowed to perform games of welcome in front of him.

They were also upset when the ship's captain bade them farewell before the boat docked at Gravesend. They had felt safe in his company and with him at the helm over the three month voyage until mid-May.

Hayman was waiting for them dockside and led them in two coaches to their base at West Malling in Kent. Lawrence continued on with the boat to London. He was due at the Surrey Cricket Club's annual dinner the night he arrived. Lawrence used the night to 'network' with the 100 guests. He drank with jolly Surrey secretary, William Burrup, who had been a keen instigator of the All-England team's 1861 tour. In correspondence begun in mid-1867, Burrup had been interested in staging the first game of the current tour against Surrey at his new, beloved Oval at London's Kennington. Lawrence, aware that every such match meant money in the bank, was delighted when they firmed up on the fixture that evening. They agreed on the dates: 25 and 26 May.

The following day he re-joined his squad and told them the good news about the Surrey match. Lawrence found them raring to play cricket. And play they would. The schedule was not well structured, and would grow as the tour progressed and the novelty of the 'troupe' was publicised. As it turned out, there was to be a 126-day itinerary from the first match at the Oval. The team was to perform on 99 of them. Take out 18 Sundays, when sports were banned, and it was left with just nine days break. Even by mid-19th century standards, this was demanding, given the time to travel from town to town. On top of this, every day would be long. The gruelling schedule allowed little else beyond playing, travelling and sleeping. In a way, it suited Lawrence. He knew he had to avoid, as much as possible, his players having idle time, where they would be tempted to 'hit the grog'. His main challenge would be keeping harmony. It said much for the Aborigines' toughness, team spirit and self-discipline that Lawrence was confident they would get through the five months without a drop-off in form.

***

West Malling was Hayman's family home and the Aborigines had an immediate impact. Few people in Britain had seen a black person. Their dual demeanour of dignified grace and ready laughter and fun-loving behaviour were a novelty. Ignorance abounded. Later in the tour, a hotel proprietor at Brighton insisted that they 'scrub off the dye' before they had baths. He thought they were white men, who had 'dyed for the occasion' – a bunch of early-day Al Jolsons. But in general, they were well received. Lawrence once walked into the local draper's shop at West Malling. The owner invited him behind the shop into his drawing room. Lawrence noted in his memoirs that the man's 'daughters were entertaining my gentlemen with a little music . . . Three of the blacks were reclining upon sofas whilst the ladies were playing and singing. They all seemed delighted with the evening's amusement and [the Aborigines] promised to call again'.

The Aborigines' colourful reputation preceded them to the Oval, where 7000 spectators turned up, many of them women who walked from all over London or arrived 'on horseback and in carriages'.

Before the first ball was bowled, the Aborigines gathered in a group, gave three cheers to the opposition and ended with a shriek that sent a laugh and a buzz through the crowd. Spectators were amused that the Aborigines fielded barefoot, but soon became appreciative of their fielding and throwing skills. They moved swiftly across the uneven outfield. Instead of the high lobs to the keeper that featured in local cricket, they would 'spear' the ball in low, fast and accurately.

A full-strength, first-class Surrey made 222. Mullagh, bowling over-arm, took 3 for 100 off 52 overs. Lawrence, in fine form with his accurate mix of over and round-armers and the odd over of slow under-arm, took 7 for 91 off 49 overs. In reply, the Australians collapsed for 83, with Mullagh making 33 and King Cole 14. The crowd was further amused by the excited chatter of the Aborigines at the crease. They yelled to each other in their own language, and made many false starts up the wicket.

The tourists were forced to follow on and did better, making 132, Mullagh this time stroking 73, Lawrence 22 and Bullocky 19. Surrey won by an innings and 5 runs. It was a result that reflected the standard the tourists would put up – below first class level but with the skill to upset quality teams. The upright Mullagh was the star with bat and ball. Lawrence, a neat, light figure, standing about 174 centimetres, would give him good support with his technically correct if slightly defensive style. Then there was Cuzens, who was the third all-rounder. After that it was hit or miss, with Red Cap, and later Twopenny, capable of a top performance here and there.

The press was generally supportive and optimistic. Reynolds News took the long view and called the match a 'new epoch in the history of cricket'. Given the touring teams that would follow from Australia into the 21st century, this was a more prophetic observation than the reporter could have imagined. The Sheffield *Telegraph*, not to be outdone, saw it as 'the Event of the Century'. But *The Times*, 112 years short of Australian ownership, was less kind. Its reporter saw 'second-rate bowling', and batting 'sadly wanting in power'. Running between the wickets was 'slow and uncertain'.

It didn't put the Oval crowds off. Twenty thousand attended over three days. A third day, 27 May, was set aside for sports. There were races, boomerang and spear throwing, high jump, running backwards, hurdles, pole vaulting, and cricket-ball throwing. A boomerang just missed decapitating a small dog that strayed onto the Oval. Spectators who under-estimated the weapon's sweeping curve were forced to duck.

Lean, bearded W. G. Grace, 20 and making his name as a champion all-rounder, competed in the ball throwing. He won the event with hurls of 116, 117 and 118 yards (106, 107 and 108 metres), beating Mullagh's 104 yards (95 metres) – below his best of 120 yards (110 metres) achieved at Harrow – and Dick-a-Dick's 107 yards (98 metres). It wasn't the last time Grace would see them on the tour. He wrote in his book, *W.G.*: 'The team went up and down the country, playing matches against clubs, including several of the Counties, and acquitted themselves very well'.

Lawrence tried other events such as his own feats with bat and ball. A ball would be thrown from a distance and he would stop it with the bat without the ball hitting the ground. The feat didn't capture the crowd's imagination. He reduced his act and it wasn't always in the show. Lawrence took note of the spectator reaction to the more popular ball dodging 'act' by Dick-a-Dick, who defended himself with a shield and leangle – a curved wooden blade, similar to an old-style cricket bat. This performance would later be given third billing behind the spear and boomerang throwing.

After expenses paid to Surrey, the police and the umpires, there was a 300 pounds (about A$700) profit. It was a strong start, but Lawrence knew it would rarely peak like this. Weather, less suitable grounds, the novelty wearing off and defeats would lower the gate.

Three days later, the Australians played an upper class team led by Lord Paget at Maidstone. The visitors, thanks to Lawrence (4 for 68 in Maidstone's 151, and 57 not out from 4 for 119), were on the way to victory, when Lord Paget decided the game should be called a 'draw' in order that the Aborigines could perform their acts and sports.

Lawrence took the team to the Derby, and was able to keep up public interest. They were intrigued by the Aborigines at a time when Darwinism was fashionable and many unscientific theories about man's origins were flying around in England's journals. Most of the comment about the tourists was polite – even glowing – though at times patronising. Yet it was always more respectful than press remarks at home.

English observations such as 'adroit hunters . . . skilled trackers . . . natural sportsmen . . . agile athletes . . . fair cricketers . . .' abounded.

Lord's, ladies and lubrication

The tourists carried on to Gravesend and were beaten by an innings by the Gentlemen of Kent, while the genteel women of Kent admired the Aborigines and their fashion. At Deer Park, in a game against Richmond early in June, the former Governor of NSW, Sir William Denison, presented each Aboriginal with 10 shillings (about A$1.10). With such interest from England's ruling classes, the ultra-conservative Marylebone Cricket Club at Lord's – cricket headquarters – relented. It agreed to a game but at a price – 50 per cent of the gate – which was twice as much as paid to Surrey at the Oval.

Before the Lord's match, the Aborigines challenged Sussex at Hove, leading on the first innings but losing the game. Then they beat Lewisham at Ladywell by 6 wickets. Mullagh and Lawrence starred both times.

***

The Lord's game of 12 and 13 June brought further big London crowds, eager to see the black tourists. (When the next white team played at Lord's, members were heard to express their shock and disappointment that the players were not black.) The MCC did not field all its 'ground' staff – the professional players retained by Lord's – a sign that it saw the foreigners as easy to beat. Instead, the lofty club selected half the side from its social and military elite: two earls, a viscount, a lieutenant colonel and an army captain, all of whom regarded the game as more than social fun. They fancied themselves with bat and ball and took their performances seriously.

Early in the game, the MCC attitude at the selection table looked like causing serious embarrassment. The home side batted first. Mullagh early on bowled the Earl of Coventry with a terrific leg-cutter that slid alarmingly off the infamous Lord's ridge (known then as the 'lip') and sent his off stump cart-wheeling. The crowd roared. Soon afterwards, Cuzens, who had been practising over-arm after watching opposition English bowlers, sent down a very quick delivery from a four pace run-up. It uprooted the Earl of Bathurst's middle stump. The Australians, sometimes referred to in the common parlance of the day as 'savages' by fascinated, onlooking anthropologists, were colourful and cheerful. They could play. The aristocrats, who may have thought themselves superior in every respect, had a sudden dose of inferiority. In the space of five minutes, the tourists earned solid respect. Now Australia was seen to produce more than just gold. It had cricketers not to be taken lightly.

The Aborigines' tour took on a different complexion. Clubs that had been a little sniffy or indifferent about playing them now lined up across the country to schedule games.

Mullagh delivered 45 overs in that MCC first innings and removed four others, including Richard Fitzgerald (50), the MCC's best bat on the day. The home team succumbed for 164. Mullagh took 5 for 32; Cuzens 4 for 52.

Lawrence thought it 'gettable' and asked the tired Mullagh for a special effort. The brilliant Aboriginal, who displayed all-round skills to match any player alive, responded with a well-crafted 75, including a strong partnership with Lawrence (31) of 60. It was enough for the tourists to reach 185 and a slender lead of 21.

At the close of play on day one, Dick-a-Dick stood in front of the members and cheekily invited any of them to throw cricket balls at him for a shilling. He offered five shillings (about 55 cents) to anyone who could hit him. In an early forerunner to the movie *The Matrix*, where the hero dodged bullets, the sprightly, lean figure again used a shield and a leangle to parry everything hurled at him. A line of members formed and dropped their money into a hat. Some cribbed closer than the 10 paces allowed, but the Aboriginal brushed off the head-high missiles with the shield and the ones directed at his legs with the leangle.

No one could hit him. Dick-a-Dick walked away with a tidy sum, which according to custom would be distributed among the players once he had bought an item or two for himself. This act brought him extra money through the tour, as did Cuzens' sprinting. He was never beaten in any race on the long tour.

The next day at Lord's, England could only manage 120, Cuzens taking 6 for 65, giving him 10 for 117 for the match. It would be a long time before an Australian in any fixture would do as well with the ball at Lord's. He was well supported by Mullagh, who took 3 for 19, giving him 8 for 101 in the two England innings.

Lawrence was nervous. His team had an even hundred to get for victory. He was savouring the meaning of a big win at Lord's against the much-vaunted MCC when his team collapsed for 45. Cuzens, 21, and Mullagh, 12, resisted. The 55 run win to the MCC was a big disappointment. Yet the competitive performance assured the tourists of a well-attended, full itinerary of games.

At the end of the game, there was a reception under a marquee where the Aborigines mingled with the English players and their families, Lord's members and other invited guests. The handsome, dignified Johnny Mullagh was the centre of attention, especially with the women. He was photographed. One of the attractive young women promised to send him a portrait of herself (as did another 'lady from Devon' whom he met during a game at Brighton). When Mullagh received the portraits, he felt strong feelings towards the women, but he knew that none of them would take it further. He told Lawrence, who on tour was every player's confidant and 'professor', that he was fond of these 'ladies' but understood he was unlikely to become involved with a member of English society. It didn't stop him enjoying the admiration, warmth and respect he was shown.

***

Apart from the odd matter of the heart, Lawrence had to contend with the ever-lurking drink problem that also emerged at Lord's. Some of the hosts insisted on drinking to the Aborigines' health. The sad irony was that it was alcohol that threatened their wellbeing. These 'cricket lovers . . . chatted with them', according to Lawrence, 'until the poor fellows got quite helpless to refuse'.

He objected to this pressure, only too aware after the experience at Edenhope of how easily too much conviviality could set them off. The hosts responded that the Aborigines 'were not slaves'. They kept plying them with drinks, saying that 'they should have what they liked'. When Lawrence further remonstrated with them, he was told that 'they [the Aborigines] were in a free country'.

It would be a constant worry for Lawrence on tour. The big drinkers, Bullocky and Harry Tiger, had to be watched. Related to this was homesickness that also emerged by mid-June. It was alarming for some of the Aborigines, who needed to relate to their home territory. They had left it in September. It concerned them to be away for months, travelling Victoria and NSW. Now, several months on and in a strange land 20,000 kilometres from Victoria's Western District, some were depressed. They missed family, traditions and the land. Lawrence counselled them as best he could, but it was a problem that would not leave the squad. It increased the likelihood of some of them getting drunk, and others becoming sick.

Death and glory

Illness unrelated to alcohol or depression was the fate of 30-year-old King Cole after the Lord's match (in which he batted well and made 14). Lawrence checked him into Guy's Hospital, London. Hayman remained in London to look after him as the 'caravan' moved on to Southsea versus East Hampshire, where the tourists were beaten easily.

As the team went down to Bishop's Stortford by 8 wickets on 20 June, King Cole was diagnosed with tuberculosis. Hayman sent a message to Lawrence that King Cole was deteriorating: he now also had pneumonia. Lawrence dropped out of the next (drawn) game at Hastings on 22 and 23 June and travelled back to London to see the ailing Aboriginal. King Cole died on 24 June. Lawrence, with a heavy heart, organised a burial in Victoria Park cemetery. He read the eulogy.

Lawrence couldn't be held responsible for such a tragedy. He had treated all his men well. Yet the warnings about the Aborigines' 'chest ailments' by Constable Kennedy and Dr Molloy would haunt him.

***

The tour had to go on, but Lawrence was now more acutely aware of each player's condition. He noted that two team members – Jim Crow and Sundown – were suffering from being away from home for so long. Lawrence needed them, but acknowledged that their health came first. The next possible ship that he could trust to take them home safely was the *Parramatta*, again under the control of Captain Williams in mid-August, still two months away. Lawrence made arrangements for their return to Australia. He was taking no risks, even if he would be left with 11 fit men for a further two months and nearly half the games.

Despite the anguish over King Cole's death, the team members began to perform better. They visited the Swansea Fun Fair, where Dick-a-Dick spent five pounds (about A$12) on the 'wheel of fortune' and won several prizes. Generous as ever, he handed them out to Mosquito, Red Cap and some of the others. He kept a Swiss imitation clock for himself and became attached to it.

Lawrence's absence against a full strength Yorkshire County team on 13 and 14 July at York had much to do with the thrashing the team received. But it was also hindered by another factor: the Aborigines were not allowed into the lunch marquee on the first day. It appeared to be the first act of racism, as opposed to ignorance, they experienced. They had encountered such positive – sometimes overwhelming – sentiment so far that it was a shock. Once over it, they were angry. Mullagh vowed not to take the field on day two. The lunch snub made the papers. Editorials attacked the Yorkshire Club. The club president denied that any discrimination had occurred, saying that the lunch had been prepared, but that the Aborigines had not turned up. He claimed they had gone to the local hotel for their meal. A supportive crowd on day two gave the Aborigines prolonged applause. But Mullagh was not among them. Lawrence regretted not being present to support his men. Later, he let the Yorkshire Club know of his feelings, although its president stood by his claim. The fact that he did showed that most people were sensitive to the race issue.

Tiger trouble

Lawrence returned to the squad and lifted their rating at Manchester in a loss against Longsight. They thrashed the Carrow Club at Norwich and then drew a tight game against Keighley in Yorkshire. On a mid-tour roll, they beat the Bootle Club by 9 wickets at Liverpool. It was a windy day and the Aborigines decided not to throw their boomerangs. The crowd booed and catcalled for some time until Mullagh, the best thrower, reluctantly bowed to spectator pressure. His first throw curved close to, but above the crowd, who first responded with an 'oooooh', then applauded and yelled for more. Mullagh obliged. The weapon was caught in a sudden wind drop. It slid into a small section of the crowd near the edge of the ground where it struck a boy wearing a straw hat. He went down, stunned and with a bleeding face. A doctor ran across the oval and treated the unintended victim for a superficial wound. His hat had saved him from something more serious.

Mullagh was emerging as the stand-out tourist, returning better figures with bat and ball than almost all top players in England in 1868. Lawrence and Cuzens backed him all the way with consistent performances, while Twopenny's bowling efforts were the surprise in the latter weeks.

Rain intervened at Bramall Lane versus Sheffield – unfortunately, as it turned out – with the Australians on track to win. Hours of idle time led to more chances than normal to booze in a summer so far mainly uninterrupted by the weather. Bullocky drank so heavily he could not leave the team lodgings. In the early hours of day two, 11 August, Harry Tiger assaulted two policemen who had found him wandering Sheffield's King Street. He thumped one of them and tried to strangle the other. Tiger was over-powered. One of the policemen used a baton to quell him. He was dragged to the police lock-up where a doctor was called to dress his head wound. Lawrence asked the Sheffield Club secretary to intervene. He paid the one-pound fine and Tiger was released.

Lawrence was furious. Tiger, like Bullocky and some of the others, blamed the 'gentlemen' – the members and spectators – for giving them too much drink. Over breakfast the next morning, he and Bullocky were warned that they would be sent home if they didn't improve their behaviour. They were so contrite that, as ever, Lawrence forgave them by the time breakfast was over. It was a constant theme, especially during 'down-time' in hotels and boarding houses on their long trek up and down England. Drink would lead to fights between team members. Lawrence would intervene. There would be sulking. Later, during card games or other leisure activity, the Aborigines, according to Lawrence, would 'profess their love for me and do anything to please me'.

He always ended up showing compassion. 'Whatever else could I do than forgive and hope for improvement', he wrote in his memoirs.

There was only one near-altercation between Lawrence and one of the team. It happened in the next game at Dewsbury versus the Savile Club. The team was in low spirits after being soundly beaten by an innings, despite a top score of 20 from a sober Tiger in the first innings, and 48 from Mullagh in the second. The team members straggled up to the station and were waiting for a train. Dick-a-Dick became agitated: he had left his beloved Swiss clock at the hotel. He went to retrieve it. Lawrence, aware that the train was already overdue, blocked his path. Dick-a-Dick remonstrated with his captain, baulked around him and sprinted off. Lawrence gave chase but couldn't catch him. The Aboriginal returned with the clock under his arm just as the train pulled in.

The match schedule ended as it had begun – at the Oval against Surrey, where the tourists were beaten again, this time by 9 wickets. The bowling was as steady and penetrative as ever. The batsmen handled speed and medium pace well. But spin and slow bowling was the team's undoing. It was the biggest single weakness of the squad for the tour.

Another disaster was averted during the boomerang throwing

when a man was struck. Again, a hat saved him. He went down from shock more than anything else. The 'very frightened' near-victim approached Lawrence and threatened him with legal action. Lawrence apologised, pulled five pounds (abut A$12) from his pocket and handed it to the man, telling him to buy a new hat.

'He went away quite satisfied', Lawrence noted, 'as the injured one was very old.'

A team of character

In all, the team played 47 matches from May to November, mainly in the rapidly growing industrial centres, and in front of fair to excellent crowds, who paid sixpence to half a crown (between 5 and 25 cents) at every venue. They won 14, lost 14 and drew 19 of their fixtures. Their form held through the arduous season. These 'Stalwart Men' as the press acclaimed them, never wavered as a unit in five months. They were performing as well (if not better) in the last month as in the first. It was a remarkable feat of character, endurance and stamina, especially as Lawrence had just 11 men to select for half the season. The problem with alcohol was ever present, but no more so than would be experienced by many Test squads later to tour England. Jack Blackham's squad in 1893, as just one example, made the Aborigines seem like choirboys by comparison.

Lawrence and Mullagh were the 1868 team's stars. Lawrence played in 40 matches and scored 1156 at an average of 20.16 an innings, with a top score of 63 versus Sussex at Hove. To appreciate his average, it must be doubled (at around 40) to judge it against performances in the 20th century because of the awful state of pitches, which gave bowlers a decided advantage. Lawrence's bowling statistics were impressive: 250 wickets at 12.1 runs a wicket. Again, the wicket-taking rate figure should be doubled (to around 24) to make a comparative analysis with today's players. Mullagh also did well. He made 1698 runs at 23.65, with a highest score of

94 versus Reading. He played in 45 matches, taking 245 wickets at 10.00. These were both outstanding all-round figures. Mullagh at least had to be rated as first-class standard. He may have acquitted himself well at Test level, but he preferred to return to the Western District and play local cricket.

The third strong performer was Johnny Cuzens, who in 80 innings made 1358 runs at 19.9 (with a top score of 87 against the Carrow Club) and took 114 wickets at 11.3. Bullocky, when sober, also had moments with the bat, scoring 579 at 9.33, as did Red Cap with bat (630 at 8.46) and ball (54 wickets at 10.7). Twopenny, especially late in the long, demanding season, lifted his rating with the ball and took 35 wickets at 6.9. He had learned to bowl over-arm during the long season, and at speed, which accounted for his improved figures. Better over-arm styles were coming into vogue during 1868. The Aborigines would take home with them advanced variations of the new technique that had only been used proficiently by Mullagh in the Western District. (Until 1864, any delivery above the shoulder line had been deemed a throw, and therefore a no-ball. For many years after 1864, any one match would see over-arm, round-arm and under-arm.)

While 'surplus' and 'profit' analysis of the trip has produced rubbery figures depending on the analyst, the tour seemed to have made about 1000 pounds (A$2500) for the investor, George Graham. Lawrence and his Aborigines received nothing beyond what they picked up as prizes, usually for non-cricket performances. Yet the tour's overall 'success' encouraged others to consider future trips.

Lawrence, aged 41 years, returned to Australia feeling that he now had to find greater security for his wife and three children. His touring, risk-taking days were over. Recalling his experience in Scotland as a railway stationmaster's assistant, he joined the NSW railways for the next 22 years until he retired in 1880. His cricket continued, this time with the Newcastle Club, where he became known as 'the Old Master'. Lawrence, it seemed, no matter who the company, performed near the top. Well into his forties, he led the

Newcastle batting average in 1870, 1871 and 1872. His stamina was remarkable. At an age when others would like plenty of spells from the bowling crease, he delivered unchanged in three games against Maitland in 1871, taking 31 wickets for 117. Lawrence played on until he was 56 in 1884, when he made his last appearance in NSW. It was a benefit match at the SCG. He scored 31. But the Lawrence name lived on in Newcastle: his son, Charles, was one of the Club's leading bats in the 1880s.

Full circle

In 1891, Charles Lawrence, now 63, with greying facial hair beyond the mutton-chops and goatee beard of his youth, was appointed coach to the 'Colts', the junior members of the Melbourne Cricket Club.

William Hayman had kept Lawrence informed about the lives of his team. Mullagh, the team's champion, became a professional at the Melbourne Cricket Club during the 1869–70 season. He was paid a pound a week (about A$2.50) and half his travelling expenses, and given free lodging. He played for the MCC for just six weeks (scoring 209 at 34.5, and taking 8 for 300) and was selected to play for Victoria. But no amount of cajoling could keep him in Melbourne or persuade him to travel to Sydney. The pull of his homeland was greater. He had been away too long and became ill, probably from the worry of being dislocated from his cultural roots. He was back in the bush at Harrow by Christmas 1869. This meant he missed playing for Victoria against NSW and was never chosen again. The MCC made sure he was in the Victorian squad for the following season 1870–71, but he refused to return to city life. Mullagh had had enough. He restricted his cricket to bush matches for Harrow, which he enjoyed in his own quiet way, except for some racial incidents that brought back memories of the incident at York. He was batting well against the Apsley Club when its captain remarked to one his bowlers: 'Let's get this nigger off the field'. Mullagh pulled away when the bowler was running in. When he faced up again he deliberately hit a catch. He let it be known to his team-mates that he didn't wish to play against a team with such attitudes. It was a quiet, dignified yet poignant protest.

On another occasion when Harrow was playing away, according to John Mulvaney and Rex Harcourt in their book, *Cricket Walkabout*, all except Mullagh was shown to bedrooms at an inn. The innkeeper ushered Mullagh to a room across the yard by stables. The Aboriginal, in another civil protest, left the premises and slept the night in the open.

Although a Colonial hero, he worked as a farmhand and rabbiter, and struggled during the 1870s. His affection for the English lured him back to Melbourne in 1878–79 to play for Victoria against Lord Harris' All-England XI. Although then in his mid-thirties and past his brilliant best, he managed a majestic 36, top score in Victoria's second innings.

The hat was passed around for him at the MCG. Fifty pounds (about A$120) was collected. A local jeweller donated a gold watch, which Mullagh treasured nearly as much as the portraits of the 'Lady from London' he met at Lord's, and the 'Lady from Devonshire' he met at Brighton. When asked later in life why he had not married, he replied with all the pathos of opportunities lost: 'a white woman won't have me, and I will never marry a black one'.

His prejudice against black women was puzzling, given his own stand against racism.

Mullagh kept playing for Harrow in the Murray Cup competition until nearly 60 in 1890. A year later, local Harrow boy, Jack Minogue, came across sheepskins hidden in a tree at James Edgar's Pine Hills Station, where Mullagh lived and worked. He told the police. They investigated and found Mullagh with more hides. He had been killing sheep to help feed himself and his dogs. Instead of being charged, he was thrown off the station. A few weeks later, Minogue found Mullagh under a tree. He was weak and complaining of a sore side. Minogue went to the station, found James Edgar and they returned, but too late. Mullagh was dead.

One of Lawrence's first acts when he arrived in Melbourne with his MCC job was to attend Mullagh's funeral at the Harrow cemetery. He joined the Harrow team, who threw sprigs of wattle and blackberry on the casket. Each year now, a Koori team plays the Glenelg XI at Harrow for the Johnny Mullagh Memorial Trophy.

***

Lawrence was interested to know what happened to his favourite, Dick-a-Dick. Hayman told him that he had 'gone bush' in the 'little desert' area of Western Victoria soon after the England tour. It was where he had once tracked and found three lost children (the 'Duff' children) – an act that brought him fame throughout Australia and England. He was later seen working as a drover and fencer along the Murray River near Mildura. Johnny Cuzens, another of Lawrence's favourites, had also been an MCC professional. Like Mullagh, he became homesick and ill. Destitute, he returned to the Western District and died of a 'cold' in 1871.

Tiger continued to live up to his name and reputation after the tour, being in and out of jail for drunken behaviour. He died in 1884. Red Cap married and had a family. He was granted 40 acres (about 16 hectares) on the Glenelg River and was a successful shearer until his death in 1893.

***

Lawrence, as an MCC professional, had come full circle since his professional days in Ireland from 1851 to 1861. He was a fine, popular coach, with an eye for technique and courage. He had seen plenty during his decades in and around the game. In 1898, at age 70, he played his last game: a charity match at the MCG, making 7 runs in a stay at the crease of just under an hour. Lawrence's strokes no longer had the brash force of his youth, yet his eye and technique, especially in defence, were a model for any of his charges.

As the years rolled on, that mighty venture of 1868 slipped into perspective for him. At 88, Lawrence began writing his memoirs. Perhaps exhausted by recalling the high dramas of that history-making venture, he gave up after 60 pages of notes – just at the point where he recalled the team docking in England. (A few other extra notes were later discovered by relatives and associates.) He died soon afterwards.

Lawrence's endeavour in touring England and his handling of a mercurial, talented Aboriginal team created a significant breakthrough in 1868. It led to 'Tests' between Australia and England less than a decade later, and soon afterwards, the Ashes – the longest running international competition in sporting history. Charles Lawrence holds the unique distinction of playing in the first England team to tour Australia, and the first Australian team to tour England. It qualifies him as a founding father of Ashes and international cricket.

THE 19TH CENTURY'S GREATEST

Impact Three: W. G. Grace

William Gilbert Grace first played for the West Gloucester Club, which had been in part created by his father, Dr Henry Mills Grace, in 1857. He was just nine years old. Some historians ranked the team as 'near first class', although such rankings were not clearly delineated in mid-19th century England. When W. G. began playing it was more like 'second class' with pretensions for a higher rating on occasions. Developments of standards would come with a rush in the last half of the century and Grace himself would be the most powerful force in the growth of cricket's popularity in England. Certainly, a high early standard was set by West Gloucestershire and invitation games were played against a touring All-England XI, which was regarded as the standard-setter.

W. G.'s maternal uncle, George Pocock, was his early coach. He was disciplined into the drills of sound batting orthodoxy: left elbow up; left shoulder well forward; body over the ball. He was steeped in the game's skills and thinking before he was 10. His father had carved a cricket pitch and oval out of an apple orchard. The pitch was said to be of top quality, which meant that W. G. was schooled in the ways of good curators long before it was an important aspect of top cricket. (Nearly two decades later in Australia, he would put this knowledge to good use when he helped a curator prepare a pitch for a game against Victoria.)

W. G. practised and played each day with his father and four brothers (there were four sisters as well), including his talented elder brother E. M., thus gaining a competitive edge at a high standard from a young age. But nothing in those early years suggested greatness in the making. It wasn't until he was nearly 12, in a game against Clifton in 1860, that W. G. showed something of what was to come for almost another five decades. He made a 'very patient and correct' 35 not out on day one. On the second day, he added 16 to be out for 51. Looking back on his career, W. G. said that knock gave him his greatest satisfaction: it was his first serious inspiration. He felt then, he said, that cricket would be his life. This vision sustained him through 1861 when he had 10 innings and averaged less than 5. In 1862 he scored 298 at less than 20, but began to be thrown the ball occasionally for his round-arm deliveries (over-arm was then banned) which netted him 22 wickets. At 14, development came with a rush as he was exposed to competition for other local clubs, and at his local private school at Downend, near Bristol. A year later, he made an excellent 32 playing at Durdham Down for '22 of Bristol' against the All-England XI.

Distinguishing lines

W. G.'s knock featured aspects of batsmanship that would distinguish him above nearly all others for the rest of the century. The 15-year-old demonstrated a sound defence mixed with an attacking flair that saw him hit a terrific straight six into the ground's tent. He also played forward or back, depending on the ball received. This in itself was a rarity. Most batsmen were known as either back or front foot players, with no mixing of styles. It meant that for the first time ever bowlers were confronted with a player to whom they could not bowl a particular 'line' for very long. W. G., who had learned much about the psychology of the game from his father and three elder brothers, was neither a slogger nor a stonewaller. His approach fell in between, although from this age he was a batsman whose natural inclination was to attack and dominate. This innings against the illustrious All-England squad was an example to W. G. of how he should better calibrate and discipline his dominant tendencies. He was bowled going for another six.

His precocious capabilities were noted. He was invited to play for All-England a year later in 1864. He also played for South Wales, which his brothers had patronised, and it was when playing for this side that he made his first impression nationally. In two innings in his first game at the Oval versus the strong Surrey Club, he made 5 and 38. Then, as a replacement for E. M., who was just off the boat from an Australian tour and not quite ready to play, W. G. came in at first wicket against Sussex at Hove and compiled a masterly century – his first ever. The fact that he did not let reaching this milestone in good company go to his head said much about his mentality, self-discipline, powers of concentration and inner expectations. He moved on relentlessly to 170, then followed this up with 56 not out in the second innings. He went on to further good scores in 1864, hitting 1189 runs and taking 122 wickets by season's end.

At just 16 years, W. G. – now a little over 183 centimetres, lean at 70 kilograms and broad-shouldered – was on the national map of cricket. Yet the appreciation for his potential was discreetly understated. The top professional, John Lillywhite, wrote in his review of the year in *Companion*, that 'Mr W. G. Grace promises to be a good bat; bowls fairly well'.

The next year saw W. G. blossom as a fast fieldsman with a strong arm. Gloucestershire wasn't considered worthy of ranking for the crude 'championship' of counties, made up in 1865 of Notts, Surrey, Middlesex, Kent, Sussex, Yorkshire and Cambridgeshire. So W. G. made the long train trips around the country to play as an amateur for the Gentlemen against the Players, the Gentlemen of the South and – once – for England against Surrey. Thus, at 17, he had reached the highest representative honours open to him. His bowling and fielding kept him afloat at the top of the game, although he also showed glimpses of form with the bat opening with E. M.

Hunger for the big one

In 1866, again playing for England against Surrey, he batted in a manner rarely seen before, scoring his first century (and double) in first-class cricket. The desire to go on beyond the 100, as if he was making up for failures on other occasions, distinguished him again from other players of the time, who were inclined to 'have a go' once that tantalising milestone was attained. W. G. showed a merciless streak that fans throughout England came to love. He was out at 224. Just to show his versatility, he got leave on the last day of the match from his skipper to compete at Crystal Palace in a hurdle race.

Three weeks later, he smashed 173 for the Gentlemen of the South versus the Players of the South at the Oval and then took 7 wickets, bowling through an innings without a break. In 1867, the poor wickets around the country worked against him with the bat and for him with the ball. W. G. had to be content with outstanding bowling figures in what he considered his 'best bowling year'. He took 131 wickets at 13.12 runs per wicket. He was now sporting a beard, perhaps to give him a more fearsome and mature appearance, in keeping with his performances.

1868 was an historic year, marking the first tour by a visiting Australian team, made up entirely of indigenous players, except for its skipper, Charles Lawrence. W. G., turning 20, competed in ball throwing competitions against them at the Oval when the tourists played Surrey. He made some appreciative remarks about the Australians in his book, *W.G.* He regarded Mullagh as 'the best all-rounder'.

In writing this, W. G. was mindful of his own good all-round season in 1868, when he scored 1825 runs in mainly minor cricket, but also first-class games at an average of around 48, while taking 143 wickets at about 14, which was much the same as his penetration in the previous year. (Mullagh's efforts saw him collect 1698 runs at just under 24, and take 245 wickets at 10, suggesting that the naturally talented Aboriginal, who was a fine attacking bat with weakness against spin, lost nothing by comparison with Grace in bowling.)

In 1869, W. G. became a member of the MCC and was still playing as an 'unpaid' amateur. Although this status was flouted to give him recompense, W. G. would remain officially outside professional ranks. His father had set a tone for the sons to follow and they would remain 'gentlemen'. The contradiction in England's quaint class system was that the rustic W. G., although middle-class, would often have more in common with the professional cricketers from working-class backgrounds than members and patronisers of Lord's.

1869 was the coming of age for the 21-year-old, who hit nine centuries, six of them first-class. It also saw him begin an amazing run of 33 seasons in which he would reach at least 1000 runs on all but a handful of occasions. In this year, he also stamped his authority at both ends of the cricketing compass, when he went to Sheffield to play for the South against the North. He crafted an accomplished 122 out of 173 against a fine Northern trio of bowlers: George Freeman, George Wootton and Thomas Emmett.

W. G. rated 1870 a 'good year' but regarded 1871 as his 'most successful'. The figures were remarkable. He made 10 centuries in all cricket, collecting 2390 first class runs at 78.9 – which was twice that of the best of the rest. W. G. this year took batting into a new dimension of big scoring that would set a standard and trend forever: no longer would averages in the 20s and 30s be considered outstanding. He also had his best first-class return with the ball, taking 79 wickets at just over 16.

There was an inevitable dip in his returns in 1872, but his returns were still healthy. W. G. and his younger brother Fred played for the United South XI, who were otherwise all professionals.

Although technically he remained an amateur, W. G. was instrumental in organising matches and he took a sizeable cut of the proceeds. Some saw him as obsessed with money, but he felt he was sacrificing much in his professional life as a future country Doctor – he was still studying intermittently – to play cricket. It was his right, W. G. thought – not unjustly – to make the most of his skills outside the surgery. And in his mid-20s he was well aware of his enormous pulling power.

The full import of the 'Grace Gates' was appreciated a half century before they were erected at Lord's.

Weight and grace

W. G. turned 25 in 1873 and ballooned up to 95.5 kilograms. His athleticism had dropped away. No longer would he hurdle or sprint at every chance in London or at meets anywhere. His paunch of prosperity, nevertheless, did not stop him from being a fine field and throw, nor diminish the exceptional stamina that often saw him bowl long stints and then open the batting for an innings lasting several hours. 1873 was the year he married Agnes Day and combined a honeymoon after the English season with a tour of Australia, for which he was to be paid 1500 pounds (about A$3500) plus all expenses for him and his new bride. It was a hefty fee, more than 10 times that of the professionals he mustered to come with them. The discrepancy, which extended to the Graces and the other amateurs travelling first class while the professionals went below deck to second-class cabins, caused some friction. Yet it was not directed at W. G. but the Australian promoters of the tour.

The tour was a huge trial and test of endurance for all concerned. Having survived the long boat trip, the team encountered dust storms in Ballarat, extreme heat, rough coach rides, ghastly sea voyages around Australia, hair-raising train rides in the Blue Mountains, poor hotel living conditions, a critical press, and competitive teams in

Victoria and NSW. Some of W. G.'s true character traits – dominance, obdurance, gamesmanship that could spill over into poor sportsmanship, and a mercenary approach – were drawn out and on show through the testing tour. His manner in playing was often dictated by the betting he had on a match, and while no hard evidence suggests he threw games and had umpires in his pocket, he certainly stretched the boundaries to make sure he won games – and accompanying wagers.

Through all this, he displayed his own impeccable style on and off the field: a leader, manipulator and organiser not given to reflection. Attacks – verbal and in the press – brushed off him, although on more than one occasion he was close to fisticuffs. Late in the tour, in a fourth game against Victoria – the first in which the local side fielded just 11 players instead of 15, 18 or 22 – he smote a century in 58 minutes just to show how good he was under equal playing conditions. This innings gave him much satisfaction, although perhaps not as much as shooting a kangaroo, which he did after many forays into the bush. He had not been content at bagging smaller game and slaughtering quail, and so much wanted to return home boasting that he had obliterated a big marsupial. Often on the long trips on horse-drawn coaches, he and others rode shotgun and used their weapons to attack anything moving in the bush, or flying.

The trip, if anything, revitalised W. G. In 1874, cricket was non-stop and only interrupted by the time taken to arrive at destinations, and the birth of a son, William Gilbert, who would be known as 'Bertie' to distinguish him from W. G. senior.

Rotten weather in 1875 'reduced' his performances with the bat, but boosted his wicket haul. After starting 1876 slowly, W. G. cranked up to two first-class triple centuries. Then, in a minor game for the United South against 22 of Grimsby, he went one better – in more ways than one. Celebrating the birth of his second son (Henry Edgar), W. G. scored 313 not out. He went on the next day and was not out at the end of the innings.

Grace came off the ground and popped into the scorer's box to see how many he had made. It was 399.

I am Freddie, hear me roar: Andrew Flintoff has Ricky Ponting caught behind during the Second Test at Edgbaston in the 2005 Ashes.

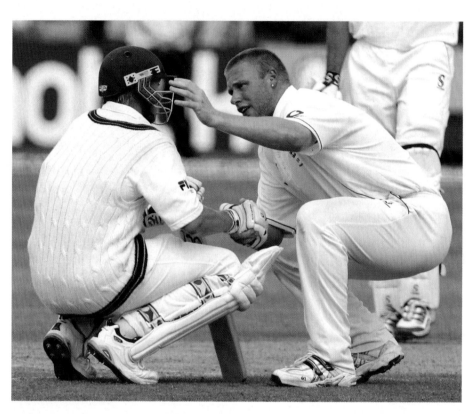

Bad luck, mate: Andrew Flintoff commiserates with Brett Lee after Lee and Michael Kasprowicz failed by two runs to win the Second Test at Edgbaston in the 2005 Ashes.

Oh, what a feeling (of relief!): Brett Lee (left) and Glenn McGrath celebrate after surviving in a last wicket stand, which forced a draw in the Third Test at Old Trafford in the 2005 Ashes.

You talkin' to me? Ricky Ponting looks back and has words with England players after being run out by substitute fielder Gary Pratt in the Fourth Test at Trent Bridge in the 2005 Ashes.

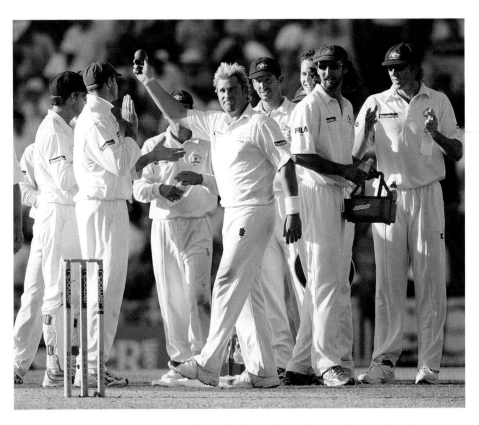

My ball, Michelle: Shane Warne holds the ball up after collecting five wickets (known as a 'Michelle') in the Fifth Test at Brit Oval in the 2005 Ashes.

The great cricket fan: Former South African President Nelson Mandela in 2003 with South African cricket captain Shaun Pollock. Mandela appreciated Bradman stopping an all-white South African cricket team touring Australia in 1971–72.

The revolutionary Mr Packer: Kerry Packer with son James (left). Packer's desire to televise cricket led to the rebel competition World Series Cricket, which changed the shape of the game and players' pay packets.

Happy Hookes: David Hookes hooks Tony Greig for four in the Centenary Test between Australia and England at the MCG on 14 March 1977.

Nice one, Dennis: Derek Randall, the batting star of the Centenary Test, on his way to 174. Here he doffs his cap to Dennis Lillee after a short ball nearly knocked it off.

'That ball': Shane Warne bowls Mike Gatting with his first delivery in Ashes cricket. It was at Manchester in the First Test of the 1993 series and ranks as one of the finest ever balls to take a wicket.

Warnie the thespian: Shane Warne shows his bowling style on the set of *Neighbours* in 2006. He said his life was 'like a soap opera', and eventually he joined one.

Brotherly love: Mark Waugh (left) and twin brother, Steve, in 1987. Both gave exceptional service to Australian cricket. Mark was nearly caught in a 'sting' by Indian illegal book-makers, but he reported failed bribe offers for him to 'throw' a Test against Pakistan.

Mark the Spark: Mark Waugh striking the ball with his brilliant flowing style in the 2001 Ashes Test at Lord's. He was a batsman in the line and style of Victor Trumper, Charlie Macartney and Greg Chappell.

Even Steve: A perfectly balanced Steve Waugh cuts the ball hard on day one of the Sydney Test in 1993 against the West Indies. He was on his way to an even 100. His batting and leadership maintained Australia's control of the Ashes over 15 years.

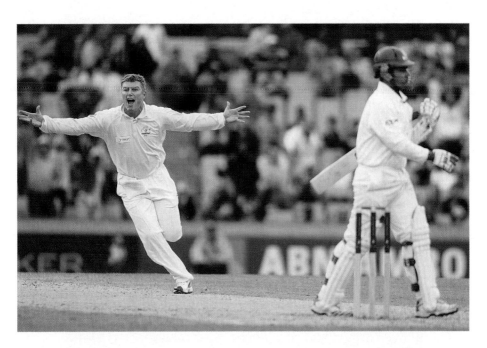

The Flying MacGilla: Stuart MacGill celebrates after dismissing the dashing Indian Virender Sehwag, caught behind for 7 in the ICC Super Test – Australia versus the World XI – on 16 October 2005. Australia won easily.

The 19th century's finest: England's W. G. Grace was the outstanding cricketer of the 19th century. He was always galvanised for games against Australia.

'Oh, make it 400', W. G. suggested.

One run was added and his score was set down as 400 not out, leaving the question of whether or not W. G. Grace ever made a quadruple century a good one for trivia buffs.

The Players were not forgotten either in W. G.'s 1876 onslaught. They suffered to the tune of 169 and, as in previous years, were none too pleased at their annual humiliation.

At 29, he showed he could still deliver with the ball too, taking 129 wickets.

New inspiration

In 1878, W. G. would turn 30, and there seemed little left to keep him in the game. His family life beckoned, and he was close to finally qualifying as a doctor. But the tour of a powerful Australian team, described by English writer Bernard Darwin 'as rugged, hirsute and serious', galvanised W. G. into an extended cricket life. In the historic MCC versus Australia game at Lord's, W. G. opened in the first innings and promptly smacked Henry Boyle for four. He hooked at the second, top-edged it and was caught at square leg. The MCC made just 33. Spofforth took 6 wickets for 4, including a hat trick. The small crowd that had turned up was stunned: the Colonials could play after all. Then the might of England fought back, dismissing Australia for 41, with Alfred Shaw and Fred Morley taking 5 wickets each. The crowd at Lord's grew from 1000 to 10,000 in the afternoon as word swept London that a terrific fight was on. England saddled up again without much confidence against the unprecedented speed and ability of Boyle and Spofforth. Spofforth, who claimed to have bowled W. G. in a net in Melbourne in 1873, had him dropped first ball by Will Murdoch behind the stumps. He bowled him next ball with one that broke in sharply from the off. W. G.'s duck set a pattern as the MCC collapsed again, this time for 19. Australia lost one wicket in mopping up the 12 needed for victory.

England, the seat of Empire, was stunned. It was as if it had lost a war against France. Many historians actually traced Great Britain's beginning of decline as the most dominant nation on earth, at least in symbolic terms, to that incredible day at Lord's. That a group of Colonials – who were not even from a nation as such – could rock England in such a devastating manner, was a huge blow to the collective ego of people in a country accustomed to dominance in everything from business and technological achievement, to international conflict and sport.

Reflecting this, Bernard Darwin wrote in his 1934 biography of W. G., *W. G. Grace*: 'Of all the shocks that a complacent England has had to suffer, in all manner of fields, in the last hundred years, this, the first of them, must have been the most sudden and appalling'.

No doubt Darwin had a little tongue in his cheek when he penned those words. Yet the events at Lord's on 27 May 1878 were the wake-up call for English cricket and W. G. From then on, the Australians would be taken seriously. England would never be complacent again. That game led to the beginning of the longest running international team sport contest in history. Intense rivalry was demonstrated even sooner, when a few weeks later, Gloucestershire was playing Surrey at the Oval. W. G. was incensed that Billy Midwinter – who was the first international cricketer to split his year between Victoria and Gloucester – was set to play that day for the Australians against Middlesex at Lord's. W. G. took a carriage with James Bush to Lord's, abused the Australian manager, John Conway, and bullied Midwinter into coming back to the Oval with him. Conway reported the incident to Australian skipper, Dave Gregory, who grabbed another carriage and gave chase across London, only to just miss stopping W. G. bundling Midwinter through the Oval gates. A bitter verbal altercation ensued. W. G., in his squeaky voice, delivered a schoolboyish parting taunt to Gregory and Conway: 'You haven't a ghost of a chance against Middlesex'.

W. G. was wrong. Australia won at Lord's and Gloucestershire was beaten, even with the dithering Midwinter, at the Oval. The Australians demanded an apology from W. G. for his 'kidnapping' and his abuse or they wouldn't play against Gloucestershire. At the beginning of the tour, this would have been laughed off. But the Australians had taken England by storm and were attracting big crowds after beating the MCC. The gates were rich. Money talked, and with a clear, loud voice to England's foremost sportsman. In a rare back-down, W. G. penned a suitable apology.

On the field, there were fewer beg-pardons as he compiled his usual fine double with bat and ball.

The birth of a daughter, Agnes Bessie, capped off a big year for W. G.

Good Dr Grace

W. G., at 30, at last became a doctor, which led to more time in his Bristol practice and less at games. The figures of the next few years reflected this as he made less than 1000 runs and took less than 100 wickets. Yet he was still top of the batting averages in 1880 – a position he held in all but three years between 1866 and 1879. Once again, the Australians turned up on England's shores, and in September, England at last deigned to play a true international contest – a Test – at home. Lord Harris captained the home team, won the toss and batted. E. M. and W. G. Grace opened with a stand of 91 and W. G. went on to a masterly 152 in his first Test innings. Ever up for a bet, especially with the Colonials for which it was a way of life, he wagered a sovereign that the Australian Captain, Will Murdoch could not beat his score. Murdoch was out for a duck in the first innings, but batted beautifully in his second knock to make 153 not out, after a thrilling ride with the tail-enders. W. G. in particular hurled his best deliveries at his opponent, who was to become a great friend.

Murdoch won the sovereign, but England took the game by 5 wickets. The honour of England and W. G., inextricably bound in that era, and so sharply taken two years earlier at Lord's, was intact once more. Notably though, Australia was without Spofforth, who thought he had W. G.'s measure.

During the season, Fred Grace, W. G.'s fit and talented younger brother, died at 29 after a cold grew into lung congestion. It was a blow for W. G. who was closest to Fred in the family.

Time off for the Test

The following years, 1881 and 1882 (in which W. G.'s fourth and last child, Charles Butler, was born), were lean in terms of runs and matches. But W. G. took time off from his medical practice to prepare for the only Test in 1882 at the Oval late in August, which Australia won in a shock for England. This led to the Ashes, born out of a Test thriller that attracted nearly 40,000 fans in two days. W. G. could take some credit for generating more than a century of hard-fought competition. His own desire to win created fire and aggravation beyond normal competition.

If anything, England's harrowing rather than humiliating loss caused W. G. to bat and bowl on. The Empire now had a more than worthy opponent comparable to the Spanish Armada and Napoleon: it had to be met by England's finest. And while W. G. was hardly 'fine' any more, having beefed up as he approached his mid-thirties, he was still his nation's most formidable cricketer and notable sportsman. He would lead from the front, but his medical practice kept him from another tour down-under in 1882–83, when four Tests were played for a two-win each result. This only fuelled interest and competitive spirit between England and its roughest, wildest colonies.

Meeting Murdoch

W. G.'s work even kept him from his annual centurion act against the hapless Players in 1883, but he was back with a career-prolonging vengeance against the new enemy led by his good mate Murdoch in three Tests at home in 1884. He scored a century against them in the lead-up games but struggled in the Tests. For the first time, his mighty image was dented. The big bearded one at 36 years was 'past it', many thought, and his critics claimed.

As if to answer them, W. G.'s batting rating lifted in 1885 with hundreds against the Players (they suffered no matter what W. G.'s state of mind), Yorkshire and Surrey, and 221 out of 348 plundered from Middlesex – a demonstration that he was still strong enough for the grand gesture.

It was a build-up for the return of the Australians in 1886, this time under Henry Scott. Once more, W. G. gained a psychological advantage with a century against the tourists before the Tests, but in the first two, couldn't repeat his form, despite England winning both games.

The pent-up passion to do well must have been profound but, as ever, well hidden, behind the granite Grace facade, when he strode out to open again at the Oval on 12 August. Not only had the Australians limited him while his team-mates were winning; Shrewsbury had taken his highest score record for England. W. G. was as determined as he had ever been when he and the ultra cautious William Scotton built a then record opening stand of 170. W. G. went on to a century and was well on his way to another before Spofforth had him caught behind by Jack Blackham. His score of 170 restored his personal record and his reputation at 38 as England's premier batsmen.

He carried this touch into the 1887 and 1888 seasons. A paunch, a dodgy knee and the passing years had not dulled his enthusiasm for hitting big scores or running in and attempting to outwit a batsman. When asked about this at the time, W. G. remarked: 'It helps to be able to think like a batsman when bowling and vice versa'.

This indicated he was using all his experience, particularly with the ball, when the zip had gone out of his deliveries. W. G. was rarely tossed the ball by his skipper against the Australians in 1886. When they returned in 1888 under Percy McDonnell for three Tests, he didn't deliver one over. The tourists always seemed to come up with a good opening bowling pair to throw at him when he batted. In the past, Spofforth and Boyle had troubled him. Now they had J. J. Ferris and Charlie 'Terror' Turner to test him. A wet wicket at Lord's in mid July didn't help. W. G., with 10 in the first innings of 53, was one of two English batsmen to reach double figures. In the second, it was the same, with W. G. top scoring with 24 out of 62 in a defiant knock. England lost by 61 runs. The home powers-that-be – in this case, the Surrey committee – made several changes, selected five Surrey players and made W. G. captain: the first time in Tests. He led the team to two big wins at the Oval and Manchester. In the latter, his skills as a batsman on a wet wicket were brilliant.

W. G. strode away from the series a proud man, having batted well and led his country to an Ashes victory. The experience was a spur. Any thoughts of retirement were supplanted by the inspiration to go on as long as he could. W. G. had his practice working well in Bristol and his family life with a wife and four children was busy yet settled. He now had a different perspective on his life. Why retire from his main love if he could manage it, his work and the rest of his private affairs?

Years 1889 and 1890 were ho-hum for him as he continued to score a thousand runs-plus – enough to justify being a first-class batsman but not near the top. He was now a bowler, not in decline but declined, because of a knee problem. Yet he was still capable of holding up an end with steady trundling, and of taking his share of wickets. There were no longer the 100 wicket first-class hauls that marked most of his seasons in the 1870s and 1880s, but half that.

Down-under again

In 1890, at 43, he was motivated for another tour down-under – his first for seven years despite many overtures in that time from promoters. This time, he was captain of a side sponsored by Lord Sheffield. W. G.'s fee was 3000 pounds (about A$7000) (twice that for 1873–74), with all expenses paid, which was far too much for him to refuse despite many thinking his reputation as England's greatest cricketer would be tarnished by such a gruelling venture.

On his first trip he had been a young man, headstrong and incompletely shaped. At 43, in a strong marriage of 18 years and with four children, he was surer of himself, and maturer, although no one could be sure if he would behave better. Agnes and their two youngest children, Bessie (13) and Charles (9), went with him. There was more grumbling about the size of W. G.'s fee, which was 10 times that of the professionals again, making a mockery of the class-driven distinction between them, and W. G. and his fellow 'amateurs'. Lord Sheffield was warned that W. G. alone would consume enough wine to 'sink a ship'. But Sheffield knew what a drawcard W. G. would be, even if some Australians, who recalled the previous tour vividly, would be turning up to see W. G. humiliated. This never quite occurred, although his team lost the Ashes 1-2 to Jack Blackham's Australians. The tour started with goodwill, but W. G.'s insistence on confrontation, insults, abuse of umpires, arrogance and games-manship that – as ever – often seemed unsporting to everyone else, meant that by the end of the tour, W. G. was bid good riddance, rather than farewell.

He had a fair tour himself, scoring 164 Test runs in 5 innings at 32.80, and taking 9 catches. But too many 'incidents' made him unpopular. He insulted Blackham's Victorians in an early game by batting on through tea himself instead of taking the time-honoured break, presumably because he was in good touch (he made 159 not out). This was tolerated by Blackham, but resented by the toiling fielders. W. G.'s bullying gamesmanship began in earnest at the MCG on New Year's Day, 1892, when Blackham produced an old penny with which to toss in the First Test. He called heads and won. W. G. objected to it, suggesting it was 'loaded' – designed to come down heads. Blackham let him toss it six times – it came down tails on four occasions – to disprove W. G.'s silly suspicion, and then decided to bat. Australia won by 54 runs. W. G. acquitted himself making 50 and 25 and retained his humour – despite the incessant barracking from a section of spectators – by 'walking' when a ball whistled over his middle stump. The crowd roared, fooled into thinking the great man was on his way. When he went back to his crease, the spectators were hushed for some time before catcalling began again. It was W. G.'s way of giving 'fingers up' to the crowd that had been at various times amusing or abusive. It demonstrated he was in charge, if not of the match, then of himself at the crease in the face of hostility.

He later challenged Australia's William Bruce, who had taken a diving catch in the outfield, saying that the ball had bounced first, when even the batsman, George Bean, had thought he himself was out. This was vintage double standard W. G. Seventeen years earlier, he had been 'outraged' when his brother Fred seemed to all on-lookers not to have saved a boundary in a game at the MCG but was taken at his word that he had saved it. Or was it just W. G. being perverse and making a point about that earlier incident? In the Second Test at the SCG, he again angered onlookers by wringing his left glove as if it had been hit when a loud LBW appeal was made. W. G.'s worst behaviour was reserved for umpires, although it could not be said he discriminated against anyone. Everyone was open to a 'serve' from the mouth inside the bushy beard. In the NSW match between the Second and Third Tests, he led several vociferous appeals that irritated umpire E. J. Briscoe. At one point, when W. G. went up for a caught behind and the appeal was rejected, he remarked loudly 'it is unpardonable, you must be blind'. Briscoe walked off later and did not umpire the rest of the game. The NSW Cricket Association demanded an apology from W. G. but he declined, denying that he had said the umpire 'was blind'. With that still simmering around him, W. G. became more capricious. According to Australian ex-batsman and skipper, Tom Horan, writing as 'Felix' in the *Australasian*, W. G. delivered a 'gratuitous insult' for not allowing umpire Flynn to stand the Third Test at Adelaide, which England won by an innings and 230 runs. The rejection of Flynn had come about when W. G. was refused another umpire, Philips. Flynn was highly reputed and respected in Australia.

Horan, the most fair-minded of observers, summed up W. G. by writing that he was 'a bad loser, and when he lost two of the Test matches in succession he lost his temper too, and kept on losing it right to the finish . . . Grace seems to have developed a condition of captiousness, fussiness and nastiness . . .'

Despite – or more likely because of – W. G.'s style and manner, the gates were high. Many flocked to see him for his performances, but the crowd also wallowed in his high-minded, dictatorial manner. He was the first 'foreigner' star to visit Australian shores who the locals loved to hate. It was akin to what would befall English Test captain Douglas Jardine 40 years later; and 50 years further on again, John McEnroe, the tantrum-prone American tennis player. W. G. gave the perception of lording it over the colonials, which touched on long-held sensitivities concerning the recent prisoner settlement past. (The last convict ships reached Perth in 1848. Many former convicts would have been spectators when W. G. played.)

Lord Sheffield's tour was judged a success and he generously split his tour profits with the professionals who ended up with more than their guaranteed 300 pounds (A\$700) each. And because money was not lost, W. G.'s whims were tolerated. His reputation as a draw-card remained, despite rumblings after he lost the Ashes.

Knee deep in trouble

W. G. somehow managed to struggle through the Australian season with that wonky knee, strapped and with an ointment of his own prescription rubbed on it. But it 'gave' more in the 1892 season, and his bowling suffered most with him managing to capture just 31 wickets – his lowest return in England since his second first-class year at home in 1866. His batting held up and he cleared 1000 runs at an average of 31, still an impressive effort for a 45-year-old.

In 1893, he was galvanised once more by a tour by Jack Blackham's Australians, who were divided more than any team from England to tour down-under because of the rivalry between Victorian and NSW players. W. G. wanted revenge again, and got it. He didn't play in the First Test at Lord's, which was drawn, but replaced Arthur Stoddart as skipper for the second at the Oval. W. G. won the toss and led from the front as usual, scoring 68 in an opening stand with Stoddart (83) of 151 that set England up for a big innings win. In the Third Test – also drawn – at Old Trafford, he notched 40 and 45, giving him 168 runs at 51.00 for the series. The Ashes win gratified him. All England placed him on a pedestal once more. At 46, he was still very much the king of cricket.

Indian summers

W. G. may well have been expected to retire after that 1893 triumph but he battled on through a mediocre 1894, declining the chance for a third tour of Australia. Instead, Stoddart led a team to an historic 3-2 victory in a great series decided in a titanic last Test struggle at Melbourne, won by England. The team was feted when it returned, but the glory was short-lived. W. G., as if determined to return the spotlight to himself, contrived the most unlikely season for a 47-year-old, which he himself called 'the crowning point' of his career. He crashed 1000 runs in May 1895, scored his hundredth hundred, reached 2346 runs for the season, and experienced the glory and satisfaction from several testimonial matches that generated more than 9000 pounds (A$21,000). The hundredth was against Somerset, and once through the nervous nineties, he went on for a big one – 288 – to mark the occasion. He also made 257 and 73 not out against Kent. An innings of 169 versus Middlesex secured his 1000 in May, and by this time, there were musings about W. G. taking a youth potion. But it apparently only worked with his batting and not his fielding and bowling, where he was down to an occasional trundle. He took 16 wickets for the season. Bad weather reduced his run production in June and July but he still managed to humble the Players with a century against them – something he had managed almost every season since 1876.

W. G. maintained this rejuvenation through 1896, perhaps to accommodate the Australians led by the tactically astute and un-assuming postman, Harry Trott.

W. G. wanted to size them up and was selected to play in Lord Sheffield's XI at Sheffield Park in the first game of the tour. He was surprised at the pace delivered by ex-miner Ernie Jones, who whistled them off a rough wicket. One went through W. G.'s beard and sailed to the boundary.

An agitated W. G. was halfway down the wicket when a four was registered.

'What! What! What!' he 'did rumble out' in a 'falsetto', according to England writer and Test player C. B. Fry, who was playing in the game.

Trott, standing close to the two men, said to Jones: 'Steady, Jonah'.

This caused the fast-bowler to say: 'Sorry, Doctor, she slipped'.

His sorrow was not deep. W. G. received a few welts by which to remember the game for some time. In the same innings, Jones cracked one of F. S. Jackson's ribs. It set the tone for a hard-fought Test series.

Trott won the toss at the First Test at Lord's and batted. Speedster Tom Richardson ran through the Australians, taking 6 for 39 and they were all out for 53. This collapse caused the crowd to grow to 30,000, most of them to see W. G. He didn't let them down. Seizing the chance to crush the great foe, he set about scoring more than them himself. Early in the innings, Jones was thought by some historians to have bowled a bumper through W. G.'s beard for the second time in the season.

'Whatever are ye at?' W. G. protested this time, according to Lord Harris, who saw the incident. Despite the big man's discomfort, the wicket was far better than at Sheffield Park and he went on to 66 before Giffen had him caught. England won comfortably by 6 wickets, and took the series 2-1.

W. G. celebrated by completing two more Indian summers. In 1898 he turned 50, and the Gentleman were pitted against the Players on his birthday at Lord's. W. G. would dearly have loved a century and a win, but had to be content with a fine 43 in 90 minutes, and a loss. If ever there was a sign that he was nearing the end, it was not being able to harvest a hundred at will against the Players.

One last hurrah at the top

But W. G. rumbled on in 1899, unable to resist the challenge of the Joe Darling-led touring Australians, for whom, a colleague noted, 'he always pulled his beard'. There was even more incentive since they had thrashed Arthur Stoddart's team 4-1 in Australia in 1898–99 a few months earlier.

After a dispute and misunderstanding with Gloucestershire, W. G. sadly resigned from the club after 30 years service and was left with playing for London County – a team of his own creation.

He took it seriously enough and in playing for the new side was as competitive as ever. Simon Wilde, in his book, *Number One, the world's best batsmen and bowlers*, noted that when a bowler (F. B. Wilson) once appealed for his wicket leg before, W. G., who had missed the ball, ran down the wicket shouting: 'Out if I hadn't hit it! Well bowled! Out if I hadn't hit it!'

The umpire's finger was up, but W. G.'s outburst caused him to drop his hand and signal not out.

Gamesmanship aside, he could still deliver, as he demonstrated with a score of 175 versus Worcestershire. It was enough to ensure his selection at Trent Bridge in the First Test in early June.

Australia chose the dashing Victor Trumper for his First Test. Darling won the toss and batted. Australia recorded a slow 252. Grace opened with C. B. Fry and they withstood an onslaught by Jones. It began with a brutal head-high bouncer that W. G. just managed to evade. He batted on, seeing Jones off, until he relaxed facing Monty Noble's gentle off-spin and was caught behind for 28. He made just 1 in the second innings before Bill Howell bowled him with a brilliant 'break-back' delivery, and England was lucky to sneak home with a draw.

W. G. still showed he had what it took to play at the top with a good 50 and the wickets of stars Clem Hill and Trumper for the MCC versus the Australians at Lord's. But behind that stern face and beard was a pragmatist. W. G. knew he was not the batsman of 1896, three years earlier. He was catcalled in the field at Trent Bridge for his ineffectiveness if the ball went other than straight to him. His experience and competitive spirit still made him good enough to make England's side, but he decided enough was enough. He retired from Test cricket. It was a shock to selectors who tried to persuade him to go on. When his old friend C. B. Fry inadvertently voted against him, the issue was settled.

The move was big news in England. Without warning, the British Empire in 1899 realised that one of its 'pillars' – a figure who gave it a sense of superiority – would never again have the impact he'd had for 30 years. Without W. G. Grace playing for England and Gloucestershire, there would be an unfillable void.

Nevertheless, there were a few encores from Crystal Palace, the home of the London County side, and elsewhere as Grace batted on. Despite his age (52) and troublesome knee, he was forever a drawcard. Amazingly, he could still provide the force for the powerful hundred as he did for London County versus the MCC and Worcestershire, and for the South versus the North.

A year later, and a few months after the death of that other 'pillar' of the 19th century – Queen Victoria – England was in need of some token from W. G., regarded now as the senior 'eminent person' of the nation. Perhaps aided by an improved ointment or strap for his knee, he provided the gesture by wheeling in for two big wicket hauls against the MCC. W. G. still lifted for the big occasion and Joe Darling's Australians provided him with another opportunity in 1902, when he took 5 for 29 for London County. In that same wet season he had a lean trot with the bat but still managed some entertaining opening stands, notably one of 120 with Will Murdoch, then aged 47 (and living and playing in England) for the MCC. W. G. motivated himself for the game against the Players, and a first encounter with the champion fast-medium bowler, S. F. Barnes. It was an intriguing tussle between arguably the two greatest cricketers England ever produced. W. G. thumped his way to 82. Barnes had him dropped once. The old stager could still match it with the very best of the era.

In 1904, he began with 52 against Surrey, then his batting fell away in May until the end of the month when he cracked 45 against Cambridge University. On 30 May, he made his final first-class performance at Lord's and it was a big game – the MCC versus South Africa. The tourists included the renowned speedster, Johannes Kotze. W. G. played him without any apparent difficulty until nicking one behind at 27.

By 1906, W. G. was fading slowly, with the odd flash of distant youth, as if not to alarm the Empire that a day would come when he would not be seen somewhere in the summer playing the national game. There was one last hurrah versus the Players when he hit 74. He was now down to a trickle of first-class games. His last big game was in 1908, a few months short of his 60th birthday. W. G. prepared for it in a way he had for nearly half a century, with several diligent practice sessions in cold March. The match was the Gentlemen versus Surrey in the first round of the season. He made 15 and 25, both in good style. Still W. G. was not done. Such was his love of the game, he fronted for the odd minor match until 1914, not long before the beginning of World War I. On 25 July, a week after his 66th birthday, he played for Eltham against Grove Park in London for his last innings. He carried his bat for 69 and also took 4 for 48.

A year later he had a stroke, which forced him to bed. He told H. D. G. Leveson-Gower that the German Zeppelin bombing raids on London bothered him. Some explosions occurred near his home. Leveson-Gower tried to lightly disabuse him of his fear, citing the fast bowlers, 'like Ernie Jones', as being more frightening.

'I could see them', W. G. noted mournfully.

Soon after this, he died.

***

W. G. played 878 first class matches – spread over 43 years – scoring 54,896 runs at an average of 39.55, with 126 centuries and 254 fifties. W. G. also took 2876 wickets at 17.92, with 246 5-wicket hauls and 126 match figures of 10 wickets or more. W. G. played in 22 Tests, scoring 1098 runs at 32.29, including two centuries. He took 9 wickets at 26.22, and 39 catches.

W. G. Grace was the greatest England all-rounder before World War I, and it would take the career of Ian Botham in the 1980s to challenge him – a century after W. G.'s peak. His impact on cricket in the 19th century was only matched by the great Don Bradman's in the 20th century.

BIRTH OF THE ASHES

Impact Four: First Thriller

The British were reticent about playing Tests when the 28-year-old William ('Will') Lloyd Murdoch and his squad of Australian cricketers landed in England in May 1882. The schedule listed the only international game beginning on 28 August. Nevertheless, the Australians went about the task of beating the lesser opposition – Oxford – with the same spirit with which they would tackle England. Hugh Massie began the tour with 206 in three hours of savagery. Then in the second game, versus Sussex at Hove, Murdoch launched into the zone of the massive scores with which he had become familiar and crafted a brilliant 286 as Australia amassed 643 to win by an innings and 355 runs (Palmer taking a hat trick). Sussex county officials were so impressed by Murdoch's batting and his mien, which projected such a positive image and bonhomie, that they approached him about playing for the county.

Murdoch liked Brighton. 'It's not Sydney', he remarked, 'but it has a vibrant sea-air, the theatre is excellent and the cricket first-rate. I shall think about it, but cannot guarantee an answer within years.'

'The offer stands as long as you do', an official responded flatteringly.

Buoyed by fine form and perhaps those overtures for his services and his exceptional companionship, Murdoch slammed a distinctive

107 not out in the next contest against the Orleans Club, which included his great combatant, Dr W. G. Grace, whom he dealt with severely.

***

The 13-man group trouped up and down Britain from Portsmouth to Edinburgh, playing 29 games, winning 18, drawing 8 and losing just 3. Cambridge, the Players of England, and Past and Present of Cambridge University defeated the tourists. This was all before encountering the national side at the Kennington Oval on 28 August in their 30th match.

Another competitive game was anticipated after the attractive encounter in the only ever Test (or international cricket game) played in England, in 1880, also at the Oval. In that game, Grace scored 152 and Murdoch 153 not out. The Australians, without their great paceman Fred Spofforth, were beaten by 5 wickets after a fight-back.

The talking point around the ground was not prospects in the match, but the war in Egypt. Thirty thousand British troops were there protecting the Suez Canal, which the first British Viceroy of Egypt, the Earl of Cromer, called 'the high road to the Far East'. His justification for British occupation seemed to be based on a desire to keep other nations, particularly France and Italy, out of Egypt rather than Britain being in.

There was a similar attitude to playing this bunch of touring 'colonists'. The British were a bit reluctant: the seat of Empire had only a vague obligation to this challenge. The one Test had been scheduled for late in the summer, but England players seemed more interested in their normal playing commitments. The attitude to giving the tourists opportunities was begrudging. There had also to be some concern – perhaps an underlying fear – that these talented, aggressive Australians might embarrass the national team in front of a home crowd. After all, the record so far in Tests was Australia four wins (all in Australia), England two wins (one each in

Australia and England), and two draws. England was yet to lose at home, but Australia had the edge in the competition between them.

A loss would be a blow to national pride – even morale – in an era when no one in war or sport was able to defeat the seat of Empire.

England, therefore, chose its strongest possible team: A. N. Hornby (captain), Lancashire; R. G. Barlow, Lancashire; W. Barnes, Nottinghamshire; Dr W. G. Grace, Gloucestershire; A. P. Lucas, Surrey; Hon A. Lyttelton, Middlesex; E. Peate, Yorkshire; J. M. Read, Surrey; A. G. Steel, Lancashire; C. T. Studd, Middlesex; G. Ulyett, Yorkshire.

Only one other player, the Nottingham speedster, Frederick Morley, would have made the side, but he was ill.

Australia's selection was: W. L. Murdoch (captain), NSW; A. C. Bannerman, NSW; J. M. Blackham, Victoria; G. J. Bonnor, Victoria; H. F. Boyle, Victoria; T. W. Garrett, NSW; G. Giffen, South Australia; T. Horan, Victoria; S. P. Jones, NSW; H. H. Massie, NSW; F. R. Spofforth, NSW.

The game was to begin on a Monday, after a gloomily wet weekend in London. The sultry, overcast morning did not deter the crowd from filling the seats, then the standing room. The newspapers may not have inspired attendance, but London's cricket supporters were there in force. They recalled the tightness of the end of the first ever Test in 1880, when England received a fright in its small, last innings run-chase of just 57 for victory.

Many had come this time to glimpse the legendary 'Demon' bowler, Fred Spofforth.

At 10 minutes to noon, and with 20,000 spectators watching, the captains inspected the wicket. It appeared waterlogged. Murdoch won the toss and decided to bat, with no great confidence. At midday, Hornby led his men out, followed by Australian openers Alexander Bannerman and Hugh Massie. Play commenced at 12.10 pm.

Bannerman first faced Ted Peate, the slow left-armer, delivering 'off-theory' from the gasometer end with the off-side stacked with fielders. He was supported by another slow left-armer, Richard

Barlow. The first session of 100 minutes was clearly England's, with the score at 6 for 41. The tourists had slipped around the pitch like a drunken octopus, with no answer to the spin coming at them. They performed no better after the lunch break, being dismissed for just 63 – off 320 balls, with Barlow taking 5 for 19, and Peate 4 for 31.

England already had a huge grip on the match.

But when it batted it did little better, struggling to withstand the ferocity of the tall, loose-limbed Spofforth. He began by scattering Grace's stumps for 4 and didn't stop, thanks to Murdoch's instinct for the bowler with stamina and desire. He let the Demon rattle off 36 (four-ball) consecutive overs for a return of 7 for 46, which included a spell of 3 wickets in four balls to go with his hat-trick in a previous Test. Just before 6 pm on day one, England was all out for 101.

It rained overnight, threatening play on day two, but the poor weather had subsided by mid-morning, when another 20,000 turned up for the contest. This swayed the umpires to resume on time, on a soggy pitch and boggy outfield.

The Australians had an obvious game plan from the first over. Bannerman, a naturally defensive batsman, would block and hold up one end. Massie, a dasher by nature, would hit at everything. Massie cut loose. He had a run-out scare early but capitalised on it by belting three fours, a cut, a sweep and a pull, in 7 deliveries. The double act worked. Massie hammered on while Bannerman put up the shutters. Australia was 0 for 50 in 40 minutes. It had wiped off the deficit, and England knew it would have some sort of run chase.

Massie's luck ran out at 55, and Australia was 1 for 66 – a lead of 28. But the only other batsman to have an impact was Murdoch (29 run out). Peate's accurate bowling collected him another 4 for 40.

Australia crumbled to 6 for 99 in the second session. Sam Jones, just 21 years old, came to the wicket and started well, collecting six in a few deliveries. Murdoch was batting with him and took a single to Grace at point. Young Jones touched his crease and walked away from it to do some farming. He patted a few spots on the pitch. Grace ran in, removed the bails and appealed. Jones looked up and wandered back to his crease, only to see the umpire's finger go up. The batsman stood his ground and looked up the wicket to see his skipper's reaction. Murdoch shrugged. Jones trudged off, head down. The astonished crowd reacted. The Australian dressing room was agitated. Spofforth was furious at what he saw as poor sportsmanship. When his skipper was run out – legitimately – soon afterwards, the speedster came up to him.

'What do you think of what happened to young Jones?' Spofforth asked Murdoch as he removed his pads.

'It wasn't the most courteous piece of sportsmanship I've seen, Fred.'

Murdoch's words were just enough to incite his main weapon.

'I swear to you, England will not win this', he said angrily.

Murdoch nodded his agreement and did not have to say anything else. He knew his charge. Spofforth was a man of his word, a no-nonsense 'bloke' and a true sportsman who, at times, had a short fuse. If ignited strategically by his leader, the effects were devastating. He had blasted through England with alacrity in the first innings. Grace's unsporting indiscretion had made Spofforth determined to be just as explosive the second time around. And it was needed. Australia only scored 122 in its second innings, leaving England just 85 for victory.

It was 3.25 pm. in the afternoon as the England team sauntered off the ground. Grace was set to open with England captain, Arthur 'Monkey' Hornby, who wanted to create a little sporting history by batting England to victory. After batting at number 10 in the first innings and being bowled by Spofforth for 2, he wished to make amends.

As the players left the arena, a spectator – 48-year-old George Spendlove – stood up to stretch for his own footnote in history after telling his friend Edwin Dyne that he didn't fell well. Spendlove had a brain haemorrhage and collapsed, bleeding from the mouth.

Dyne called, 'Doctor! Doctor!' Others in the crowd took up the cry. Grace heard them and bustled towards the stricken gentleman. After a cursory look at him, Grace ordered that Spendlove be carried to the room above the pavilion. The good doctor forgot about donning his pads. He had more important work to do. He examined the patient, but the man was beyond help and was dead a few minutes later. Grace had to clean up, before padding up and walking out to bat. Instead of a normal 10-minute delay between innings, it stretched to 20 minutes.

Grace let his new opening partner take the brunt of Spofforth's early overs, grabbing quick runs off Boyle at the other end. He watched as Spofforth uprooted Hornby's stumps with a ball described by a journalist 'as the quickest on English soil in a decade'. More hyperbole would follow as the Demon then bowled Barlow for a duck. England was 2 for 15.

Ulyett – the best player against Australia in Test cricket's short history – joined Grace, who sensed the ill-feeling from the Australians over his controversial run-out. This made him just as determined as Spofforth to win. He dug in and played shots to the few balls that allowed them.

These two put on 36, taking the score to 51, which the spectators thought would see the home side sail home. Murdoch noted that the sky was darkening. He cajoled Spofforth into bowling up the slope from the pavilion end. This way, his long right arm would be less easy to pick up in the poorer light. The Demon responded by lifting his rating even further. Surrey Secretary, Charles Alcock, founder of *Cricket* magazine, noted how rattled the English dressing room became watching Spofforth as he tore away from them and in at the wavering batsmen.

'Our finest lost their nerve', Alcock said. 'The collective cool dissipated.'

Spofforth bowled his famous 'break-back' ball – which cut into the right-hander from outside off stump – 10 times in succession then zipped through a straight one. It confused Ulyett (11). He was good enough to get an edge to Blackham, who was literally breathing down the batsman's neck, and displaying his great skill standing up to the wicket for Spofforth, who was above medium-pace.

England was 3 for 51. There was still no need for panic, with 34 to make and 7 wickets in hand. With the score at 53, Grace (32) drove at Boyle but failed to get to the pitch of the ball. A catch was struck to Bannerman at mid-off. He snaffled it. 4 for 53. Grace had batted at his best, and seemed unfazed by the need for his professional services, and the losing of a patient, just before he batted.

Lyttelton off-drove Boyle for 4, and he and 'Bunny' (his nickname, not his batting status) Lucas, coming in at number five, lifted the score slowly. There were six wickets in hand. Murdoch urged his team to concentrate and his bowlers to deliver accurately. His hope was that this would force errors.

Twelve successive maidens were bowled.

Lyttelton had managed to avoid Spofforth. The speedster had a quiet word to Murdoch. The skipper then spoke to three players forward of the wicket, including Bannerman. Boyle delivered a slower ball. Lyttelton drove to Bannerman, who misfielded deliberately, letting the batsman take a single. Lyttelton had to face Spofforth. Four maidens followed. Lyttelton was stranded at one end facing the Demon, who finally delivered an unplayable break-back that crashed into the batsman's stumps.

England was 5 for 66 – 19 short with half the side still to bat and no time restraint.

J. M. (Maurice) Read, batting at number seven, had made an impressive 19 not out in the first innings. He ran hard as Lucas took 2s. After an over, he had to face Spofforth. The first ball to him shaved his off stump. The next one bowled him, sending the middle stump metres back.

England was 6 for 70, still 15 short of victory. Next ball, Spofforth bowled Steel for a duck. 7 for 70.

'With such bowling', Alcock wrote, 'it could have been 150 [to get].'

England was still in the box seat, however. Lucas was still in.

He had been joined by number nine, William Barnes – a top-class professional. The number 10, Charles Studd, had made two centuries against Australia and in theory would be able to polish off the few runs needed. But his nerve had gone. He was walking around the pavilion with a blanket over his head, trying to keep warm while blocking out the view of Spofforth charging in and the cries from the stunned crowd. Studd was praying he would not have to bat. Someone handed him a glass of champagne, a welcome nerve 'steadier' in the circumstances.

Lucas and Barnes scrambled 5 runs off Boyle's over, taking the score to 75. Spofforth, showing no signs of fatigue, charged in and forced Lucas (5) to play on to the last ball of his over. England was 8 for 75, 10 away from a win. The big crowd was now full of tension. People nibbled on fingernails. One fellow even gnawed at his umbrella handle.

Studd, having consumed two glasses of champagne, walked to the player's gate, the blanket still round his body. He dropped it on a seat and walked out, his legs jelly and his brain spinning.

'I'm facing, Mr Studd', Barnes informed the newcomer.

'Oh, thank God!' Studd said.

Barnes made a decision to keep the strike. Studd, normally a fine stroke-maker, was not up to it this day.

Barnes took the beginning of Boyle's 20th over. The first ball jumped awkwardly. Barnes fended it off. The ball flew off his glove to a gleeful Murdoch at point. England was 9 for 75. Peate – England's last batsman – came to the wicket. He had a wild swing and collected 2 to leg.

The score was 77. England had 8 to win, 7 to draw.

Peate played and missed the next ball and then swung mightily at a third. It bowled him. The crowed was hushed for a moment. Then they jumped the fence, yelling and screaming. Spofforth was lifted shoulder-high and carried to the pavilion.

Once inside, he danced a jig of victory, thrilled with his magnificent 7 for 44, giving him 14 for 90 for the match. He was the best player of the game. He was appeased for what he saw as Grace's unsporting transgression in the Jones run-out. He had vowed vengeance and achieved it.

Spofforth and Boyle had taken 6 wickets with their last 20 balls while just two scoring shots were made for 4 and 2, thus ensuring an amazing Australian victory by just 7 runs.

The electricity generated by such a close encounter boosted cricket to an unprecedented level of interest in England and Australia. This infuriating, taxing game that could bore to tears demonstrated to a wide audience that it could also excite like no other sporting contest.

The next day, some excited newspapers gave the result equal front-page billing with comment about the Sir Garnet Wolseley-led British victory at the Battle of Tel-el Kebir. It made the historic loss at the Oval a fraction more palatable – although still unacceptable – for British gentlemen devouring the news analysis on 30 August.

The game invoked songs, scenes in the NSW parliament and even poetry by poet laureate, John Masefield. He penned '85 to win', a dramatic reconstruction including a line for poor Spendlove, who died prior to the real excitement, which began an hour after his death.

After the amazing contest, death was a continuing theme.

A writer at *Sporting Times* published a mock obituary notice:

In Affectionate Remembrance
Of
ENGLISH CRICKET
Which died at the Oval, 28th August, 1882
Deeply lamented by a large circle of
Sorrowing friends and acquaintances
R.I.P.
NB – The body will be cremated and the
Ashes taken to Australia.

Thus Spofforth's brilliance, Massie's daring, and Murdoch's pressure and leadership skills in the tense final hour led to the introduction of 'the Ashes' competition.

Murdoch and his squad played another eight matches and then returned home via the US. The trip had lasted eight months. The players were heroes after the narrow Oval success and feted in every Australian capital city on their return. In Melbourne, they were given a torchlight procession and awarded medals. A jubilant John Monash, aged 17, and no cricket fan, joined the procession. He cut out newspaper clippings of the victory and placed them in a scrapbook. The 1882 Oval win meant an enormous amount to Australians who wished to be see their six colonies federated and independent of the UK.

The victory, by the only entity then to represent Australia, was an emotional precursor to nationhood 19 years later.

***

The Oval Test sparked so much passion that Ivo Bligh's England team was set to play four Tests during the 1882–83 southern summer.

In the first, 'Mr Murdoch's XI', as it was officially called, was successful by 9 wickets against 'The Hon Ivo F. W. Bligh's Team', in front of a total MCG crowd of 54,000 over the New Year.

Australia lost the Second Test in Melbourne, beginning 19 January 1893 when England notched 293 and then bundled out Murdoch and co for 114 and 153. The teams barely had time to get off the train before they were at it again in Sydney in the Third Test. England kept the pressure on, scoring 247. The world's best bowler, Spofforth, finding the SCG wicket much more to his liking, took 4 for 73.

The home team, with opener Bannerman (94) in form, struggled to 218. Spofforth (7 for 44) then reduced England to 123 in its second innings, which set Australia 153 to win. It was the time for Australia's collective nerve to fail. It only reached 83, with Barlow (7 for 40) the destroyer. England won by 69 runs and took the series 2-1.

In keeping with the spirit created at the Oval and the notice in the *Sporting Times*, an attractive group of young Melbourne women, led by Florence Rose Morphy, presented an urn containing burned bails to England's Bligh, 23. (Morphy and Bligh married a year later.) Now the Ashes had 'substance' – they existed.

The urn would eventually be given to the MCC at Lord's. England and Australia would fight for it from then on, although it was destined never to leave Lord's again until 2006, when it would tour Australia over the period of the Ashes (2006–07).

THE MAVERICK
MAGICIAN

England's S. F. Barnes was one of the finest bowlers of all time. He could deliver in-swingers, out-swingers, along with fast leg-breaks and off-spin. He was the dominant bowler of the Golden Age of cricket in the late 19th century and before World War I.

***

Sydney Francis Barnes was born in 1873 in Smethwick, Staffordshire and brought up as the second of five children. His father, Richard, worked for the Birmingham Muntz Metal Company, and encouraged his son's cricket career, but with the proviso that he always have a trade. Professional cricket was acceptable to the working-class patriarch, but it was not to be relied upon because of the game's short earning time. Richard expected his son to last a decade as a professional cricketer, and Sydney found work as a clerk in a Staffordshire colliery – a solid back-up for his cricketing wages.

Barnes grew into a robust, powerful man of 186 centimetres. He bowled off a shortish run, but made full use of his height by 'hooking' the ball down from a high right hand. He extracted bounce and imparted spin using his strong hands and fingers, without seeming to use his wrists. This allowed him greater deception. Batsmen found it difficult to pick which way his fingers were propelling the ball, as opposed to watching the more obvious conventional break of the wrist. He was unerringly accurate and had the uncanny capacity –

much like Shane Warne in the modern era – to drop the ball on a length from his first delivery and maintain it there for long spells.

Barnes claimed to always 'bowl at the batsman's stroke', in order to create a false move. But the record is more ambiguous. He clean-bowled and captured LBW a fair proportion of his victims, suggesting that he delivered at the stumps just as much. More pertinent perhaps was his capacity to bowl at the batsman's weakness. If the batsman was unsure of the lifting ball, Barnes would use it. If he fidgeted outside off, Barnes employed the out-swinger. If he was a back-foot player, Barnes loved ripping a fast off-spinner or in-swinger at him. He boasted that he could send down a distinctively different delivery for every ball in an over. No one dared doubt him. He was a master bowler whether at league, county or Test level.

Barnes had an unconventional career, playing mainly league and minor county rather than county cricket, except for two successful seasons. He made his debut for Warwickshire (against Leicestershire) at 20 in 1893, but it was not yet a first-class county. In 1894, he slipped back to Lancashire league playing for Rishton and only played a couple of county games. Barnes preferred the security of the league, with its steady wage and hypocrisy-free atmosphere, to the uncertainty of county cricket which offered him less, and was confused by the rankings of amateurs and professionals, who were looked down on for playing for money. Rishton paid him three pounds and ten shillings (about A$8) a week, which was well over three times the average skilled worker's wage, and substantially more than he would have been paid at Warwickshire. It entered the county championship in 1895 and was not rich enough to pay top salaries. The other advantage in the eyes of Barnes and his father was that league cricket was played on weekends, which allowed him to maintain a steady job.

Barnes was well aware of the problems encountered by professionals. He noted that 'after fleeting years as famous cricketers, feted and fussed over, they dropped out, returned to the mine or factory, or, at best, a fourth-rate beerhouse, trading as best they could upon their faded glories'.

This mind-set of what to avoid in English cricket dictated Barnes' approach throughout his long, illustrious career. He would be hard to sway from his rock-solid path of steady income. This fitted with his somewhat dour character. There was little flamboyance in Barnes' make-up (although as he mellowed later in his career, a dry wit surfaced here and there). Cricket, essentially, was still a sport to be played part-time – not a life.

Nevertheless, pressure was put on him to change. Archie MacLaren, captain of Lancashire and England, found a way to seduce Barnes to break his set pattern of play and work. MacLaren asked him to play for Lancashire against Leicestershire in the final county game of 1901. Barnes slipped easily into the first-class contest, and bowled magnificently. He impressed with his easy, high action, control and menace. He took 6 for 70 in Leicestershire's first innings. MacLaren then realised that the description of 'fast-medium' was about one-tenth the story.

He wanted to persuade Barnes to play for Lancashire in 1902. He found a sweetener to the deal that would be tough for Barnes to refuse: the 'trip of a lifetime' down-under for a Test tour in 1901–02. Barnes was 28 in 1901 when he was asked by MacLaren, who wanted players to replace Yorkshire's Wilfred Rhodes and George Hirst – both star bowlers. Yorkshire's Lord Hawke, the county's supremo who put county before country, would not allow them to tour because it might harm Yorkshire's chances of victory in the 1902 championship. This left openings for the Australian trip. Barnes agreed to go.

MacLaren was criticised. In 1899, he had failed to take back the Ashes that had been relinquished by England in 1897–98. The press asked who Barnes was beyond a league cricketer approaching 30 who had had moderate success in half a dozen county games.

MacLaren, who had toured Australia twice, was making the biggest selection gamble in cricket. He was backing his judgment on one county game and the experience of facing Barnes in the nets.

Barnes-storming

In the lead-up games to the Tests, Australian cricket followers were in no doubt about Barnes and his capacities. He took bags of wickets against Victoria, South Australia and NSW and his determined demeanour gained respect from opposition, spectators and the press. MacLaren had no hesitation in choosing Barnes for the First Test at Sydney beginning 13 December 1901 – but then again, he had few options. Gloucestershire's skipper, Gilbert Jessop, a fast bowler who was renowned for his big hitting, had played just one Test. Somerset's Len Braund, who bowled medium pace and leg-spin, and Colin 'Charlie' Blythe, a slow left-armer from Kent, were also both on debut at Brisbane. It was a thin attack. The Australians, with their powerful batting line-up – including Syd Gregory, Victor Trumper, Clem Hill, Monty Noble and Joe Darling – were confident of victory.

MacLaren won the toss, batted and England racked up 464. When Australia was just 3 in reply, Barnes deceived Trumper with a slower one. The greatest batsman of the era pushed too early and sent back a return catch. Barnes took it one-handed. The casual method of the catch saw Barnes receive a reprimand from MacLaren.

'Well I caught it, didn't I?' Barnes retorted. He may have been a professional but he would stand his ground against anyone, anywhere. MacLaren, an amateur, was one of the few men in the cricket establishment who knew how to handle this dark, brooding figure. There would be no forelock tugging or 'sorry sir' from this straight-backed Staffordshireman.

MacLaren was jubilant to see the back of Trumper who, with his brilliant 135 not out at Lord's in 1899, had been a key to Australia winning the Ashes 1-0. Barnes went on to remove half the Australians and included Hill and Darling in his haul as Australia staggered to all out 168. It was a sensational debut by an Englishman in Australia. MacLaren enforced the follow-on and a shell-shocked Australia was rolled for an innings and plenty.

There was more to come in Melbourne. There had been rain overnight and the pitch was rain-affected on day one – New Year's Day, 1902. MacLaren won the toss again and this time sent the Australians in. Barnes stunned the big crowd by having Trumper out caught by Tyldesley for 0 off his second ball. Barnes again repeated his Brisbane act by bowling Hill, this time for 15. Australia never recovered and was sent back for 112, Barnes this time snaring 6 wickets, bowling unchanged. But if Australia's effort was meagre, England's was wafer thin thanks to rangy Monty Noble who took 7 for 17 with his off-spinners. The tourists could only manage 61 in 15.4 overs.

It was still only day one when Australia batted again. Its skipper, Joe Darling, switched the batting order around after losing early wickets. It went to stumps 5 for 48. Twenty-five wickets had fallen in the day. Spectators weren't likely to forget the entry into 1902 in a hurry. On day two, and in better conditions, Clem Hill led a fight-back with 99, while Reg Duff, batting at number 10, scored 104. Barnes was always dangerous and managed to dismiss Trumper cheaply for the third time in four innings. He finished with 7 for 121 off 64 overs. Yet Australia compiled 353, giving it a 400 plus lead. England were beaten easily. Both Barnes and Noble (they got on well but didn't start an American book store chain) took 13 wickets for the game.

Barnes had 19 wickets (at 17) for the series, but that was to be his final tally (with another 22 wickets on the first-class tour). He broke down with a knee injury at Adelaide in the Third Test and the playing side of the tour was over for him. Without him, England didn't have enough answers to Australia's long batting line-up. It lost the series 1-4. Had Barnes been fit, England would have achieved a much closer result. Instead, they lost the Ashes for the third successive series.

Yet Barnes personally sailed home with a big reputation and an improved bowling repertoire, including an off-cutter taught to him by Monty Noble.

Barnes' knee kept him out of the 1902 Ashes until the Third Test at Bramall Lane, Sheffield – in the one and only Test there: the first two Tests had been washed out. Barnes was not selected in the original 12, but when MacLaren woke to an overcast sky he made a snap decision to cable Barnes, asking him to make his way to the ground. MacLaren won the toss and sent Australia in. Just before going onto the field he informed Yorkshire fast-medium bowler Schofield Haigh he would be 12th man. But Barnes was late. Haigh moved out onto the field with the team. Lord Hawke – who had personally picked Haigh – and his fellow selectors looked on and thought all was in order. They had no idea that Barnes had been selected and Haigh given drinks duties. Barnes arrived five minutes late but was summoned onto the field, replacing Haigh.

This was a brave move by MacLaren given that Haigh was in front of a home crowd and, more poignantly, that he was Hawke's choice. It was a coup, albeit a temporary and risky one. If Barnes flopped, MacLaren's leadership position would have been in jeopardy.

As soon as Barnes appeared, MacLaren threw the ball to him, thus thwarting any possible counter-move by Hawke, who was watching, flabbergasted. Once Barnes delivered a ball, there could be no doubt in the minds of umpires or onlookers that Barnes was in the XI and not Haigh.

Barnes was just too late on the field to dismiss Trumper (bowled Braund for a duck), who was having a bumper season. But he proceeded to dismiss Duff, Hill, Darling and Syd Gregory cheaply, leaving Australia at one juncture 5 for 73 and in disarray. They recovered, thanks to a brave 47 from Monty Noble, and reached 194. Barnes walked away with the handsome figures of 6 for 49 off 20 overs. Rarely had a player made such an impact on debut in both Australia and England. Now his home country understood the reason for the fuss over Barnes after his Australian tour. He had, inside four appearances for England, established himself as a truly great bowler against one of the best batting line-ups in the history of cricket.

Yet even he was unable to prevent Australia winning by a healthy 143 runs, thanks to a blinding second innings start by Trumper (62) – his 50 coming up in 40 minutes – and a fine 119 by Hill. Trumper exacted some revenge for his drubbings at the hands of Barnes so far, and the big bowler took a thumping. He ended with 1 for 50 off 12 overs, four of them maidens after Trumper had done his worst. Barnes was not happy, but gained no small measure of satisfaction in bowling Darling for a duck. Noble once more proved the difference in a Test, taking 11 wickets.

Then came the shock of Lord Hawke's revenge: Barnes was inexplicably dropped from the last two Tests. Had this type of incredible selection decision been in isolation it may have caused outcry. But English cricket was used to such moves while Lord Hawke was involved. It passed by with not much more than a ripple in the press. Those who a year earlier questioned Barnes' selection now queried his omission. But it was too late. Australia had won another series 2-1 – making it four on end. Again, had Barnes been playing, England may well have won.

Not in his league

Barnes, now 29, had to make do with playing for Lancashire for 1902, and then once more in 1903. He was the first bowler in the country to take 100 wickets in 1903 and managed 131 at 17 for the season. Many of those wickets were due to a new style of delivery dubbed 'the Barnes Ball'. It was a leg-break that swung into the batsman then cut away and lifted with some pace. By the time his county contract was over he had taken 226 wickets at 19.41. Barnes always had the fall-back of the league and this seemed to dictate his sometimes too-direct airing of views on and off the field. He got up the tilted noses of his gentleman amateur team-mates. He was scathing about them if they didn't play hard to win, and he resented the attitude towards him when he did, which was most of the time. His irreverent mien didn't make him popular with his fellow professionals. On the contrary, they couldn't cope with his behaviour towards the amateurs when they were being deferential and subservient.

Barnes' independence cost him further immediate Test selection. MacLaren was no longer in charge of the national team after the loss to Australia. His place had been taken by Pelham Warner, who was under the misapprehension that Barnes could not bowl an off-break. This alleged shortcoming was a false story pushed by *Wisden*, the establishment mouthpiece, which had never favoured Barnes and his maverick, anti-authoritarian ways. Consequently, Warner didn't argue for him to go on the tour and he was left out. A few days after the team was announced, Barnes met Warner in a game at Lord's. Barnes delivered three leg-breaks. His fourth ball was a beautiful off-break that bounced back Warner's middle stump. The point was made, but too late.

Near the end of the 1903 season he tried to renegotiate his contract for 1904, asking the county to find him employment during the winter and also to grant a benefit match after eight years. This was instead of the miserly one pound (A$2.30) a week during the winter offered by the county. Lancashire said 'no'. Barnes 'walked'.

England's stunning 3-2 win under Warner in 1903–04 and the triumphant bringing home of the Ashes didn't help Barnes' cause.

MacLaren tried to patch it up with Barnes early in 1904, offering the bowler the same pay as the top professionals at the Club. But Barnes rejected his old skipper and returned to the Lancashire league. This isolated him and gave those who didn't like him an excuse for not selecting him at the national level.

Barnes was left out of the entire 1905 Ashes, despite many good judges – among them Test cricketer and writer C. B. Fry – insisting he was England's best bowler in that year and others that followed. But England won the series 2-0 without him, so there was no press or public cry for his return. It was no surprise to see him omitted from the 1905–06 tour of South Africa. England was thrashed 4-1 and there was good reason to urge Barnes' return for the next series in England – also against South Africa – in 1907. But despite taking a record 119 wickets at a remarkable 7.83 for Staffordshire in the minor counties in 1906, with no exposure at the top county level, he was rejected once more.

The long overdue return

While England struggled to win the 1907 three Test series 1-0, Barnes claimed 112 wickets at a staggering and miserly 3.91 runs a wicket playing for Porthill Park in the North Staffordshire league. This included all 10 wickets for 26 against a strong Yorkshire Second XI at Wakefield. News reached Lord Hawke, still the country's key selector.

Barnes had missed Test selection for five years. He was now 34, but not forgotten. He had cut a swathe through Lancashire league teams and minor counties, returning figures that were more akin to school than professional cricket. His enormous talent had a mystique about it. He played to packed houses in Lancashire but the only news the rest of England heard about him was in regular small press items that said 'Barnes Takes Eight', or 'Barnes Breaks Record'.

A lack of talent willing or able to tour Australia in 1907–08 caused Barnes' name to float to the surface after too long an absence. But first, he cut a good deal for himself: a 300 pound (A$700) cash payment at the end of the tour, a first-class return ticket, 30 shillings (A$3.50) a week during the sea voyage and 40 shillings (A$4.70) a week expenses while in Australia. With this agreement secured, he was selected for his second tour down-under. It was a big challenge for Barnes and he relished the thought of doing battle with Australia's outstanding batting line-up again. Only another five of the 15-man squad had been to Australia previously – Arthur Jones, Wilfred Rhodes, Len Braund, 'Charlie' Blythe and Arthur Fielder.

The First Test was a thriller. Barnes contributed, without being penetrating, yet he had the satisfaction of bowling Trumper for just 3 and Noble for 27 in Australia's second innings. Australia seemed beaten when 8 for 219 and still 55 short of victory, but ninth wicket pair Hazlitt and Cotter steered their team to a 2-wicket victory. The Second Test at Melbourne, beginning New Year's Day, 1908 belonged to Barnes for a fine all-round effort. He bowled tightly in the first innings, taking 0 for 30 and then took 5 for 72 off 27.4 overs in Australia's second innings of 397. It was his fifth 5-wicket haul in just six Tests.

England was left with 282 to make for victory. Barnes came to the wicket at 7 for 198 with 84 still needed. At 209, Crawford was out. Barnes was joined by Humphries of Derbyshire. They added a spirited 34. Then big Warwick Armstrong, bowling his leg-spinners, trapped Humphries LBW for 16. The score was 9 for 243. Kent's Arthur Fielder, who was not a complete bunny, came to the wicket. It was a tall order for England to win, although not an impossible one, considering Barnes' run-making for Staffordshire had been commendable if unscientific. They edged the score up until Barnes hit the winning run off Armstrong, who was particularly dejected in front of his adoring home crowd. England won by 1 wicket and Barnes was cheered from the ground after playing a big hand in the series' second thriller.

Australia exacted revenge with a 245 win at Adelaide in the Third Test, but again, Barnes was not disgraced. He turned stock bowler in the face of a Clem Hill (160)/Roger Hartigan (116) 243 partnership that set Australia up. Among his five victims for the match was Trumper once again, this time bowled for a duck in Australia's second innings.

Back at the MCG for the Fourth Test, Barnes struggled, taking 1 wicket in each innings. Australia won easily and took back the Ashes. Barnes rallied in the dead rubber at Sydney, removing 7. His grand haul of wickets included Trumper (10), Noble (35), Hill (12), Charlie Macartney (1) and Gregory (44). Unfortunately for England, he could not repeat this performance in Australia's second innings. A brilliant 166 by Trumper turned the tables and set Australia up for an eventual 49 run win.

Barnes would once more sail home in a soundly beaten squad. But again, he was far from disgraced with Test figures of 24 wickets at the more than respectable rate of 26.08 runs per wicket against a powerful batting side. He had now taken 50 wickets at less than 21 in just nine Tests since his debut in Sydney in 1901.

The Australians returned to England in 1909 to defend the Ashes. Lord Hawke reinstated Archie MacLaren as England's skipper, but failed to select Barnes, now 36, until the Third Test. There were rumours that Barnes was not well, having caught whooping cough from his son, but he was playing at league level. The series was one-all, and while the horse had not bolted, Barnes' presence at Lord's, where Australia won by 9 wickets, may have made a huge difference. He did make a difference in the Third Test at Headingley, and it was not his fault that England failed by 126 runs. Barnes took 5 of the first 6 wickets to fall in Australia's second innings. His final bag of 6 included Trumper, Noble, Warren Bardsley and Vic Ransford. England collapsed in its second effort under the guileful left-hand spin of Macartney and was thrashed.

Relishing his return to the international arena once more, Barnes continued on at Old Trafford in the Fourth Test where he had left off at Headingley – this time collecting Trumper, Bardsley, Ransford and Macartney. The Fifth Test at the Oval was drawn (giving Australia the series 2-1) and Barnes was more than serviceable, taking 2 wickets in each innings, including Trumper (73) as they continued their decade-old arm wrestle.

In just three Tests, Barnes took 17 wickets at 20. He now had 67 Test wickets at 20.73.

Australia for the third time

Wisden, long a detractor, finally faced the truth about his abilities and got on the Barnes bandwagon by naming him one of its 'Five

Cricketers of the Year' for his efforts in 1909. He declined to go on the tour of South Africa in 1910–11, but was available for the next tour of Australia in 1911–12. Only Barnes, Warner, Rhodes, Hobbs and George Gunn had toured Australia before.

Olympic boxing gold medallist Johnny Douglas led England in the First Test at Sydney in place of Pelham Warner who was ill, and made his presence felt with a decision in keeping with his amateur status. Douglas decided to open the bowling himself.

Barnes objected and said: 'That's all very well, Mr Douglas, but what am I 'ere for?'

The skipper ignored him. Frank Foster, also an amateur but a good pace bowler, opened at the other end. Australia, pleasantly surprised at Douglas' shunning of Barnes, managed a fair start. Trumper, coming in down the order and relieved not to face his old nemesis, was well set when Barnes was belatedly summoned to bowl and managed to secure 3 wickets. But it was too little, too late. Trumper went on to his sixth century against England and his eighth in Tests. Australia reached 447.

England replied with 318. Then Australia placed itself in an unassailable position by scoring 308 in it second innings after Douglas insisted on himself and Foster once more using the new ball first, thus again reducing Barnes' impact. England fought hard but was never going to reach the target. Had Douglas given Barnes the new ball in either innings, the result would have been much closer. But it was true 'amateur hour'. England, along with a disgruntled Barnes, suffered the consequences.

Douglas read the Australian press that mocked his arrogance in making Barnes a second stringer and took part in a heated argument with his senior players over his misjudgment. Douglas was no tactical genius but got the point. He took things more seriously in the Second Test at Melbourne. After losing the toss he threw the ball to Barnes who, despite suffering from flu, opened from the members end. His first ball was an in-swinger that bowled Bardsley off his pads. He went on to bowl Hill with an in-swinging yorker, trap

Kelleway LBW and have Armstrong caught at the wicket. The Melbourne crowd, who had long admired Barnes' fierce competitive nature, applauded him as if he were one of their own – a rare accolade for an Englishman. These 5 wickets fell in 5 overs while a solitary run was conceded. Barnes managed alarming lift off the wicket and hit every batsman. Australia did recover to reach 184, but the damage was done.

England cruised to an 8 wicket win.

Barnes was revved up for Adelaide after his success in Melbourne and was instrumental in helping to win this Test too, taking 3 for 71 and yet another 'Michelle' or 'five-for'. He produced a further match-winning effort at the return Test at the MCG, his favourite wicket-hunting ground, once more removing half the Australians in the first innings. Hobbs (178) and Rhodes (179) set England off with an opening stand of 323. This led to a big tally – 589: enough to win comfortably.

A jubilant England now led 3-1 and had won back the Ashes. They rubbed the Australians' faces in it by winning again at Sydney in the Fifth Test. Barnes was again the best bowler taking another match haul of 7 wickets. During the game he took his 100th Test wicket – Warwick Armstrong. He had taken 77 wickets in Australia in only 13 appearances.

This series debacle left Australia in total disarray and culminated in a boardroom fist-fight between skipper Clem Hill and selector Peter McAlister.

After watching Barnes throughout the series, Warner wrote: 'He is, on all wickets, the finest bowler in the world today – that, at all events, is the opinion of the Australians'.

Barnes sailed off for home much happier than on his two previous trips. He had been the dominant bowler of the series, taking 34 wickets at 22.88 (in all, 101 at 21.44) and now he was returning a hero in a team that had won back the Ashes.

Home run

Barnes was 39 when he saddled up for another minor county season, but he was going to see more Tests than ever before, three against Australia and three against South Africa in the Triangular Tournament of 1912. The first two Tests against Australia were washouts and he had little impact. But he was devastating against the South Africans.

Wisden noted his performance at the Oval: 'Barnes surpassed himself, bowling in even more deadly form than in the previous Test matches. He broke both ways and his length was irreproachable. The South Africans thought that they had never faced bowling quite so difficult'.

Barnes could have been back in the league fixture, such were his results. His 34 wickets at 8.28 represented a return unmatched in Tests for the rest of the 20th century. The final game at the Oval – the Third Test against the Australians – was to be the decider. Barnes, in his final contest with the Australians, fittingly took 5 for 30 in Australia's first innings, bowling unchanged and sending down 27 overs. His dismissals included Syd Gregory, Charlie Macartney, who played him better than any other Australian in the era, Charlie Kelleway and Bardsley. Barnes thus played a big part in England's win, which gave it victory in the tournament.

Wisden, now completely won over, praised Barnes by agreeing with what many other good judges had been saying for a decade: he was 'the best bowler in the world'.

Veldt victorious

With such success behind him, Barnes agreed, on good terms, to tour South Africa in 1913–14. He revelled in the warm, dry conditions, taking 125 wickets at 9.64 – 104 in the first-class games at 10.74. He found the matting wickets very much to his liking. In the first four of the five Tests he took 49 at 10.93 – a world record that has also lasted into the 21st century. He took 17 wickets in the Second Test at Johannesburg. His stamina was astounding for a 40-year-old and he seemed as fit at the end of the tour as at the start. Only one or two blemishes spoiled his tour. A single batsman, Herbie Taylor, played him with relative ease on a few occasions and frustrated Barnes to the point where he once threw the ball down in disgust. Yet Barnes still dismissed him five times in eight innings. Only once – in the first innings of the series – did Taylor take control and score a century. But two other innings of 70 and 93 had Barnes in a quandary how to get rid of him. The world's finest bowler had not been conquered, but at least he had been countered on occasions.

Barnes was told to expect a special 'reward' for his performances, and when it was not forthcoming he refused to play in the final Test at Port Elizabeth. It was an unfortunate end to his Test career. Yet it was in keeping with his mercurial nature.

Wisden overlooked his minor tantrum and waxed lyrical about his tour, coining a future pop song title in the process: 'He was simply irresistible . . .'

Wisden showed it couldn't resist him by putting him in its advertisements for its own brand of cricket balls. The ad ran for the next 11 years.

War and after

Barnes at 41 was too old for active service, but would have been fitter than half those who marched off to the various war fronts. Barnes' nine season verbal contract with Porthill Park was terminated in 1914. He had collected 893 wickets at just 5, and surprised with the bat, scoring 5625 at the fine average of 42.61. Porthill had won the North Staffordshire league championship six times and were runners up on the other three times during Barnes' stay. Pre-Barnes, the club had won the title once in 15 years. Now, with a wife and child to support, he had to find 'work'. He answered a newspaper advertisement for a 'left-arm bowler' to play with Saltaire in the Bradford league. Barnes cabled the club, asking, 'Will I do?' Saltaire didn't hesitate to sign him up. The association lasted from 1915 to 1923.

Looking ahead, Barnes – despite his fitness – knew his cricket earning time would end one day. He decided to take a trade and did an apprenticeship as a sign-writer and calligraphist. Once qualified, he found work inscribing illuminated scrolls in the Legal Department of Staffordshire County Council, a job that lasted another 50 years. Barnes developed outstanding skill as a calligrapher. His beautifully written letters became a prized possession for any recipient.

He continued to ply his other trade during the war years until 1918, taking 404 wickets at 5.17. In 1918, he took all 10 wickets in an innings against Keighley, which included Test players Jack Hearne and Schofield Haigh. In the same year he smashed 168, his highest score ever, against Baildon Green in a Priestley Cup match.

In 1920, Barnes was invited to tour Australia post-war. There was no doubt that he was still good enough for the highest level, yet the demands of a fourth Australian tour – they lasted for nine or 10 months – were too great; he considered this too long a time to be away from his family. He asked that his wife and child be taken on the trip and paid for. The MCC rejected his request. Barnes, as ever, was 80 years ahead in his thinking and demands. England's loss was Australia's gain: the tourists, bereft of bowlers, lost 0-5 to Warwick Armstrong's team.

Barnes was not too old at 47 to return to Test cricket at home in 1921, but his disagreement over terms for the 1920–21 tour put him out of favour with the establishment once more. He continued to plunder the Bradford league while Armstrong's team thrashed England 3-0. Had he played, that scoreline again could have been different. His mere presence would have sent shudders through the Australian dressing room as it had since he first appeared two decades earlier.

Barnes, at 51 in 1924, returned to Staffordshire to compete again in the minor counties championship. He began where he had left off a decade earlier and took 73 wickets at 7.17. He emulated these kinds of returns, along with good service with the bat, until 1933. Then, at age 60, a phenomenal age for a fast-medium bowler, he played in only three games for Staffordshire and concentrated on his performances for league team Rawtenstall. In 1935, aged 62, he retired after 22 seasons with Staffordshire, in which he took 1441 wickets at 8.15. He kept playing league cricket on weekends until 1940 when, at age 67, with war consuming the game once more, he reluctantly retired. 1939 marked the first year of World War II, and the first year since 1895 that Barnes did not have a contract to play professional cricket. For 44 years of his adult and working life, he was proud that a team or club was prepared to pay him to play the game he loved.

In 1957, while still working for Staffordshire County Council as a calligrapher, he had another proud moment when he presented Queen Elizabeth II with a hand-written scroll he had produced describing a visit to Stafford 400 years earlier by Queen Elizabeth I.

Barnes, by all accounts, mellowed in his old age, and he was chuffed to learn in 1963 that esteemed English writer, Neville Cardus, had selected him as one of 'Six giants of the *Wisden* Century', to mark 100 years of the publication. The other five were W. G. Grace, Bradman, Hobbs, Trumper and England fast bowler, Tom Richardson.

Thirty-seven years later, Bradman named Barnes in his best England team of all time. His record speaks for itself. He took 189 Test wickets at 16.43, while making 242 runs at 8.06. In first-class cricket, Barnes took 719 wickets at 17.09, and made 1573 runs at 12.78.

Sydney Francis Barnes, who lived to be 94, would be a dominating force in any era.

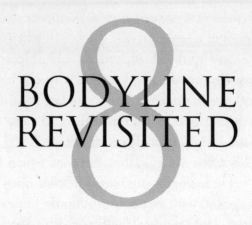

BODYLINE
REVISITED

Impact Five: Bodyline

The 1932–33 Ashes marked the ugliest, most aggro-riddled series in the history of the competition. It was all because England needed a method to defeat the new run-making machine, Don Bradman. They used bodyline – a tactic meant to bruise batsmen into submission or cause them to fend off a catch. Its origins lay in an August 1929 game between Nottinghamshire and Northamptonshire. The two Notts ex-miners and speed bowlers, Harold Larwood and Bill Voce, unleashed deliveries bounced at the batsman's body. In that first recorded sustained incident, the main target was 18-year-old Harrow schoolboy, Victor Rothschild, the scion of the banking dynasty, who was the only batsman to counter them. Young Victor noted the six fielders placed close on the leg and stepped away to slice cuts through the off-side. The future third Lord Rothschild was hit at least a dozen times in an hour of defiance in which he scored 36. After he was out caught he showed his mass of multi-coloured welts to his sister, [the honourable] Miriam. When a fellow player asked Rothschild what he thought of the tactics – euphemistically called 'fast leg theory' – instigated by Notts and former England skipper Arthur Carr, his rueful reply was: 'You mean fast leg, chest and head theory.'

In that game, Larwood and Voce collected 15 wickets between

them. Carr shrewdly did not direct this destruction more than a few times a season. This avoided the game's then ruling body, the Marylebone Cricket Club (MCC), taking action against it, despite Rothschild protesting in writing.

But circumstances changed during the 1930 Ashes in England. The 21-year-old Don Bradman spiflicated bowlers up and down the country, beginning with a glorious 236 not out under the Cathedral at Worcester. In his first innings at the historic Oval in London under the less than prepossessing gasometer, he thumped 252 not out against Surrey, forcing its skipper Percy Fender to eat his words of criticism. Fender, employing psychological warfare before the Tests, suggested Bradman would fail: his stroke play was flawed. The son of a Bowral carpenter let his bat respond by scoring 974 runs in 7 Test innings at an average of 139.14 – a record still to be surpassed in any Test series. Bradman delivered four different kinds of innings that remain classics of the game. At Nottingham, he made 131 in a rearguard fight and at Lord's he delivered a technically perfect innings of 254 at not far short of a run a ball. At Leeds, he smashed a remarkable 334 (309 in a day) and in the final deciding Test at the Oval, crafted 232 in a near-perfect mix of defence and attack. In these performances, Bradman targeted England's tearaway Larwood and drove him out of the attack in every encounter. The Nottingham Express was derailed. His paltry 4 wickets cost him 73 runs apiece.

Against all odds, Australia – which seemed inferior on paper – had taken the Ashes, thanks to Bradman and guileful leg-spinner Clarrie Grimmett, who dominated England's chief destroyer, batsman Wally Hammond. Bradman's dominance shook and humiliated the seat of Empire. What's more, this brilliant young athlete promised to do it for another 20 years unless England countered. But how?

The MCC's first step was to appoint a new captain who did not carry the scars of England's 1930 obliteration. The MCC used Fender, thirsty for revenge, and former Test skipper, Plum Warner (Rugby school/Oxford educated son of the former attorney-general of Trinidad) to try to persuade Douglas Jardine (Westminster school/Oxford educated Bombay-born lawyer) to lead the MCC on the now dreaded tour down-under. In May 1932, these three establishment figures met for lunch at Lord's. They discussed the Bradman problem. The telephone numbers he scored in Tests against the West Indies and South Africa in the Australian summers of 1930–31 and 1931–32 were demoralising. The sharp, aquiline-featured Jardine agreed with the others that Bradman could well 'score a thousand in a series' on Australia's harder pitches.

Warner, who would manage the tour, offered Jardine the leadership. Jardine declined, saying he had 'better things to do in the winter than suffer the heat and flies and the ill-humoured crowds'. Warner was more determined that his genial exterior suggested. After the Lord's meeting, he told Fender he would see Jardine's father who knew much about 'heat, flies and crowds'. M. R. Jardine was the former Advocate-General of Bombay.

M. R. met with his 32-year-old son at the Garrick Club in London's West End and reminded him of his duty to 'King and Empire'. Jardine admitted that the real problem was that 'little bastard', Bradman. M. R. urged the doubting Douglas to treat the tour with the discipline and precision of a 'good military campaign'. Soon after their meeting, the MCC announced that Douglas Jardine would lead the tourists on the 1932–33 tour.

The new skipper did his homework during the English summer. Fender urged him to use leg theory. Jardine consulted the fine pre–World War I left-hand fast bowler, Frank Foster of Warwickshire, who was an expert – although not in the way Fender was urging the method be used. Jardine met with Arthur Carr, who explained how Larwood and Voce intimidated and cornered batsmen with short-pitched bowling and a closely packed leg-side field.

'But you can't just use any bowlers', Carr told him. They had to be quick and pinpoint accurate. The method should be used as a shock rather than a stock tactic, particularly early in an innings. Jardine wanted to know if Carr's two star bowlers would be willing to use fast-leg theory as part of a strategy to win back the Ashes. Carr thought they would. Larwood was reluctant to tour after his shellacking from Bradman. Any plan to defeat the Australian would be acceptable. The two men arranged a meeting with Larwood and Voce at the grillroom of the Piccadilly Hotel after the traditional Surrey versus Notts Bank Holiday fixture at the Oval in August, 1932. The discussion centred on how to restrict Bradman.

Jardine asked Larwood if he could 'bowl on the leg-stump and make the ball come up into the body all the time so that Bradman had to play his shots to leg'. Larwood, eager to please his new captain, said he could. His accuracy had improved and his stamina was good. Larwood recalled Bradman 'flinching' when hit at the Oval in the final Test of the 1930 series. That pleased Jardine. It made no difference that Bradman had been hit on the forearm in wet, difficult conditions while carving out a gutsy, stunning 98 in the pre-lunch session en route to a series-winning 232. The 'flinch' would be the whispered justification for the sustained attack on him.

***

While Bradman's demise was being plotted, he was on his honeymoon with his wife Jessie in Canada and the US sight-seeing, meeting Babe Ruth the superstar baseballer and Hollywood stars such as Boris Karloff and Leslie Howard. He and Jessie were with an unofficial Australian squad organised by former Test leg-spinner, Arthur Mailey. Bradman played lots of cricket, perhaps too much. In 51 innings on the North American tour he crunched 3779 runs at an average of 102.1. He returned to Australia fatigued, and dogged by a mystery illness. It didn't help that he ran into a dispute with the Australian Board of Control over its rule that cricketers couldn't be employed in the media to comment on the game.

The question of whether he would play in the Ashes series hung over his head when he travelled to Perth to play in a 'Combined Australian XI' against England. Jardine, fearing Bradman would start a season as he usually did by belting the opposition, left out of the game his three exponents of fast leg theory – Larwood, Bill Voce and Yorkshire's Bill Bowes. In late October, the Australians were caught on a 'sticky' in front of packed Perth crowds that had come from all over Western Australia to see Bradman. Out of sorts, he made 3 and 10, and for the first time was dismissed twice in day. The left-arm Yorkshire spinner, Hedley Verity – whom Bradman named in his best ever England team – removed him both times in their first ever contest. England won easily. Jardine was delighted. He had the mental advantage over Bradman and the Australians much earlier than expected, even before his grand plan was revealed. He also noted the Don's demeanour. Gone was the youthful self-confidence of England in 1930: he was pale, underweight and uncertain.

Jardine was cunning. In press conferences, he played up Verity's importance, suggesting the spinner was his wild card for the Ashes.

'He [Verity] has a margin of 10 feet (3 metres) on faster Australian pitches in which to vary the length of his deliveries', Jardine informed the press, 'rather than five feet (1.5 metres) in England.'

Hedley from Headingley was projected as Australia's bogeyman as a diversion from what was to come.

Jardine selected an all pace line-up for England's next encounter with Bradman when it played 'an Australian XI' at Melbourne in mid-November. Verity was not selected and Jardine himself did not play. Instead, he went trout fishing on the Kiewa River in country Victoria, but not before leaving instructions to his pacemen to attack Bradman at every opportunity. Larwood took this to mean plenty of short stuff at the rib cage and head with five men in close catching positions. His partner for the match, England's fourth ranked paceman, Gubby Allen (who refused to use this tactic), would bowl accurate bouncers on a fast, bouncy wicket.

As soon as Bradman came to the wicket in a tense atmosphere at the MCG, Larwood set his field with five men close and two men out for the hook – all on the leg-side. Bradman ducked and weaved. He was unsettled, never having seen or experienced this set-up, but adapted by stepping to leg and belting the ball into the unguarded off-side.

Larwood recalled that bowling bouncers at other batsmen 'was like potting pheasants. But Bradman was more like a wild duck'. He was tougher to strike, and therefore debilitate.

Bradman scored 36 in quick time but received a poor LBW decision and was on his way.

An observer dubbed the tactic 'bodyline'. Fast-leg theory suddenly had a more pertinent name, and image.

Bradman tried the same elusive method of scoring in his second innings, but was bowled by Larwood for 13. The Nottingham Express was back on track and ecstatic. It was payback for all the beltings Bradman had given him in two Ashes series and every encounter since 1928. Bradman never looked secure. Verity, watching from the dressing room, thought he seemed 'rattled'. Jardine learned of bodyline's success by phone. He was thrilled.

A week later, on 25 November, Bradman was in the fray again against the now confident tourists, this time for NSW. Jardine was proving a master strategist. He left Larwood out of the game, saving him for the First Test that would begin just three days after this match.

Bradman contracted flu just before the NSW game and managed only 18 (LBW to Maurice Tate) and bowled for 23 by Voce in a bodyline burst. Now Verity, Allen, Voce, Larwood and Tate – five of England's six key bowlers – had dismissed him in the lead-up to the Tests. England had a psychological grip on the urn of burnt bails – for which these two countries fought so hard – even before the 1932–33 Ashes began.

Bradman's flu worsened and he missed the First Test at Sydney, in which Larwood dominated, taking 10 wickets. Only Stan McCabe, with a 'stand and swing' 187 not out, defied bodyline. A spectator brought rare mirth for the match by calling out to Jardine to 'leave our flies alone' as he swatted at them in the heat. Yet the England captain would not let up on the Australian batsmen, who capitulated.

Bradman decided that there was no way bodyline could be defeated through five Tests unless a daring counter-attack could be devised. His counter was to move inside the ball and drive it on the off-side where there were no fielders.

In my interviews with him, he commented: 'I saw no advantage to me or the team whatsoever in standing still and being struck. If you view film of Larwood bowling to me [in an ABC TV documentary], you'll notice where the ball passes [at 155 kph] when I move away. If I had remained where I was, I would have been struck in the chest or head. The only sensible way was to move into position to avoid the fast-rising delivery or in order to play scoring strokes'.

Bradman pointed out that his counteraction would, in fact, increase the chance of being hit.

'The orthodox manner of playing the fast-lifting ball is to move across to the off and out of the line of flight. The ball on middle and leg will go by and you're unlikely to get hit. The danger of being hit is if you stand precisely where you are, or if you back away a bit to the leg-side to try to play it on the off, because the ball is then following you. What I planned put me in much greater danger of being hit than if I adopted an orthodox method. But there was no way I was going to get runs playing orthodox cricket.'

He added: 'I decided to play some tennis shots'.

Bradman would run across the crease and attempt to hook and cut from unorthodox positions. Perhaps only this batting genius, with his lightning footwork and amazing 'eye', could attempt this against deliveries from Larwood, who had been clocked at 160 kph.

Bradman came back for the Second Test at Melbourne over the New Year leading into 1933 in front of a full house. After a shock first ball duck in the first innings, he made a superb, dominant unbeaten century using his counter methods. The most unusual aspect of Bradman's approach was that for the first time in his career he was hitting the ball in the air – hooking and cutting. The desperate measures worked. Larwood was beaten. Australia won. Yet bodyline was taking its toll on the other Australian bats, who did not have Bradman's freakish skills. They were getting hit or out cheaply to awkward deliveries.

In the 10-day break before the Third Test at Adelaide, the press built up the game in anticipation of more drama. There had been accusations that British economic policy and advice, taken up by Australian governments and banks, had helped cause the Depression. England was billed as the 'enemy'. The embodiment of British Imperialism, allegedly responsible for Australia's economic malaise, took the shape of tall, lean Jardine, who insisted on wearing his harlequin cap and silk cravat.

The police turned up in numbers, keeping their mounted troops and squads out of sight outside the ground, yet ready for trouble. Mid-afternoon on the second day of the game in front of a capacity crowd, Australia began its first innings. Allen had Australian opener Jack Fingleton caught behind for a duck. This brought Bradman to the wicket to tremendous applause. Lines of police began curling into position around the ground. He hadn't been at the wicket long when Jardine clapped his hands above his head, signalling bodyline positions for his fielders. The crowd reacted, booing and jeering. Again, one moment of humour punctuated the electric atmosphere in a lull before Larwood delivered. A flock of seagulls flew overhead.

'There's Jardine at mid-off', a spectator yelled. 'Go for him!'

Moments later, Larwood bowled a vicious bouncer that crashed into Australian skipper Bill Woodfull's chest. He dropped his bat and staggered from the wicket. The spectators erupted. It seemed they might invade the ground. Jardine sidled up to Larwood to offer support.

'Well bowled, Harold', he said.

It wasn't long before Bradman was out for just 8, caught in the leg-trap off Larwood. The crowd was incensed, but with Allen refusing to bowl bodyline, there was some respite every second over. Had Jardine used Voce with Larwood, then some fans may have turned into a murderous mob. The courageous Woodfull (the schoolmaster son of a preacher) battled through to the tea break.

Plum Warner visited him in the dressing room, where the Australian captain uttered the immortal words: 'There are two teams out there. One is trying to play cricket and one is not. It is too great a game for spoiling by the tactics your team is adopting. I don't approve of them. It might be better if I do not play the game'.

The 'I' here meant the captain and his team.

Later in the day, Australian keeper Bert Oldfield had his skull fractured by Larwood, who was counted out several times. After play, the Board of Control over-reacted by sending a telegram to the MCC, which said the tactics were 'unsportsmanlike'.

'Unless stopped at once', the regrettable message stated, 'it is likely to upset friendly relations between Britain and Australia.'

Australia was set 512 to win. Only a big double hundred from Bradman in his second innings could challenge such a target. He brought gasps from spectators as he pulled away from the wicket to slice and cut Larwood. Soon after he had reached 50 in quick time, Larwood was removed from the bowling crease. Bradman had won another battle. But his normal control, which had seen him check rushes of blood in the past, deserted him. He hit Larwood's replacement Verity for six – his first in Test cricket – then tried another and was caught and bowled for 66. Despite Woodfull demonstrating his courage and application by batting through the innings unconquered with 73 not out, Australia was thrashed.

After the game, an intense debate developed in the Australian camp about how they should fight back. With two Tests to play, the Ashes were still there to be won. Batsman Vic Richardson wanted Victorian paceman and champion, Swans footballer Laurie Nash – an athletic Merv Hughes of his day – in the Australian team to fight fire with fire. Nash was a dashing centre-half back for the Swans in their Aussie Rules Premiership of 1933. Sometimes he played his cricket as if he was still on the footy field.

The fastest bowler in the country, Aboriginal Eddie Gilbert from Queensland, was another name that came up. Gilbert was short and wiry with long arms. He had a chest-on, whipping, suspect action from only four paces. A chucker or not, he was swift enough to knock the bat from Bradman's hand and dismiss him for a duck when they first faced each other in 1931.

The press, reflecting public opinion, picked up on the retaliatory theme, but Woodfull would not hear of it. Bradman and leg-spinner Bill O'Reilly supported him. They thought the game would be reduced to thuggery and an awful spectacle if both teams used bodyline.

In the last two Tests at Brisbane and Sydney, Bradman batted well but could not calibrate his mind and game for the gesture of the big match-winning innings, scoring 76, 24, 48 and 71. A shell-shocked Australia went down 4-1. Bradman had the best batting record of batsmen from both sides with an average of 56.57, yet he had been reduced to half his usual effectiveness. Jardine and his pacemen had won back the Ashes and were feted in England.

Yet bodyline caused repercussions. The talented West Indies fast bowlers, Manny Martindale and Learie Constantine, used the tactic in the Second Test at Old Trafford in July 1933. Now, the English batsmen suffered. Martindale split Wally Hammond's chin. The champion batsman said he wouldn't play again if bodyline was not outlawed. Jardine, showing grim determination, scored his only Test century in facing it, thus making a strong point in defending his methods. But he was a lone voice as Larwood and Voce continued to use bodyline in the 1933 English county games. Battered batsmen complained. By the time Australia turned up for the Ashes tour of 1934, bodyline was outlawed, and Jardine had been dumped by the MCC as skipper. The technique's main exponents, Larwood and Voce, were told they would not be chosen for their country if they didn't apologise for using bodyline. This was hypocritical, given that the MCC had supported Jardine in Australia. Larwood refused and never bowled for England again. Voce agreed. Despite letting go a barrage of bumpers with a near-bodyline field for Nottingham against the Australians in August 1934, he would live to fight in the Ashes again.

After an indifferent first half of the 1934 tour, Bradman's capacity to calibrate the massive score at Test level returned.

The night before the Fourth Test at Leeds, famed English cricket and music critic Neville Cardus spoke with Bradman, who expressed the need to make a big score for his country to win the series. Cardus reminded him that his last Test innings of 334 at the same venue meant another mega-score was 'against the law of averages'.

Bradman's response summed up his mentality: 'I don't believe in the law of averages'.

This was not bombast or false modesty. He had been defying such laws throughout his cricketing career. He smacked 304 to make his point, then followed it up with 244 at the Oval to win back the Ashes.

Soon after these efforts, he collapsed with peritonitis and was fortunate to survive an operation. He only fully recovered in time for the next Ashes in Australia in 1936–37. Now, at 28, he was Australian captain, and Gubby Allen, the bowler who had openly opposed bodyline, was England's skipper. The series restored the goodwill between the two teams lost during 1932–33, but the situation came very close to turning nasty once more during the fifth and deciding Test at Melbourne. The series was 2-all. In the week before the Test, Laurie Nash – playing for Victoria against England – had let go a brutal barrage of short-pitched bowling. This was a rude demonstration of what would have happened had he been chosen for Australia in 1932–33 and urged to blast out the England bats in retaliation. Allen and Hammond protested to the Board of Control and demanded that Nash not be picked to play in the final Test. Bradman, sensing panic in the England camp, pushed hard for Nash's selection. The Board refused to name him in the team of 12. Bradman suggested it name 13, with Nash in the squad. The Board reluctantly agreed. Allen and Hammond were furious. They demanded a meeting with Bradman, which took place at the Windsor Hotel, Melbourne. Over lunch, Allen said Nash could not be chosen, otherwise there would be a 'bumper war'. He threatened to unleash Voce. Bradman replied that 'no Englishman will ever dictate who is or is not selected for Australia'. This sobered the discussion. Bradman promised that there would not be a bumper war, which appeased Allen and Hammond, although there was agreement that some bumpers would be allowed. Hours later, Bradman fronted the Board and put his case for Nash being in the 12. After he left the Board meeting there was a heated debate on whether to accede to Bradman's request.

When one director posed the question of who was more powerful – Bradman or the Board – the room fell silent. There was a fear that Bradman might stand down if he didn't get his way. That evening, the Board announced the 12: Nash was in it. On the morning of the match, Bradman won the toss and decided to bat. The skippers exchanged teams sheets. Nash was in the Australian XI.

'Are you going to have a go at us?' Allen asked angrily.

Bradman repeated there would be no bumper war. He dominated Australia's innings of 604, scoring 169 to follow his 270 and 212 in the two previous Tests. When England batted, Nash bowled fast, if erratically, taking 4 for 70. He let go only a handful of bumpers but nothing prolonged. Yet his physical presence and aggressive manner put England off. Bradman had learned much about the subtleties and nuances of intimidation since the Bodyline series.

***

Bradman and Jardine had one last encounter, when they both covered the 1953 Ashes in England as journalists and sat in the same press boxes.

'We couldn't agree on anything we saw on the field', Bradman told me. When I asked him what he thought of Jardine, he replied that he was 'a very fine batsman'. It was the Don's way of expressing his lasting dislike for the England skipper. Yet he grew friendly towards Larwood, whom he did not blame for the Bodyline fiasco.

Bradman's death in 2001 meant that all the antagonists of that fateful 1932–33 series had gone. Jardine died of lung cancer in

1958. Larwood, who migrated to Australia in the early 1950s, was a popular figure in Sydney among cricketers until his death in 1995. Belatedly, he was awarded an MBE in 1993.

Bodyline's reverberations were felt down the decades with each side keen to gain the ascendancy using speed. Ray Lindwall, whom Bradman named in his best world and Australian teams, modelled his style on Larwood. His speed and control was a problem for England's batsmen for seven years after World War II. England's fastest ever bowler, Frank Tyson, and Fred Trueman, who Bradman ranked as its best ever paceman, retaliated against the Australians in the 1950s and 1960s. John Snow threatened Ian Chappell's team in 1970–71, while a few years later the lethal combination of Dennis Lillee and Jeff Thomson were a menace to the opposition. Then it was the turn of Bob Willis for England in 1981. A decade later, Australia's Merv Hughes snarled and ear-kissed his way through a couple of Ashes contests.

Australia now has Brett Lee for intimidation. England has Steve Harmison.

The ill-feeling generated between the two countries in 1932–33 has long since died. Yet the rivalry, which bodyline accentuated so dramatically, is very much alive, as seen in the 2005 Ashes, and the build-up to the 2006–07 contest.

THE 20TH CENTURY'S GREATEST

Impact Six: Don Bradman

Statistics can be made to lie or distort, especially in the figures-riddled cricket industry. But in analysing the run output of Don Bradman, no one has ever needed to embellish or mislead. His production is a constant reminder that there is a standard in cricket's art of batting, indeed *all* sport. It is the Bradman standard.

By any measure, Donald Bradman is the greatest batsman the world has ever seen. He batted 338 times in first-class cricket over 22 years from 1927 to 1949, scoring 28,067 and averaging 95.14. He hit 117 centuries at better than one every three innings, a rate that no other batsman has remotely approached.

His English rival for the title of the world's best-ever cricketer, W. G. Grace, had *one thousand and fifty* more first-class innings than Bradman and yet scored only nine more centuries. On paper that makes Bradman about *four times* better than Grace at hitting three-figure scores.

In the modern era, Brian Lara has had about a hundred more first-class innings than Bradman while scoring about half the number of centuries, a difference reflected in the averages where Bradman's is nearly twice Lara's.

Analysis of Bradman's scores of 200 or more takes him into a further dimension of his own. He hit 37 scores of 200 or more. His nearest rival in this field, Wally Hammond, hit 36 double hundreds or more in *three times* as many first-class innings.

Bradman's rate of accumulation adds to his supremacy. He maintained a rate of 42 runs an hour (84 runs a session, or 252 runs in a day, at a strike-rate of 75 runs per hundred balls – respectable even in modern *one-day* cricket.)

In 52 Tests he managed 6996 runs at 99.94 – or, rounded off, a century every time he went out to bat in his eighty innings. He actually hit 29 Test centuries, including twelve doubles, two triples and a score of 299 not out. Even in grade cricket and what was once called 'second-class' matches, he kept up this relentless run accumulation and average at a pace unmatched by anyone else.

Bradman's unearthly Test average returns are roughly four times that of the best batsmen of the 19th century and twice the best of the rest in the 20th century.

In effect, statistically he is worth two of the best of the rest since the inception of Test cricket. 'Worth' is the key word here, for it would be misleading to claim he was twice as good, other than in statistical terms. Nevertheless, if you picked any great team in history – that actually or hypothetically played – he would be equal in value to any two other batsmen chosen. Any team containing Bradman would win over a series, given the rest of the two squads chosen were more or less of the same standard. (This was the case while Bradman played in full Test series from 1928 to 1948. Australia never lost except for the Bodyline series in which his average was pulled back to 56.57, or in the range of the next best players in history.) Would any other sport have a player at the top worth the value of the next two performers together? In tennis, would Laver be worth Newcombe plus McEnroe, or McEnroe be equal to Becker and Rafter? In Boxing, would Muhammad Ali ever be considered the equivalent of Rocky Marciano and Mike Tyson together? Or in golf, could Jack Nicklaus be the equal to Greg Norman plus Tiger Woods? Never.

There are arguments about the conditions in different eras and whether it was easier or harder for batsmen in The Don's time. Those who say it was tougher for Bradman point to uncovered wickets and the barest protection provided by equipment against real speed generated by bowlers such as Harold Larwood. Then there are the bigger, better implements – the bats themselves – today. They are much better suited to big scoring. There was also more variety in bowling in the past, especially with medium-pace swing bowlers and spinners in the Bradman era (1928–1948). Most of Bradman's matches were against a strong England team, whereas in modern times there are easy opportunities for batsmen to polish and improve averages against teams such as Zimbabwe and Bangladesh.

Those who suggest Bradman had it easier argue that a speed quartet such as that produced by the West Indies in the 1980s would make it tough for him to average a hundred. The counter-argument is that a varied attack would do better than even those *awesome foursomes*, provided the third and fourth bowlers (a medium-pacer and spinner, say, an Alec Bedser and a Shane Warne) were top-class.

Yet after 130 years of analysis of international and first-class figures, batting averages have remained more or less the same with the 'norm' being 40 to 60 for the best in any era post–World War I.

South Australian biochemist Charles Davies went further in analysis and created a bell curve on a graph, which weighted Bradman's average against the best of the rest. Bradman's record is so far from the norm that we would have to wait for another million Test batsmen before someone approaching it would emerge. The bell curve could be applied to all sports. Analysis shows that the best performers in other sports such as football, tennis, swimming, running and the high jump could not get anywhere near the statistical superiority over their competitors as Bradman had over other cricketers.

The question is why? How did he manage to be so far ahead of the pack? Consideration of some of his key characteristics may help comprehend this. They include concentration, character, courage and determination, technique, knowledge of the game, natural athleticism, competitiveness, leadership skills and intelligence. Woven together they provide at least part of the answer to Don Bradman's sporting uniqueness and genius.

Concentration

During my long interviews of up to seven hours with him, he never wavered, or seemed to tire. The answers were sometimes long but never complicated. Our discussions occurred when he was in his late eighties. It wasn't difficult to imagine what he was like when concentrating at anything – including batting – from age 11 to 40. Yet he differed from other batsmen like Boycott, Barrington and Lawry, who could stay at the crease for long periods, minimising mistakes. Bradman was error conscious yet also an attacking player to rank in his destructive skills with all the great belligerents from Hammond and McCabe to Viv Richards and Barry Richards, Tendulkar, Lara and Ponting. The longer he stayed and accumulated, the faster his rate of accumulation. To do this without 'having a bash' took a power of concentration where his batting harmony and symphony built to a crescendo. Bradman's last fifty in all his massive scores above 200 – about fifty in all forms of cricket, which included nine triple centuries and one quadruple – often came in half an hour. Yet he never lost control unless he wanted to. Bradman would often throw his wicket away, that is, let loose without concern for losing his wicket or posting an average preserving 'not out'. Nor did he make those big innings for the sake of them or for records. Bradman played big innings when it was necessary to set up a win. Even when he made that whopping 452 not out for NSW against Queensland in January 1930, his team won easily with more than a day's cricket to spare.

Bradman's aim always was to win and in the most entertaining way possible. This approach dictated his thoughts on the game. Cricketers must give the paying public the best value possible for money. Everything must be done to keep them coming through the gates, especially in the modern era where there is so much competition (on television or otherwise) from other sports and entertainment.

Character

Neville Cardus, who knew Bradman well, once said of an innings of his, 'He was never uninteresting; he merely abstained from vanity and rhetoric.'

This succinctly summed up Bradman from my own interviews, chats and communication with him over several years. He always got to the point, without flim-flam. He never slipped into beating his own chest, or even subtle comments about how good he was. Bradman, in terms of the smart Nike commercials, just did it. The indisputable record was there for all to peruse. That was enough. Nor was this a case of false modesty or manufactured humility. His vanity-free mentality had to be distilled from his ego, for The Don had a strong sense of self. Yet he was not egoistic. In conversation, he never unnecessarily wallowed in the 'I' and the 'me'. He listened to and absorbed comments, as he did suggestions when he was captain or running Australian cricket. He would be critical of others but never with malice. Bradman viewed everything from his own unique perspective. His standards of excellence were on a different plane.

A contradiction in his nature was his self-proclaimed pessimism. Yet it was his way of preparing for a failure or loss when he aimed higher than anyone else in the game. How many players in cricket history set their sights on a triple or big double century at the most critical point in a Test series and achieved the aim? The pessimism was his way of softening any possible fall. This was linked by some close to him with an alleged hypochondria. Yet when I asked him about his health, I understood his responses to be like a weather report. You asked and you received an answer. I never felt he was looking for sympathy. On the contrary, he seemed surprised, even bemused that continual illness of different kinds could be happening to him. It should be remembered that we were in contact when he was 86 to 92 years old.

In competition, as in conversation, he cut to the point. In cricket, that was to make as many runs as possible in time to dismiss your opponent's XI twice. All else was superfluous. Bradman batted and captained with this in mind. Rarely could a bowler con him into a shot he didn't wish to play. Rarer still were rushes of blood to the head after, say, two well-hit fours. Bradman knew all about focus decades before it became an American management cliché. There was never a temptation to play beyond his limitations or those of the moment. Vanity never got the better of him. He remained patient when necessary. There was always a time to tear an attack to pieces, whether from the first ball or when he had reached a century and the opposition was demoralised.

Conversations with him, like his batting, were never dull and were often unpredictable. There were countless examples of this. One was his response to a question about the problem of gambling corruption in cricket in the 1990s. I didn't expect him to respond piously, nor did I anticipate him saying, 'You should read more cricket history. The game grew on the back of gambling in the 19th century. This [corruption] will be overcome. The game will survive, prosper and be better for it.'

There was never hesitation in his organised, layered answers to questions. If he didn't have an answer he would say so, just as if he were playing back in defence. If he had an answer it came quickly and articulately, sometimes with the subtlety of a late cut, often surprisingly like a cover drive off a leg-cutter. He was always friendly and obliging to deal with, but because of the nature of the relationship – biographer and subject – there was conflict. Bradman could be tough, yet never unreasonable. It was the biographer's task to delve. He might not always appreciate it. Differences invariably were over publicity. If I wanted to write something about him for newspapers he was never happy. The reason, as explained, was the direct correlation between publicity and an increase in the dreaded mail he received. When, in 1996, he agreed to be interviewed by Ray Martin on TV, I thought there was a story in how Kerry Packer stitched up a deal to pay the Bradman Museum more than a million dollars for the interview. Don had not been enamoured with Packer since the media mogul created World Series Cricket in 1977. Yet the Museum and producers at the Nine Network were keen for him to do the interview. The commercial TV channels had been trying for forty years to lure Bradman in front of the cameras, but he had refused to appear, partly because he had been offered money, implying that he could be bought. The figures went up and up. Producers were going on their principle that 'everyone has a price'. But it was an empty cliché when applied to Bradman. He knocked back Bob Hawke, Ray Martin and Mike Munro. Then Nine's producers and executives became aware that there was a chance he would be interviewed if a payment were made to the museum in Bowral. It meant the museum could finish the second and main building. (Bradman did not receive a cent of the donation.) But Ray or Bob or Mike were not up to persuading Bradman. That job could only fall to the Nine Network's owner, Kerry Packer. Could super-salesman Kerry turn Bradman around? More pertinently, would Australia's most famous figure be reconciled with the country's richest? The mountain had to go to Mohamed in leafy Kensington Park, Adelaide. Packer, excited yet apprehensive after the fallout over World Series Cricket twenty years earlier, flew over. He was treated to the exceptional Bradman hospitality, courtesy of the charming Jessie, that had been experienced by prime ministers and paupers alike.

In May 1996 I rang Bradman to chat to him about the deal and the meeting with Packer, with the view to writing an article about it.

'I'm not saying anything about it,' he told me brusquely, 'and Packer won't tell you anything. So how are you going to write it?'

Business executive Bob Mansfield was present at that fascinating meeting with Packer at Bradman's home and he filled in a few details.

After 1996 I stopped writing articles about Bradman because of his complaints about the increase in mail he received whenever anything appeared. He couldn't understand, nor did I try to explain to him, why his name came up every day in papers in England and Australia. Mention of him and discussions about him had been out of control since the 1927–28 cricket season when he first played for NSW. Part of the reason for his popularity and the fascination with him is the fact that his record has 'grown' in the more than five decades since his retirement. When he bowed out in 1948, no one realised that a cricketer with a Test century average over a career would not be seen again for a long time, maybe forever. Great players burst on the scene, were worked out by bowlers and pegged back to averages between 40 and 60. Some were dubbed the new Bradman in hope and expectation. Less than a decade after The Don retired, the public was hungry for a new champion and the media fed it. Ian Craig, in 1956, was the 'baby Bradman'. He was promising and stylish but it was too much of a burden. Norm O'Neill was next, and he could certainly belt the ball harder than most. His scoring was heavy early, and his Test start in 1958–59 against England hinted at something like the Bowral Boy's thirty years earlier. Yet he levelled out with a strong Test career average in the mid-40s. Then in the mid-1960s, easy-going Doug Walters started with two terrific hundreds against England. He even looked like Bradman in the baggy green. Yet Walters also disappointed, not because he wasn't popular or attacking or first rate. The poor fellow simply averaged in the 40s rather than 100. It has taken nearly 60 years for this enthusiastic comparison to disappear. Fortunately for new young players such as Australia's Michael Clarke, there is no bracketing with Bradman, even by the most clichéd commentators. The failure to live up to the comparison has made it a curse, *a kiss of death*, for those bursting on the scene with a blaze of big scores.

Half a century went by and analysts began to acknowledge that the finest batsmen ever born would always fall into this good to excellent, 40 to 60 range. Then there was Bradman, way off the graph. This superiority, coupled with his need for privacy after decades of close media attention created an aura of mystery around him. People judged his behaviour as 'reclusive', which it never was.

Some disparaging remarks were made when he didn't come to his 90th birthday celebration in Adelaide. There seemed to be no concession for the stroke in late 1995 that had left him with an almost imperceptible speech impediment. Bradman didn't feel he could live up to the high standard of speeches he had made over his life. He didn't want the strain of a night where he was the focal point of attention for a thousand celebrators who, despite meaning well, could not understand what it was to be Don Bradman at 90. Fans and the media wanted him to somehow always live up to the image of his playing days or, at worst, the sprightly octogenarian he was. Few concessions were made for his humanness. In reality, while still mentally vigorous, he was a frail old man who just wanted 'peace and privacy'.

Bradman the legend

The nation had never had such an enduring legend. He was not allowed to grow old or behave like a person in his twilight years. Part of the problem was that Bradman has eschewed publicity, even though it pursued him doggedly. And he hated the whole ordeal of exposure, made worse for him by a stroke at 87. In one way he was closer to 1930s screen actress Greta Garbo, who unwittingly created an enigma by 'retiring' as a youngish filmstar, stating that she 'wanted to be alone'. Yet Bradman did not actually retire from cricket. He was a key administrator (as a state and national selector and member of the Australian Cricket Board) until he was well into his seventies in the early-1980s. He could hardly be considered a loner and without influence. But he still preferred the backroom to the media room. It wasn't that he couldn't handle the media. Nobody did it better when it came to a succinct thought, direct statement or good photo opportunity if required. It was just that he thought the media limelight was mostly superfluous, to be used as a vehicle for a message, not for projecting his vanity or for ego boosting.

Bradman chose stockbroking as his profession. At 26 he disappeared (when he wasn't playing cricket) into the confidential world of stocks and shares. If you wished to avoid media attention it was as good as the morgue, and nearly as closed off as the upper echelons of banking.

This attempt to become anonymous failed to give him privacy but instead enhanced his aura until to many commentators his image seemed akin to an Australian version of royalty. There were differences. The British royals were more or less born into it. Bradman's elevation was due to substance. He earned it. The royals had to exude that doubtful trait of 'charm'. Bradman's charm was that, apart from exhibiting all the normal niceties at public events, he was always transparently *him*. He seemed incapable of small talk – another reason for avoiding, if he could, functions where small-talking champions aired their skills. Perhaps the only royals he was really like were the Duke of Edinburgh and his daughter, particularly the latter. Bradman, like Princess Anne, was capable of telling media people to 'naff off'. This endeared him (and her) to the media more. In a way, this attitude embodied what intrinsic royal 'power' was about. The media were there to serve as a vehicle and, as servants, were not to be pandered to. As long as this power was not abused, at least not in public, it would be maintained.

A key divergence here is that Bradman never needed the media; it needed him. Without media support, or without a continual presence through the media, the British royals would have been reduced to riding bikes and smaller habitation, like their counterparts in Holland.

Bradman also avoided politics. Both major parties wanted him. Labor Party officials listened to his accent, took into account his roots and thought he was ideal for them. The conservatives looked at his job, noticed how all 'classes' of Australian society admired him and claimed him as one of their own. Bradman gave a decided *nyet* to becoming a politician, although he did flirt with being a diplomat – as Australia's high commissioner to the UK. By not becoming a political partisan Bradman enhanced, or at least maintained, his image as the 'greatest Australian ever born'. Where half the population might admire a Gough Whitlam, the other half – for reasons of their political sympathies – would not. Thus Bradman by the end of the twentieth century was far more universally popular – polls suggest at least twice as popular – than any politician from Billy Hughes to John Howard.

The substance beneath the mythology was created by the perfect coincidence between Bradman's incredible feats with the bat and Australia's decline into a miserable economic depression that lasted for a seven-year period from the late-1920s to the mid-1930s. He and another nearly infallible sporting champion, the mighty horse Phar Lap, gave hope to a young nation in desperate need of inspiration.

Courage and determination

Bradman's determination placed him with the most courageous and tough-minded individuals ever to play the game. Perhaps his most remarkable performance in this regard came in the Fourth Ashes Test of 1934 – one that Australia could not afford to lose. Batting at Leeds, he scored 304 not out in a game with the series at stake. He had been weakened by a mystery illness that reduced his weight and left him with an alarmingly gaunt appearance. He still managed a masterful innings, despite cramps and extreme fatigue, reaching 271 not out in a day. Instead of tiring himself by running two and three's, he crashed 43 fours. He collapsed after the day's play and had to be undressed by team-mates. Bradman went on to his second triple century in Tests. In the next Test he ensured Australia would win the Ashes by hitting 244 and 77, while similarly debilitated, and soon afterwards was rushed to hospital for surgery. He was found to have a lingering peritonitis. Bradman was not expected to live but pulled through.

Five years later he won the South Australian squash championship in a one-hour game that observers said was the most ferocious and fast final ever played in Australia until then. Bradman said it was so tough that he would never play squash again in official competition. He was so determined to win that he would go beyond normal levels of endurance.

His enemies questioned his courage and criticised his methods against the bodyline tactics of Larwood, Voce and Bowes in the 1932–33 Ashes series.

Bodyline would have ruined the game. Fortunately, it was outlawed by the next year (1934) and faded into history. Bradman survived Bodyline and illness, and went on to dominate another five Ashes series. During the early years of World War II, he was a fitness instructor, and his competitive nature was nearly the complete undoing of him. He insisted on showing the way, competing in foot races and other physical events. He developed debilitating back problems that plagued the rest of his cricket career.

Technique

Bradman's batting technique was both orthodox and unorthodox. Early in his career, he was criticised for playing 'cross-bat' shots when pulling balls around from the off-side to the on. Bradman reduced the alleged transgression to absurdity by asking, 'How else do you score on the on-side when a ball is well outside off-stump?'

If Bradman faced a strong off-side field, he was not going to worry about playing a cross-bat shot through the on-side if that was the only way to score. However, it must be conceded that Bradman could play such shots with impunity because of his extraordinary skills. His batting methods were more effective than anything before or since.

He had no backlift in the technical sense. Bradman used the top hand on the batting handle to lever the bat up when playing a shot. This sped up the time for him to be ready to play a shot. It also took the strain off muscles in the arms and shoulders. Bradman played every shot in the manual, and some that were not, to perfection.

His grip gave him a less attractive appearance in stroke execution. The right or lower hand was turned over so far that the handle pressed against the base of the thumb, instead of resting against it. The left or upper hand was turned so that the wrist was behind the handle. Only someone with suppleness and power in the wrists could even try to play shots using this method and not feel awkward.

If this grip is tried by someone coached in orthodoxy, or even by a natural batting talent without training, it is a most uncomfortable, unnatural feeling. Any conscientious coach would quickly disabuse a child trying it now. Did anyone attempt this with the young Don?

'No,' he said. 'I was never coached. I did experiment with other methods, but I went back quickly to my own style. It was natural to me. I used it with an axe for my daily chore of chopping wood [at home from about age 8 to 18]. 'That's one reason I gained strength [in forearms and wrists].'

This Bradman grip produced three unique outcomes in attack or defence. First, the bat sloped at about 45 degrees to the ground, ensuring the ball was kept down. Second, when the player hooked or cut, the wrists rolled the bat over the ball so that with normal contact the ball was again kept down. Third, with a clean drive straight, or to off or on, Bradman didn't loft the ball because the top or left-hand grip acted as a brake. He only lofted when he wanted to. He applied the brake and kept the ball down for most of his career, particularly early on, and only hit 44 sixes in his 338 innings. Instead he stroked fours – 2580 of them – and two fives, mostly along the ground.

Bradman once suggested to a young Greg Chappell that he should change his grip to the Bradman grip – with both hands forming a 'V' on the bat handle. He told Chappell that the only other player to whom he had given this advice – and who had not taken it – was no longer in the South Australian team any more. Chappell took the advice and his technique improved to the point where he could play drives on the off side as well as the on side, which he favoured almost exclusively before Bradman's intervention.

Bradman's unorthodoxy didn't end with the way he held the willow. He developed a 'closed face' technique where he would move across to the off-side and turn the front of the bat to the on-side when making contact. On contact he would follow through over the ball. Bradman observed modern players who were coached to keep an open face and play everything square on, which seemed to restrict the capacity to follow through over the ball.

'[In addition] if the ball leaves, [modern players] tend to open the blade a little to advance the ball behind point and down to gully or third man,' he noted. 'This exposes the edge of the bat more than I used to. This in turn exposes them more to being caught behind the wicket more [than Bradman was].'

Bradman also thought that modern bats were too heavy for his liking. It was acceptable to play perpendicular shots with a heavy bat, but it was tougher to play horizontal shots. It made batsmen lazier in their defensive patterns.

There were other features in Bradman's technique. He usually took block middle to leg, an alignment that he thought lessened the likelihood of him being trapped LBW. Bradman was more interested in the position of his stumps that most players. He made more use of the crease than perhaps any player before him, sometimes ending with a foot someway *behind* the stumps at the finish of a shot.

At the point of the bowler's delivery, Bradman moved his right (back) foot back and across to the off. At the instant a ball left the bowler's hand, the bottom of the blade was levered up level with the top of the stumps. It was this preparation, coupled with his lightning feet, body movements and good 'eye' (rather than his average eyesight) that gave him technical and physical advantages.

His technique left him more unscathed than most. In twenty years of Test and first-class batting – 338 innings – he may have been only hit on the hands once. The main reason was that he almost always hit the ball, which is remarkable in itself. There were, of course, occasions when he was hit on the body, when hands and bat were not involved. One instance was at the Oval in 1930 when he made 232. In a tough pre-lunch session, in which Bradman scored 90 on a dangerous wicket, Larwood hit him on the upper arm. In the Fifth Test of the 1932–33 Bodyline series, Larwood hit him again on the forearm. Yet for the rest of his career, even on sticky wickets, Bradman got bat to ball. Many keepers, from George Duckworth to Don Tallon, attest to his not letting anything go through to them.

Another result of his technique was his 'wagon-wheel' – the sketch of his shots around the wicket during an innings. The English county court circuit judge B. J. Wakley wrote a book on the statistics of Bradman's career and found his range of shots 'varied more than any other cricketer' from innings to innings. Bradman had his favourites but rarely indulged them if the conditions were not right. He reset his mental computer and range of shots for each visit to the crease to always meet the needs of the moment, with the aim to attack and score fast, unless in a rearguard action.

Knowledge of the game

Bradman made himself an intellectual master of the game by reading about its history, how it developed, and by sitting the NSW state umpire's exam in 1932 at age 24. His study gave him ideas, an annoying thing for cricket establishments that were very slow to change. In 1933 he wrote a humble letter to the MCC suggesting that batsmen using their pads against balls pitched outside the line of the off-stump should be judged LBW, if, in the umpire's opinion, the delivery was going to hit the wicket. This suggested law was not in a batsman's interest, but it made for far brighter cricket. Batsmen were forced to play the ball and not use pads. It was several decades before his advice was heeded and a rule was introduced, which included the proviso that the batsman would be judged out if he was not playing a shot.

Bradman wrote books on the game and did a fair amount of journalism over the decades. This research and his experiences off the field, as a selector and as a member of the Australian Cricket Board, widened his comprehension of cricket and its influences, especially when he had to analyse such things as the throwing controversy of the 1960s and the South African apartheid problem in the 1970s. It also gave him exceptional vision. Bradman was often decades ahead in his thinking with suggestions on marketing and, for instance, the use of video and camera technology to help umpires make quick, accurate decisions.

However, he lacked perspicacity when it came to the game's overall evolution. Match payments and player conditions did not keep pace with the growth of the game. Bradman, like all the world's administrators, was caught in a time warp. Players were treated like amateurs at a time when the game needed a global, professional approach to survive and prosper in a world of rapidly increasing media competition. Part-time amateur managers could not run the game after the 1960s.

Natural athleticism

Bradman was a natural athlete and good at all sports. He had a small, compact, lithe frame that was deceptively powerful. For the first decade of his Test career he was considered one of the best fielders, if not *the* best fielder, in first-class cricket. He had a deadly fast throw and moved like Jonty Rhodes and Ricky Ponting of recent times. His strength and hardiness developed from his early 20th century country boyhood. He could live off the land by shooting game and fishing if he wished. Bradman's background built into him an endurance and constitution that helped him survive severe illnesses and live a long, mainly healthy life. He ate well, enjoyed good wines in his later decades and was never diet conscious. Even at 90, if he felt like a three-course meal at lunch or dinner, he'd have it. (In the interest of trivia, his favourite meals were shepherd's pie or lamb cutlets followed by bread-and-butter pudding or strawberries and ice cream, along with more than one glass of Henschke Hill of Grace shiraz, or a Coonawarra Estate.)

His body was taut with noticeably strong forearms until 90, the only concession to his good living being a very slight paunch. At 90, however, his muscle condition deteriorated and, like most people in old age, he had the odd fall that left lasting, painful bruises.

He often said 'old age is not funny', and I believed him. The body's weaknesses that such maturity brings were particularly galling to him because of his long history in sport and general fitness. In his school years he was a good runner in sprints and long distance, a top cricketer and tennis player. He was a NSW country under-16 tennis champion but had to decide at that age if he would pursue it or cricket. Tennis lost, but Bradman beat every Australian Wimbledon player of his era in 'friendlies', even though he never played in an official competition after he turned 16. Later, he played squash for fitness, but could not resist competing in 1939 for the South Australian championship, which he won. He first took up golf, his second sporting love, on the Ashes tour in 1930 and regularly drove the ball more than 260 metres. His concentration, consistency and precision from tee to the green were impressive. Yet his putting early on, according to former Test player Arthur Mailey, 'tended to be erratic'. Nevertheless, Mailey suggested he would have been a champion if he put his mind to it.

'It was incredible to watch Don if he pushed one into a sand bunker,' Mailey said. 'He would never get despondent and drop his game. Instead, he would enjoy stroking his way out of the predicament and the challenge not to drop a shot.'

Mailey criticised that strange grip and stance that Bradman carried over into golf, and observed that his batting strokes 'would take a while to iron out of him . . . When he's driving his left foot is well forward, as if he's hammering a straight boundary'. There would be no major changes in his golf game while he played first-class cricket, and his technique would have needed much work if he were then ever to challenge the world's best. Still, in 1935 at the age of 26, he won his first major trophy – the Mount Osmond (Adelaide) club championship – while recuperating after his life-threatening peritonitis. By 1940 he had reduced his handicap from 14 to 5. In 1949, after retiring from cricket, he coached those restrictive batting shots out of himself and worked hard on looking like a golfer, not a brilliant batsman who played golf as a leisurely interest. By 1960, at age 52, he reduced his handicap to scratch and was playing his best golf at pennant level. Bradman aimed at beating the course par rounds wherever he played and achieved this at Kooyonga (par 73) with 69, Peninsula (par 73) in Victoria with 69, Victoria (par 73) with 71, and Kingston Heath (par 74) in Victoria with 70. He retained his scratch rating well into his seventies.

More than 60 years after his first championship win, he was still winning at the club based on an age handicap. Until the age of 88 he played rounds twice a week at Kooyonga off 23. He would always walk the course and occasionally came in below his age.

In mid-1997, I asked, as I always did, how his golf was going.

'Terrible,' he said.

Why?

'I have to use a buggy,' he replied, miffed by the realisation that he would never again be able to stride over eighteen holes. The Don was finding it harder than most to bend to the uncompromising forces of old age. He had a severe flu in a cold 1998 Adelaide winter and a torn calf muscle just before his 90th birthday on 27 August. Any exercise became infeasible. He was depressed in the knowledge that his golfing days might be over after 70 years of playing.

Competitiveness

Test cricketer Ian Johnson related a story about his father, Bill, watching a private billiards game between Bradman and Walter Lindrum, the world's greatest player. This was in the winter of 1935 at the Adelaide home of Bradman's sharebroker boss, Harry Hodgetts. Lindrum made a break of 100, which Bradman couldn't match. It riled his competitive spirit so much that he had a billiards room built into his new home that was being constructed at the time. Bradman bought a table and, according to Lady Bradman, 'practised every night for the next year' until, like Lindrum, he was able to break 100 with ease.

Lord (Colin) Cowdrey told a similar story. It happened when he asked Bradman to play him at Royal Tennis in the late-1960s in London.

'But I don't know the rules,' Bradman responded. 'What are they?'

Cowdrey gave him a thick rule book about the ancient, elitist game that originally was played for the amusement of France's Royal Court. Bradman studied it overnight.

'He knew the rules better than I when we played,' Cowdrey remarked. This was typical of Bradman's tenacity, whether he was playing socially or in a Test match. To him, competition was not worth bothering about unless you were prepared and played to your potential, always aiming to win. He was obsessive and it didn't always please those pitted against him. Keith Miller, for one, thought him too competitive when they played billiards. Yet Bradman always took a loss well. Win or lose, he was never other than generous and honest in remarks about opponents. Though he performed for the moment as if his life depended on it (as in the 1939 South Australian squash championship), at the end of the day, he competed for enjoyment. Bradman, despite a fierceness that would have made him a formidable performer in professional ranks today, was forever an amateur at heart.

Bradman on others

Despite his scholarly comprehension of his chosen sport, Bradman never could explain why his record is so much better than anyone else's. He said he had seen 'plenty' of cricketers who looked better than him, even two whose natural home ended up as grade cricket. One player who Bradman judged 'superior' was Rayford Robinson from Newcastle. He played just one Test, aged 22, at Brisbane in the 1936–37 Ashes series. He was caught by Hammond off Voce in each innings, making 2 and 3. Robinson was dropped and never played Test cricket again. He represented both NSW and South Australia and scored 2441 at a 31.70 average. Robinson was judged by many to rank in stroke-play and timing with Trumper, Jackson and Kippax.

Bradman couldn't explain why Robinson and others like him didn't make it. Perhaps Robinson's flaws derived more from his character than anything else. Off the field he worked on the wharves and preferred the company of gangsters and criminals to his cricket companions. He was once charged with stealing. He had a sad end sleeping rough in the parks and under bridges in his native Newcastle. Robinson died there aged 51 in 1965.

Others, Bradman said, lacked concentration or had never learned to pace an innings. If players with the finest style kept being dismissed early, they would soon disappear. Indiscretion, lack of discipline, over-flamboyance, and lack of concentration – you see it all the time at park or even second grade or club level. Players look like champions, until they get out. It's not a matter of luck. These types will spend decades displaying all the strokes for a bright 30 or 40 and then play a hopeless shot that will end their innings.

'Great players learned to avoid errors,' Bradman said, 'or they had innate intuition, which allowed them preserve their wickets without necessarily playing defensively.'

Leadership

Bradman took on the captaincy of Australia in his 29th Test and applied the same integrity, skill, aggression, intelligence, shrewdness and efficiency to leadership as he did in making himself the best batsman of all time. He captained Australia in 24 Tests for 15 wins, three losses and six draws for a win ratio of 62.50 per cent, which was second to none among leaders who had skippered in 20 Tests or more and who were retired at the end of the 20th century. Like most captains, his performances, statistically at least, improved once he took on the top job. Bradman's average while captain in his last 24 Tests (101.51) was higher than in his first 28 games (98.69). He scored 14 centuries while skipper, at a better rate than his 15 before that.

He was skipper in five Test series. Four of them were won decisively. Two of the five teams he led – in 1936–37 and 1938 – were among the weakest in Australia's Test history, but for one factor, they had Bradman in them.

His leadership ranked among the most successful and astute captains in history. It is not easy to compare from era to era, but Bradman would sit among the supreme tacticians such as W. G. Grace, Douglas Jardine and Mike Brearley from England; and Trott, Ian Chappell, Richie Benaud, Mark Taylor and Steve Waugh from Australia. He would also be bracketed with the game's finest strategists – including Pelham Warner and Jardine from England; along with Allan Border from Australia. It is more difficult to rank Bradman with the best 'instinctive' leaders such as Benaud and two outstanding individuals in this department who never captained Australia – Keith Miller and Shane Warne. But Bradman was not without spontaneity, despite being a planner and a plotter by nature.

Yet his advantage as a leader were his own performances. When the big match or series-winning innings was needed, Bradman would deliver it.

In 1936–37 and 1938 particularly, he could have led Australia's second XI and the series result would have been the same. He won one series and saved another. After WWII, when he led three stronger sides against England in 1946–47 and 1948 and against India in 1947–48, the distance between Australia and the opposition was huge. Bradman's output at 40 remained more or less the same with a better batting line up around him and a far better, more rounded bowling array to throw at the opposition.

After a rotten start in his first series as Captain in 1936–37 in which Australia lost the first two games to England, he scored 270, 212 and 169 to dominate victories in the last three Tests. In the drawn (one-all) 1938 Ashes he scored a century in each of the three Tests in which he batted. In the last game at the Oval, Wally Hammond let England bat on to a record 7 for 903. He feared that Bradman, given two innings, would make a huge score in at least one of them. The game ended in anticlimax when Bradman tore ankle ligaments in the field and did not bat.

There was never a more shrewd leader than The Don. He supported Bill Woodfull when he opposed Jardine's bodyline tactics. When he became skipper, his attitude was more flexible. He included bowlers in his line-up who could intimidate the opposition.

Bradman's mind was sharp and sagacious. On the boat to England in 1948, he discussed tactics with his main weapon, fast bowler Ray Lindwall. He would be used in an attempt to destroy England's trump, Len Hutton, who had scored 364 – and taken Bradman's world record score of 334 – in 1938 during that mammoth construction of 7 for 903. Bradman wanted Lindwall confident and prepared for the Tests. He didn't want him to be a spent mental force before the Test matches as Ernie McCormick had been in 1938, when he was no-balled 35 times in his first game at Worcester.

Lindwall had a suspect 'drag' of his trailing leg when bowling, which made him liable to no-balling. Bradman told him to concentrate on 'passing' the umpires in the opening games. Taking wickets was of secondary importance. The captain told him his place in the

Test team was assured, no matter what his figures were early in the tour. Lindwall did as instructed and was passed by the umpires. He went on to play a significant part in the Tests.

Bradman also let Lindwall bowl bouncers at Hutton at Lord's. The star opener was troubled and dropped prematurely by selectors after failing in three of his four innings of the first two Tests. By the time Hutton was restored to the Test side, Australia had retained the Ashes.

In the Third Test, Lindwall bounced and struck Bill Edrich. When Australia batted, Edrich then bowled five bouncers at Lindwall, hitting him once. When Edrich came to the wicket in England's second innings, Bradman told Lindwall and Miller to ease up on the use of bouncers after Edrich was hit again. The captain allowed intimidation, but would not cross the line into a bumper war that would 'not be in the spirit of the game'. Bradman was also aware that the media would pounce on the swapping of throat balls.

There was evidence of a more subtle use of psychology in the way he handled Lindwall in 1948. The bowler strained his groin in the First Test. Bradman gave him a tough physical examination at Lord's before the Second Test. He passed but Bradman, who knew all about leg injuries and recovery times, was sceptical.

'Leave me out on form if you want to,' Lindwall said, 'but not fitness.'

Bradman picked him. When Lindwall bowled he pulled up during the follow through of his first delivery. He tried to hide his discomfort. Bradman, who never missed a trick on the field, pretended he hadn't seen anything. Lindwall did everything to cover up his problem, including taking wickets – five of them for 70.

Years later, Lindwall, on prompting from Bradman, admitted he had hurt his groin again with that first ball.

'Why didn't you say something at the time?' Lindwall asked.

'I noticed that you were trying so hard to hide it from me,' Bradman explained, 'and I reckoned you might bowl better if you thought I didn't know about it. I wasn't far wrong, was I?'

Bradman was also the great pragmatist. He more than once rearranged the batting order to preserve his own wicket and those of his key batsmen when his team had to bat on a poor wicket. He had no time for the heroic skipper, such as Joe Darling, who would go in first on a sticky to set an example to his men. This was a suicide mission. By contrast, Bradman dropped himself down the list to avoid the worst of the wicket. Invariably he succeeded, the classic case being the Third Test of the 1936–37 series at the MCG. Bradman sent in bunnies 'Chuck' Fleetwood-Smith and Bill O'Reilly to open, and Frank Ward, a third man with no batting pretensions, at number three. He dropped opener Jack Fingleton to six, himself to seven and further protected Stan McCabe at eight and Len Darling at nine. Australia lost 3 for 38, 4 for 97 and 5 for 97. Bradman (270) then joined Fingleton (136) on a dried out, flat wicket for a mighty partnership of 346. Australia went on to win by, not coincidentally, about the size of the Bradman–Fingleton link.

'Some were unkind enough to suggest that my purpose was to avoid batting on a wet wicket,' Bradman remarked. 'Of course it was; but only because such avoidance was *necessary in the interests of the team.*'

The main interest of the team was a win. Had Australia lost that game, the Ashes would have been lost. Bradman's mind, unfettered by vanity, the need to preserve an average, fear of failure, or bravado, speared right to the heart of the matter. He had to give his best batsmen a chance on a better wicket.

Bradman was not known for his nurturing skills, but he did dispense advice, sometimes gratuitously, usually when asked. Bradman kept it simple, often getting to the point in a word or two. If an individual absorbed what was said and acted on it, he was better for it. In 1948 Neil Harvey, the 19-year-old 'baby' of the squad, had a shaky start to the tour. He was too nervous to ask Bradman himself for advice, so he prevailed on his Victorian friend Sam Loxton to intervene with 'the boss' and find out what he should do to improve his batting results.

Bradman told Loxton to tell Harvey to keep the ball along the ground. The teenager was baffled. Was that it?

'That's what the boss said,' Loxton said with head tilt and a shoulder shrug.

A bemused Harvey took the advice. Bradman's reasoning as ever was pertinent. There was nothing wrong with Harvey's batting at all, and Bradman regarded him highly and without any weaknesses. To confuse him with unnecessary science about stroke-play on low, slow wickets, which he knew anyway, would be superfluous and counter-productive. To say nothing at all might lower the young man's confidence. Bradman's minimalist edict caused Harvey to concentrate on a basic. His scores improved. He was selected for the Fourth Test and hit 112 in his first ever Ashes match and helped Australia to one of the great wins in history. No observer could recall any lofted shots from the teenage star.

During the 1970–71 season Bradman met a youthful Dennis Lillee at a function, just before his first Test at Adelaide. There was much media and paper talk about Lillee being selected as a counter to the aggressive fast-bowling of England's John Snow. Lillee was not quite sure what his approach should be.

The 62-year-old Bradman took the new demon bowler aside and said, 'Forget about all the newspaper talk about bowling bumpers. Concentrate on what you've done. It's got you into the Test side.'

'It was a good, logical piece of advice,' Lillee remarked in his book *Over and Out*. 'It relaxed me for the huge job ahead. I was 21 and the responsibility of opening the bowling for Australia was bigger than anything I had shouldered before. My chat with Bradman eased the inner tensions but put me deeper in awe of the man himself.'

Lillee bowled brilliantly in his first effort, taking 5 for 84, and never looked back.

***

Bradman's amazing ability to make big scores at will and an average with twice the capacity of the best in history has been discussed by everyone interested in cricket, including kings and philosophers. Australian expatriate Brian O'Shaughnessy, regarded as England's best and most radical modern philosopher, in his book *Consciousness and the World*, dwelt on Bradman when examining human skills and the power we have over our limbs to achieve goals using those skills. O'Shaughnessy said, 'I was using Sir Donald as an example in which the distinction was almost negated – so great did his power of choice seem to be.'

The philosopher noted:

The great batsman Donald Bradman signalled his arrival in England in 1930, 1934, 1938, with innings of 236, 205, 258; and at the age of 39 in 1948 relented to the extent of notching a mere 107. Each of these innings were played at Worcester; they were the first first-class innings in each tour, and he made four tours in all. And yet cricket is supposedly noteworthy for its marvellous 'uncertainty'! But this was the man who hit over 300 in a day in a Test match against the truly great bowling of Larwood and Tate, and without taking any risks. And it was he of whom Constantine wrote, on witnessing his 254 in the Lord's Test Match in 1930: 'It was like an angel batting.' Indeed, it was Bradman who said of McCabe, who played three innings of genius in Test matches, that he had the impression that he 'played beyond his means'. And it is entirely credible to claim that he did, and that Bradman did not do this. After all, we are talking surely of the greatest sportsman who ever lived.

O'Shaughnessy here touched on the distinctions Bradman had over other leaders and batsmen related to his willpower, determination and single-mindness, along with outstanding powers of concentration.

Intelligence

The dictionary meaning of 'genius' is *'exalted intellectual power, instinctive and extraordinary imaginative, creative or inventive capacity'*. It's overused, but if the label ever applied to a sportsman, it did to Bradman and his approach to cricket. Intellectual strength alone would mean little if an individual didn't have the innate and acquired physical skills to play at the top. If they happen to be coupled together, as they were in him, the result would be an exceptional individual of brilliance, voracity and mental stamina. Add the other features mentioned and you a have big part of the package that made Bradman the true master of cricket in the 20th century. Yet examining his character and statistics to fully explain his genius is a bit like a surgeon dissecting a brain to find a soul. It can't be done.

10
MILLER'S LUCK

My book, Miller's Luck: the life and loves of Keith Miller, Australia's greatest all-rounder, *was published in August, 2005. The following is my speech for launches in Melbourne and Sydney.*

***

Keith Ross Miller was born a few hours after my father on 28 November 1919. They were acquaintances and had several other things in common, including serving in the Air Force in World War II. Miller died, aged 84 years, in 2004 on my birthday, 11 October. To anyone else, this would mean nothing. But it did mean something to me. The media, everywhere cricket is played, celebrated his life rather than simply reporting his passing. It was an inspiration.

My first memory, aged nine, of Miller was on a wet day at Christmas 1955 in a state game: Victoria versus NSW. Ten thousand spectators were at the game, held at the Junction Oval, St Kilda. It began to rain. My grandfather wanted to leave, saying that the game would be stopped. There were pools of water near the boundary line. But NSW captain Miller kept his team on the ground. The crowd roared their approval for this almost eccentric conduct in cricket. Playing in the rain.

Miller had command of his players, the opposition, the umpires and, it seemed, the match itself. The next day in the papers, journalists gave him accolades for staying on the field. It was an act of largesse and very much typical of Miller, who always had a connection with spectators.

My next memory of him was his winning a Test match at Lord's

172

in 1956. I, like countless others, listened to the commentary on a whistling radio. Miller took his only 10 wicket haul in a Test. It was his last game at an arena with which he had a special rapport. Lord's fans loved him.

A photo of him captured the real Miller and stayed with me for half a century. He is coming off the ground. He has just taken a bail from an umpire. With shoulders square, he nonchalantly flicks the bail into the crowd. It's a symbol of a showman, when showmen in sport were rare. It's also symbolic of his special link with Lord's spectators who supported him as if he were one of their own from the middle of World War II.

That photo is in the book.

Another Miller portrait, a painting, is one of three Australians hung in the Long Room at Lord's. The other two are Don Bradman and, within the last few months, Shane Warne. Victor Trumper's portrait is in the Lord's museum.

Miller remains Australia's greatest all-round cricketer. He may even be considered as the greatest of all all-rounders. It's conventional wisdom to speak of Garry Sobers as number one. But when you compare their records there is really nothing in it. Miller has a better bowling record; Sobers has a better batting record. They were both fine fielders. Miller was the better leader, in my analysis. It is impossible to place one clearly above the other.

Miller was also an outstanding Australian Rules footballer. He played for St Kilda and Sydney, and for Victoria and NSW. He had a remarkable entry into top football. Early in 1940, he was playing for the then VFA Club, Brighton, against Coburg. Miller was a raw 20-year-old, about 183 centimetres, and just 70 kilograms – a tall, skinny kid. His job early in the season was to play against the great Bob Pratt. Pratt was one of the three or four superstars of the 1930s. He had been with the Swans kicking bags of goals. He was only 27 and at the peak of his career.

The game was being watched by St Kilda selectors wondering if they could poach any Brighton players. Miller played a brilliant game, holding Pratt to six possessions and one goal. Miller was best on ground. The selectors came into the dressing room and signed him that afternoon with the Saints.

War and cricket prevented him from being regarded as one of the greatest footballers of all time.

Now, Miller the character. There would have been few performers as popular as Miller: with his team-mates, with the opposition and the fans here, in England and everywhere. His attitude was the key. Fight like hell to win, but enjoy it and enjoy the after-match festivity, especially with the on-field foe. The nearest contemporary personality in the game is Shane Warne. Miller, like Warne, had as many mates in the opposition as he did in his own team.

John Bradman, at Miller's state funeral, made a telling point, saying that Keith was a man's man who nonetheless expressed friendship more openly than any other man he had known. Neil Harvey augmented this by saying Miller was a man's man and a ladies man – but presumably nothing in between.

Miller's character and attitude were modified greatly, if not changed, by war. He had an amazing, hair-raising 30 months as a trainee and war mission pilot based in England from early 1943 to mid 1945. All the while he was in action or heading towards it, countless mates, friends and acquaintances all over the combat zones of Europe and the Pacific, at home and on English soil, were dying or being killed. Some were shot. Others crashed their planes. Some drowned, fooling about in planes. Others were beheaded. Some were blown up. Still others went out on missions, never to return.

The reason 'Dusty' Miller, as he was known during the war years, kept on going was his American fiance (later his wife), Peg Wagner, from a well-to-do Boston family. She wrote to him, sending him love and hope and beautiful thoughts of a future together. If it were not for Peg, Miller would never have made it. She was the main love and person in his life. She bore him four sons. Peg was loyal well beyond the call of duty. She was a woman of outstanding character, class and values. *Miller's Luck* is dedicated to her.

English cricket commentator John Arlott observed in the war and after it that 'Dusty' Miller was living life as if he were running out of it. And in Miller's mind, he was living on borrowed time, every hour of every day. He and everyone else in the Air Force called his survival Miller's Luck. That was the simple way of describing his freakish good fortune in surviving malfunctioning planes, mid-air collisions, crashes, enemy fire, napalm bombs that stuck to the wings of his plane and would not drop, bombs destroying a pub when he should have been in it but wasn't, bombs destroying a London cinema when he was in a pub and should have been in the cinema.

He even got caught in a Naval battle in the English Channel between a British destroyer and German U-boat. The U-boat ended at the bottom of the ocean, but Miller's ship could just as easily have gone down. That time, he was just taking a look at how the Navy operated in war, during leave from the air force.

He and his mate, Gus Glendinning, were always looking for the next adrenalin rush. Miller didn't have much time between those thrill fixes. He was on flying missions some days and playing cricket at Lord's and elsewhere the next day.

Some days war and cricket collided.

In July 1944, he was playing a brilliant innings on a wet wicket in a match at Lord's. He had reached 96. He had not yet scored a century at this hallowed ground. An air-raid warning sounded. It was followed by the engine buzz of a German guided missile, known then as a 'flying bomb'.

Play stopped. Spectators and players looked up. They could see the missile swooping over Lord's. It detonated just south of the ground. Play went on. Miller smacked a four to achieve that coveted first century at the home of cricket. He raised his bat to the appreciative crowd, just as another missile buzzed overhead and exploded much closer.

The nervous nineties would never be a problem for Miller after that experience. It was one reason among many for his not taking sport too seriously after the war.

Cricket went on at Lord's throughout the war. It was a deliberate show of 'calm' under the threat of destruction. It would have been a huge moral victory for the Germans if the game had been stopped.

***

Recently, I was in London during the terrorist bombings. It was pleasing to see that cricket continued at Lord's in the one-dayers and on 21 July 2005 – the first day of the first Ashes Test – when the terrorists struck a second time. It was a further demonstration of defiance in the face of threats, 61 years after Miller made that spectacular hundred.

***

Miller was a multifaceted character who loved classical music and poetry as much as a bet and a beer. As combat for him drew closer, he went – at every chance – to concerts and performances from maestros and musicians such as violinist Yehudi Menuhin. Miller even went AWOL for a London show. His attitude was that it might be the last performance he ever heard.

He once took Glendinning to the Buckingham village of Stoke Poges to see the grave of poet Thomas Gray. This was where Gray wrote his famous 'Elegy Written in a Country Churchyard'.

One verse reverberated in Miller's mind:

> 'The boast of Heraldry, the Pomp of Power,
> And all that beauty, and all that wealth e'er gave,
> Awaits alike th'inevitable hour –
> The Paths of glory lead but to the grave . . .'

It was Miller's way of gearing his mind to the strong possibility of his amazing fortune running out when he was inevitably sent aloft on combat missions.

Despite his fears, Miller survived. He came out of the war running at the top speed life could sustain and then leapt on a rollercoaster to superstardom. And his amazing good luck continued.

He played in the 1945 Victory Tests. 2005 marks the 60th anniversary since that unheralded – yet fabulous – series between England and Australia where each nation was represented by servicemen.

During those Victory Tests, Miller made his most famous remark after being asked by a reporter about how he handled the pressure playing international cricket.

'Pressure?' he responded dismissively. 'Sport is not pressure. Pressure is when a Messerschmitt is up your arse.'

As the war progressed, Miller developed a strong sense of the clinical condition known as 'survivor's guilt': how come *I* don't get snuffed out, when others do?

These feelings – this emotional confusion – accentuated Miller's affinity, his compassion, his sense of fraternity with the living who were still fighting and surviving like him, and also those who had died in the cause. And every day he made it through the war and after it, this affinity grew – mainly because he was living a wonderful existence. Miller, for decades after the war, would seek out the graves of mates and place flowers on them – in Australia, in southern England, in northern England, in France.

A few weeks after the war, Miller crashed his plane, ripping off both wings as it slid across a field and a road. He walked from the wreckage unscathed, played soccer half an hour later, and collapsed from shock in the middle of the game. A day later, still in shock, he was on a train to Lord's where he scored a brilliant 79.

Within weeks of that, he played the greatest innings of his life, scoring 185 with 7 sixes and 13 fours in 165 minutes of controlled mayhem at Lord's, playing for the Dominions against England.

Miller carried his luck onto the racetrack. The horses had always attracted him: as a kid, his main dream was to be a jockey. Keith was a tiny tacker, only about 150 centimetres (4 feet 11 inches) until into his 17th year. So he held that dream for longer than most. Then he grew about 33 centimetres (13 inches) in just over a year, and any reverie about winning a Melbourne Cup evaporated. But he stayed close to jockeys and the racing fraternity. And he was a gambler.

Not surprisingly, after the war and that rollercoaster 1945 summer, Miller was always on edge. His post-war nervous energy was channelled into some of the most devastating short periods in the history of cricket, with ball and bat.

On top of all that, Keith Ross Miller just happened to be one of the most attractive characters ever to represent Australia at anything. Many called him the Errol Flynn of sport. When Elvis Presley and Marlon Brando emerged in the mid-1950s, he was compared to them. But there was a major difference: Miller was not a celluloid, unreachable star. He was a real character who had done startling things in war and in international sport.

Along with his looks and character, Miller had style and charisma. This made him attractive to women of all ages. And he liked their company. Miller charmed across the board. Not even princesses in India and England found him resistible. The most often asked question I had during the writing of the book was about Princess Margaret, the Queen's sister. Did he have a relationship with her? Certainly, they saw each other often during Miller's three tours of England in 1948, 1953 and 1956. On each occasion, the princess initiated the link, once using Lord Mountbatten to approach Miller to join him for a dinner at his home where Margaret was a guest. (You'll have to read *Miller's Luck* to find out more.)

Keith Miller believed that all men were equal as characters no matter what their background or station in life. That's why he mixed with garbos and Royalty alike.

Miller wrote in 1956 that he had 'numerous failings', and that he had never 'set himself up as a shining example of propriety'.

These failings remained for the next half century.

Miller's Luck demonstrates that his shortcomings were outweighed by his human virtues of fellowship, of courage, of conviction and of sacrifice.

Australia has never produced a better all-round sportsman. He was a once-in-a-generation cricketer. More than that, Keith Ross Miller, was a once-in-a-lifetime character.

THE VICTORY TESTS

War in Europe ended on 8 May 1945, and within days of the last shots being fired, a Test series between English and Australian servicemen was arranged. The series was played in an unprecedented atmosphere of sportsmanship and goodwill. Because of the Victory Tests' competitiveness, the tension made them as exciting as any contest ever seen between these two long-term rivals, and the standard reached was high. Keith Miller emerged as the superstar of the series, out-batting the mature, still great Wally Hammond, and also – with the ball – drawing comparisons with the magnificent speedster, Harold Larwood.

Praise in the two main departments of the game could not be higher than this.

With the Victory Tests, cricket was once again called into service as a symbol of the British Empire. Throughout the war, Sir Pelham Warner, the leading name in MCC (Marylebone Cricket Club) administration, had been instrumental in keeping the game alive at Lord's to demonstrate British defiance against the belting by German bombers. The national game would go on, regardless. Now it was a humane way of celebrating victory, lifting the national spirit and taking the collective mind off the destruction and deprivations in immediate post-war Britain.

The precedent of such England–Australia competition 26 years earlier was still clear in the minds of Warner and others. Then, in

1919, a team known as the First AIF Australian XI was selected from the 170,000 diggers in the process of being repatriated, or educated before returning to Australia after World War I. The Australians were happy to play official Tests, but the MCC – which controlled the game – was not. It pointed to just one available player with Test experience: 33-year-old all-rounder, Charlie Kelleway. There was also one other established first-class player, the stolid 30-year-old batsman, Herbie Collins. The MCC would have been willing to play the series had big names such as Charlie Macartney been available. It didn't have access to a crystal ball, which would have alerted it to the serious talent among the servicemen such as dashing all-rounder Jack Gregory, the attacking batsman and outstanding cover field Johnny Taylor, the top-class keeper Bert Oldfield, the strong driving C. E. 'Nip' Pellew, or the batsman/keeper Hampden 'Hammy' Love, and others. They all shone for the First AIF squad of 19 that in 1919 toured England, South Africa and Australia. It showed its strength by playing 47 matches, winning 25, and losing just four. This success accelerated the return to cricket normality post the 1914–18 war.

Digger underdog

In 1945, it was not the MCC but Australian cricket administrators who would not allow the four (eventually five) three-day matches set down to rank as official 'Tests'. The war may have finished in Europe, but there was still fierce fighting in the Pacific with Japan, which did not make it a propitious time for Australia to celebrate with the highest level contest in cricket. Another factor was the inadequate number of recognised top-class players to choose from the 15,000 Australian servicemen in England. They were not representative of Australia's full talent.

The 2nd AIF and the RAAF fused in the interests of providing better competition for a near-complete England Test team. Even then, the Australians admitted to a sizeable inferiority complex towards the old enemy, whose squad included Len Hutton, Cyril Washbrook, Wally Hammond, Les Ames, Bill Edrich, Walter Robins and Doug Wright.

The RAAF provided six players in the Australian XI, and the AIF five. The lowly ranked warrant officer class II, Lindsay Hassett, who had played four Ashes Tests in England in 1938, was selected as captain despite some rumblings about the suitability of Keith Carmody for the job. Carmody, who was due back in England soon, had been shot down early in 1945 during an attack on four German ships off the Hook of Holland. He was rescued by the enemy and put in solitary confinement at Venlo and Frankfurt. Weeks later, he was marched 240 kilometres to a concentration camp near Berlin. The Russians, advancing from the east on a crumbling Germany, released him when they overran Berlin late in March, but then held him throughout April for a possible prisoner exchange with the Allies. Carmody did not like the prospects of this arrangement and the chances of him being shipped to Siberia. He escaped and managed to find an American force coming from the West. He was a hero in the eyes of his fellow airmen, and also a commissioned officer.

Yet Hassett was the only Test player available, and he was appointed. The fact that he had not lobbied for the position helped the other RAAF players accept him. The other personnel with first-class experience were Keith Miller (Victoria, nine matches); Stan Sismey (NSW, eight matches); Albert Cheetham (NSW, 18 matches); and Cecil Pepper (NSW, 10 matches). Pepper bowled leg-spin, but with variations, such as an excellent wrong'un, and a front-of-the-hand flipper, that he could deliver almost like an off-break. There was also medium-fast bowler Graham Williams (15 matches) and opening bat, Dick Whitington (32 matches) from South Australia.

Champagne cricket

Thousands of Australian (in dark blue), British and Canadian (in khaki) servicemen swelled the numbers at Lord's on 19 May 1945 for the first day of the first Victory Test. The usual crowd of members and notables, including Lord (Louis) Mountbatten, filled the Long Room and private boxes. They broke open the champagne and chicken sandwiches. It may not have been an official Test, but it was an important match between two teams representing England and Australia. The weather was chilly and overcast, the feeling festive – yet with the suspense always associated with the first day of a big series. With the Union Jack and Southern Cross flags fluttering, the celebration of Victory over European fascism so soon after VE Day created a palpably happy atmosphere. Cricket commentator John Arlott described the emotion of the morning as 'a general euphoria generated by relief and nostalgia'.

The Tests were expected to mark a new post-war era of cricket. It had been seven years since the dour drawn Ashes of 1938, when opposing captains Hammond and Bradman refused to give an inch. There was now a hope that the competition would be more carefree and daring. There was all and nothing to play for. No little urn containing burnt bails was at stake. Hammond was playing, but Bradman, the winner's winner, was not. Both sides, particularly England, were expected to present new, dashing cricketers. The spectators were aware of an imbalance between the two old enemies, but wistfully hoping for miracles. Those supporting England were expecting a special win.

Flying Officer Keith Miller was the only Australian with a relaxed smile in the dressing room. After two seasons, he felt at home at Lord's. Besides that, he had found batting form in between flying missions with a 50 for the RAAF side against England, and also a dashing 52 against Lancashire. He was one of those that Arlott recognised as 'relieved' to be simply alive and there at the home of the cricket.

Another was pilot Graham Williams, who had just been released after four years as a prisoner-of-war, where he had distinguished himself teaching Braille to blinded bombing victims – mostly children – in Germany. He had been shot down in the Western Desert during the Libyan Campaign. The 193 centimetre beanpole Williams looked emaciated, having lost much weight during his long ordeal. His last-minute act before taking the field was to swallow a cup of glucose in the hope of restoring energy to a body he was unsure would cope with physical exertion.

Williams' wonder; Miller's moment

Hammond won the toss, and decided to bat. Cheetham (a Rat of Tobruk), the tall, efficient medium-pacer, had the honour of sending down the first ball in a new era to Hutton. But it was Williams who thrilled the Australians in the crowd next over when he had Hutton caught behind for 1. The recent POW must have pinched himself. Only a few weeks earlier, he had been wondering if he would escape Germany alive. Now he was being cheered at Lord's for dismissing cheaply the holder of the world record Test score (364 at the Oval in 1938). Later, he got rid of Hammond for just 29, uprooting his off stump.

Miller came on as the usual fifth change, after Cheetham, Williams, Ellis and Pepper, and promptly bowled Bill Edrich (who had been a pilot at Great Massingham, Norfolk, which was where Miller was also based) for 45 just when he and Ames looked like taking the game away from Australia. Yet there was no real thought of using Miller earlier. His good economy rate was due to him being both erratic and quick. On both counts, he was tough to score off.

England reached 267. Australia was 2 for 82 at stumps on the Friday. On day two, a good crowd of more than 25,000 jammed into Lord's, demonstrating that Plum Warner's optimism about a successful series so soon after VE Day was well placed.

A big occasion player

Miller loved the challenge of a big occasion and audience. He arrived at the crease at 3 for 136, and joined a subdued Hassett, who seemed to have lost his pre-war verve. This Miller innings would create no fireworks. He let technique supersede aggression as he took on two outstanding leg-spinners in Doug Wright and Walter Robins who, in his time, had dealt blows to Bradman and Stan McCabe. Miller, who at this stage of his career still struggled against top spin bowling, was keen to make a good impression here. It could have some impact when real Tests returned.

Miller harvested rather than blasted until, at 5 for 270 and past England's score, his stroke-play blossomed. He unleashed shots that had electrified crowds in England in the past two summers. Urged on by the man mountain, Cec 'the Ox' Pepper – who had a sound defence but loved to attack – Miller drew applause from some of the most critical observers in the Long Room. Comparisons were made with Victor Trumper, Archie Jackson and McCabe.

At one point, Colonel John Stephenson (later to become MCC secretary and a good Miller mate) bowled Miller a late out-swinger, which just missed hitting the off-stump. Miller strolled down the pitch and patted the spot where the ball had landed, tossed back his mane, and glared at the Colonel.

'I bowled Miller an identical ball', the Colonel recalled. 'He drove it into the stand for six.'

Miller again strode down the pitch towards the bowler.

'A better ball', Miller called to the Colonel, 'but the better the ball the bigger the six.'

Miller made 105 in 210 minutes. He struggled in the 90s for 40 minutes, yet it had the required impact. Spectators – particularly the Australians – seemed pleased enough. They drank the ground's beer supply and applauded all the Australian performances.

A tear for a survivor

One memory of that rapturous day at Lord's would stay in Miller's mind forever. It was not that brilliant straight drive off Stephenson, or raising his bat when he reached his initial first-class century at Lord's. It was the reception for lanky Graham Williams as he emerged out of the Long Room to bat.

'I have heard touching applause at Lord's, in fact all around the world', Miller said, 'but this was hand-clapping with a difference. I have never heard it before or since . . . magical, heart-felt hand-clapping. It is a scene I will never forget.'

There had been press reports on Williams' plight as a POW, and he was being warmly welcomed back 'home' and to freedom. But the impact of the response would have had a deeper impact on Miller. His gentle tears for Williams were for himself too. Miller's last dice with death, when he limped home from a bombing mission, was just two weeks before. He, indeed no one, could explain why some survived and some did not.

Williams, not known for his batting, celebrated with a delightful 53. He was living a fantasy and could do no wrong with ball or bat.

Thrills and spills

Miller's 'notices' were good. The *London Times* thought his knock 'as good a century as has been seen at Lord's in many a long day'. *Wisden* liked his 'elegant, emphatic style'. The London *Daily Telegraph* looked ahead and would have pleased Miller: 'It proves how valuable he will be to Australia in future official Tests'.

His sterling effort at the crease (along with Hassett's 77 and contributions of 35 or more from six other batsmen) helped Australia to a healthy 455. England's second innings of 294 was a fraction better than the first. It left Australia 77 minutes to reach a target of 107. Hassett's men took up the challenge. The impetuous Pepper led the way with his usual attacking approach. He hit one prodigious six into the top deck of the grandstand. It was the strike that symbolised Australia's intent, which at certain moments led to panic and two run-outs. Anyone thinking that the game would be played to the finish in an atmosphere of total generosity, or that the spirit of the game counted more than winning, would have raised eyebrows at England captain Hammond's placing of eight on the boundary. It slowed the run-rate, caused frustration and helped England to a point where it could force a draw.

At 4 for 76, Australia needed 31 in 12 minutes for victory. Pepper was in everything. He thumped a straight four, then followed it with a cover drive. Lieutenant Errol Holmes, wearing a cream cravat, moved around the boundary to cut it off, but the ball evaded his ungainly lunge and slipped over the boundary rope. The Australians needed 23 from 18 deliveries.

'What's that around neck?' a Yorkshireman called, 'cravat or noose?'

Holmes nodded a rueful acknowledgment of his error in the tense final minutes.

'Why don't you tighten it, Guv'nor?' the spectator yelled.

Beating the field, the clock and expectations

The tight finish soon boiled down to six deliveries and five runs to get.

England's 'affable Alf' Gover, an England Surrey medium-pacer, was thrown the ball for the final over. He put the first one in the block hole. Pepper's partner Charles Price just dug it out. No run. The second ball was pushed to mid-off for a scampered single. Four balls to make 4 runs. Hammond fiddled with the field, bringing two of his eight boundary riders closer in. Everyone, including Pepper himself, knew that he would swing at the next ball, no matter what was delivered. The big, talented all-rounder proved far more predictable as a batsman than as a wily spinner. He launched into an on-drive, but mis-timed it. The ball flew high, but directly above Doug Wright at mid-wicket. The fielder ran forward, then back, reached up with his left hand, lost his balance, and clutched at his second attempt. Wright had it at a third attempt but it was a juggle too much as he toppled to ground. The ball spilled free. Wright accidentally kicked it away in his fall. Pepper called Price through for a second run. Three balls remained; two runs were required.

Hammond held up play again, moving everyone in to cut off the single. The 17,000 crowd were hushed and expectant. Gover delivered his fourth ball on middle stump. Pepper, who would never die wondering about anything, went onto the back-foot and cross-batted the ball. It squeezed through the mid-wicket, running down towards the boundary rope in front of the seats where the Australian servicemen were predominant. They were on their feet cheering as the batsman ran 2.

Australia had scraped in with 2 balls to spare and 6 wickets in hand. *The Times* noted that Hassett's men had beaten the fieldsmen, the clock and expectations. Miller, Pepper, Hassett and co celebrated long into the London spring night.

England gets serious

The competitive but fine spirit of the game, marred only slightly by Hammond's defensive field placements in the last half hour, was outstanding, and drew comparisons with the dour 1938 Ashes series. Commentators spoke with authority rather than hope of 'a new post-war era'. The three days drew 67,660 spectators, who paid a shilling (about 10 cents) each to pack Lord's. The total gate for the game was 3383 pounds (almost A$8000). After tax and expenses, 1935 pounds (about A$4500) went to the Red Cross and five Australian charities.

The game had been a spectacular success. Plum Warner and Keith

Carmody, two prime movers over the years in setting up the series, were pleased. England showed it was taking the competition most seriously by making changes for the second Victory Test more in keeping with an Ashes contest than a peace celebration. They dumped Test players Gover, Ames and Robins and replaced them with medium-pacer George Pope, paceman Dick Pollard and batsman Maurice Leyland, whose last outing against Australia in the 1938 Oval Test produced a thumping 187. But Leyland withdrew unfit, as did Stephenson. England and Surrey batsman, Errol Holmes, and Lancashire's left-arm spinner, W. B. Roberts, replaced them. Australia brought in Carmody who was back in England after his escape adventure. He replaced the battler batsman, Ross Stanford.

***

The second Victory Test began on 23 June at Sheffield's Bramall Lane, a venue which had been hammered by the Luftwaffe. The grandstands had areas that were charred and dented; the ground was pock-marked.

Hassett won the toss and pleased the Yorkshire crowd by sending England in. The local hero, Len Hutton, didn't get going, but the crowd was content with a domineering even century by Hammond. Warner classed it as one of his best ever, and raved about a strong 63 by Cyril Washbrook. Miller was thrown the ball as fifth change to hold up an end. He was again quick but too erratic to take a wicket or cause other than the occasional discomfort.

Hammond singled out Pepper for special praise, saying that his bowling 'was some of the finest spin I have ever faced'.

Considering Clarrie Grimmett had won his tussle with Hammond during the 1930 Ashes in England, and that he had also faced O'Reilly at his best, this was a high accolade indeed.

Miller, not always the best runner, found himself batting in the second innings with someone less reliable in Carmody (42), who ran him out for 17 when he looked set for another big innings.

Australia struggled to 147. Pope, living up to comparisons with the great S. F. Barnes, removed half the Australians.

England's openers had reached 41 without loss in its second innings, when Hassett – for no apparent reason beyond using the surprise element – threw the ball to Miller to replace Williams. Miller had injured his back in a wrestling match in late 1943, but if he did not overwork it, he could generate considerable speed.

He considered it a challenge to be given a chance first change rather than fifth, and with some shine still on the ball. Taking the role a fraction more seriously, Miller raced in from nine paces instead of a leisurely six. He was off-line and didn't trouble Washbrook. The next over, Ellis was on in another change, and he tied up Hutton.

Miller's second over was quicker and shorter. He hit Washbrook a painful blow on the thigh. The batsman hobbled for a bye, leaving Hutton to face. He ducked a very quick head-high bumper. Miller, nostrils flaring and hair flopping, looked back at the batsman as he returned to his mark, more or less. In what was becoming a Miller trademark, he flicked his hair, running a small concealed comb through it, and then charged in. Hutton was hit on the left forearm, the one he had injured in 1940 in a gymnasium accident while training to be a commando. He stumbled a bye and dropped his bat at the bowler's end. Miller examined the hit, and rubbed the welt. The Yorkshire crowd reacted to its champion being struck.

There were yells of 'Larwood! Go off, Larwood!' in reference to Nottinghamshire's pace demon of the 1930s who had terrorised Yorkshire in county games. Miller now had both batsmen uncertain. When Hutton was ready, but still sore, Miller walked to his mark, shoved back his mane and steamed in, more in reaction to the crowd than any desire to do further damage. The ball to Washbrook was another head high bouncer. He ducked, but into the ball, which cannoned into his crown.

The crowd roared. The ball flew clear. Hutton set off for another bye, but seeing that Washbrook was dazed and in trouble, he returned to his crease. Miller was catcalled and booed. Play was held up as the hardy Washbrook took some moments to clear his head which fielders, Hutton, Miller and the umpires examined as if it were a damaged bowling ball.

Miller's third over was better mannered. Each ball was of good length. The crowd settled down and watched as Washbrook flicked at a very quick delivery outside the off-stump. The ball flew straight to keeper Sismey. It popped out of his gloves as Pepper dived from slip and just failed to snaffle it.

Miller stood mid-pitch, hands on hips. But instead of snarling, he pushed back his hair with his left hand and that comb, and waved to Sismey with his right. The bowler knew that both batsmen had been softened to the point of vulnerability.

Miller's fourth over was his best so far. He kept a good length with three deliveries. Then he released another dangerous short one at Washbrook, which would have arched his nerves. The crowd was temperate in their response, perhaps sensing that Miller was now bowling with some science. The next ball was a quick away swinger. It had the nervous batsman pushing again. The edge went to Sismey, who held it this time.

Hammond came in. Miller delivered a variety of pace and bump at the super-batsman, who looked uncomfortable.

There was a tea break. Ellis removed Hutton (46) and Miller beat Jack Robertson with sheer speed, trapping him LBW for 1. Hammond (38) never looked happy against Miller's pace or the spin of Pepper and Ellis, and was bowled by the latter. England stumbled to 190.

***

The more astute observers of this game felt it was the turning point for Miller as a bowler. But most of the press still regarded him as a batsman, who was brought on to rest the four main bowlers. One scribe who thought otherwise was the aptly named South African former speedster, Bob Crisp, writing in the *Daily Express*. He advised Miller to lengthen and mark his run to 15 paces, a novelty for the bowler on two counts – distance and calibration. Crisp also notified Hassett that he should open the bowling with Miller. More than Washbrook's head, it seemed, had been struck by Miller's effort.

Australia was set 330 to win in 360 minutes on the final day. Whitington (61) and Workman (living up to his name with a dogged, yeoman 63) gave the servicemen a fine start and a fair chance. But Miller was bowled by Pollard for just 8, and while many players managed starts, Australia fell 41 runs short in another thriller.

The series was square. The result caused Hassett to consider using Miller more proactively with the ball.

***

Australia made one change for the Third Test back at Lord's: RAAF match-winner Bob Cristofani replaced injured spinner Price. England's veterans came under criticism, and the selectors swung the axe, dropping Errol Holmes and Jack Robertson. Pope, further in the tradition of Barnes, withdrew to play a professional Lancashire league match. One way or another, the selectors decided on infusing the team with a deal of class. In came Donald Bryce Carr, aged 18, the captain of a leading private school, Repton; the Honourable Luke Robert White, the fifth Baron Annaly, 17, in his first year at Cambridge University; and John Gordon Dewes, 18, a Portsmouth Naval cadet. The selectors thought that this was the time to blood promising youngsters. The thought had merit, given the likely resumption of official Tests in 1946.

Bob Crisp, in the *Daily Express* on the morning of the match, maintained his campaign to have Miller opening the bowling. He had a different view of England's injection of well-bred teenagers. What better time to give Miller the new ball, Crisp suggested, 'than against this cavalcade of youth'.

Hammond won the toss and batted despite a rain storm, which held up the start on a Saturday for 40 minutes. The weather did not stop spectators pouring in and packing the stands. Hutton opened the batting with Washbrook. Hassett ignored the newspaperman's crisp advice and let Williams and Albert Cheetham have the new ball.

Williams had Washbrook caught behind for 8, but Hutton was his immovable self. When bowling changes were due, the Australian skipper once more demonstrated that he thought Miller's form at Bramall Lane was a fluke by choosing the spinners Ellis, Pepper and Cristofani before him. Miller was thrown the ball as the sixth option. England was 2 for 100. Hutton was set. New left-hander Dewes was looking the part.

Miller paced out a 12-step run-up. It wasn't the 15 recommended by Crisp, but the fact that it was longer and marked with a swipe of his boot, indicated he had accepted the gratuitous advice. He tore in faster than ever before. The Long Room members, near fossils and younger observers alike, held their breath. Miller made the ball zip and rear off a good length. He was relying on speed, causing Dewes – who said he had never faced anything like it – and Hutton – who was too experienced to comment – to play, miss and edge. Miller hit Dewes before cartwheeling his off-stump for 27. England was 3 for 107.

After tea, a refreshed Miller sprinted in again. He uprooted young Carr's middle stump for 4, and then Hutton's prized middle and off stumps for 104. Miller was near unplayable, and accurate enough to bowl all his three victims. The buzz at Bramall Lane, which brought back unpleasant memories of Larwood for Yorkshire supporters, was transmitted to cricket headquarters. Yet the observers here mumbled 'Larwood' more in awe than anger. Miller, the batsman who was being compared to the great Wally Hammond, could also bowl like the man who was responsible for England's last Ashes victory, now in the dimming past of 1932–33.

Miller put a dent in England's youth policy and created a few concerns for Hutton, who nevertheless achieved his typical century in 209 minutes. The shrewd old pro, knowing that he was likely to face Miller in the future, was not about to praise him. Yet he had never experienced express and unpredictable bowling like this, not even from Ernie McCormick.

***

England made 254, and Australia responded with just 194, which would not have been reached but for Hassett's best innings (68) of the season. Lancashire's Pollard overshadowed Miller's efforts with 6 for 75, and bowled him cheaply (for 7, with one that kept low) for the second innings in succession. Pollard's long, flat-footed run-up was deceptive. He delivered swing both ways and would build his pace over a spell.

The question now was whether or not Hassett would open the bowling with Miller in the second innings. Williams and Cheetham had toiled hard but for a return of 1 for 92 between them during the first innings. Crisp once more pushed for Miller to open. This time Hassett obliged, and with little to lose. England was without Hammond, who had a severe attack of lumbago which not even a valiant effort by Australia's physiotherapist, Larry Maddison, could remedy. Washbrook, with an injured thumb, wisely dropped himself down the list. This left England's new chum, Dewes, more vulnerable to speed. He coped with Williams well enough. But Miller with a new ball was something else. Now the speedster could employ swing with pace. A blur of a late out-swinger knocked back Dewes' middle stump for 0.

Hutton scraped through Miller's opening burst with courage, luck and skill in about equal measure. The bowler came back in a second spell to bowl the in-form and gritty Edrich (58), then later took delight in flattening Pollard's stumps for 9.

England was reduced to just 164, thanks to the spin of Cristofani. All Miller's six victims were clean bowled, which was testimony to his accuracy and pace. Crisp, in the press box, could be forgiven for saying 'I told you so'.

Miller was suddenly a paceman to be reckoned with, but there were consequences for the effort. His back was in spasm and pain during England's second innings. Yet it would take more than this to stop him batting. Australia was set 225 to win in 300 minutes. Miller came to the wicket at 3 for 104 after three hours of stubborn batting. He had two hours to secure victory, and batted accordingly with a crafted innings (71 not out) of controlled drives, giving Australia victory by 4 wickets.

Miller had provided the best performance with bat and ball in a single match of his cricket career.

By 16 July 1945, at Lord's, an all-rounder of enormous skill and capacity had been born.

***

The Fourth Test, which was again at Lord's, began on 5 August. Australia was weakened by the loss of Cheetham, who went back to Australia, and Carmody, who was rested. Stanford returned and was joined by Jack Pettiford, a leg-spinning all-rounder.

Miller had put paid to England's youth policy. The three youngsters were dropped and replaced by a more traditional, mature look of Pope (34 years), Robertson (28), and – in a seemingly retrograde step – Surrey left-hander, Laurie Fishlock, who was 38.

Australia led the series 2-1. England needed to win or draw to keep the series alive. Hassett won the toss and batted, and the Australian plan was apparent early. One player would hold up an end, while his partners kept the scoreboard moving. The designated 'stayers' were opener Workman, and Sismey, batting at three. The latter did the job when Workman was out for 6 at 15. Sismey saw Whitington (46) and Hassett (20) go before Miller got up from his seat on the pavilion balcony with the score at 3 for 108.

***

Miller emerged from the dressing room through the Long Room along the rubber mat and down the pavilion steps to strong applause from the 5 August Bank Holiday Monday crowd of 34,000. The buzz of 'Miller's in' had become synonymous with brilliance and class.

He had to counter the swing of Pope, who had already seen off Whitington and Hassett. In earlier games, Pope had been a mystery. No one in Australia bowled like him. He caused Miller to push and probe at balls, which swung either way or came straight on. By luck and his good eye, Miller squeezed through an early examination and settled down. His cover-driving was a dream. It was used to collect 8 of his 10 fours as he piled on another century. It took him 170 minutes which, as planned, made up for the slow rate generated by Sismey, who scratched together 59 in four hours, injuring his thumb in the retarded process.

Pope eventually bowled Miller for 118 after a 200-minute exhibition of grace and power. Pepper rubbed salt into English wounds with a quickfire, six-laden 57. Australia reached 388 in 420 minutes at a respectable rate of 55.43 runs an hour. But the English press, reverting to a negative, nationalistic style now that the series looked like going Australia's way, criticised the batting approach and run rate. Miller's magnificence received minor status. Sismey's doggedness was attacked instead.

Wisden didn't like the scoring rate. It accused Australia of playing to avoid defeat – which was harsh, given Miller's performance. Whitington, a wordsmith, was driven to write to the *Daily Telegraph* and explain that there had been no Aussie plan to play for a draw. But he shouldn't have bothered. His excuse that his side set out to put England in a position where it had to take risks to win seemed to give credence to the whinging.

Rain and bad light delayed play until after lunch on day two. Miller opened the bowling. He delivered with fire, pace and accuracy. Although he didn't take a wicket, he was unlucky with two catches being put down by keeper Workman, who was standing in for Sismey.

The 30,000 plus crowd was impressed by Miller's application, and the confirmation that he was an opening bowler of distinction. None of the top England batsmen was comfortable against him.

***

Workman's struggle behind the stumps saw extras take on the proportion of a good individual batting score for England. He let through 51 by the end of the day. Hammond, who was batting, allowed Hassett to use twelfth man Carmody as a keeper the next morning.

'There is only one thing stopping you from using Carmody behind the wicket', Hammond told Hassett. 'That is my permission, and you have it.'

It was an act of sporting generosity rarely seen at the top level of the sport. Commentators dived for the records to find that this had been done just once in England/Australia Tests in the Oval game of 1905. Then, Australian skipper Joe Darling allowed England's twelfth man Arthur Jones to stand in for injured Arthur 'Dick' Lilley.

Hammond had encouraged and enjoyed the fraternising of the two teams each evening in the shared dressing room and elsewhere. The change was welcome after the grimly fought Ashes Tests that had developed in the wake of the sporting disaster of Bodyline, when ill-feeling between the teams was at its peak.

The irony of this largesse in allowing Carmody to keep was that it prevented Hammond from scoring a century. He was in sparkling form on 83, when he cut a ball from Ellis. Workman, happily replaced as keeper, flew horizontally and held a one-handed 'blinder'. Hammond had been in a strong partnership of 157 with Washbrook (112 in four hours).

England went on after tea on the last day to 7 for 468 declared – a lead of 80, which meant it had no serious intention of striving for a win. The folly of not declaring earlier seemed apparent when Australia collapsed in its second innings, losing 4 wickets before it had wiped off the deficit. But Miller held the side together in a textbook example of sensible batting, remaining 35 not out from Australia's 4 for 140 at the close. This gave him 153 runs for once out for the game. His bowling figures of 0 for 49 off 23 overs with five maidens did not reflect his impact with the ball.

The run rates for the two first innings (Australia 1 run for every

2 balls; England, 1 every 1.9) were similar enough to support Australia's argument that the onus was on England to fight harder for a win. The inherent competitive nature of games between the two countries had turned exhibition three-day games into well-fought scraps, albeit in good spirits, that might only be resolved by five-day contests.

Australia's tactic of forcing a draw or a desperate response from England had worked. It led 2-1, with one Test to play.

A record attendance for a three-day match at Lord's of 93,000 demonstrated the huge public appeal throughout the series, which led to a Fifth Test being tacked on at Old Trafford, Manchester.

***

The Lord's game finished on 8 August, two days after an atomic bomb – carried from Tinian Island in the Pacific's Marianas in a US B-29 plane – was dropped on Hiroshima, Japan. The bomb killed 80,000 people and injured another 70,000. On 9 August, a second bomb was dropped on Nagasaki, killing 40,000. By the next day, the Japanese government appreciated the impact of these horrific new weapons of mass destruction. It began moves to surrender. The Pacific War was over.

***

The end of major hostilities worldwide meant that the final Victory Test at Old Trafford beginning 20 August would be played in an increased atmosphere of celebration. This applied especially to the Australian servicemen in Europe who would have been called upon to enter the Pacific war theatre, had fighting with Japan continued until the end of 1945.

Hassett again won the toss and batted under fair skies. The crowd of 28,000 was a sell-out. Another 10,000 unlucky cricket fans swarmed around the gates and tried to gain admittance as play began.

After a fair start, a mini collapse saw Miller at the wicket with the score at 4 for 66. New man Eddie Phillipson (who replaced Roberts) joined Pollard, his opening bowling partner at Lancashire, to give England a decided home ground advantage. There was no Manchester black cloud to assist, yet still they were a formidable combination, especially when backed up by the brilliant Pope, who could swing the ball in any atmosphere. The wicket was soft. The bowlers' boots were cutting it up, which assisted the three professionals, who managed swing and cut, and a swathe of wickets. Yet Miller began his innings with intent, slamming 14 off the first over he faced, from Phillipson. Miller showed he was a quick learner and becoming a master in all conditions by conquering the three specialist bowlers. He proceeded to dominate the Australian innings as wickets fell steadily, reaching 77 not out (7 fours) in 115 minutes in the team's meagre tally of 173. Square cuts and strong drives were a feature of his batting.

Given the state of the wicket and the opposition, this was Miller's finest innings yet. He never seemed in trouble, and used his excellent eye and reflexes to counter Pope's prodigious swing late off the back, and swiftly off the front foot in a manner few in the history of the game could have matched.

Invigorated by his batting, Miller came onto the field revved up to blast England out. It seemed the only option. He smashed through Fishlock (9), but Hutton (64) and Hammond (57) demonstrated why they, too, were class acts by defying Miller's tearaway tactics.

England stumbled to 243 (Cristofani 5 for 55), a lead of 70, which on a responsive wicket and with the permanent threat of rain, was strong. Half of day two was lost when Australia limped to 3 for 37 at stumps, drawn 20 minutes early because of rain and bad light. Miller, much to his chagrin the next morning, made just 4, caught behind off a big away-swinger from Phillipson. It was the first time Miller had failed at a critical moment in an important international.

Australia fell apart and was 8 for 105, when Cristofani, who had starred with the ball, took charge. His method was to stand a stride forward of the crease, forcing the three swingers to bowl short and lose their length. The tactic worked. Cristofani hooked with short-arm jabs, cut off the front and back foot, and reached the pitch of the ball to off-drive. Inspired by previous innings by Miller and Pepper, the young spinner played the shot of the match by hooking Pope for six into the terraces.

Cristofani remained 110 not out in Australia's 210.

His gallant effort was not enough. England mopped up the 141 required, losing 4 wickets in the 150 minutes left. This drew the magnificent and evenly fought series, which was watched by 367,000.

'This is cricket as it should be', Hassett wrote after the match: 'These games have shown that international cricket can be played as between real friends – so let's have no more talk of "war" in cricket.'

Miller was undoubtedly 'player of the series'. He topped the batting averages with 443 runs at 63.28, well ahead in aggregate and average of Test batsmen Edrich (331 at 47.28), Washbrook (329 at 47.00), Hammond (369 at 46.12), Hutton (380 at 42.22), and Hassett (277 at 27.70.)

Hassett summed up Miller's efforts with the bat, saying: 'In our team, Miller stands out. He hasn't Hutton's solidity yet, but as a stroke player he is second to none in the world today'.

Miller's returns with the ball (fourth on the Australian list with 10 wickets at 27.70 each) were more modest, yet masked his imprint as a real all-rounder.

The Victory Tests were a resounding success for cricket and in helping restore the UK's morale.

12

LORD OF LORD'S

Within days of the last Victory Test, a mainly Australian XI again took on England at Lord's. Miller's glorious 1945 summer continued with one of the finest innings ever seen at Lord's.

***

Keith Miller took two steps down onto the Lord's arena. He was greeted by such applause that anyone not knowing he was an Australian would think he was English. The date was 27 August 1945. It was the last hour of the second day of a match between England and a 'Dominion' combination, made up of eight Australians, one New Zealander, one West Indian and one South African. Miller was conscious of the fact that W. G. Grace, Victor Trumper, Wally Hammond and Don Bradman had also made those two modest steps for cricket. It gave the tall, lithe and graceful athlete a thrill to again be walking – with his characteristic erect back and loose limbs – the same walk. Miller loved the spirit at this ground: the epicentre of the cricket world. He had made it his own during the World War II years with brilliant performances that had seen him compared with the all the greats of the game.

The favourite of Lord's, ladies and gentlemen

Most of the 34,000 packed into the ground had stayed in the hope of seeing Miller. They were full of expectation as he tugged at his sleeve, used his teeth to wriggle on his batting gloves, and strode to the wicket with the lope of a man relishing the moment. Male fans were riveted to him as he rolled his broad shoulders and glanced skywards, as if searching for enemy planes and missiles – something he and they had done for the past several years. Female fans clapped and shrieked as he took off a glove and gave his ample dark locks a smoothing over, reflecting the behaviour, just before a performance, of the concert conductors he so admired. Miller took block and settled into his upright, classic stance. There was no agitated tap of the bat. His stillness spelt murderous intent, as did his easy grip, which was that of the tail-ender, signalling that at every chance he would attempt to belt the cover off the ball and often send it skyward. Yet Miller was establishing himself as a batsman of the highest order. His readiness for mayhem reflected his character rather than his magnificent stroke-making prowess.

The score was 2 for 60 in the Dominions' second innings. It led England by 80. A Miller special was needed. Already this summer at Lord's, he had scores for the RAAF, Australia and now a Dominion side of 105, 1 (run out), 7, 71 not out, 78 not out, 75, 63, 118, 35 not out and 26. In previous seasons, he had scored several centuries here. He had just been man-of-the-series in five Victory Tests for Australia against England, which celebrated the end of World War II in Europe. Miller was the runaway favourite player of the English summer and had come to symbolise the best of British life and sport. He may have been an antipodean of Scottish descent, but he had fought for the Royal Air Force as a pilot in a bomber squadron over enemy skies in Europe. The United Kingdom and Lord's had claimed him as their own. The matinee idol good looks, ready smile and willingness to engage with the spectators all conspired with his outstanding performances to make him the centre of attention with the bat, the ball or even just fielding. It was said he could catch swallows in slips.

Miller had every motivation to perform. It would be his last big game at Lord's for the summer; the finale to his war-time stay in England. Hammond had provided a typically fine century in England's first innings. Miller had tussled with him for pre-eminence as a batsman all season, and wished to leave his adopted cricket 'home' with a statement. There was little to lose. If he failed, he would still be ranked as equal to the English great. Miller could deliver a swashbuckling show or go down trying.

He moved onto the front foot against the excellent bowling of Test leg-spinners Doug Wright and Eric Hollies.

He was in touch from his first cover drive to the fence, second ball he faced. Miller was a player of moods. His footwork demonstrated his finesse on this day, as each movement brought his head and shoulders over the ball, which at first sight seemed exaggerated until the observer realised that this was the norm. Miller's back-foot movement also seemed overdone when, in rare moments, the spinners forced him to retreat. The elbow was erect as if an extension of a very vertical bat. Even this defence was a form of attack. The ball was rebounding through the field.

Miller was lunging at deliveries with full confidence and decisive punch, whether to kill Hollies' spin or cover-drive Wright with power and the straightest of bats.

Another early hint that he was in form was his late cutting. The artistry and precision of this fine shot were usually the preserve of shorter players such as Don Bradman or Denis Compton. Yet the taller Miller was equally adept at it.

Miller reached 49 in 49 minutes. At that score, he took one step down the wicket and lifted Hollies high and straight. Members in front of the pavilion scattered as the ball cleared the fence, and bounced right. Three balls later he repeated the feat.

Miller was 61 not out, and the Dominions 3 for 145 at stumps on day two.

Morning mayhem

He always slept on 'a few beers' before a game, but whatever he had on the night of 27 August, it put him in a plundering mood on the third and final morning of the match. New Zealand's dashing little left-hander Martin Donnelly (29) was yorked early by Wright. This brought West Indian Learie Constantine, the Dominions' captain, to the wicket. Miller went into overdrive, smashing Hollies and Wright with contempt to all parts of the ground. Hammond had no slip. Every fielder was in the deep, in the hope that this flop-haired belligerent would mistime a stroke and sky a catch.

As writer Denzil Batchelor put it: 'The nearest fieldsman seemed in Mesopotamia, while the farther bodies were pretty well astral'.

Miller was in an ebullient mood for the second successive day. He asked umpire Archie Fowler if it were true that no one had cleared the pavilion roof with a hit since Australian Albert Trott had done it playing for Middlesex against Australia in 1899.

'Correct', Fowler replied. 'He hit a ball from Monty Noble. It struck a chimney pot and fell to the back of the pavilion.'

'Well, Archie', Miller said, 'I'm going to clear it myself this morning.'

He set about his task. One of Miller's sixes carried over the 170 metre boundary and hit Block Q to the right of the pavilion. Then he set himself for the biggest one ever seen at Lord's. It was a swing over mid-on, which kept climbing and climbing towards the broadcast position, causing commentator Rex Alston to choke on his words and duck. Only half a metre at the top of the pavilion and a small roof on the broadcasting box above the players' dressing room stopped the ball from leaving the arena and ending up on a doubledecker bus in the streets of St John's Wood. The press box had not been there for Trott's hit, which indicated that Miller's launch might well have been greater.

'On hitting the pavilion', former England captain A. E. R. Gilligan, who was in the box, noted, 'it fell into a hole that had been made in the roof of the commentary position by shrapnel [from a German bomber]. The ball had to be poked out with a stick.'

It was the only poking that ball experienced.

Had Miller's match been played on another pitch to the left, the ball would not have been impeded by anything on its flight into folklore. Yet the innings itself was headed there. Experts in the pavilion, when not ducking for cover, were spellbound. Former England captain and MCC chairman Plum Warner, who had 60 years experience in first-class cricket, was prompted to say as Miller's carnage continued: 'I have never seen such hitting'.

Another member repeatedly called: 'Why don't you give Langridge a bowl?'

Hammond obliged, throwing the ball to the left-arm Test spinner, whom nobody at the ground could recall being 'seen to' by a rampant batsman. Miller corrected this by sending two of his first four balls soaring straight and over mid-on to the pavilion, causing members – including the vociferous Langridge supporter – to scatter. Constantine joined in with another six in the same over.

The destruction saw 117 runs scored in 45 minutes. Miller connected with 13 fours and 7 sixes, most of which collected the seats below or adjoining the Long Room windows. Dick Whiting-ton, who had performed with Miller in the Australian Services team in the Victory Tests, observed: 'Several elderly gentlemen who had experienced some of the severest Germany artillery bombardment [on the Western Front] of the Kaiser War [World War I], were forced to desert their favourite positions and seek sanctuary in the Members' Bar'.

Part of Miller's appeal was the pure 'Englishness' of his batting. Right through his frenetic stay he stood tall at the crease, in classic side-on pose. Each time after a huge hit, he reverted to that still position. His batting this innings and in all others was based on front-foot play, with the emphasis on the drive. Yet he still made room for the back-foot cut, which was one of his favourite hits. And from the beginning of his innings the day before, Miller had drawn appreciative applause from the connoisseurs in the Lord's Pavilion Long Room for his sweet dab of a fine late cut, which was in contrast to the lusty belting of those massive sixes. This delicacy seemed incongruous for such a square-shouldered big bloke. Yet it was part of the character of Miller, who had several gears and nuances beyond the one-dimensional in his play and his life. His shots had authority and style on both sides of the wicket, but if he were to be remembered for other than his sending good deliveries into orbit, it would be for the cover-drive. He played it with textbook precision and power, opening the blade and giving full expression to the most glorious of strokes.

Even the experts watching on this sunny morning at Lord's might have been fooled by his occasional lofted shot to leg. The terrific twist of his upper body, and the thrust of shoulders, arms and whipping wrists, caused him to end up playing the shot with just his powerful left arm. To the unaccustomed eye this seemed like a loss of control; a wild hoick more in keeping with what would be expected from the village blacksmith. But Miller knew what he was doing. He executed it on purpose.

There wasn't much to hook in this innings, but Miller demonstrated a liking for this shot too, with the few chances he had. It required confidence, courage, good foot-work, reflexes, eye, punch and more than a touch of the daredevil and risk-taking.

Miller went on to 185 before cracking a faster Langridge ball straight to Wright, giving two of the tormented opposition a minor consolation. Miller had scored 124 in 115 minutes before lunch. In all, the innings had taken just 165 minutes.

Storybook batsman

He left the arena to a standing ovation, his eyes searching the sky for non-existent Luftwaffe again, now a sign of embarrassment rather than light adjustment. With a pluck of his unbuttoned shirt away from his sweating torso, a jerk of his head to throw back his hair and a wave of his bat to the cheering fans he disappeared up the Pavilion steps into the Long Room.

Whatever followed from Hammond in England's second innings, it would be physically impossible for him, aged 42, to match this sustained power hitting. Miller was being applauded as king of the 1945 season, and for the third successive season, a dominator at Lord's.

The Times correspondent, Beau Vincent, the next morning wrote: 'We were beginning to wonder whether Lord's is big enough to take such terrific hitting'.

Former England Test player and a legend of the game, C. B. Fry, added some perspective for those in Australia who had not witnessed Miller's 1945 summer of brilliance.

'In our eyes, Miller is Australia's star turn', he said in a BBC World broadcast. 'We know we have been watching a batsman already great, who is likely, later on (when official Tests resume post-war), to challenge the feats of Australia's champions of the past. Apart from his technical excellence, Keith Miller has something of the dash and generous abandon that were part of Victor Trumper's charms.'

One of the game's finest ever observers, R. C. Robertson-Glasgow, watched Miller's dominance of the summer and remarked: 'He has over-matched the best bowlers in England. He has quelled them with a casual accuracy peculiarly his own. His abundant runs have kept England from victory in the (Victory) Tests; the manner of their making has revived the affection of the faithful and excited the interest of the doubtful. Miller is a storybook batsman; were he not fine fact, he would be first rate fiction'.

***

Miller was 25 years old. His triumph at Lord's was the pinnacle of his career, and the innings an expression of his character, which had been modified by his experiences in World War II as a night fighter pilot. After nearly losing his life on at least six occasions when many of his mates and colleagues were not so fortunate, Miller was living life on a day-by-day basis. It had become a habit forced upon him in the 30 months in the Air Force based in England.

BRADMAN AND MILLER: A COMPARISON

Much has been written in the last 60 years about a feud between Don Bradman and Keith Miller – two great Australians, who were very different. Because of certain incidents in Australia and England during his war service, Miller developed a strong dislike for authority figures. And Bradman, in Miller's eyes, was the ultimate authority figure in cricket.

Their contrary positions were drawn into public view during the Adelaide Fourth Test of the 1946–47 Ashes series. Miller had bowled flat out in the heat near the end of the day for the reward of just 1 wicket – Alec Bedser's. He was relaxing in the dressing room when team manager Bill Jeanes, the Secretary of the Australian Board of Control, urged him to hurry for a taxi that would take him and others back to the team hotel. Miller wouldn't budge. An argument ensued. Jeanes reported him to Bradman, who sent a message for Miller to come to his broking office before play the next day. (Bradman would reach his desk at 7 am, squeeze in as much work as possible and then walk to the ground, ready for the morning session.)

Bradman had not intended it to be a summons; it was more convenient to meet Miller at his office. It was also away from the team hotel and the ground, which would allow the minor issue to be settled in private.

Miller reluctantly obeyed the directive. He found Bradman

buried in paperwork in his office on Grenfell Street. Bradman explained that Jeanes had been ill recently. He agreed that the Board Secretary might have erred in rushing Miller when he wanted to relax after some hard work at the bowling crease. Bradman suggested Miller forget the incident but Miller left the meeting still unhappy.

'Here I am just back from the war', he thought to himself, 'a war which had been dangerous for me in parts, and I am sent for like an erring schoolboy called to the head's study.'

Given that the complaint had come from the Board's Secretary and team manager, Bradman felt he had to show some authority, although there was no penalty nor even a reprimand. He was conscious of not imposing too many rules on his charges, especially the ex-servicemen. His only directive was that they turn up fit to play when they had to. But Miller resented any show of authority at all. He was still haunted by the harshness of the sentence he received after an altercation with his commanding officer at Ouston, England.

The Jeanes incident also contributed to a festering attitude towards Bradman, for whom he had mixed feelings. It had begun back in early 1939 when Bradman had caught him off Grimmett, in what Miller suspected was gamesmanship after hitting a bump ball. It offended Miller's sporting sensibilities. That incident had been accentuated by Bradman's approach to winning the Ashes, when Miller had so much wanted to be part of a repeat of the spirit engendered in the Victory Tests at the end of the war. He didn't like Bradman's attitude of driving the opposition into the turf at every chance. Nor did he appreciate or care about the history of fiercely fought Ashes contests in the decades before the war.

Both sportsmen had the 'killer instinct'. The difference was that Bradman had it all the time, in whatever level of any game or contest in which he participated, from squash and tennis to billiards and tiddlywinks. Miller reserved his desire to beat an opponent for certain occasions, and did not believe in one-sided contests. As a batsman, Bradman treated every bowling opponent the same, from country and club to state and Test cricket. He wanted to accumulate a winning score as fast as possible. Miller often didn't care for more than a cameo performance – a bright 70 runs in 80 minutes was good enough, even in first-class games. (Although he also had the patience for the big double hundred in first-class cricket, but not Tests.) If he was bowling, he often only wanted to be at the crease if there was a worthy batsman facing him.

Bradman planned his cricket with an obsessive attention to detail. His style fitted that of ancient Chinese philosopher, Sun Tzu, who said: 'Those who triumph, compute at their headquarters a great number of factors prior to a challenge'. Like the greatest general of World War I, Sir John Monash, Bradman always thought it better to have a plan, than no plan at all.

Miller, by contrast, went by the maxim in the Koran: 'Man makes plans, God laughs'.

Bradman calculated with the sharpest of minds how to beat an opponent before a game began, and how to destroy him when it was on. Miller was more instinctive. He had to have the right atmosphere and mood to let his great gifts loose. He was more the artist, whereas Bradman was more the artistic technician. Neither man was enslaved by technique, but Miller allowed himself the luxury of letting power dominate technique more often than Bradman. The evidence for this was Bradman's utter control of his six hitting, especially in Tests. He only despatched a handful in his career, and went by the dictate that you can't be out if you keep the ball along the carpet. That was part of his success in accumulation.

Miller always had his eye on hitting at least one six an innings. Along with that, he liked to loft the ball to all points of the compass. The 'along the carpet' directive had been drilled into him since his youth, and even then it irritated him.

'Strictly and austerely speaking', English writer Neville Cardus wrote, 'his [Miller's] technique is sometimes not above suspicion. It works less by reason than by instinct. You might as well refer to the technique of a young panther on the "kill" or in repose! Miller is a cricketer of reflex action. I don't intend to suggest that he puts no intelligence into his play, but only that at his best he is swayed rather by the logic of the heart than by the logic of the head.'

By contrast, Bradman was in himself unerringly logical in everything he did. No sportsman ever entered any contest better prepared than him. His consistent force of will to achieve what he set out to do is unmatched in the annals of sport.

Bradman performed to the beat of his own drum, not that of the spectator. He was a crowd satisfier, more than a crowd pleaser. It mattered not a jot to him what fans thought when he batted. Yet he was an entertainer. He was the fastest accumulator of the huge run-making batsmen of the late 19th century and first half of the 20th century. His dexterity with the blade, and uncanny precision in piercing the field rather than going over it, enchanted those with a fair knowledge of the game. The connoisseurs loved his all-round stroke-making skills, which in essence were copybook and second to none. Bradman was also appreciated as an innovator with his shots, which demonstrated a certain flexibility of mind and body. His genius was evident and somewhat exposed with bodyline when he changed his batting style and had more success than any other batsman against that difficult, potentially lethal form of bowling.

Australians love a winner, and Bradman was the winner's winner. He could program and discipline himself for the massive score, which cricket lovers enjoyed. It is part of cricket's peculiarity to keep going at the crease when dehydrated, or with aching muscles or when the brain is tired. Stamina, patience, hunger, even greed for runs and occupying the crease, are essential to reach 100, let alone 150, 200, 300 – Bradman did it nine times in all cricket, with one 299 not out in a Test – and once, 400.

Bradman felt his obligations to the public were restricted to what he did on the playing field. Off it, he defended his privacy fiercely, yet went out of his way to respond to people who wrote to him, especially children. He also signed autographs endlessly and quietly. Behind the scenes, he assisted in much charity work.

Miller didn't just satisfy spectators, he excited them. He

performed according to the way he felt on the day. He was also a crowd pleaser. According to the Melbourne *Herald*'s Percy Millard and cricket writer Dick Whitington, he needed to feel 'liked', even though he was uncomfortable with applause, which indicated too much focus was on him. This was perhaps an over-statement, even of his early years (and was certainly not symptomatic of his later years after 1946–47 when he riled and bated crowds with his hostile bowling). Yet both observers had seen him go out of his way and even take risks, when in those formative years between the ages of 16 and 27, to manoeuvre the baying mob to support him. This characteristic had often seen him lose his wicket. When bowling at Lord's in 1945, he was urged by the Australian Servicemen in the crowd to bowl bumpers and he obliged. He responded when fans at Sydney or Bramall Lane bellowed for big-hitting.

Miller cared little for averages and record-breaking. He was not enchanted with those who did, even though his boyhood hero, Ponsford, like Bradman, was keen on lifting the bar to the outer limits. Bradman had been miffed early in 1930 when his skipper, Alan Kippax, had declared a NSW innings closed while Bradman was on 452 not out. It was then the highest ever first-class score. He had wanted to go on to 600 and shut out all challengers for a few hundred years. Miller, when in the right frame of mind, would hit a double hundred, but never felt the urge to go on for a record. Cricket was to be played more for enjoyment and camaraderie. He also lacked the consistency needed to conquer and annihilate, achievements which were features of Bradman's play.

Despite the obvious differences in their characters and attitudes, the two men did have one thing in common: competitiveness. Like Bradman, who loved taking on the greatest bowlers of spin and speed in history such as O'Reilly and Larwood, Miller was a competitor's competitor. He loved the one-on-one challenge within a contest. Even in his years with perennial VFL losers St Kilda, he was the stand-out performer in a defeated team. Both men feasted on the greatest opponents. But that was where the similarity ended.

Winning as comprehensively as possible within the rules was always Bradman's over-riding desire. Miller loved the personal battle within a war, and cared less for the outcome of the conflict as a whole.

Bradman didn't drink alcohol (although when he retired, he enjoyed catching up on lost opportunities), and was a 'Melbourne Cup Day mug punter'. His battle to earn a living in the 1920s and the Depression made him frugal – because he had to be. He didn't 'mix with the boys' in the traditional Aussie sense, preferring to be at home with his family or working. Although Miller and others found Bradman a good travelling companion, he was more at ease with his own company and often sought it on tour. He found solace in concerts music, playing the piano, reading and letter writing. In many ways, he was a sports professional more in keeping with the 21st century. He kept his body in top condition in order to perform at his best.

Miller, by contrast, loved a drink and a bet. He was generous with gifts and money, even when he didn't have it. He was restless for the convivial company of both sexes. Even an oddball stranger could phone Miller and interest him in a good time, as happened during the 1946–47 Melbourne Test. Bradman would never accept such an offer. In fact, there were so many invitations that he could be blunt in turning them down. He never felt the need or urge to be spontaneous. He liked his life ordered. Chances are that there was always something planned each evening.

Miller also loved classical music, especially in grand settings at the opera and concert halls. He made a virtue of having a good time, no matter what the occasion the next day. He often turned up hungover for a match, but he had a strong constitution; his sodden condition did not ever appear to spoil a performance. His conviviality was a characteristic. There have been few players as popular with both his team-mates and any opposition, at home or abroad.

Their private lives were vastly different. They had both chosen warm, loving life partners. Bradman was a family man and devoted to wife Jessie and their two children. Miller was a 'player', who loved women and womanising. Unsettled by war and his uneasiness with what 'fame' meant, Miller would never be faithful in the conventional sense. He had chosen and pursued his Bostonian wife-to-be, Peg, romantically across the world although there were scores of attractive women in London and Melbourne who would have settled for the dashing sportsman. It was as if he were driven by the future life he desired for himself. Peg was from a family that was socially above his own. She would bring class and strong values to the marriage, and tender care to prospective children. Peg would always represent the mother-image that Miller desired in a wife, in what his psychologist niece Jan Beames described as 'the Madonna/whore complex'.

Peg was the idealised mother and wife figure. He would play with many other women, who were not 'whores' as such, but simply play-objects for fun-loving Miller. He would always return home to earth mother Peg. In his own way, he was committed only to his wife, and whatever family was to come.

Miller had tasted real fame in the summer of 1945, and the adulation and easy access to admiring women which it brought him. Instead of giving up a Peter Pan or playboy existence for married life, Miller took on both, almost on a seasonal basis.

***

Miller and Bradman were men of very different temperaments and outlooks. They were bound not to see eye to eye. Their minor encounters on the field, Miller's disagreement with Bradman's approach to the 1946–47 series, and the reprimand-that-wasn't, rankled with Miller.

Whitington and Millard, who followed Miller's early playing career (1936 to 1946) more closely than any other observers, put this rebellious nature and 'chip on the shoulder' down to his being such a midget for so long as a kid. Right through those formative years as 'Weedy', he was bullied and picked on. It wasn't until he left school and joined the workforce that he fully transformed from runt to burly bloke. Millard also thought that setbacks when trying to break into district and state cricket added to Miller's being at odds with authority. Miller was a relatively late achiever, and had not cemented his place in the Victorian team in 1940–41 at age 21. The war forced him to miss several seasons and it was not until he was 27 in 1946–47 that he was selected in the state team. He never felt appreciated by state administrators.

It was suggested, too, that his experience as a late developer was the reason Miller often sided with the underdog.

Pilot Gus Glendinning's experiences as Miller's closest mate over two years of war fitted a pattern: Miller tended to be a hell-raiser and confrontational. He disdained taking orders, and disliked anyone in any capacity standing over him. It provoked reaction whatever the consequences. He was indeed a rebel, with or without a cause.

Hence those mixed feeling towards Bradman. He appreciated his skipper for his greatness as a cricketer and importance to the nation in historical terms. But as a character, Bradman was not to his liking. Miller would never be a 'yes' man, or keep an opinion to himself.

Bradman respected Miller as a cricketer and named him as the all-rounder in his best-ever Australian XI. But Miller's flamboyant, even wild, side would never sit well with him.

***

Late in life, Miller complained in private about his former captain, so much so that Miller's brother Les told him to 'lay off the obsession!' Nevertheless, Miller maintained a connection to Bradman and often phoned him for a chat.

In deference to an Australian tradition, Miller was generous to his Captain, even though his attitude was not always reciprocated.

After Bradman's death early in 2001, Miller continued to demonstrate a largesse by helping the Bradman Museum with contacts in England that led to cricket matches on Paul Getty's Estate.

Miller may not have loved the Don, but he appreciated his great and lasting legacy.

BRADMAN, APARTHEID AND A CHANGE OF MIND

The toughest decision of Sir Donald Bradman's cricketing life did not concern bodyline or whether he, at nearly 40, should tour England in 1948 when his fitness was suspect. It was whether or not he should ban the all-white South African Test cricket team from touring Australia in 1971. Whichever move he made would have ramifications for the already strained relationship with his son John, who supported the ban.

Bradman was anti-apartheid, yet felt that South African cricketers were exempt because they had shown their opposition to racism.

'They have tried harder than our protesters to do something about it', he wrote in 1971 in correspondence with Melbourne *Herald* journalist Rohan Rivett (placed by the Rivett family in the National Library, Canberra, in late 2003). 'Why should they be crucified? I cannot see why they [white cricketers] should be blamed for attitudes of a Government with which they disagree.'

Bradman, accompanied by the South African ambassador, had witnessed a rugby Test between Australia and South Africa in Sydney and Bradman was shocked at the violence of protesters.

'The ground was protected by barbed-wire barricades', he told me, 'and the police were ready for smoke bombs and flares. But the barricades didn't stop the protesters. They invaded the area.'

Bradman left that scene concerned that it would be hard to police a cricket match. He knew the sport would be the worse for such violent interruptions. Yet the protest didn't make him change his mind. Bradman was in his last year as Australian Cricket Board (now Cricket Australia) chairman. The South African government, by inviting him to watch the rugby game, was preparing him for what to expect in the coming summer of 1971–72. The experience had the desired effect. Bradman stood firm. The tour was still on.

Bradman pointed out to Rivett that 'the rugby team "comprised mainly of [apartheid supporting] Afrikaners". The white cricketers were "basically of English descent and a minority group among the whites. Their party – the United Party – is not opposed to mixed sport as are the [Afrikaner] Nationalists"'.

'Politics should not come into sport', he concluded. This placed Bradman in the 70 per cent majority of Australians polled at the time who favoured white-only cricket tours and who felt that Australia should not interfere in other nations' internal problems. He believed the South African cricketers should be 'encouraged to pursue their opposition to racism in sport'.

Yet the young protesters on the barricades caught his attention. He was familiar with attitudes of protest and change. His son, John, then 32, was a tutor in Constitutional Law at Adelaide University. He was against the Vietnam War and Australia's participation in it. John's anti-apartheid views placed him in the nation's minority that mainly comprised of church groups and intellectuals. These and other issues were the subject of hot discussions around the Bradman family dinner table. They added to the tensions between father and son. Don, then 63, was crusty and direct. His running of Australian cricket was only part-time and unpaid. His main job was as an adviser on stocks and shares, and he was regarded as one of the best, if not the best, in Adelaide. He had been 20 years a stockbroker until a near-nervous breakdown forced him out of the business in 1954. His daily contact was mainly with those conservative in thinking and unlikely to take kindly to radicals. John's work, which included an expertise in Aboriginal law, saw him associate with intellectuals who were usually on the lookout for what they saw as social and political change for the better. Their worlds were alien to each other. The courteous, affable Jessie (Lady Bradman) was often the mediator. She lived mainly in Don's world, but always sympathised with John.

(My own impressions around dinner tables with Don and Jessie a quarter century later were of the lion and the lioness. She knew how to work around him if she thought he was being stubborn. John would probably have been the only person in Don's daily life who would contradict him.)

At this time too, John felt the pressure of being the son of the most famous character in the land. Whenever his name was mentioned, he was asked the inevitable question: 'Are you related to . . .?'

Having to live with this had troubled John in his youth. He was a promising young cricketer and athlete (Olympic material as a hurdler until he injured a knee), and comparisons with his freakishly skilled father were premature and unfair. When John contracted polio at age 12 in 1951, and was laid up and nursed by his father and mother all year, it was a relief to the boy that expectations would never be so high again. Yet the Bradman name dogged him until his early 30s. He discussed it with his parents. They were understanding. John claimed his father even suggested he change his name (Don would certainly not have meant it). Such a comment may have been made in a moment of exasperation or to test John's thinking. Yet it helped John reflect on the possibilities.

Bradman wrote to Rivett about his son's quandary and expressed views that exemplified the generational gulf over issues that affected many father and son relationships at a time of upheaval and change in the world. It was not long after the near revolutions in France and Czechoslovakia, the Tet Offensive in Vietnam, and the tempestuous US Presidential election (won by Richard Nixon) in 1968. Australia's involvement in Vietnam was another divisive issue.

'I have done so much for that boy physically, mentally and financially,' Bradman wrote, 'yet I cannot perceive a spark of gratitude –

nothing but cynical criticism of everything I do or say and an apparent hatred of the legacy I have given him in my name, and a detestation of all the things I believe in and stand for.'

Bradman guessed that his son's stance might be part of the general rejection of the establishment. He felt John was emotionally a revolutionary and that even his beard reflected the way he was thinking. Yet, equally, Bradman's attitude reflected a desire to maintain a status quo without serious debate on the merits of the opposing argument.

Bradman added: 'He has a very fine brain actually, which, if properly directed, would achieve great things. But he is so utterly obsessed with his lack of individuality that it seems to have completely dominated his thinking.'

Yet the debate heated up in Bradman's mind. John's stance, along with Rivett's views, challanged Bradman. He had a flexible mind when he applied it. He decided to go beyond conventional opinion and investigate the issue himself.

He wrote to the anti-apartheid protest movement in Australia, asking them why they were demonstrating. Meredith Burgmann – then a protest organiser, much later President of the NSW Legislative Council – was astonished to receive such a request from someone she regarded as typically, trenchantly establishment.

She recalled: 'We had this dialogue, which went on for some time, and I'd send him information about what was happening in South Africa.'

Bradman was intrigued. He flew to South Africa to meet with the prime minister of the Republic, John Vorster, a former war-time political extremist, who supported and admired the Nazis and Adolf Hitler. Vorster welcomed Bradman, believing he would support the cricket tour. But the meeting quickly became tense, then turned sour. Bradman asked questions in his direct way about why the blacks had not been given a chance to represent their country. Vorster suggested that they were intellectually inferior and could not cope with the intricacies of cricket. Bradman laughed at this. He asked Vorster, 'Have you ever heard of Garry Sobers [the West

Indian, whom Bradman regarded as the leading cricketer of all time]?'

Vorster's racist attitudes, which Bradman thought 'ignorant and repugnant', led to his change of mind, which had been precipitated by John, Burgmann and Rivett and others with whom he corresponded. Bradman flew on to the UK to meet with British prime ministers Harold Wilson and Ted Heath, who had dealt with the protest problem in England. He returned to Australia with his mind made up.

He spoke to fellow members of the ACB, reached an agreement and then called a media conference. After a short preamble in which he announced that the South African tour had been cancelled, Bradman made a simple one-line statement: 'We will not play them [South Africa] until they choose a team on a non-racist basis'.

In South Africa, Vorster vented his anger publicly against Bradman while the main anti-apartheid organisation, the [black] African National Congress, rejoiced.

Burgmann, unaware that Bradman had met Vorster, Wilson and Heath, was again surprised. 'We expected him to use the excuse of not being able to guarantee the safety of the cricketers', she said, 'but he made this wonderful statement, which pleased us [the protesters].'

Burgmann and Rivett congratulated him.

'I appreciate the compliments', he wrote to Rivett in September 1971, 'but, no offence meant, I'm not really in the mood to feel elated. I've seen too much of both sides of the issue [which included the impact on the banned, innocent white cricketers], the good and bad of each. I was not cut out to be a politician or banner-carrier.'

'In my few moments of triumph (if any) in the modern arena', Bradman lamented, 'I have sought seclusion and peace – not publicity. But hate it as I might, publicity seems to be my lot.'

Bradman knew he had ruined the Test careers of some of the finest cricketers ever, including Mike Proctor, Barry Richards, Hilton Ackerman and Graeme and Peter Pollock. South Africa's team was the dominant Test side in the world. Now it was in tatters and would have to disband.

Bradman had another pressing problem: the decision would also put the ACB in a terrible hole financially unless they could find another team to tour. He solved this by inviting a magnificent multiracial combination, led by Sobers and including Ackerman and the Pollock brothers, to play against Ian Chappell's young Australian team. The tour was a financial success.

On the bigger issue, Bradman had succeeded where politicians and protesters had failed by going beyond entrenched arguments to discover the integrity of the matter. His reputation and fame meant the unexpected move was a blow to apartheid on the international stage.

There was still personal fall-out in the Bradman family as Don became front-page news throughout the 1971–72 season because of his anti-apartheid decision, and the fill-in World versus Australia five Test Series. Bradman had retired from the ACB after banning the tour, but instead of fading from public view as he fervently wished, he was now as prominent as in his Test playing days (1928–48).

By the end of the season, with all the extra publicity for his father, John was more fed up than ever about his perceived loss of identity, and being 'the son of . . .'

Lady Bradman described the critical moment to me: 'A legal VIP from the UK was visiting [Adelaide University, early in 1972]. Some of the Law Faculty were introduced to him. When he met John, the person doing the introductions said "And this is the son of Sir Donald Bradman". That was the last straw for John. He went out and changed his name by deed-poll to Bradsen'.

John felt he had been 'popped in a metaphorical glass cage to be peered at or discussed'. He was 'no longer prepared to accept being seriously introduced as simply someone's son'. John said he was 'an individual, not a social souvenir'.

His parents were stunned, but remained supportive. Bradman did wonder why he chose a name so close to the original and not 'Smith' or 'Jones'. But Bradsen it was.

Jessie was, as ever, sympathetic; Bradman was less so. But John's plight was driven home by a story in their city's newspaper, the Adelaide *Advertiser*. It was headlined 'Bradman's Son Changes Name'.

Bradman thought it was 'the most cruel article' he had ever read. 'If ever an article was meant to crucify and ridicule a decent person, this is it. It is something for which I shall never forgive them.'

Bradman added, 'We are quite prepared to accept the hurt to ourselves, and all it will mean. But will it prove to be a panacea to John's problems? If it doesn't, he may find himself worse off. Then what?' After brooding for a few weeks, Bradman showed more of his feelings, writing that he could 'scarcely ever think the same about him again. Even though I understand, the rejection of my name and all the hopes and ambitions that any father would normally have for a son, are a deep wound, which I will have to bear silently to the end.'

A week later, in early April 1972, Bradman was even unhappier. He wrote, 'I think his best interests would be served by a kick in the pants, and a polite invitation to have the guts to stand up to the world and not run away from it.'

He later said: 'As the years go by I believe he may regret what he has done – may even reverse his steps'.

The cool relations continued for several months until John, at 33, left the family home, moved to a Bradman-owned farm at Crafers near Mt Lofty, and married his wife, Judith, as 'Bradsen'.

The father/son relationship was at best strained and at worst estranged.

The issue that helped establish this rift – apartheid – remained, but slow progress was made. In April 1986, a group of seven 'eminent persons' from the Commonwealth – including former Australian prime minister Malcolm Fraser – were allowed to visit the imprisoned deputy president of the African National Congress, Nelson Mandela. Despite being locked up for 24 years, he had a commanding presence. His first question to the surprised group was:

'Is Don Bradman still alive?' Bradman had been Mandela's sporting hero, and he had been endeared further to him because of his 1971 decision. Fraser was able to assure him that Bradman was definitely still functioning, and he arranged for a bat signed by him to be sent to the African leader.

Three years later, Mandela was released and apartheid was over. In late 1993, a South African team, chosen on a non-racist basis – 22 years after Bradman's one-line official directive – began a tour of Australia.

***

When gravely ill in 1997, Jessie Bradman called for a rapprochement between the long-estranged Don and John, asking her son to get together with his father and record Don's life. The two men obeyed her wish and sat down with a tape recorder for about a week. She died in September 1997. The father/son relationship improved to a point in 1999 where John decided to change his name back to Bradman, thus fulfilling his father's prediction and wish.

The surnames of John's children, Greta and Tom (with Judith), and Nicholas (with partner, Megan Webster) also reverted to Bradman. This pleased Don, who was depressed at the thought of his three grandchildren, and future generations, not carrying his name.

***

When the gracious Mandela visited Australia in 2000, he wanted to meet Bradman and thank him for his courageous act in 1971. Don, 92, was too ill to see him. He was humbled by the desired attention from one of the most outstanding individuals of the 20th century, and someone he 'admired greatly'.

ONE HUNDRED YEARS OF FORTITUDE

Impact Seven: Centenary Test 1977

The first cricket international – later to be known as a 'Test' – began one sunny day in mid March 1877 at the Melbourne Cricket Ground, then the Richmond Police Paddock. The teams were the professional England side, led by James Lillywhite, and Australia, captained by David Gregory. It all began when an overweight, bearded Alfred Shaw from Nottingham, wearing a tie and black sash to keep his trousers up over his pot belly, ran in to deliver a ball to Australia's Charles Bannerman. For the first time in clashes between countries, the crowd hushed. Australia was then a ragbag of colonies and was 24 years from federating as a nation – an event that this sporting contest would help accelerate. Bannerman, with a total disregard for his place in history as the first batsman to receive a Test delivery, blocked it. He pushed the second delivery to the leg-side for a single. A cheer went up to mark the first run. Little did everyone present know that the competition would become the keenest in the world and the longest running. England would be playing to keep the prenatal 'Australia' in its place as just a far-flung land that had been colonised. Australia would be hell-bent on showing the seat of the mighty British Empire a thing or two. The Empire's attitude was more or less uniform: it would not stand anything challenging its supremacy, from Napoleon and the

Spanish Armada in war, to representatives of a penal settlement in the 'Far East'.

Remnants of respective attitudes of the two nations remained, with Australia over time proving more often than not a match for its more populated former 'motherland'.

That first big game in Melbourne (at the MCG) ended with Australia winning by 45 runs. The interest in this initial international competition ignited a fire throughout the Australian colonies that was never to expire. Once England played in front of fascinated home crowds against the Australians in the 1880s, the competition had a future. The rivalry was acute and never diminished. The flag of Ashes combat would only be lowered during two World Wars (1914–1918 and 1939–1945) over the next 100 years.

***

Australian Hans Ebeling, vice-president of the Melbourne Cricket Club and a former Test player, had the marvellous idea to play a Centenary Test at the MCG in March 1977 to mark the 100th anniversary. Ebeling successfully put forward the concept of every living player in Ashes history being invited to the game. It was to be sponsored by airlines Qantas and TAA; the Melbourne Hilton Hotel; and tobacco company Benson & Hedges. Two hundred and forty-four players converged on Melbourne. Only 26 players rejected the offer, mostly because they were too old or not well enough to make the trip to the biggest reunion in cricket history. Sadly, the great Frank Woolley's health was not up to the trip from Canada. Herbert Sutcliffe was grounded in England for the same reason.

Eighty-four-year-old, almost totally blind Percy Fender, who had toured Australia in 1920–21, was the oldest England player to make the arduous 25-hour plane journey. Former Test captain and selector Jack Ryder, at 87, was the oldest Australian at the event. The hotels provided functions – lunches, cocktail parties, dinners and receptions – for a week when past competitors swapped stories and remembered feats funny and fabulous, terrifying and tragic. Most of the game's greatest – including characters such as O'Reilly, Trueman, Snow, Tyson, Loader, Knight, Lock, Edrich, Barrington, Evans, Grimmett, Morris, Benaud, Harvey, Hawke and O'Neill – attended. Don Bradman was seen chatting happily with his bodyline tormentor, Harold Larwood. Mates Keith Miller and Denis Compton enjoyed themselves along with all the others, which proved to be the most splendid festival of nostalgia ever. The question on everyone's lips was whether the game they had come to witness would match the spectacle and good time being had by all the invitees.

***

Australia was represented (in batting order) by Davis, McCosker, Cosier, Greg Chappell (captain), Hookes (on debut), Walters, Marsh, Gilmour, O'Keefe, Lillee and Walker. England's team was Woolmer, Brearley, Randall, Amiss, Fletcher, Greig (captain), Knott, Old, Lever, Underwood and Willis.

More than 60,000 fans turned up for day one – 12 March 1977 – to see ex-Test captains accompany the teams onto the arena, followed by all the ex-players.

The applause was so loud that the competing teams could hardly hear themselves speak. Very few words were spoken between them.

'There was an uneasy feeling', Australian opener, Ian Davis, noted in his autobiography, *More Than Cricket*. 'It wasn't like they were our mortal enemies, but it also wasn't a time for pleasantries. There was too much at stake.'

This tension set the tone for something special. Both teams put aside the partying for a serious attack on each other, even though the Ashes were not being fought for.

South African born Tony Greig pushed and prodded the green-tinged pitch, an act that would later become his specialty as a commentator. He noticed the moisture. He won the toss and sent Australia in. Greig feared his batsmen facing Dennis Lillee, whose pace and cut could prove impossible to handle under such conditions.

A roar greeted Davis and McCosker as they walked out to bat.

McCosker had never opened for his country so Davis gallantly volunteered to take guard first. He became the Bannerman equivalent, while left-armer John Lever took up the role of Alfred Shaw, albeit in a far fitter condition. The Australians were not prepared for the pace of lanky Bob Willis from the other end. He was quick with a difficult, steepling bouncer. The batsmen grafted for 28 minutes before Davis became the first victim of the match – a doubtful LBW decision – at 11. Then McCosker, who looked uncomfortable, was bowled a short, very fast ball by Willis, which crashed into his jaw, and then dropped onto the stumps, dislodging a bail. In the dressing room, a doctor and dentist examined McCosker, who was sent to hospital. His jaw was fractured in three places and it was doubtful that he could continue in the game.

The second wicket had fallen at 13. Australia was soon in trouble at 3 for 23, then 4 for 45 and a disastrous 5 for 51. The procession back to the pavilion was steady with only Chappell (40 in just under four hours) and Marsh (28) offering resistance en route to a miserable 138 all out. England's four bowlers shared the spoils and quietened the crowd.

There were few alarms for England, which was 1 for 29 at stumps. The next morning, Lillee demonstrated why he was regarded as one of the best speedsters of all time by ripping through the England line-up with a combination of pace, swing and movement off the wicket. Big Max ('Tangles') Walker, with his gangling run-up, removed the nightwatchman Derek Underwood and backed Lillee up, taking 4 for 54. Lillee secured 6 for 26 off 13.3 overs. The object of the England bats was to get up the other end to avoid him, but they then faced Walker, whose prodigious swing did not provide much relief.

England buckled then collapsed for a paltry 95. Australia was back in the game. As the Australians walked off the ground, captain Greg Chappell told spinner Kerry O'Keefe that he would be opening Australia's second innings with Ian Davis, replacing the injured McCosker.

Bob Willis bowled with hostility again and had the openers jumping about with short-pitchers. O'Keefe showed courage and application, staying at the crease for just under an hour while making 14. But two quick dismissals of Chappell and Cosier left Australia at 3 for 53 and in trouble again.

Walters (32 not out) joined Davis (45 not out) and they batted sensibly through to stumps giving Australia a lead of 150 at the end of day two. Next morning, Davis started well by being the first player to reach 50 for the game. He had battled hard against the dangerous Willis, who had been well-supported by Old and Lever. When the less menacing beanstalk Tony Greig was on, the batsmen, perhaps relieved not to be dodging Willis, became a fraction over-confident. Greig's height – about 200 centimetres – allowed him to achieve bounce and swing. He had Davis caught behind driving at him for 68. Walters fell the same way for 66.

This brought left-handers David Hookes and Rod Marsh together.

Greig sledged Hookes: 'Here comes another Australian left-hander who can't bat'.

Twenty-one-year-old Hookes responded: 'At least I'm Australian playing for Australia. I'm not a South African captaining England'.

After that verbal joust, Hookes stroked his way into cricket folklore by hitting five successive boundaries off Greig. This shifted the momentum to Australia and the crowd loved Hookes, in his first ever Test, for his controlled shot-making. Every stroke – to off, a pull, cover, mid-wicket and cover – saw the ball sail over the grass. None was airborne through a rush of blood. England was stunned, not the least reason being that its captain was such a good and miserly bowler, whether delivering medium-pacers or off-spin.

Hookes raced to 56, before left-arm spinner Underwood had him caught. His bravado had momentarily changed the game's psychology, but it took Marsh, in the innings of his life, to steer Australia into a strong position.

The MCG exploded in a roar with the emergence from the pavilion of McCosker, with his jaw wired and swathed in bandages like a latter-day Egyptian mummy, yet still wearing his baggy green.

The score was 8 for 353. In the days before helmets, he was exposed to further injury. But such was the importance of this historic game in the players' minds that any similarly handicapped player on either side would have shown the same guts.

The crowd began singing: 'Waltzing McCosker, Waltzing McCosker, we'll come a waltzing McCosker with you . . .'

McCosker hung in for 88 minutes for his 25, allowing Marsh to reach a century, the first ever by an Australian keeper in a Test against England.

Chappell declared at 9 for 419, with Marsh on 110 not out, setting England 463 to win.

England reached 2 for 191 at stumps, with Nottingham's Derek Randall on 87 not out.

With the Queen and Prince Philip watching on the final day, Randall – a knock-about, unlikely hero – turned on a terrific display of batsmanship against the odds. He cut, drove, hooked and – for contrast – jabbed his way to a big 100, forcing Lillee to cut his run-up bowling on a slow, low pitch.

One of his hooks off Lillee sped to the mid-wicket boundary and drew applause from all the watching ex-Test stars. Another short ball knocked off Randall's hat. His response was to retrieve it and bow to Lillee. Randall's capacity to lighten up on the field reduced the tension on the final day, yet did not stop Lillee trying to remove him. A bouncer hit him in the skull and knocked him down. Randall, like a rubber-man, jumped to his feet, rubbed the affected part vigorously and went on batting.

Apart from his swashbuckling play, Randall's effort will be remembered for another incident. He appeared to be caught behind at 161, and was given out by umpire Tony Brooks. But as he removed his gloves and marched off, Marsh indicated to the umpire that he had not completed the catch. Randall was called back in.

'It was Rodney's way', Randall remarked. 'He was such a tough competitor, but above all he values cricket.'

The Queen and Prince Philip were introduced to the players at the tea break. Dennis Lillee caused a comical stir by asking the Queen for her signature. The Queen refused with a charming smile, but later sent him a signed photograph of herself.

O'Keefe finally had Randall caught for a gallant 174, including 21 fours, in 446 minutes.

A weary Randall trudged off the arena to thunderous applause, perhaps more in relief for Australian fans, who feared he might take the game away from them. He took the wrong exit and climbed the stairs to the enclosure where the Queen and Prince Philip were viewing the game.

Randall apologised. The Queen gave him a big smile and a 'well batted' as a dignitary showed him the way to the England dressing room.

Jaunty Randall was ably supported by Brearley (43), Amiss (64), Greig (41) and Knott (42). England's innings was proving to be a magnificent effort, and one of the best last innings performances in Test cricket. But when Lillee had Knott LBW with England at 417, one of the finest Tests ever played was over.

Randall was awarded $1600 and adjudged Man of the Match, ahead of Lillee with his 11 wickets for 185 for the game.

Australia had won the 226th Test between the two countries by 45 runs.

It was the same winning margin as the very first Test in 1877.

The dressing rooms soon filled with the stars of yesteryear – from Bradman to Len Hutton, from Benaud to Illingworth. They congratulated the players for a terrific contest. The Australians were celebrating. Courageous McCosker had his jaw wired and was sipping champagne through a straw out of a beer glass. He was fighting the pain. Doug Walters was trying to make him laugh by saying: 'It [the 45-run-win] just goes to show that the Poms haven't improved one bloody run in a hundred years!'

CLASH OF CRICKET'S OLD AND NEW

Impact Eight: The Packer Revolution

In the turbulent 1970s, players and others became restless for change in cricket. For too long, the best performers in the game had been grossly underpaid. Their disgruntlement about keeping jobs and making ends meet while they played cricket for Australia coincided with media baron Kerry Packer's own irritation at the intransigent behaviour of the conservative Australian Cricket Board (ACB, now Cricket Australia). It refused to let him buy the exclusive rights to televise Test cricket. In hindsight, it was understandable that the two antagonists to the ACB should combine in some way. They formed a breakaway cricket system that threatened to take over the entire game. In essence, the Packer intervention revolutionised the game, making it more professional in every way.

***

'There's a little bit of the whore in all of us', Kerry Francis Bullmore Packer told the Australian Cricket Board in May 1976, when bidding for the TV rights to broadcast Test cricket. 'Gentlemen, name your price.'

Being told they were part-prostitutes would have been a new experience for members of the conservative ACB, who rejected the offer. The 38-year-old media mogul was not amused. After all, he had offered the ACB A\$2,500,000 over five years for the rights to

232

televise cricket on his Channel 9 only to find that they had already been granted to the Australian Broadcasting Commission (ABC) for A$207,000 over three years. This was about A$70,000 annually as opposed to Packer's A$500,000. The knock-back was frustrating for the media owner who had originally asked for a meeting with the Board in February 1976. He had waited three months before he was given a hearing. In that time, a deal had been done with the ABC.

Packer had expansive plans for the coverage of Test cricket, with a future eye to exploiting the popular appeal of one-day games which promised a vast, additional, younger audience that would attract advertisers to his network. The Board's decision to filibuster the commercial TV owner in favour of signing for a lot less with the national broadcaster smacked of a snub. Perhaps the Board feared Packer's influence and that he might wrest power from it.

Packer, a hulking man of passion and impulse, reacted first by turning to tennis. He had been working on a deal with Lawn Tennis Association of Australia (LTAA). New courts were being built at Sydney's White City with a view to bringing top-ranked world stars to compete at tournaments in Australia.

At the same time, there was a growing unrest among Australia's top cricketers about match payments. They were being asked to travel and play the game for a relative pittance with such increased demands on their time that holding down a reasonable job, full-time or otherwise, was impossible. Dennis Lillee complained to John Cornell, Perth journalist and manager of comedian Paul Hogan, that he was left with $30 a day in a Test after tax and deductions for expenses. In 1976, most experts ranked Lillee as the top bowler in the world. He had a family and was, for a time, running a cleaning business, but it was tough to make ends meet. His case was typical of Australia's best players, who were meeting a brick wall in dealing with the Board. The ruling cricket body's attitude was rooted in an arcane, out-dated, amateur view of the game. Traditionally, crick-eters were expected to have working lives and jobs away from the game. The honour in playing for Australia was deemed enough recompense. But there was a diminishing rationale in this argument. Players and their families had to survive. They were being offered what amounted to pocket money or, as Ian Chappell called it, 'fish and chips money'. The trend would mean that only a handful of stars would wish to stay in the game for more than a few years. They simply could not afford to play Test cricket.

There were other factors causing player disgruntlement. Many felt that they were being treated in a manner bordering on contempt.

'In India [in late 1969] we stayed in terrible conditions', former attacking Test opening bat, Keith Stackpole, noted in a Radio National interview with journalist Amanda Smith. 'The conditions were not two-star, or one-star. Some of it was pig-sty stuff.'

Australia captain Bill Lawry put the team complaints about travel, food and accommodation in writing after the gruelling five Test series, which Australia – miraculously, under the conditions – won 3-1. Players were run down and suffering from malnutrition after India but within days were expected to embark on a demanding four Test series in South Africa. The home team was very strong, but the 4-0 belting – Australia was thrashed in each Test – was not reflective of the teams' respective strengths.

When Australia faltered in the Ashes in the next home summer 1970–71 (won by Ray Illingworth's England team 2-0 in six Tests), Lawry was dumped as captain and as a player without notice before the final Test. The rest of the team were unhappy with this treatment of a popular man who had given his best for his country for next to nothing. With unreasonable and growing demands being placed on the players, some of the glory of representing Australia was being tarnished.

Stackpole recalls having a poor series in New Zealand (50 runs in 6 innings) in 1973–74. He returned to Sydney and had the following exchange with Alan Barnes, then Board Secretary:

'Have you organised my trip back to Melbourne?' Stackpole asked.

'No', Barnes replied. 'You can do that.'

'That's your job!'

'Well, you don't have to play if you don't want to.'

That final response spoke volumes to Stackpole, then 33, and with a few years at the top still in him. He decided there and then to retire.

Stackpole and Lawry were not alone in suffering unnecessary humiliation at the hands of the Board. It added to the undercurrents of discontent, which were exacerbated when recently retired Test batsman, Bob Cowper – himself forced out of cricket prematurely at just 28 to follow a career as a stockbroker – was appointed by players to represent them in negotiations with the Board. Cowper interviewed five Australian state captains before submitting proposals for increased match fees, tour proposals (with the problems in India and South Africa in mind) and sponsorships (to increase player fees). The Board rejected everything.

Packer met with Cowper. They had long discussions. Packer began to consider a radical move. Cornell and his Perth associate, Austin Robertson, joined the chats, which were turning into strategy meetings. Recent Australian captain Ian Chappell was also an early participant who, like Lawry, had voiced his concerns about poor pay packets and unfair demands on players. He too had left the Test team, although he could have played on for another half a decade at least under better conditions and with more sympathetic administrators.

Chappell wrote, in *The Bulletin* magazine's special tribute to Packer (after his death on Boxing Day 2005), of wearing jeans, a checked shirt and denim jacket when he first met Packer at his Park Street Sydney office.

'What are you?' Packer asked. 'A [expletive] cowboy?' before shaking hands.

Packer had decided that Ian, rather than his brother Greg, would captain the squad he was formulating.

'Who do you want in your [expletive] team?' Packer asked.

The mogul's use of the vernacular put Chappell at ease.

'From the beginning', he wrote of the meeting, 'I knew we spoke the same language.'

In late 1976, the discussions led to the concept of World Series Cricket (WSC). It would play matches with more than 60 representatives from all the top playing nations, including the banned South Africa. In effect, it would be a rival competition to Test cricket, although it was not portrayed this way in the beginning.

Chappell and Cowper drew up a list of players to be targeted. Cornell and Robertson were directed by Packer to offer specific contracts to the players, with an up-front lump sum 'sweetener' on signing of a contract.

One of the first targets was Greg Chappell, captain of the Test team. Chappell was one of the finest batsmen in history, as well as being more than a handy medium-pace bowler and an outstanding slips fielder. He was only 28. In theory, he had another seven or eight years in top cricket ahead of him. If he left to join WSC, it would be a huge wrench. Chappell knew the mentality of the Board, and how its members would hate the new concept. He could well be finished as a Test player, and might never again captain his country. In addition, there was no guarantee that WSC would work. It was more likely to fail. And if it did, where would that leave him? He had taken over the Test captaincy from brother Ian only a year earlier. Was it wise to throw all that away? On the other hand, Chappell had a young family to consider. There was no security in his sport for him, as it stood in the mid-70s.

The pressures on Greg Chappell were weighty.

On 25 February 1977, Robertson met with him secretly at Eden Park, Auckland during the Second Test of the series between New Zealand and Australia. A three-year contract at A$35,000 annually was offered. This would be seven times his average yearly Test cricket income. Robertson dangled a signing-on cheque of one-third of his yearly contract – A$11,666.66 – in front of him. It was more than twice his annual Test fees – for doing nothing, and an offer he could not refuse. Chappell signed on. Along with Lillee, he would be the highest paid Australian WSC player. Their acquisition was a major coup for Packer. He had secured the services of Australia's best batsman and bowler.

Top cricket, which had evolved slowly over the previous century, was about to go through a revolution.

On the same day that Chappell was signed up, batsman Doug Walters was offered A$25,000 a year for three years, which was about five times his earnings playing Test cricket. The attacking, popular New South Welshman was nearing the end of a fine career. He had little to lose. Walters signed in another early break for Packer.

Also contracted around this time were Ian Chappell, Rod Marsh, Max Walker, David Hookes, Kerry O'Keefe, Rick McCosker, Len Pascoe, Ian Redpath, Gary Gilmour, Ross Edwards and Ray Bright. Australia would be able to field a strong team. If Packer representatives could now sign players from other nations at the same rate, WSC would have a competition.

Operation TCCB

Packer's main aim always had been to televise Test cricket, and even while he was secretly setting up his alternative competition, he was trying to secure the Australian TV rights to the 1977 Ashes, beginning in a few months. He offered the English Test and County Cricket Board (TCCB) A$118,000. It was twice the ABC's offer. The TCCB referred the offer to the Australian Board for approval. The Board was told the decision was theirs, but TCCB then added the suggestion that Channel 9 and the ABC could broadcast the cricket in a shared arrangement. Packer was incensed and would not accept this. He doubled the offer to A$236,000 for the exclusive rights – excluding the ABC. The TCCB accepted the revised offer.

Packer now had control of Australian TV rights for Test cricket until the end of August 1977. His plan was to televise WSC a few months later. Whatever happened, his network would be putting some form of big cricket on Australians screens for the next year.

Not all targeted WSC players signed on the spot (Jeff Thomson, perhaps the most feared speedster in world cricket, slipped through the early net, but would later join up). Australia's talented opening bat, Ian Davis, presented a different challenge from that of Greg Chappell and Walters. Davis was just 23 and establishing himself as a Test player. He was married and planning a family. When Robertson approached him on the rest day of the Centenary Test – 15 March 1977 – he had just made a courageous 68 in the big game and was on a confidence high. At a clandestine meeting at Melbourne's Windsor Hotel, Robertson and Cornell offered him A$22,000 plus performance bonuses each year for three years. Davis was tempted, especially when Cornell told him Ian Chappell would be his captain, and that he wanted him in the team. But the young man was uncertain. He wanted time to consider the offer.

At the end of the thrilling Centenary Test, Davis was having a beer and enjoying the Australian victory celebrations in the dressing room. Robertson handed him an envelope, telling him it contained theatre tickets.

'When I opened the envelope, I nearly fell off my chair', Davis said in a speech at Bowral's Bradman Museum in 2005. Inside was a cheque for A$8000, a 'good faith' first payment – even though Davis was yet to agree to be part of WSC. He later rang Robertson and said he was 'in'.

Max Walker recalled the contract presented to the players: 'In effect, it said: "55 days of your life, play World Series Cricket. The very best players in the world. You are able to earn some money"'.

Walker, like all the others, was swayed. He had started on A$400 a Test in his first game in 1973. It was the same pay as he would receive in the Centenary Test.

'After the Whitlam [federal government] years [1972–1975], costs had gone through the roof', Walker recalled. 'We were a fair product.

Yet the ACB was telling us we couldn't get better deals. We were told that if we didn't wish to play for Australia there were 50,000 others who would. But the point was, how many were as good as a Lillee or a Greg Chappell?'

Meanwhile, the Board heard whispers about the WSC developments. It gave players increased payments in revised contracts, but it was too little too late.

The WSC concept took another leap forward with the signing of Tony Greig, England's captain, just after the Centenary Test. Greig was a vital acquisition if WSC was to succeed. Apart from being a feisty character when necessary on the pitch, he had the sort of off-field strength and personality to take on the ultra-conservative TCCB. It was useful timing for Greig. He had wanted to meet Packer anyway concerning the possibility of a career as a TV cricket commentator. He was told he would captain a World XI. He would help in recruiting the best cricketers in Pakistan, the West Indies, England and South Africa. Greig's usefulness to WSC was manifold. He had some standing in his home country of South Africa as well as in his adopted UK.

Greig and Robertson (Packer's bagman) were given a 45-minute video showing Ian Chappell testifying to the authentic intentions of Packer and the integrity of the deals being offered. Chappell, well respected by his peers worldwide, had added his reputation to the WSC enterprise. The video helped Greig and Robertson do very well on a trip to the Port-of-Spain, Trinidad, where the West Indies was playing host in a Test against Pakistan.

The West Indians, then providing more outstanding talent than just about any nation, were the poorest paid players in the world. Many wanted to join WSC. The problem was who not to contract.

Greig and Robertson secured further top-line players including Viv Richards, Andy Roberts, Clive Lloyd and Michael Holding from the West Indies. Mushtaq Mohammad, Imran Khan and Asif Iqbal from Pakistan also joined up. Majid Khan, Javed Miandad and Zaheer Abbas would follow.

The Pakistanis look upon elders as avuncular figures and Packer was suddenly an honorary relative.

'He was uncle Kerry to me', Javed Miandad commented.

Talking money

Robertson and Greig, receiving strong lessons in how money talks, then flew on to London where there were several juicy English and South African targets. Greig first worked on the England players, including pace bowler John Snow (his Sussex team-mate), Kent keeper/batsman Alan Knott, and spinner Derek Underwood. South Africa had been banned from Test cricket because of apartheid for several years. This was a chance for some outstanding players to resurrect international careers. Barry Richards, Clive Rice, Kepler Wessels, Eddie Barlow, Mike Proctor and Garth Le Roux were among those who signed on. Le Roux was a strapping 22-year-old pace bowler needing challenges beyond South Africa's domestic Currie Cup competition and playing county cricket for Sussex. His country's isolation made it ludicrous, Le Roux said, not to join WSC. His 21-year-old county partner Kepler Wessels, a left-handed opening bat, had already looked into the possibility of settling in Australia. Packer provided a perfect vehicle for him. Wessels reckoned he would have played for nothing, so desperate was he to play international cricket. But he didn't tell his benefactors, who paid him handsomely for making the switch to WSC.

Unfortunately, South Africa's finest player of the era, or perhaps any era – Graeme Pollock – missed out, as did Denys Hobson. They would go to Australia but Jamaican Prime Minister, Michael Manley, objected to these two participating in WSC. They had remained in South Africa under the apartheid regime and were thus branded by Manley as not having broken from apartheid. The others were living in England playing county cricket alongside blacks and were considered acceptable.

Pollock was disappointed but had experienced cancelled tours since 1970. It was nothing new. Packer would pay him out in full. Pollock took in the bigger, more altruistic picture and saw such pedantic opposition to apartheid as being more important than his chance for an international career.

The other South Africans, who were not discarded for their 'South African-ness' as Manley put it, were pleased at the chance to play cricket with the world's elite.

'Where do I sign?' Barlow asked Greig when they met at London's Churchill Hotel.

By April 1977, just before Greg Chappell led his conventional Ashes team to England, Robertson had the signatures on WSC contracts of 66 players – the 28 Australians that Ian Chappell and Cowper had originally listed; 18 West Indians and a further 20 from the rest of the world – mainly England, South Africa and Pakistan.

Packer's commitment to risk millions of dollars to set up WSC could now ensure at least two seasons of the breakaway competition.

***

The conventional cricket world was in turmoil when the WSC project was first heard of at Hove, where the Australians were playing, via the press and media on 9 May 1977.

A column in *The Times* of London carried a mock obituary notice: 'In affectionate remembrance of international cricket, which died at Hove, on 9 May 1977. Deeply lamented by a large circle of friends and acquaintances. Rest in Peace. Note: The body will be cremated and the Ashes taken to Australia and scattered around the studios of TCN Channel 9 in Sydney'.

This was a send-up of the original notice that was placed in England's *The Sporting Times* in 1882 after Australia defeated England for the first time in a Test on English soil. It led to the legend of the Ashes.

Benaud's break

The news of the Packer breakaway soured the 1977 Ashes. The media hounded Greg Chappell and his Australian players. UK newspapers were against Packer and his mission. Australian papers reacted as if those involved were 'traitors'. Peter MacFarline, a journalist with the Melbourne *Age*, was the first to make a personal attack on Packer by writing: 'He not only looked like a hammerhead shark but acted like one'.

The UK *Daily Mail* kept up the oceanic predator metaphor with a blazing front-page headline: 'World's Top Cricketers Turn Pirate'.

Another unacceptable, rich Australian, it seemed, was hijacking England's national game. Invective usually reserved for Rupert Murdoch was turned on Packer. Picking up from where MacFarline had left off in Australia, personal attacks in British newspapers became frequent. Packer was dubbed 'the man in the rubber mask'. Extravagant stories – apocryphal, mythical or otherwise – began to circulate in London. They included rumours of him losing A$30,000,000 in a 72-hour Baccarat binge in Las Vegas. He was a familiar face at the London club, Croxford's, where the maximum bet on any hand was £250,000 (about A$650,000). Packer was known to have dealt all seven hands at once – a maximum bet of £1,750,000 (A$4,550,000). Tales of him tipping waiters were legendary. If he won, it was not unusual for him to hand over big sums to those who waited on him at tables. Once, in Las Vegas, he asked a croupier the amount of the mortgage on her house.

'Fifty thousand dollars', the woman replied.

Packer pushed chips to that value her way. But the female croupier explained to him that she couldn't accept it. All tips had to be pooled and shared. Packer called for the manager. He demanded that the woman be fired. The nervous manager refused, saying that she was a member of a union, and that there was no reason to fire her.

Packer pointed to a casino across the road.

'If you don't fire her', he said, 'I'll take my business across there.'

The manager fired her. Packer then pushed the US$50,000 worth of chips to her again.

'Now you can accept it.'

Then he turned to the manager and said: 'Now re-hire her'.

Then there was the tale, on another occasion, about the Texas oilman at a casino, who was bragging about his wealth.

'How much are you worth?' Packer asked him.

'One hundred million dollars.'

'Really?' Packer said. 'That much?'

'You bet, sir.'

'I'll toss you for it', Packer said.

These stories were supposed to paint him as a reckless hedonist. Yet it demonstrated a cavalier attitude to money, and life. It sent a signal that Kerry Packer, media mogul, was prepared to dig deep in his deep pockets and gamble to achieve what he wanted.

He was deliberately inflammatory with quotes at the time such as: 'I've read a lot about Genghis Khan. He wasn't very loveable, but he was bloody efficient'.

A cartoon in *The Times* once showed a sword-wielding Rupert Murdoch on the gangplank of a convict ship, which was re-docking at an English port. It depicted Australian convicts lining the deck, ready to jump onto land. The cartoon caption read: 'We're Back!'

But unlike Murdoch, who was set to plunder more newspapers in the UK, Packer was on a hit-and-run raid that would rob England of its finest cricketers.

One of his closest confidants was Richie Benaud, a respected figure in England for his cricket career until 1964, and for his TV commentary. Benaud's dry style, wry, observant wit, and flair as a commentator who had an outstanding comprehension of the game, made him popular in England. It was a shock for the British to learn that even he was a defector. When the *Daily Mail*'s leading sports columnist Ian Wooldridge found out, he was incredulous that the coup had been kept secret. He would have been more amazed, then, to learn that Benaud had been a key strategist, with a consultancy fee of A$30,000, advising Packer on how to attempt negotiations with the Board, and on setting up the WSC series. Benaud had public relations as well as journalism experience.

He predicted that the secret would leak, as it did.

'It would be unwise to write off the [Australian] Board simply because you have the players signed up on contract', Benaud told Packer. 'The Board of 14 have in their number Bob Parish, a tireless worker; Sir Donald Bradman, a brilliant administrator and business-man, chairman of several boards; Ray Steele, solicitor and one of the best administrators in the world. There are weaknesses because the structure demands a certain number of representatives from each state [which was public-relations-speak for saying the others made up the numbers and were not very effective administrators], but they will close ranks on a matter of this kind . . .'

Benaud knew well that Parish, Bradman and Steele – all staunch establishment men – would ally themselves with their English counterparts in an effort to stop Packer.

Benaud also explained how the media would react.

'As this [WSC] is a Channel 9 exclusive production, there will be resistance from other media, despite the quality of the players . . . you shouldn't think that there won't be some sniping from all sections of the media . . .'

Benaud was talking only about Australia. In the meantime, now that the story was in the open, Packer had to deal with the onslaught in the UK, and its possible effect on the players he had already signed up, who would be reading everything in the press to gain a wider grasp of the venture.

Packer persuasion

British writer, commentator and bon vivant John Arlott was scathing about the WSC concept, calling it a 'circus'. He predicted that if it got off the ground in competition with Test cricket, it would fail. The esteemed E. W. Swanton of the *Daily Telegraph*, a good friend to Bradman, attacked the concept and said Packer's sole motivation was to gain the TV rights to Test cricket in Australia. This suggested that the establishment did not believe that Packer would actually ever go on with WSC. It was a seen as giant bluff. Swanton would not speak to Greig, with whom he had been on good terms. Bradman, who had always been fond of Benaud, would not answer his phone calls. The schism in world cricket would ruin relationships and forge new ones. Supporters in Australia split down the middle, and along age groups. More mature fans hated the concept. The young were more inclined to give it a chance.

Two weeks after the news of the great cricket rebellion broke, some of the 13 Australians on tour with Greg Chappell had second thoughts. Packer arrived in London. The 13 players were summoned on a tour rest-day to meet him at the Dorchester Hotel.

Packer got straight to the point. He had heard, he said, that some of them wanted to break their contracts with his WSC. If that were so, he told the assembled cricketers, he would have no hesitation in taking them to court to recover damages.

Davis recalled Packer telling them that he would 'take your house, your car . . . everything you've got'.

Later, Packer was led to believe that 22-year-old David Hookes may have been offered the official Australian captaincy by the ACB. Packer summoned Hookes from Adelaide to his office in Sydney. Hookes was accompanied by his accountant.

'David, look at me', Packer said. 'I have invested a lot of money in you. I hear that you are thinking about not playing World Series Cricket. You have some doubts. Look at this . . .'

Packer showed his visitors five 30-second commercials featuring Hookes and Greig.

'I have spent a lot of money – a lot of creativity – in making you the face of WSC', Packer said. 'If you bail out of this I will sue you for everything you've got. What I don't get off you, I will get off the

ACB.' He stood up. 'You've got two minutes to think about it.' Packer walked out of his office, slamming the door behind him.

Hookes and his accountant were left speechless. Not a word passed between them before Packer stormed back into his office in less than a minute.

'Well', Packer challenged them, 'have you made a decision?'

Hookes and his accountant looked at each other.

'David', the accountant said, 'you are really going to enjoy playing World Series Cricket.'

Packer's bullying made sure that all the contracted players were completely committed to WSC.

The snub

Not surprisingly, Greg Chappell's team did not fare well in the 1977 Ashes, being thrashed 3-0. It was tough for the skipper. The team manager, Len Maddocks, gave him a dressing down. The Board felt Chappell had been disloyal and that he had misled it, especially as he had signed to represent the Board and WSC, while denying to the Board that he had a WSC deal. But Chappell was not in breach of any contract. He intended to, and did, fulfil his obligations as Test captain until September and resigned after the 1977 Ashes tour. Then he planned to take up the obligations to WSC.

The ACB and the UK TCCB were in accord: Packer had to be stopped. Their survival as ruling bodies of cricket in the two countries, and the survival of the game as they had controlled it until then, was in jeopardy. The British media continued its vilification campaign against Packer. In Australia, players were snubbed even at club level. Ian Chappell was fired as North Melbourne's captain-coach. The Melbourne Cricket Club would not pick Max Walker. Ray Bright couldn't get a club game; he had to turn out for Footscray Technical College. Richie Robinson took a coaching job at North Alphington, and was transported back to his under-age days playing on malthoid pitches. It was rough, but he was able to get in some cricket.

The Board tried to prevent WSC from using training facilities. The MCG and SCG were not available for its use. The International Cricket Council (ICC), in conjunction with the TCCB, rewrote its rules to prevent cricketers from playing WSC. But Packer was playing a close checking game. He counter-attacked, directing his lawyers to seek an injunction and damages in a London High Court action against the ICC and the TCCB. The Court saw their action as 'an unreasonable restraint of trade'. Packer's group was awarded costs of A$350,000. The contracted players were free to perform, if WSC could find somewhere play.

***

Packer secured AFL's Waverley Park, in Melbourne's outer suburbs, for its first 'Super Test' between Australia and the West Indies. He took all participants to a top restaurant. The players presented him with a signed cricket bat.

'This is one bat I won't be parting with', Packer said. 'It has cost me one point nine million dollars before a ball has been bowled.'

If ever anyone had put his money where his verbal intentions were it was this TV mogul. He was a gambler, but this venture was the riskiest of his career. It could make or break him.

The Garner ambulance

At the start, WSC seemed a shaky venture. It hired TV commentators Keith Stackpole, Fred Trueman, Bill Lawry and Richie Benaud, who gave the rebel teams a pep-talk before the game, inciting them to show the 'cricket establishment' that they were not 'disapproved persons'.

Stackpole recalled turning up early for the match, expecting a big crowd. There was no traffic, no spectators. He even thought he might have had the wrong day.

'It was amazing', he said, 'just walking into AFL Park, and there was just no atmosphere. There was nothing there except those 22 cricketers out on the ground. It was strange, eerie . . .'

It was a disappointing beginning. Nine's cameras had to find ways to avoid showing the empty terraces in the VFL stadium, which had held football crowds of more than 70,000. Yet TV spectators tuned in for curiosity's sake. They did not know if the games would be authentic, especially with critics and the Board suggesting it could not be fair dinkum. What they saw was definitely competition. It was tough, uncompromising and fierce. Batsmen were forced to wear helmets regularly for the first time in cricket competition, as the fastest bowlers in the world unleashed thunderbolts at heads and upper bodies.

Max Walker remembers 'big Joel Garner, all 6 ft 9 inches (206 centimetres) of him, standing in front of a black sight screen. All I can see is a huge piano keyboard [his smile] looking at me. He called to me: "Maxie, Maxie – one ball you dead man! I will put you in hospital". He painted a cross on his forehead. I was terrified'.

The aggression and derring-do was very much in the Packer mould. He liked flying gliders and driving motorised go-karts. He played football and cricket hard and well at school. Packer became a more than fair golfer with a small handicap, and a fair horseman and polo player. He tried facing a bowling machine at the pace of Larwood and Thompson – about 160 kph – just to see what facing fast bumpers from them would be like. He was hit under the heart and had to be carried off the pitch. (Some observers wondered if this was the beginning of his heart problems.)

There were lasting WSC innovations such as coloured clothing, cricket under lights and white balls. In the one-day game, fielders had to be inside inner circles marked on the ground for the first 15 overs, which encouraged batsmen to go over the top to ensure fast scoring and big hitting. Incentives for sixes and fast scoring were introduced. Cameras were used at both ends of the ground, and others were set up at different angles. Close-ups became part of the various new visual options. Pitch microphones were used to pick up the banter, sledging and abuse between players.

Channel 9's ratings began to increase. While WSC ran at a loss in the first full season (1977–78), advertising revenue began to offset losses. Nine executives reckoned that they were attracting enough sponsors to make cricket much more cost effective than costlier programming of home-grown and imported TV dramas. They were also unearthing a whole new market of young viewers who loved the changes from the less exciting presentation of Tests during the 1960s and the first half of the 1970s. This new demographic would not have been attracted to the ABC coverage, which suited older traditionalists. This in turn attracted advertisers eager to thrust their products at an audience with growing 'disposable income'. They were more likely to spend than the audience watching the ABC, which had no advertising anyway.

While the network may have been uncertain about immediate returns from its experiment, the risks would pay off in younger viewers gained. They would stay loyal to Nine as long as it led the way in sports coverage.

Board bites back

The Board attempted to counteract the WSC with its own Test series – against India. Don Bradman was seconded to entice Bob Simpson back to captain the official Australian team, which was now virtually a Second XI. Simpson was 41, and had not performed at Test level for a decade. But he had been playing club cricket in Sydney, which kept him in touch. The Indian team was weak, which meant that the sides were evenly matched. A close competition drew fair crowds. Simpson hit the Brisbane First Test's highest score (89) and Australia scraped in by 16 runs. There was another close call in the Second Test at Perth where Australia scored the highest fourth innings score (8 for 342) to win a Test in Australia. The victory was by just

2 wickets. Simpson was again the star, scoring 176 and 39 (run out). India hit back in the Melbourne Third Test to win by 222 runs, and this provided a serious competition for the final two Tests. Because of the tight games, there was more hinging on results than that produced in the higher standard WSC Super-Tests. India did the right thing by the Board by thrashing Australia in the Sydney Fourth Test, thus setting up the Adelaide Fifth Test, beginning at the end of January 1978, for a thrilling, riveting contest in the series decider.

India obliged again by fighting back magnificently in the final innings of the series, scoring 445, and falling 47 short.

The Board made claims about higher revenue for the 1977–78 season. But if anything, with a plethora of watchable cricket, the battle between the highly competitive conventional Tests and the hard-hitting Super-Tests was a 'draw'. There was no decisive winner for the season. WSC was still alive. Official Tests had not lost that much in crowd appeal, with Indian spinners providing plenty of action against some adventuresome batting.

The official Australian team was scheduled for a tour of the West Indies early in 1978. The home side had the benefit of all the WSC stars for the first two Tests, which saw the Australians easily beaten in both games. But the WSC players were in dispute with the West Indies Cricket Board and they walked out of the last three games, which allowed a more even competition, with one win each and a draw. The West Indies Board lost A$100,000 and there was residual acrimony about the impact of WSC.

The crunch came for the official Australian team in the 1978–79 Ashes against England, led by Mike Brearley. It was thrashed 5-0. This abject failure saw 150,000 more fans for the season turning out to WSC games. On top of that, Nine's ratings were much higher than the ABC's when it came to cricket viewers.

Packer appeared to be winning. He had managed – in his inimitable style – to win over the SCG and the Gabba grounds to the WSC. There was some initial trouble in getting the lights on for day–night games at the SCG, but Packer's persuasive ways prevailed, and to enormous effect. A spillover crowd of more than 50,000 turned up at the SCG on 28 November 1978 to watch a one-day game. This night marked the success of the WSC in the eyes of the public, and even the media opposed to the Packer venture. It led to the Board losing A$445,000 whereas the marketing group running WSC was profitable.

Packer sent his troupe to the West Indies early in 1979 for five Super-Tests, which was again a profitable venture. At the same time, the official Australian team slugged out a two Test competition in Australia versus Pakistan (one win each), which once more lost money.

The Board was concerned about the future of official Tests. A demoralised and weakened Australia had now been crushed by England at home and abroad in Ashes Tests, and it had struggled against India and Pakistan. With the talent pool so diminished by WSC, there was little hope of redressing the problem for several more series, when new young stars would make a natural progression to the top. In the meantime, Australia might look forward to a decade of struggle and no hope of winning back the Ashes. Already, there had been damaging losses for the Board, and also the states in running their competitions, which had a flow-on effect to club level around the nation.

Australian cricket was bleeding to death, and not slowly.

Gladiators

What of the WSC cricket itself, beyond the razzle dazzle of change and presentation? WSC was to last 17 months, beginning mid-November 1977 and ending in Antigua on 10 April 1979. In that rarefied period, the world was to see the greatest cricketing gladiators battle for team and individual supremacy in close, sometimes brutal, combat. Dressing rooms would be like hospitals and the pitch area was like a zone between World War I trenches. It also allowed pairings that without WSC would not have been dreamed of. The classic was the grand sight of the ultra-talented Barry Richards batting with the mighty Viv Richards for the World XI in the first season. It occurred most dramatically at Gloucester Park, Perth in January 1978. Barry belted a superb 207, while Viv stroked and crunched his way to 177. Both showed immaculate timing. Observers could not separate them easily or rank one above the other. Greg Chappell, with his exceptional fluency, had to be bracketed with them, and he showed why at Gloucester Park with a stunning 174 in a losing team. Chappell and Viv each hit four centuries and averaged in the mid-50s in the tournaments, which pitted Australia against the World or the West Indies.

Dennis Lillee was confirmed as the greatest bowler in the game and earned every cent Packer paid him. He played in 14 matches, taking 67 wickets at 26.87 each. This was superior to the array of brilliant West Indians, who all lived up to their elevated reputations.

Rapprochement

By early 1979, the Australian Board had no choice but to deal with Packer, and he was happy to meet them halfway. WSC was battling, despite getting over some humps after two seasons. The future was bleak for it. There were only two national teams in the competition – Australia and the West Indies. The World team had plenty of stars, but they did not have quite the edge in unity and ambition of a national squad. No official teams in the rest of the world were going to join WSC, which meant that the triangular competition, including a disparate World team, would have trouble sustaining itself. The competition was in danger of petering out. Packer had the additional problem of supporting the second rank of about 30 players in the WSC squad. They played in Australian country competitions, which were difficult to make better than exhibitions.

With this as a background, Packer flew to Adelaide for a secret thirty-minute meeting with Don Bradman at his home in Kensington

Park. Packer, a natural powermonger, knew exactly where the true potency lay in the Australian cricket establishment. Over tea and scones with Bradman, an agreement was struck. Bradman then persuaded the ACB to support it.

Packer received the rights to televise official Tests in Australia, which he had wanted three years earlier. He also obtained the right to televise day–night games – which had proved so lucrative – with all the attractive accoutrements, such as coloured clothing. Packer's marketing group, PBL, also gained responsibility for the promotion of all first-class cricket. These were strong gains for Packer, even if he had gone about it the hard way. He was now in a dominant position in the media concerning control of the TV broadcast of Tests, and the highly popular innovation of one-day cricket, which would prove a ratings winner and cash cow for all concerned for the next quarter century.

The Board, with Bradman guiding Parish and Steele, negotiated back the right to select teams and deal with sponsors. On the surface, the cricket world was back to square one. In other ways, it had changed forever, and in the medium and long terms, for the better.

Australia had to recreate its official national team. But cricket's stabilising took less time than anticipated, especially with the increased income generated from the TV rights. Money was distributed to the states, which in turn flowed down to club level. Packer's innovative methods of bringing cricket to the public attracted far more sponsors to the national and state teams. Over the years that followed, every major ground in the country was refurbished. The facilities were bigger and better for the public. The Nine network's revenues increased due to more advertisers wanting to display their wares.

The amalgamation of the WSC and official teams seemed at first to go smoothly with mixed success. The 1979–80 Australian season saw Greg Chappell take over from Kim Hughes to lead the Test team to a 3-0 series win against England, but a 2-0 loss to the West Indies, which had emerged in the WSC period as the strongest team in the world. Australia lost again in Pakistan 1-0 in another three Test series.

The Australian side was less competitive abroad, especially as Greg Chappell would not tour. Team harmony, with Kim Hughes leading former WSC stars Lillee and Marsh, was not at its best. The defeat by England (3-1), with Ian Botham dominant, in the 1981 Ashes was a shock to the tourists, when they looked set to retain the Ashes. Australia managed to draw a three Test series with the West Indies in the 1981–82 home season that followed. In the next summer, Australia beat England 2-1 in a five Test Ashes series, and there seemed to be a sustained healthy recovery post-WSC, which ran through to the end of the Australian season 1983–84 and a decisive series victory against Pakistan.

That season saw the retirements of WSC senior stars Greg Chappell, Lillee and Marsh. Australia, again led by Hughes, was thrashed 3-0 in the West Indies. When the Caribbean players toured Australia in 1984–85, the brittleness of the Australian team was apparent against the world's best. All the batsmen were in trouble against the finest fast bowling line-up of all time – Marshall, Garner, Holding and Walsh. Australia managed to win at Sydney on a spinner's wicket – the only Test it had won in the last 10 games against the world champions. Hughes made himself a scapegoat by resigning as captain mid-series, when in reality Australia did not have the calibre of batsmen to take on the supreme speed quartet.

Allan Border took over a Test team that struggled for the next four years against all countries. But by the end of the 1980s it began to emerge as a challenger to the West Indies.

The radical change, without WSC, continued in the 1980s, with cricketers playing up to three times more Tests than their counterparts of earlier decades, along with one-day competitions, which remained a big drawcard, bringing a vast new audience to the game. Channel 9's programmers were scheduling 600 hours of cricket each summer. Payment for this was filling Board coffers in a way that met player pay-rise demands. For the first time, apart from the brief

WSC period, Australia had a group of cricketers who were paid well enough not to worry about taking jobs to survive. Apart from annual Board contracts, this elite group added to their incomes by appearances in Test, one-day and state teams, along with deals to sponsor equipment.

Thanks to Border's messianic commitment to making his nation number one, Australia was on equal footing with the Caribbean champions by 1992. Three years later, Mark Taylor's team was the best in the world. It had not relinquished this status after more than a decade under Taylor, Steve Waugh and Ricky Ponting.

Parallel with this long-term, on-field success, there was an upward spiral of revenue for the Nine Network and the Board, and players' increased requests for higher payment were met easily. Even players not destined to rise above the state level were on contracts that would mean they could have just one form of employment – cricket. The system now spawned a generation of millionaires from the sport, which was a far cry from the days when top players in the mid-1970s battled off-field to make ends meet.

***

The Board attitude in 1976 – of not countenancing professionalism in the game in its approach to TV broadcasting and player payments – was the root cause of the reaction from the top players, and Packer. His drive to get things done in his own direct way proved to be a positive factor for all concerned. The Board, now Cricket Australia, is a strong marketing operation run by professionals looking to improve and expand the game in every way. This is a far cry from the insular, closed star chamber that ran the game for the first three-quarters of the 20th century.

Talented young cricketers now have attainable dreams about playing top cricket in Australia, and playing for the national team, over a period approaching 20 years.

It is all the result of the Packer revolution.

THE BLITZ OF 1981

Impact Nine: Ian Botham

Ian Botham became an England legend during the 1981 Ashes when his Herculean efforts turned a series, which Australia appeared to have won after three of the six Tests were played. In the history of Ashes cricket, only Don Bradman's almost single-handed performances in the 1936–37 series would rank higher than Botham's. Then, when Australia was down two Tests to nil, Bradman scored 270, 212 and 169 in the final three games to give his country three wins and the Ashes. Bradman's mighty batting displays were complemented by his outstanding captaincy in his first Ashes as leader. Botham, likewise, was a dominant force in two departments of the game – batting and bowling – after losing the captaincy three games into the 1981 Ashes. Like Bradman, Botham came back hard to dominate the last three Tests of a series.

***

Ian Botham approached the wicket in a relaxed mood with England 5 for 105. It was half an hour after lunch on day three of the Third Test of the 1981 Ashes series at Headingley, Leeds. England was all but beaten. Australia had made 9 for 401 declared. England had made 174 in the first innings and was following on towards defeat. Botham had returned to form in this game with 6 for 95 and a blistering 50 in 54 minutes after a miserable start to the series. This, plus the fact that he had been relieved of the England captaincy after not recording a win in 12 games as leader, had unburdened the strongly built 186 centimetre, 100 kilogram all-rounder. He was resigned to defeat but would go down fighting. Botham began with a couple of slogs to the boundary. A cautionary comment by English umpire Barry Meyer, who indignantly asked him if he were going to play himself in, caused Botham to settle in with a touch more discretion. He was doing his bit, but England crumbled to 7 for 135 – still 92 from making Australia bat again. The expected loss would put England down 0-2 with three Tests to play in the six Test series. Botham continued to restrain himself until tea when he was 39 not out in 87 minutes. His partner, Graham Dilley, had been the more attacking of the two. After tea, they both decided that there was no point in trying to defend. They would have a bit of fun. Botham led the way with an assault on all Australian bowlers – Dennis Lillee, Terry Alderman and Geoff Lawson. Australian captain, Kim Hughes, held back spinner Ray Bright. Botham moved from controlled power hitting into something more murderous. He swung at everything and usually connected, sending the ball to all points of the compass.

When Dilley (56) played on to Lawson, he and Botham had added 117 in 80 minutes. Since tea, they had added 76 in 44 minutes. It was a period of devil-may-care slather and whack that had succeeded without any science or serious planning. They had transformed the game's mood but not yet the winning equilibrium. England was 8 for 252, just 25 ahead, and effectively 8 for 25.

Botham was joined by Chris Old and raced through his century. During this link, the Australian wheels fell off: Hughes lost control of his troops. Old observed that the Australians began bitching at each other. Keeper Rod Marsh, paceman Lillee and Trevor Chappell 'ignored' Hughes' directives. He in turn still failed to use spinner Ray Bright, which the English players and skipper Mike Brearley thought was a tactical error, given Botham's rampage. Botham and Old, sensing the demoralisation, continued to plunder the bowling, which became loose. At 319, Old (29) was bowled by Lawson.

Their 67 run partnership had given England the lead by 92.

Bob Willis came to the wicket with 20 minutes to go. Botham had not thought of slowing down as stumps approached. There was no point. The Australians were down. Botham put the boot right in with some more swashbuckling while shielding bunny Willis from all but 5 balls. Another 31 were added. Botham galloped to 145 not out. The score, as stumps were drawn, was 9 for 352. England's lead was 125. Botham, criticised for his weight, his form, his apparent lack of leadership skills and his attitude, was suddenly a national hero of a dimension unparalleled in English cricket in 25 years. Not since Jim Laker had taken 19 for 90 at Manchester in the Fourth Test of the 1956 Ashes series had an England player been so praised. Yet Botham's performance had more impact. Laker's effort was against a weak Australian team down for the count and kept there on a spinner's dustbowl paradise. As exciting as falling wickets are for a fielding team and its supporters, there is nothing quite like a powerful batsman bludgeoning an opposition into submission. And Botham's performance came when England, not the Australians, had been all but counted out. His size – he was known as 'Guy Gorilla' and 'Beefy' – gave him a fighter's image: just the sort of bloke the English loved to see knock the stuffing out of the Aussies. He was their gladiator, the toughest character playing for England since Fred Trueman terrorised opposing batsmen.

The morning after the mayhem, Botham (149 not out) crunched one more boundary before Alderman removed Willis. England had reached 356.

Australia had 130 to make for victory.

Willis felt that unless he bowled exceptionally well he would be dropped. His Test career was on the line. Motivated by this fear and inspired by Botham's batting feat, Willis delivered a great performance, taking 8 for 43 from 14.1 overs. He kept his place. England won by 18 runs in the most amazing turnaround in Ashes cricket history. Botham's attitude, and his preparedness to risk everything to gain all, triggered an unlikely win and boosted England's confidence.

It went on to win the 1981 series 3-1, thanks largely to Ian Botham's force and exceptional skill.

The MCC 'boy'

Cheshire born Ian Botham was just six when he told his parents, Marie and Les, that he was going to be a professional sportsman. The Yorkshire couple didn't ever disabuse him of this course. They were both into a variety of sports. Les, an engineer and former Navy man, was a good park cricketer, runner and soccer player. Marie liked cricket, badminton and hockey. They encouraged their physically precocious son to 'go for it', and it happened that young Ian chose cricket – the sport common to both his parents – as his number one summer interest. He saw his initial first-class game at Bradford at age eight. At nine he was getting a game with adults at the Milford Recreational Ground in Yeovil, Somerset where he was brought up. At 12 he made the Yeovil Second XI, and played matches with his father. A year later, young Botham captained the under 16 team at Buckler's Mead Secondary School. He was soon picked up for the schools team of his county, Somerset. He crashed 80 in his first ever knock. Botham was unfairly ignored as a bowler.

At 15 he was just as keen on soccer. He supported the flamboyant good-time 'glamour' boys at Chelsea Football Club, who exhilarated the King's Road on Saturdays in the late 1960s and early 1970s. Crystal Palace wanted to sign him up. Botham was only in his mid-teens and already his prophecy that he would live by his sport seemed a likelihood. His lack of academic application began to be of less and less concern to his parents. This highly determined, talented youngster had the mindset to achieve what he wished.

The ultimate desire, with which his parents concurred, lay with cricket.

A big national opportunity to shine for decades in England centred on the annual England Schools match between boys from private and public schools – the toffs versus the yobs, as one observer called it. Important cricket figures, often including Test selectors looking for the new Hobbs, Compton, May or Cowdrey, watched the game. Botham did well in trial games for selection of the England Schools team, especially with the ball. He had been billed as a batsman, not a bowler or all-rounder. There just wasn't a Lord Hawke or a Pelham Warner with the cricketing nous to spot a future champion. Botham felt let down, but as with other greats before him (Bradman being a notable example), and others after him (Steve Waugh being one) who had received selection setbacks in their teens, his talent had plenty of time to be acknowledged. His next step was to spend two seasons as a 'Lord's Ground Staff Boy' – a job that included being a cricketing 'dog's body' on call for MCC members wanting a 'hit' in the nets. Botham at 16 in 1971 was paid 12 pounds (about A$28) a week to survive in expensive London – a salary that had to be subsidised by his parents. He didn't shine, or impress his coaches or anyone else. Yet his staggering self-belief when no one else saw any greatness in him was the key. Despite building a reputation for being wild, Botham worked hard on his skills in the nets. He listened to the coaches he respected, especially those who took a more laidback, less dictatorial approach. The mentality at Lord's was diametrically opposed to his, from the superior attitude of members, to the coaching which attempted to disabuse him of his natural aggression with the bat, and strangely, his capacity to swing the ball. He was a quick learner but his talent was ignored. He became frustrated, and his irritation from the experience never left him. But he surmounted it, absorbed the positive side – which was personal development in the technical elements of the game – and moved on.

Ian Botham knew he was destined for far bigger things, even if no one at Lord's did. His attitude was that he would 'show them'. It was the kind of incentive he would revel in for much of his career.

Sun up at Somerset

Botham left Lord's with plenty of good mates – something that was important to that exuberant youth. He loved the game, the competition and the camaraderie.

At 17, in 1963, he played in Somerset's seconds, along with a brilliant young West Indian bat, Vivian Richards. They became close mates. Each respected the other's toughness, brilliance and competitiveness. Botham was blooded in two Sunday league games for the county at the end of 1973. Then he made the big step up to first-class cricket at 18 in 1974 under the expert guidance of coach Tom Cartwright, who helped develop Botham's bowling. Another influence was Somerset captain Brian Close, a legend in post-war cricket.

1974 was the year Botham emerged as a teenage force and hope for Somerset and England. He played in a Benson & Hedges one-day quarter-final against Hampshire. First, he bowled the best bat in England at the time, Barry Richards of Hampshire, which restricted that county to just 182. When Somerset batted, Botham came in at 7 for 113, with just 15 overs to go and 70 to win. Andy Roberts, the fastest bowler in England that year, hit him with a bouncer that smashed into his mouth. The helmetless Botham spat out blood and teeth, continued and dominated the final overs. He hit the winning run with 7 balls to spare and was an instant hero.

The old-timers at the club told him about roosters one day, feather dusters the next. They didn't want the super-confident youngster to get a swollen head. But the young Botham didn't change. He expected to perform like this. It was exhilarating, but no big deal for him. If he couldn't come in and take control of a game at a critical point, what was the point of playing? Botham wasn't in the game for averages or awards or draws or tactical defensive measures. He didn't believe in reverse gears or putting up the shutters or any other negative thoughts. He visualised himself as a match-winner, someone for the extra big occasion.

He was becoming a legend for being a wild drinker in Taunton, but meeting a young Yorkshire woman, Kathryn Waller, steadied him just enough at a critical time. Botham didn't transform into an angel, but his relationship with her matured him fast. He became engaged to Kathryn and faced responsibilities at a young age. His cricket benefited. Botham, like any professional sportsperson taking on marriage, had to succeed for reasons other than self-aggrandisement. Perhaps he tried too hard and was impatient. His second season, 1975, fell short of expectations. He did well enough with the ball, but his batting was subdued. Somerset didn't cap him (make him professional), and he was struggling financially. But he and Kathryn married in early 1976, pushing Botham to lift his rating. He did better early in 1976 and was capped. His salary increased. Over the summer his bowling figures were almost identical to those of 1975, but his batting went up a notch, helped by a dashing 167 not out against Nottinghamshire in August. It was his maiden first-class hundred, and a beauty. It allowed him to break the 1000 run barrier (1022 in all) at an average of 34.06.

His aggregate included a timely 97 off Sussex, led by England's skipper, Tony Greig. Greig pushed for his selection in the end-of-season one-day internationals against the West Indies. Botham played in two of them, but didn't shine. It was his slim chance to impress selectors but he gave them little to go on. He missed the 1976–77 tour of India and the centenary Test in Melbourne to mark the anniversary of the first international ever played.

Test break

Botham saw his main chance of playing Test cricket for England in 1977 against the touring Australians. First, he took up a Whitbread scholarship to play club cricket in Melbourne early in 1977, yet did not distinguish himself on or off the field. He was involved in a pub altercation with former Australian captain, Ian Chappell.

Unfazed by his apparent lack of progress, Botham returned to

England for the 1977 season. He played well for Somerset against the Australian tourists but overdid the bouncer, and paid for it in boundaries in the MCC versus Australia game. He maintained his batting improvement with a century and several 50s and tightened up his bowling. It was enough for Botham to be selected for his debut Test, the third in the Ashes series that England led 1-0. The venue was Trent Bridge, Nottingham. It was a good environment for Botham, 21, to make his first big international appearance. Australia was on the run. Morale in the tourists' camp was low. England skipper Mike Brearley, who struggled with the bat at Test level, nevertheless was out-generalling his counterpart Greg Chappell. Furthermore, Yorkshire opener Geoffrey Boycott was set to return to Test cricket after a self-imposed exile of 30 matches. His (at times) painstaking but usually effective run-making technique was likely to put the tourists under more pressure.

The Australians could blame their poor form, in part, on the looming Packer crisis. The best world players had been contracted to play in a breakaway international competition, and some were suffering from guilt or uncertainty, as well as being given the 'cold shoulder' by Australian officials. Both teams had defectors, but there were only a handful of English rebels who had signed with Packer to play a series after the Ashes, compared to Australia's entire First XI.

Australia batted first and Botham was on early. He bowled erratically, but settled down after he took his first wicket, Greg Chappell, one of the world's three top batsmen (the others at the time being Barry Richards and Viv Richards), with a long hop wide of off-stump. Chappell dragged it onto his stumps. Later, Botham gave left-hander Rod Marsh the old one-two: a bouncer, then a pitched up in-swinger that trapped the vigorous Aussie keeper LBW. Botham ended with the fine figures of 5 for 54 off 20 overs. He was somewhat of a hero when he met the Queen and the Duke of Edinburgh during the last session of the day.

It was a red-letter day for the novice and one he would remember. Botham made 25 in his only innings. England went on to win comfortably. He made a duck in the Fourth Test at Headingley but relished the cloudy atmosphere when he bowled. He was able to get his out-swinger going. This time he took an excellent 5 for 21 off 11 overs. Included in his bag were Doug Walters and left-handers David Hookes and Rodney Marsh. England went on to win by an innings, and took the Ashes 3-0.

Botham broke a bone in his foot and missed the Fifth Test. His 10 wickets were taken at 20.20 and he could be more than satisfied with his sensational entry to the international level. Early autumn was also a joyous occasion in the Botham household when Kathryn gave birth to a son, Liam. (They would later have two daughters, Sarah and Beccy.) About this time, he accidentally entered a hospital ward full of children with leukaemia and realised how fortunate he was that his own son was healthy. The plight of these youngsters generated in Botham a level of compassion unappreciated beyond his inner circle of friends and family. He arranged for a regular anonymous fund for Christmas parties in that ward.

Botham's place as England's all-rounder was entrenched with the defection of Greig to Packer's World Series Cricket. But severe dysentery stopped him from exploiting the break on England's tour of Pakistan in 1977–78. He had to sit out the three Tests there and wait until the touring party moved on to less challenging accommodation conditions in New Zealand. Botham, 22, returned to the team and took two more 5 wicket hauls, in addition to his first Test century – 103 at Christchurch in the Second Test. It was a responsible, patient knock of 312 minutes, made more laudable by his 'rope-a-dope' tactics against paceman Richard Hadlee, who tried to bounce him out. Botham waited until Hadlee had tired then picked him off with ease, hitting several boundaries.

England needed quick runs in its second innings. When Boycott, the acting captain in place of the injured Brearley, couldn't get them, Botham came in at number four and deliberately ran out his skipper to get others in to up the tempo. Botham led the way by belting 30 not out off 36. England went on to win by 174 runs. Botham became the second England player after Tony Greig to score a century and take 5 wickets in an innings in the same Test.

Botham finished the three Test series with 17 wickets at 18.29, and a batting average of 53. He also took several splendid catches. These returns were those of a true all-round champion.

The lad from Yeovil had arrived as a top-line Test all-rounder.

Consolidation at the top

Botham continued his good Test batting into the 1978 season at home with a century in the first of the three Test series versus Pakistan. Then, at Lord's in the Second Test, he went one better than his Christchurch effort by scoring 108. This second successive century took just 104 deliveries and came in bizarre circumstances. Botham and Chris Old went out drinking after the first day – 15 June – was washed out. They thought that day two would also be wet. Instead, it was sunny. England captain Mike Brearley knew his opening bowlers had been out revelling until the early hours. He batted when he won the toss. Thus, Botham's third Test century surprised Old and his skipper when it came after a particularly convivial evening. It helped reinforce the Botham legend as an individual with the constitution and recuperative powers of an ox.

His performances didn't end there. In Pakistan's second innings he took 8 for 34, including a final spell of 6 wickets for 8 in 53 deliveries. It was the best ever analysis at Lord's. Botham was able to get the ball to swing late and at genuine pace. Some of the deliveries in his last spell were unplayable, even for a master batsman. Botham became the first player to score 100 and take 8 wickets in an innings in a match. At just 22, he was in serious company in the record books for great all-rounders. Again, his Test figures were outstanding. He continued the devastation with the ball in three Tests against New Zealand later in the summer, including an 11 wicket haul at Lord's. Botham gained enormous satisfaction with his outstanding displays twice in the one summer at the home of cricket. Five years earlier, he had been just another lowly hopeful on the ground staff. Now those members who had yelled 'Boy!' when they wanted him to bowl to them were standing to applaud him. In the summer of 1978, Ian Botham was king of Lord's and had no peer.

In his debut year he had taken five wickets or more eight times in just 11 Tests and had scored three centuries.

Down-under plunder

With this record behind him, Botham looked forward to touring Australia under Brearley and causing some devastation there, especially as he would be playing against that country's Second XI. Its top 12 players had all gone over to Packer's WSC.

England won the series 5-1, with the inexperienced new Australian skipper Graham Yallop no match for the wily Brearley. Botham and off-spinner Geoff Miller took the most wickets for England, yet Botham could not put Australia's bowlers to the sword as he hoped and he managed just two 50s in 10 knocks. Part of the reason was the surprisingly high standard of bowlers he faced. The WSC defections had created chances for some worthy Australian bowlers such as Rodney Hogg, Alan Hurst and spinner Jimmy Higgs. They helped ensure that Australia was not slaughtered. In fact, England failed to reach 400 runs in any innings. It was a bowlers' series. Australia's bats were the weak link that handed England the Ashes.

Botham continued on his merry way in 1979 at home, this time against India. Now he seemed assured not to 'fail' with bat and ball in any Test. If he didn't make a big score he took a 'five for'. If he didn't take a wicket, as in the drawn Third Test at Headingley, he made runs – 137 in this instance. This powerhouse knock included 5 sixes and 16 fours. It took only 152 balls. He was a 23-year-old in a hurry and preferred getting there with boundaries – 94 runs worth.

England won the four Test series 1-0. Botham was at the peak of his powers with both bat and ball, and a regular match-winner. At the Oval in the final game of the series, India was set 438 to win and looked likely to do it when its score was 1 for 365. A few wickets fell but the runs kept coming. Brearley threw the ball to Botham with the score at 3 for 399 and eight overs to go. India had to make 39 off 48 balls – which was tight but gettable. Botham's chest went out, as it seemed to in these moments. He roared in like a bull, putting pressure on the Indians, who faltered. Botham took 3 for 17, including Sunil Gavaskar caught for a magnificent 221, and also effected a brilliant stop and run out of Venkat. India reached 8 for 429, and fell 10 short of the target. The game was drawn.

Put asunder down-under

Botham travelled again to Australia for a three Test series in 1979–1980 against a side strengthened by the ending of the Packer experiment. He couldn't prevent a thrashing of England but performed admirably himself, especially with the ball. Yet Botham struggled with the bat in the first five innings of the series, compiling just 68 runs. It prompted him to ask for help from former batting great Ken Barrington, the England team's assistant manager. Barrington suggested he was falling forward when playing a shot, rather than remaining still. Botham corrected the fault by taking guard on leg-stump. This meant he was not into the shot too quickly and therefore, in theory, less likely to topple forward after playing it. It worked. In the Third Test at Melbourne in February 1980, he made 119 not out in grand style off 188 balls in 199 minutes. This was against a rampant Lillee bowling leg-cutters on a slow, low Melbourne wicket.

It was Botham's first hundred against Australia.

With lessons learned and reputation intact, he and the team moved on to Bombay in mid-February for the Golden Jubilee Test to mark the formation of India's cricket Board of Control. Botham strode like a colossus through this game and became the first player to score a century and take 10 wickets or more in a Test. England won by 10 wickets. He returned home for a challenging summer against the West Indies, which had established itself as the dominant world cricketing nation in the aftermath of WSC.

Captain Botham

Brearley, one of the more cerebral captains England ever had, stepped aside to pursue a qualification in psychotherapy, and Botham was appointed captain in 1980. He had the toughest assignment in world cricket and could not force a win against the West Indies during the five Test series, lost 0-1. England then drew with Australia in the 1980 Centenary Test that celebrated the first Test ever played in England. Botham again battled to find touch with the bat. He began the 1980 season well enough, scoring a 50 in the first innings of the First Test at Trent Bridge. But his form fell away against a barrage from Andy Roberts, Michael Holding, Joel Garner, Colin Croft and Malcolm Marshall – a formidable speed force. He was also less penetrating with the ball. A consolation was his dismissal three times of his close friend Viv Richards.

Botham's trials against the formidable Caribbean combination continued in another five Test series from February to April 1981. The tour was calamitous, beginning with the cancellation of the Second Test at Georgetown, Guyana when paceman Robin Jackman was deported from that country. This occurred after it was discovered he had played and coached in South Africa over the previous 11 years. Then Ken Barrington died after a heart attack in his hotel room during the second evening of the Barbados Third Test. Barrington had been a cricketing mentor for Botham and his death touched the England skipper deeply.

England was soundly beaten 2-0. Botham's form fell away further with the bat. He had now gone 17 innings while scoring just one 50. His bowling returns were fair for him, but in 10 Tests now he had failed to take a 'five-for' in an innings.

Botham returned to England and was straight into the 1981 season, which would feature six Tests against the Australians. There were calls for his sacking as leader. Fairer minds pointed out that he had to be given a further chance, considering the difficult task of taking on the West Indies at their peak in his first two series.

Australia won the First Test at Trent Bridge and honours were even at Lord's in a drawn game, but Botham's form with the bat – he managed a 'pair' at Lord's – and ball convinced selectors that he should be relieved of the leadership. After no wins, four losses and eight draws from 12 games, Botham's short tenure as England skipper was over. It was a miserable time for him. He was angered by the Lord's members' cold reaction to his second innings duck, bowled round his legs first ball by spinner Ray Bright. Not one pair of hands went together in a gesture of sympathy for one of the country's greatest players down on his luck. Botham was bitter about this and concerned about his form. He accepted the 'chop' and was consoled by the return of Brearley to the helm. It meant Botham was free to be his flamboyant self as an all-round champion.

Sacked but back

Instead of wallowing in self-pity, he was into the fray nine days later in the Third Test at Headingley. He was now unfettered by the strictures and problems of leadership. His determination returned and he dominated this game as probably no player had done with bat and ball in any Test before him. He took 6 for 95 and 1 for 14, and made 50 and that thumping 149 not out. This, plus Willis' 8 for 43 in Australia's second innings, won the game for England and levelled the series, one win each, with one draw.

Botham's explosive return to form and confidence seemed to falter

THE ASHES: A CELEBRATION

in the Fourth Test at Leeds when he scored 26 and 3 and took 1 for 64 in Australia's first innings. The tourists were 4 for 105 in their second innings, needing just 46 for victory, when Brearley brought Botham on to keep the runs down in the hope that off-spinner John Emburey could pull off a near miracle at the other end. Emburey had the tenacious Allan Border caught of a difficult ball that bounced sharply. Australia was 5 for 105, and still with 46 to get.

Brearley's introduction of Botham, his jousting knight, did strange things to the Australian bats. The aggressive Marsh seemed intent on smashing him out of the firing line. He hit across the line of an ordinary ball and was bowled. Martin Kent did the same. Lillee wanted to hit him too, and went out of his way to nick a near wide to keeper Bob Taylor. Tail-ender Bright was beaten by a quicker one and trapped LBW. Finally, Terry Alderman only needed a straight one, which he duly got, and he was bowled for a duck. Botham had taken 5 wickets in 28 deliveries while conceding 1 run. That only one wicket – Bright's – merited a dismissal was testimony to the psychological impact Botham had in the tight circumstances. Brearley's intuitive skills and Botham had won another Test for England. It now had a 2-1 grip on the series with two to play. Gone were the horrors of Lord's for Botham. He had triumphed. But he had much more to prove in those final two games.

At Old Trafford in the Fifth Test, Lillee had him caught for a duck but he fought back with 3 for 28, including the now prized Australian wicket of Border for 11. Botham came to the wicket in England's second innings at 5 for 205 – a comfortable lead of 306 with five wickets intact. The pitch was true. He began sedately, scoring three in singles. He stepped up his rating and reached 28 off 53 deliveries before the new ball was taken. Lillee steamed in and let go two bouncers. Botham smashed each of them over long leg for six and hooked another – all inside two overs. Soon the crowd was clapping his 50. The mayhem didn't stop as he crunched the others – Alderman, Mike Whitney on debut, and Bright, en route to a century. He hooked and drove on the off, or hit straight drives over or past the bowler. It took just 86 balls. His last 72 had taken just 33 balls in only 37 minutes, which would be a terrific rate for two bats in a one-day rush for runs. But this was Botham on his own in a Test, and in a hurry. Fans had their hearts in their mouths twice as he mishit high catches to mid-off and third man, only to see these gettable chances grassed. Apart from that, it was a top innings of that rare combination of power and class. Bradman observed, as he had with Sobers a decade earlier at the MCG in an Australia v Rest of the World double century, that Botham's innings was a case of awesome bludgeoning power in control of technique. This applied off the front or back foot. Bradman called the innings 'enthralling'. He saw a difference from a batsman simply 'having a go' to Botham's approach of clinical execution.

Botham's innings ended on 118 when he was caught behind off Whitney. It took 123 minutes and 102 balls. He hit 13 fours and six sixes – then a record number of sixes in England and against Australia anywhere.

Australia was left with a near-impossible target of 506 for victory, and it went down bravely by 102 runs. England had won the Ashes. Botham, with three successive 'player of the match' awards in the Third, Fourth and Fifth Tests, did more than anyone to achieve the series victory. He was the difference between a series won and lost. Without his spirit, the result could easily have gone the other way.

He finished off the series with two failures with the bat and two fine bowling performances that netted him 10 wickets. It was Botham's 41st Test and he reached the 200-wicket milestone. He was still just 25. He had been in Test cricket just four years, although this larger than life figure seemed to have been around for a decade. Perhaps it was because when he performed 'big' it was huge, and when he failed it looked horrendous. So much was expected of him. Now, after his dramatic return to dominance, especially against Australia, he was billed as England's finest all-round cricketer of the 20th century. Certainly, no one seemed as forceful a character in the minds of English cricket historians since W. G. Grace in the 19th century.

Post-1981

Botham found it tough to maintain the form that destroyed Australia, when he toured India in 1981–82. Yet he still demonstrated the ability to deliver the grand performance when he put his body and mind to it. His bowling figures were not up to his usual high standard. But his batting was consistent and strong. He finished the series with a dashing century at Kanpur.

A few months later, the demanding grind continued through another summer. In 1982 England played three Tests each against India and Pakistan. Botham faced challenges to his position as the world's leading all-rounder from India's Kapil Dev and Pakistan's Imran Khan. Once more he lifted his rating, first against India when he hit 67 and 5 for 46 at Lord's, then with a century at Old Trafford and – at the Oval – his highest score in Tests: 208. The double came up in 220 balls and 268 minutes. He was kept on his toes by Kapil Dev, who hit three 50s including a dashing 97 in 93 balls. Botham bowled better against Pakistan and twice more passed 50. Imran Khan did better with the ball and also cracked two 50s.

***

Botham was approaching 27, and feeling the pressure of non-stop touring and almost all-year playing at first-class and Test level. He was now a superstar who had widened his circle of friends to include people such as singer Elton John, and he found it tough cranking up for the 1982–83 season on his third tour to Australia in four years. It showed in his results, which were mediocre.

England was beaten 1-2 and lost the Ashes after the heroics of 1981.

From 1983 on, for the next decade, his outstanding performances were more sporadic but he could still turn it on here and there – except with the ball against the strong West Indian line-ups of the 1980s. He met another challenge from New Zealand's Richard Hadlee, who outshone him over two series in England and New Zealand in three of the four 'contested' sets of analysis. Hadlee won out in England in the four Test series of 1983 with both bat and ball. In New Zealand over 1983–84, Botham was superior with the bat while Hadlee did better with the ball.

In recognition of his outstanding service, Botham had a record £90,000 (A$212,000) raised for him by Somerset in 'benefit' matches in 1984. In 1985, after bowing out of a tour of India and Sri Lanka to recuperate after eight years non-stop travelling, he came back for a strong all-round effort against Australia. Botham took 31 wickets at 27.58, by far the best figures for England as it won back the Ashes 3-1.

Hannibal Botham

In 1986 he was suspended from cricket for admitting in a newspaper article that he had smoked marijuana. But this was overshadowed when Botham became heroic off the field in support of leukaemia research, with a 1398 kilometre walk from John o' Groats to Land's End. Botham had never lost his feeling for victims of this disease. This to some extent countered the poor aspect of his media-generated image over a decade as a pot smoking, hard-drinking lout given to fits of violence. Botham set himself a gruelling schedule, travelling 48 kilometres a day. After this success, he involved himself in further challenging walks over the years and raised considerable amounts for leukaemia research. The year also marked a sad end in his long association with Somerset. The county sacked its West Indian pair, Joel Garner and Viv Richards, and Botham walked out in sympathy. He joined Warwickshire.

On a fifth tour to Australia in 1986–87, he showed all his old touch with a dashing 138 at Brisbane in the first Test of the series and brought back plenty of 1981 nightmares for the Australians. But it was his last show of power against the old enemy. His other five innings saw him accumulate just 51 runs. He took only 9 wickets at 32.89.

Botham had a moderate season with Queensland in 1987–88 but it was impaired by alcohol-fuelled thuggish behaviour on a long plane trip from Melbourne to Perth in March 1988. This saw him charged with assault and offensive behaviour. Botham was bailed out of jail by Dennis Lillee, who arrived with a crate of beer. He was fined A$320 after pleading guilty. The incident resulted in him being sacked from his three-year contract with Queensland. Undeterred, Botham took off for another walking assignment, complete with accompanying elephants and a herd of media people, this time from Perpignan in the South of France across the Alps to Turin in Italy. It was a distance of 720 kilometres over 21 days – a rate of 33 to 35 kilometres a day. This was an even more demanding effort than his mighty stroll from John o' Groats to Land's End. He was following the route taken by Hannibal, the Carthaginian general, in the spring of 218 BC.

***

Botham's courage was unmistakable, especially since he had been nagged by a serious back injury for years. Not long after the walk he underwent surgery. His days of being threatening with the ball seemed over, mainly because of the back problem. Botham did play again in the 1989 Ashes but was ineffective. In 1992 he moved to Durham for their inaugural year of first-class cricket and played his last Test. He retired halfway through the 1993 season.

In 102 Tests he scored 5200 runs at 33.54, including 15 centuries, and took a then world record of 383 wickets at 28.40. He was always an athletic catch, snaffling 120 victims. In first-class cricket he hit 19,399 runs at 33.97, including 38 centuries. His tally of wickets was 1172 at 27.22, and he took 354 catches.

After retirement he even did some pantomime, and became a regular television commentator.

Ian Botham was England's finest all-rounder of the 20th century.

18

'THAT BALL'

Impact Ten: Shane Warne

In 1993, Shane Warne burst onto the international cricket scene with his very first ball in Ashes cricket. It was one of the finest deliveries ever seen. Before that, in 1992, he had already had an impact in winning a Test in Melbourne against the reigning world champions, the West Indies. In that game, he delivered one of the best flippers ever to Richie Richardson. Since those early days in his career he has consistently come up with amazing deliveries that would be unplayable even for Don Bradman at his best. Yet that one delivery at Old Trafford, which bowled Mike Gatting, has immortalised Warne, now regarded by many as the top spinner of all time.

***

Shane Warne, nicknamed 'Hollywood' because of his blond hair and matching flair, began rolling his arms like a butterfly swimmer, then stretching as his captain Allan Border glanced over at him. Moments earlier, after 74 minutes of England's first innings of the opening Test of the Ashes series 1993 at Old Trafford, speedster Merv Hughes had opener Mike Atherton caught behind. This brought the pugnacious Mike Gatting to the wicket to join his skipper Graham Gooch, who looked in command. His team had started well with 1 for 71 following Australia's mediocre innings of 289.

Warne felt a nervous tingle. Border, the on-field general, concentrated so much on the game plan that he rarely made eye contact, unless it meant a bowling change. Paceman Craig McDermott, who had not looked penetrating, finished an over. Border motioned to Warne.

'Warnie, you're on next over', the captain mouthed. Warne took a deep breath as he moved to his position behind square leg. Hughes steamed in for another over and the leg-spinner felt a slight clamminess in the fingers. This was it. He was about to bowl in an Ashes Test for the first time. Border wasn't going to protect him by waiting until the quicks might have broken into the middle order. He was throwing Warne into the front line early to take on two of the best players of spin in cricket.

Gooch took a four and a two off Hughes and the over ended. Gatting would be facing Warne. The gritty Englishman, with his gladiator forearms and nose flattened like the front metal of a Roman helmet, had won a place back in the test team after bludgeoning bowlers in the counties in the first month of the season. He had led England to its last Ashes victory over Australia in 1986–87. Now the 'Gatt' was back to continue where he left off as the Aussie tormentor. He and Gooch had a prearranged plan to destroy Warne. Batsman Graeme Hick had carted Warne all over the riverside field in the opening 1993 tour game under the Norman Cathedral at Worcestershire. That was not a Test, but the intent was the same: belt him into submission.

Warne rolled his arm over to Hughes, who roared a few words of encouragement, more like a football coach than a cricketer. 'Carn, Hollywood, you can do it!' But Hollywood was not thinking about glittering success. He just wanted to get the ball on the pitch on a good length. Border set the field and looked across to see if Warne approved. He scanned the placings, nodded, rubbed his right palm on the grass and began flipping the ball in the air. Gatting settled in, substantial derriere jutting back and face forward, all grim determination. It was that challenging look that caused Warne to focus.

'Pitch it on leg-stump and spin it hard', was the thought on his adrenalin-pumped mind. One last look around the field, a supportive grunt from Hughes, and in. It was a faster swagger to the wicket than normal. Warne dropped his shoulder, trying not to over-pitch. The ball curled with a left to right drift and landed well outside the leg stump in the beginnings of the rough. Gatting lunged forward to block it. The ball darted like a cobra past Gatting's copybook positioning of bat and pads. It clipped the off stump, sending the bail high as keeper Healy leapt in the air with it. The ball had snapped about 58 centimetres. Yet it was the dip and curve that had left the Englishman standing frozen like a statue. He heard the death rattle, but didn't believe it.

Healy rushed the length of the pitch to embrace Warne. Gatting stood there, only making eye contact with the umpires, first at the bowler's end, then at square leg. The look asked, 'Had keeper Healy knocked the stumps? The ball couldn't have done that, could it?'

Neither umpire reacted. There was no raising of the finger for a confirmation of what everyone on the field – apart from the batsman – knew. He had been clean-bowled.

Gatting finally moved, more of a bewildered straggle than a march, back to the pavilion. Only the English manager, Keith Fletcher, dared go near his charge, who was undoing his pads. Gatting was not angry, just stunned.

'What happened?' Fletcher proffered. 'It seemed to spin a yard!'

'I don't know', Gatting responded. 'It must have.'

'Your front pad was . . .'

'I had it covered.'

'It must have hit the rough.'

'It turned all right.'

'It must've spun at least a yard.'

Fletcher added some words of comfort and let Gatting settle down alone in the dressing room.

On the field, Warne's nerves evaporated as Smith took block. If Gatting could club you to death, Smith could go on to a massacre.

He had already done this in a one-dayer, hammering Australia's finest for a record 167 not out. He was fresh and ready to continue that in the Test. Yet there was a problem, perhaps just a tactical one, but a problem nevertheless. Warne had not played in the one-dayer. Smith had not faced a ball from him since 1990 when the leg-spinner was a novice at the Cricket Academy.

Smith blocked the first and crunched a straight drive for four off Warne's second. The English crowd roared their approval. This was more like it. Gooch played out another over at the other end and then Smith faced the spinner again. Smith groped at another ball, which hit the deck more or less in the same spot as that ball to Gatting. It too spun sharply. Instead of cannoning into the stumps, it took the outside edge of the bat and carried to Taylor at slip.

Warne liked this delivery as much as the one that dismissed Gatting and all the glory.

After play that night, the England players came into the Australian dressing room for a drink.

'Bloody hell, Warnie', Gatting said, 'what happened?'

Warne was stuck for words, even a little embarrassed.

'Sorry, mate', Warne said. 'Bad luck.'

The media wanted to know all about *that ball*. England's manager Keith Fletcher remarked: 'It turned three feet comfortably. "Gatt" couldn't believe it, nor could anyone else.'

The quote was recorded in all the papers along with analysis that concentrated on Warne's skill and sudden success. The English team, reading the comments the next morning at breakfast and watching the interminable replays of *that ball* on TV news, was psychologically damaged.

Richie Benaud remarked on BBC TV: 'It's one of the best balls I've ever seen in Test cricket, and I've seen some.' By Sunday two days later, cricket writer Robin Marler in the *Sunday Times* took it a notch further, calling the delivery 'the ball of the century'. Not to be outdone, Richard Williams in the *Independent on Sunday* announced it as 'the best ball ever seen in cricket history'.

The tabloids went even further over the top.

Warne himself, when quizzed about it, said: 'I got a bit lucky with Gatting', and a score of scribes scribbled the immortal words.

Such hype meant that England players would find it hard facing Warne for the rest of the six Test Series.

***

Warne established himself with *that ball* in 1993 as the best spinner in the world, a position he maintained for the next 13 years. He took 34 wickets in the 1993 series. Twelve years later in the great 2005 Ashes (won 2-1 by England), he easily topped the list of wicket-takers for both sides with 40 for the five Test series, and was the one Australian to keep his side in the contest until the last session of the final Test. His ripping leg breaks in 2005, at age 35, were at least as good as he delivered in that 1993 series.

SHANE WARNE:
THE LONG-
RUNNING SOAPIE

Amidst the worst image crisis in Shane Warne's career, he declared his life had become 'like a soap opera'. It was late 1998. He had just been exposed for taking money from an Indian bookie in exchange for match day information – weather and pitch reports – in 1994. Warne loved TV soapies – *Melrose Place* was his favourite. His declaration was a wonderfully disembodied statement, as he was not sure whether he was watching his own life unfold on TV rather than actually living it.

Film star Russell Crowe also saw the dramatic possibilities in Warne. In the 22 March 1999 edition of *Woman's Day*, magazine columnist Peter Ford wrote that the actor was interested in a movie based on my biography of Warne: *Bold Warnie*. Crowe is a big cricket fan and has two cousins, Martin and Jeff Crowe, who were Test players for New Zealand. If the report were true, he would have been excited by Warne's parallel lives on and off the field, similar to a contemporary version of the successful TV drama *Bodyline*. Except that there would be much more off-field drama in *Warnie* than in *Bodyline*. Dramatising the game – especially Test cricket – is notoriously hard. As good as Gary Sweet's performance was playing Don Bradman in *Bodyline*, he could never come remotely close to appearing like him at the crease. Only one player in history, India's Sachin Tendulkar, looked in style, technique and footwork similar to Bradman. But Crowe, a well-built fellow about Warne's size, could play it chunkier if he wished, and probably get away with it if there were a limited number of scenes simulating on-field events. There is no doubt he would have worked hard on attempting to emulate Warne's sliders, flippers, wrong'uns and leg breaks. Perhaps Terry Jenner, or Warne himself, would have coached him.

In *Bodyline*, there was no avoiding the central drama of events on the pitch, with Larwood trying to hit Bradman and other Australian batsman. Events portrayed on the field were minor weaknesses in an otherwise successful production. In fact, it is probably the most successful dramatisation on a sporting theme, along with The Club (about a footy club, written by David Williamson) in the history of drama for film or TV in Australia.

Sweet's Don Bradman was the 'star' of *Bodyline*, and was played as the 'good guy'. By 1999, Warnie had the image of a larrikin, who could be portrayed – at least in the celluloid version of his life – as having been innocently drawn into a demimonde of evil. For an actor like Crowe, then trying to improve his range, Warne must have offered potential. It could have been a long-running soapie, or even a black comedy.

But any thoughts of taking the film/mini-series idea further were shelved when Crowe received two big offers: one where he would fatten up and blond his hair to play a cigarette industry whistle-blower in *The Insider*; the other where he had to muscle up to play the lead role in *Gladiator*, the movie that launched Crowe to super-stardom.

By coincidence, these two roles would have been perfect training in several ways for an intriguing, filmed version of Warne's life.

***

Warne's symbiosis with matters celluloid was evident when, as an unknown 19-year-old semi-professional, he played league cricket in England in 1989. Then, he was taking lots of wickets and developing the kind of deliveries that would later bring him world fame. He was fat – and getting fatter – on junk food and plenty of Aussie beer.

Warne was a hit with the local girls. He seemed like a chubby version of an actor in *Neighbours*, starring Kylie Minogue and Jason Donovan, the Australian soapie that had been a long running hit in England. Most of Britain's viewing public would watch the early-evening show as it soared to new heights of banality, and with it the all-important ratings.

The sanitised series, with its emphasis on sun and hints of sin, had captured the popular imagination. Everywhere Warne went, he was asked about Kylie and Jason as if he had stepped out of the show himself. He seemed like a surfie, although the boy from bayside Melbourne had never been near a board.

Yet it was more than just the look that attracted. Warne had a fun-loving Aussie manner that was idealised in *Neighbours*.

Warne came back to Australia thinking he would make the St Kilda Cricket Club Firsts, but was shocked to find that he had been dumped to the Thirds. The club took one look at his ballooned figure and refused to take him seriously. His weight topped 100 kilograms, which would have challenged Russell Crowe in *The Insider*, or even Robert De Niro playing Jake Lamotta in *Raging Bull*.

This was a devastating moment for Warne. He had flown off to England early in 1989 after failing in a gut-wrenching effort to make the St Kilda Football Club's list. His dream to play top Aussie Rules for the 'Sainters' was over. A hurt Warne overcame the misery by eating and drinking to excess and 'losing' himself in league cricket. This second rejection, by the cricket club, pushed him to a low ebb.

Yet Warne clung to a fading dream: he wanted more than anything else to be a sporting hero. He knew in his heart that he could spin a cricket ball like nobody else. This skill had been seen here and there before his summer in England. It consolidated for the first time when he bowled as he wished on all those village greens.

All through the seminal 1989 summer, Warne had one eye on Allan Border's Australians winning the Ashes. The team had one leg-break bowler – Trevor Hohns – who was useful, but not a match-winner. Warne kept comparing his own efforts and felt he could do better. He hoped to achieve club selection first and then push for the state side.

That scenario now seemed to have been hit for six, even before the home 1989–90 season began. In this down moment, Warne contemplated chucking it all in and playing social cricket with his old school mates. Then he could drink and eat all he liked, and enjoy the game.

Yet, even in the nets, he was well aware that no batsman at St Kilda could handle his ripping deliveries. He decided on one more season. If he didn't progress, he would 'retire' from serious com-petition and become a 'coulda been' champion – someone with unrefined skills having a whack in park cricket.

Underneath those layers of self-indulgence brought on by all the hurt of rejection, Warne had a strong character. St Kilda, like all club cricket teams, moved into the 1990s more conscious of physical fitness. He responded to demands for running and exercising outside games and shed just enough kilograms to show the club he was at least conscientious. Injuries to other players allowed him to slip into the St Kilda Firsts by Christmas 1989. His third game was against Waverly-Dandenong, captained by Test fast bowler Rodney Hogg. After facing a few deliveries from Warne, Hogg remarked: 'This bloke should be in the Test side, turning 'em like that!'

If the comment had come from anyone else but a Test player, it would have been a throwaway line. But Hogg meant it. In 20 years of cricket, he had never seen or faced any spinner as gifted as Warne. In any other era, these words would have drifted into the ether to be lost forever.

***

Enter Allan Border, Australian Test captain. This honest, solid, determined individual had spent the past five years dragging the national team out of the doldrums of one of its worst periods in history. Border wished to take Australia to the top. He was looking to beat the West Indies and win the world cricket crown. Border couldn't match the Caribbean champions with speed. It had to be spin.

Word about Warne spread fast. Border heard about him. Victoria was urged to fast-track him into the state squad. Its manager, Bill Lawry, obliged. Warne had taken only a handful of wickets at club level. But by the end of the 1989–90 season he was chosen for the Australian Institute of Sports Cricket Academy for the 1990 winter. It was too quick for Warne. He responded poorly to the advanced fitness training, pinch tests, diets, restricted nightclub hours and discipline. Warne walked out before he was thrown out. The main black mark against the 20-year-old was that while on tour in Darwin, he insulted three women by a hotel pool when a prank backfired. The fast-tracking had been too fast for an immature 'Jack the lad'.

In other decades this incident may have seen Warne stamped as too hot to handle. He would have been ostracised. But Border wanted a top leggie in his armoury. He knew they matured 'late' (in the performance-on-the-field sense) and were better bowlers at 30 than 20. The Australian skipper and the selectors would not wait. If Warne could produce anything like that elusive 'potential', there would be a place for him in the Test side. He made the state team by default towards the end of the 1990–91 season.

Rather than take jobs delivering pizzas and working in retail stores (which were not altogether successful ventures for him) as before, Warne spent another season – 1991 – in professional cricket, this time in the Lancashire league. This was followed by a tour to Zimbabwe in an Australian Second XI captained by Mark Taylor. Warne was under scrutiny, and in competition with another leggie, Peter McIntyre. Both performed well, Warne taking a career best of 7 for 49 in a first-class game. He had proved he could be a destroyer, and in front of Taylor and a national selector, John Benaud.

***

India was touring Australia in 1991–92. Border and Co dearly wanted to groom a spinner in this Test series, with one eye on the following season against the West Indies. The Australian prime minister, Bob Hawke, colluded with national selectors and Border in selecting Warne in his XI to play a one-day game against the West Indies. The alacrity of Warne's rise without a trace of sustained wicket-taking ability was too much for the Victorian state selectors, who reckoned that he had not justified a place on merit. There was tension between state selectors and frustrated national selectors who by-passed the state and put Warne in a team to play the West Indies at Hobart late in 1991. He acquitted himself well against the West Indian stars, taking 7 for 56 over the two innings. He troubled the big names such as Lara and Richardson. It was enough. A tubby 95 kilogram Warne, at 22, was selected to play against India in the Third Test at the SCG, scheduled to start on New Year's Day 1992.

Warne threw a party at his parents' home and celebrated hard. The next morning he was driven, hung over, by his father to the ACB for a baggy green cap fitting. The media wanted to interview him. Warne asked the ACB to stall them while he threw up in the toilet.

This marked the end of his pre-Test career as an unknown, happy-go-lucky bloke, and the beginning of a life in the limelight.

***

Warne flew to Sydney on New Year's Eve and was looked after by Geoff Marsh. The dry, steady-nerved opening bat, David Boon (the team's beer drinking champion), and big fast-bowler, Merv Hughes (the team's ear-kissing clown and pest), provided relief and relaxed him a little.

Warne's nerves were eased by Australia batting first. He ran the edginess out of himself, making 20 runs in an invaluable 72 minutes at the wicket. No amount of counselling – if there had been any – cajoling or boosting could have been as useful as this effort with the bat. He was terribly nervous when he came on to bowl for the first time in big cricket. Leg-spinners are notorious for rotten starts. The palms ooze sweat, the fingers grip the ball too hard. Half-track deliveries and even wides are not uncommon in first-up performances.

Yet he still managed to deliver steadily enough, drawing some qualified praise from the great leggie, Bill O'Reilly: in a Fairfax newspaper article, he welcomed Warne into the Leg-spinner's Club. The only problem was the fact that Warne ran into a rampant India. Its batsmen gained the ascendancy. All bowlers, including Warne, suffered at the hands of Ravi Shastri (205) and brilliant teenager Sachin Tendulkar (148 not out).

Warne ended with the ignoble figures of 1 for 150.

But he didn't sulk or make excuses. He remained cheerful. Border admired his pluck and decided to persevere.

At the end of the 1991–92 season, blunt-talking team coach Bob Simpson told Warne to lose at least 10 kilograms or he would be discarded. (A decade later, Simpson would give the same brutal message to another champion, England's Andrew Flintoff.)

Warne was sent back to the Cricket Academy under Rod Marsh and put through a gruelling routine straight out of *Rocky*. Warne responded, shed the weight and emerged looking like a rock-hard Sylvester Stallone – without the lisp. Warne's Teutonic good looks of green eyes and fair locks (his mother, Brigitte, was an immigrant from post-war Germany) emerged more prominently.

The new Warne played Tests in Sri Lanka and dismissed three tail-enders for a few runs to win a Test. But it wasn't enough to convince selectors that he had 'the goods'. He missed out on the first Test of the all-important series versus the West Indies in the home 1992–93 season. Border asked publicly for his return to the national XI and he was selected to play in the Boxing Day Test at the MCG. On the last day, he provided great sporting drama by delivering one of the best balls in years – a magnificent flipper that bowled an in-form Richie Richardson.

Warne went on in that MCG match against the West Indies to take 7 for 52 and Australia won. He was a match-winner at 23 years and had justified the faith Border and others had shown in him. It was the real moment of arrival for the leg-spinner, and a counterpoint to the bad old days of the fun-loving jester.

Warne now had a certain stardom, and was given free drinks cards at bars in Melbourne's posh South Yarra. The glitter attracted the sorts of people he liked – including curvaceous blondes like stunning Simone Callahan. She was a female mirror image of Warne. They fell instantly 'in like', in a manner American film director Woody Allen would have thrived upon. Warne secured Simone's telephone number, then promptly lost it. But he couldn't get her out of his mind. They met again, and this time he made sure he called her. They quickly became an 'item'.

***

Meanwhile, back on he field, Border plotted his next big use of Warne – in the 1993 Ashes in England – with more thought, style and intrigue than a John Le Carre espionage novel. The skipper hid Warne during the lead-up to the Tests, and when he did play, he only bowled his stock leg-break. When Border unleashed him in the Tests, Warne's first ball – a leg-break to England's Mike Gatting – was one of the greatest deliveries ever seen.

'That ball', as it became known (see previous chapter), was replayed so often that England was demoralised from the series' beginning. Warne went on to dominate the Ashes with 34 wickets at 25.7 runs a wicket. Australia won 4-1. Off-field, the British media decided that Warne was its pin-up for the summer. The papers and magazines chased, photographed and wrote about him ad nauseam. Warne was dubbed a single, eligible Adonis in the glossies. The grubbier papers found stories of romance. Warne's Melbourne girl-friend, Simone, turned up in England to ward off the competition, real or imagined. Warne asked her to marry him and they became engaged. The media, unfazed, changed step, took him off the stud list and beat up different angles, such as 'How Simone Tamed Her Man'.

Warne continued to perform on the field, but by his own admission he began a period in 1994 as a 'bighead'. His success caused an on-field arrogance that culminated in him abusing South African bat

Andrew Hudson as he left the Wanderers field after being dismissed. Warne was fined and reprimanded.

***

The year 1994 marked also the beginning of another dramatic, more 'film noir' theme in Warne's life. He was gambling at a casino in Colombo, Sri Lanka when approached by an Indian bookie named 'John'. By this time Warne, earning more than A$400,000 with his ACB contract, plus triple that from ads and endorsements, had developed a big betting habit. Wherever he was, he headed for the garish, glittering casinos with mates such as Mark Waugh, another big punter.

This may have been the part of Warne's story that gripped Russell Crowe the most. Warne, the big-spending gambler and sports star, was set up for a sting by an illegal bookmaking ring controlled by the main Indian 'mafia'. Warne and Mark Waugh seemed like perfect targets. Both were match-winners who could swing games by individual efforts. If they could be controlled to fix matches, huge money could be wagered and won. First, there would be the hook.

Warne was introduced to 'John', the Indian bookie, in a dimly lit casino behind the Oberoi Hotel. Peter Sellers would have played him brilliantly, as he grovelled to, fawned on and flattered Warne with lines such as, 'Oh, Mr Warne, you are my very favourite cricketer, the best. I love the way you play'.

The Indian looked on as Warne dropped US$5000 at the roulette table. The next day he invited Warne to his hotel room and continued the feigned sycophancy, telling him he was 'his biggest fan'. Then he shoved an envelope into his hand, saying: 'Here is a token of my appreciation'.

Warne gave the money back. 'John' returned it. 'Please take it', the Indian insisted. After a moment of to-ing and fro-ing, Warne took the money. It was the bait. Warne would now feel some obligation to 'John'. And the US$5000? Warne blew it at roulette that night.

Here, the *Neighbours/Melrose Place* soapie turned into more of a thriller, with major ramifications in real life. Soon after, Australia played Pakistan in a Test at Karachi, beginning 28 September 1994.

Enter, 'the Rat' – Salim Malik – the 'baddie' in the story. He had been so nicknamed because, as Warne later told a Pakistani court, some of the Australians thought he looked like the said rodent. His subsequent behaviour had cricketers suggesting Malik was 'as flash as a rat with a gold tooth'.

Malik was Pakistan's best bat and the link to the Indian under-world in fixing cricket matches. Aware that Warne was 'hooked', he rang him at the Pearl Continental Hotel where they were both staying and invited him to his room. It was 10.30 on the night before the vital last day of the Test, which was poised on a knife-edge.

At that meeting, Malik suggested that Warne and Tim May, Warne's room-mate, should bowl badly and thus deliver the game to Pakistan – for US$200,000. Warne returned to his room and discussed it with May. They both agreed to reject the proposal. Warne rang Malik and told him that he and May rejected the offer. Malik told him he was making a 'mistake'. Warne told him to go forth and receive fornication.

The next day, Pakistan needed 157 to win with 3 wickets in hand. The game swung this way and that and was won by Pakistan by 1 wicket. Warne gave it everything, taking 5 for 89 and winning the man-of-the-match award.

That night at the hotel, Malik ran into Warne and told him: 'You were stupid [not taking the money]. You lost'. Warne reminded the Pakistani that his team had been very lucky. Malik again chided him over the money.

In a Hollywood script, the Rat would make a duck in the next Test at Rawalpindi, Australia would go on to win the three Test series, and justice would be done. But this was real life. Malik made a brilliant 237 in the Second Test, which was drawn, as was the third.

Malik's in-your-face bribery attempts continued. Having failed with Warne, he now went after Mark Waugh, the other player 'hooked'. Waugh also gave Malik short shrift when he offered him, his brother Steve, Warne and May US$50,000 each (again, a US$200,000 attempted bribe) to throw a one-day match.

During the 1994–95 summer of Ashes Tests in Australia (won 3-1 by the home team, Warne taking a hat-trick at Melbourne), Warne and Waugh were rung by 'John' who wanted weather and pitch reports. Clearly, the bookies felt that they could still manipulate them, despite their rejections of Malik's bribery overtures. But early in 1995, the story of the attempted bribery was brought to the attention of the ACB. Officials swept it all under the carpet to protect the careers of two of its superstars.

Salim Malik was, for the first time, named as the 'bad boy' of international cricket – and accused by the Australians. In secret, Warne and Waugh confessed to the ACB that they had taken money from 'John'. They were fined the equivalent of the money they had been given. The issue was covered up. It was now a ticking time bomb. So many people knew of the incident that it was bound to be made public, some day.

***

Back on the field, this time in the Caribbean, Warne was an important part of the team that beat the West Indies for the first time in 29 Test series and 15 years. He had been vital to Australia's revival following the dark days of the mid-1980s.

Warne married Simone a few days short of his 26th birthday in September 1995, and then prepared for another round with Malik and the Pakistanis, who arrived in Australia in late 1995. Malik made no effort to confront his accusers. During the games, the Australians snubbed him on the field, even refusing to 'sledge' him. This 'cold shoulder' treatment caused Malik to say to an umpire, 'Nice to have someone to talk to'.

***

In 1996, hampered by nagging injuries, Warne had to decide which went under the knife first: his spinning finger or his shoulder. He chose the finger and he was a late starter in the 1996–97 season against the West Indies.

It was worrying for Warne. If his finger didn't recover well, his career would be over. He did everything right in rehabilitation, overcame the operation and was back starring in Australia's 3-2 second successive series win over the West Indies. That season spilled into another in South Africa in early 1997, then a further Ashes tour of England. Warne, the pin-up boy of 1993, was now under attack by the fickle English media. They were sick of his grip over England and tried everything they could to lower his morale by putting down his skills and ignoring any of his good form. Sections of crowds turned nasty; Warne was abused. Mark Taylor, the skipper, was ridiculed for his poor form.

The Australians began badly, losing the one-day series 3-0 and the First Test. Warne and the rest of the team were struggling. They drew at Lord's. He was distracted by the birth of his daughter, Brooke, during June, but prepared well for the Third Test at Old Trafford, Manchester. Australia began to fight back, with Steve Waugh scoring a gutsy century in each innings. Warne ran into form. All his histrionics returned. There was the confident body language; the querying looks down the wicket; the stroking of the chin as he considered that batsman's efforts against him; the grins, the frowns and grimaces; the charges down the wicket to appeal; the chit-chat with keeper Ian Healy ('You were right about that, Heals'); and the chirpy remarks for the ears of the batsman at the other end ('Bit of a turner now').

He returned 6 for 38 from 30 overs and, with Waugh, won the match. Warne suffered fearful abuse at Taunton versus Somerset – with references to his weight and sexuality – from a group of profane, unfunny morons. Acting skipper Steve Waugh threatened to take his team from the field if it continued. The offenders were evicted.

Australia went on to win the next two Tests at Leeds and Trent Bridge, and took the series and the Ashes. Warne celebrated by doing the 'dance of the derriere' on the balcony in response to the continued abuse from spectators. It was twisted by the English media into a dance of derision for the vanquished foe languishing in the dressing room below. The photos went out across the cricket world. Warne was portrayed as an arrogant gloater. The accusations were wrong on both counts – Warne was never arrogant in victory – but the impression would stay in the public mind.

***

Undaunted, Warne returned to Australia for the 1997–98 season to take on the Kiwis and South Africa, where he reached the heights, taking 39 wickets in six Tests, and raced through to 300 wickets for his career. He lifted particularly for the Proteas who, for the Australians, were the most competitive team next to the West Indies. Warne kept his batting 'bunny' Darryl Cullinan contained in his hutch, beat Hansie Cronje and demoralised the South Africans.

When the selectors decided to pick 'horses for courses' in their one-day side, they dumped Mark Taylor, and made Steve Waugh captain and Warne his deputy. Steve was injured and Warne showed his prowess as a leader. The style was pure Aussie Rules, as he exhorted his players to 'put in' and led with infectious enthusiasm. Australia rocked the Proteas by beating them 2-1 in the finals. Warne, as usual, came on to take telling wickets at vital moments. Had he reached his zenith on the cricket field? It was difficult to imagine him, or any spinner, ever doing better.

If Warne thought he had been through some character tests in the past, they were nothing compared to the next year. It began in April 1998 with a thumping from Sachin Tendulkar in India in Tests and one-dayers, and the decision he had been dreading and putting off for years: surgery for his shoulder.

No one in big sport, from javelin throwers to footballers, had ever recovered to perform as well as before this particular operation. Most had faded away. Warne had the operation in June and weeks later began the long, demanding rehabilitation. He put off his return to cricket until he could truly make it. In early games he was tentative about letting his re-made shoulder 'rip'.

If that were not enough tension for one mind, he had another pressure to contend with in December 1998 when it was learned that he and Mark Waugh had taken money from bookies for match-day information on the weather and pitches back in 1994. The media came down heavily on Warne in particular. He was in line to captain the country in Tests and was already filling in often for Steve Waugh as leader of the one-day team. Critics demanded that he never be made captain of Australia's Test team.

In the middle of all this his second child, a son, was born. A day later, he was selected to make his comeback for Australia in the Fifth Test of 1998–99 Ashes at Sydney. It was at this moment that Warne made the remark, 'my life has become like a soap opera in recent times'.

In one sense, it was good for him that he saw events this way. Life was episodic; there would always be up days and down days. For the moment, he ignored the media and focused on his comeback.

A packed crowd on day one at the SCG early in 1999 was thrilled to see Mark Taylor bring Warne on before lunch. There was tension all round as he waddled in for his flat-footed three-step walk-up. Then followed the little quick step to his delivery stride and finally, the mighty shoulder heave and hip rotation accompanied by that familiar grunt of strained effort as the ball whirred on its way.

Warne did make the first breakthrough in each England innings at Sydney. But a cruel fact was clear. He was a shadow of his former self. It had little to do with the off-field furore swirling around him. Either his shoulder had not come up the way everyone hoped, or he had lost 'it'. For Warne, 'it' was the amazing power to turn a cricket ball – or send down a different ball if needed – for every delivery in an over. But none of this was happening. His famed 'drift' in the air was not there. To make his appearance worse, fellow leg-spinner

Stuart MacGill was turning the ball square and taking wickets the way Warne used to. The champion was feeling redundant and the media was reminding him of it every day.

What must have struck Russell Crowe was the pure drama surrounding Warne at this time, when he was down and almost out.

He was still news, even when he was sidelined or not taking wickets. And just to make sure he was on the back and front pages, and the lead item on the nightly TV news, Mark Taylor stood down as Test skipper, leaving the way open for a new leader. Steve Waugh looked certain to take over. But Warne – on the canvas for the count in December – was up and challenging through January 1999. By chance Waugh was injured, leaving Warne to lead the one-day side in several matches. He performed well, not losing a game and leading with aplomb.

Off the field, the bribery and corruption scandal was hotting up. Pakistan was investigating its own players and needed testimony from Warne, Mark Waugh and Tim May, who had been approached by Malik. This led to a Pakistani courtroom being set up in downtown Melbourne, complete with a picture of Mohammad Ali Jinnah, the founder of Pakistan, and prayers to 'Almighty Allah'. Now the long-running soap-cum-thriller had another dimension – the ever-useful dramatic counterpoint of a court. It was more colourful and combative than anything contrived on *Law and Order*.

Pakistani lawyers grilled the players. They seemed more intent on proving the Australians were corrupt than on enlightening the investigation regarding the criminal activities of Malik and Co. Under pressure, Warne was pure Warne – direct, ingenious and confident. He was neither disrespectful nor genuflecting towards the aggressive interrogation. He came out of it well and more indignant about his own position. He had been forced by his employer, the ACB, to say he was 'naive and stupid' when he would rather have defended his actions.

Warne was not thrilled about the way he and Mark Waugh had been portrayed. After all, he pointed out, he had never been involved in match fixing. He should have been painted as heroic for exposing Malik's nefarious activities.

This kept Warne on the front pages. If you missed him there, he could be seen in TV ads for Nike, 'just doing it'. If you only read papers, he was also there in advertisements for the company making patches to prevent smoking. Warne's on-field efforts, courtroom appearances, battle for the captaincy and constant media attention assured advertisers of maximum exposure. During all of this, Warne vowed to give up smoking for the sake of his family – for a tidy sum of A$250,000. No one bothered to ask him why he needed to be 'bribed' into giving up his little vice if he was concerned for his family's health.

***

Warne lobbied openly for the captaincy. He did not utter any of the usual hypocrisy and false modesty about how he felt about the job and his capacity to do it. He wanted it. But in the end, Steve Waugh was appointed and Warne became his deputy. Their first assignment together was a tough one in the Caribbean.

Warne's form deteriorated during the Tests. Waugh was forced to drop his deputy for the last game at Antigua, making the hurtful remark that the vice-captaincy was 'just a title'. Healy was the player whose advice he valued most. The resultant stress from his first dumping since 1992 drove Warne back to cigarettes. He was caught in photographs at a nightclub like a naughty boy behind a shelter-shed. Warne was ropable about his dismissal. Yet he faced the fact that the only way back was to find form.

He did this to a degree in the one-day series that followed the tied 2-all Test series. He was the player of the competition, despite the official award going to Sherwin Campbell.

***

The Australian team flew on to England for the 1999 World Cup and performed poorly early. Warne took fearful hammerings in some games, soon after the News of the World ran a story: 'Cricket Ace Warne's Games With Wicket Maiden'. The tabloids were at it again, trying to unsettle Warne with a beat-up about his alleged affair with 'porn star Kelly Handley'.

It was the last formula ingredient, except for religion and drugs, missing from the Warne scenario. This time, the media caused Warne serious concern. His confidence on the field, up in the one-dayers in the Caribbean, had been shredded. Now, this unwanted attention off the field put pressure of a more personal kind on him. Warne wanted to throw in the towel. It was too much. Then skipper Steve Waugh took him for a long walk in Kensington Gardens near the team's London hotel.

The captain cajoled his star spinner into playing on in the World Cup. After the rejection in the West Indies and Waugh's insensitivity this was the correct approach. Warne believed he was wanted. He came back late in the tournament to be a star and earned man-of-the-match awards as Australia streaked to a win. Despite epitaphs written by a hopeful British media, he returned with all the vengeance of Clint Eastwood in one of his Westerns. His form allowed him to nose in front of the unlucky MacGill for a Test spot in Sri Lanka and Zimbabwe in August and September 1999. His form held and he retained his place for the summer of 1999–2000.

***

Warne lifted for the big contests, especially in the greatest of all in pure cricket terms – versus his old nemesis, Sachin Tendulkar. Warne used every ounce of experience and ability to dismiss the world champion bat in the Second Test against India in Melbourne. In doing so, he gained revenge against one of three outstanding bats to give him an even tussle (the other two being Brian Lara and Salim Malik) in nearly a decade as the world's finest spin bowler. In New Zealand, he broke Dennis Lillee's Australian wicket-taking record of 355 victims and looked set for 100 more.

Right at the end of the long run of games from September 1999 to April 2000, the match-fixing scandal blew up. South African captain Hansie Cronje was accused by the Indian police of corruption. Further stories of murder and bribery emerged. The Pakistani government was prompted in late May 2000 to allow the release of the investigation by the brave justice Malik Mohammed Qayyum. In it, Salim Malik was found guilty and banned from playing cricket for life.

Salim Malik was the main culprit, the Qayyum report noted. 'There is clear evidence of match fixing against him. He has brought the Pakistani national team into disrepute.' At last, the courage shown by Warne, Waugh and Tim May (there had been murders in this saga) had brought justice to the game, or perhaps the business of cricket.

This would be a fitting end for any soap, drama or thriller concerning Warne. But it was only the year 2000. There were at least another seven years of episodes in the story, during which Warne would be still playing top cricket.

***

Any thespian's range would be tested by Warne's behaviour as reported in yet another British tabloid exposé during the 2000 cricket season in England. This time, the London *Mirror* newspaper bought the story of a nurse, Donna Wright, who had met Warne at a Leicester nightclub. She claimed that he left her several lewd mobile phone messages after she rejected his overtures for a dalliance. Who flirted with whom first was in contention. As Warne's biographer, I was interviewed on Channel 9's *Today* program by Tracey Grimshaw. I suggested the issue was clouded by the fact that Ms Wright sold her story to the newspapers and did not go to the police. This discounted the possibility of harassment by Warne and threw the story into the realms of sleazy beat-up. I further suggested, after conducting my own interviews with the *Mirror*'s editors, that they seemed to have a vendetta against Warne. The *Mirror*'s tenacious editors and reporters would stalk him whenever he landed in England. It had become a common occurrence now that he was a Hampshire county player.

This Donna Wright 'issue' had the potential to tarnish the heroic image of Warne once and for all. In Peter Weir's *The Truman Show*, every moment, utterance and peccadillo of a naive man is caught on camera for a vast audience. Watching the film, you squirm for Truman at the intrusion, the embarrassment and the exposure. He doesn't know he is on TV every moment of his life. The exposure Warne received was as near as modern technology will allow to Truman's experience. The big difference with Warne was that he knew. In effect, Warne is Truman, and he knows it.

When the pressure was on, he withdrew to a transparent bubble with everyone looking in. His method with the Wright issue was to dig in and slip into 'denial' mode, his only way of 'handling' the media. He had lived in the bubble for more than a decade, ever since moving from the 'real world' into the 'unreal' one. In effect, he transferred from the school locker room to the locker rooms of the travelling circus that is cricket without much of a reality check. Warne had never held down a conventional job. In this unreal but affluent world, he became hooked on hotels, nightclubs, junk food, fast women, video games and gambling. The insulating bubble was sustained by a mainly fawning media at worst and a fickle one at best. It needed him for good copy. Those who criticised him were on his black list. For a time, only grovellers were given a hearing. They helped him feel comfortable in the bubble. And Warne always knew that one more terrific performance on the pitch would make other calamities in his life appear to fade.

***

Several more episodes vied for any film-script writer's attention. Some had an eerily familiar ring, especially the sexual encounters. But what would the scribe leave out? Certainly not the infamous tale of how Warne's mum Brigitte gave him a prescription-only slimming pill to help him look good for a media conference in which he announced his retirement from one-day cricket. The drug showed up in a random test on Warne in late 2002. This was just before the World Cup in South Africa early in 2003.

The family angle would be too human to edit from the soapie. The consumed pill happened to be a masking agent commonly taken to hide the use of steroids. As the ACB investigated, Warne lived with the prospect that he could receive a two-year ban from all cricket. In the end, the ACB decided he was 'half pregnant'. He wasn't a drug cheat, it found, but he was guilty of taking a banned substance.

Just as with the cash-for-match-day-information scandal, Warne was in the dock again. He received a one-year ban. Warne's supporters – among them Victorian state coach, David Hookes – said he was an innocent victim. Most of the media condemned him and were keen to write off his career. On ABC's *The 7.30 Report* in an interview with Kerry O'Brien, I maintained that he would again come back better and stronger after the enforced 'rest'. Warne was the Teflon sportsman of the age. The public, especially cricket fans with chronic short-term memory loss, would forget Warne's transgressions as soon as he started taking wickets.

The unscheduled lay-off meant Warne had lots of idle time, much of which he spent in his home film suite watching videos of his great cricket performances and playing video games. He also took the opportunity to train and work hard at building up his fitness.

But he was soon back in the headlines with another alleged 'scandal'. It appeared that Warne could well be the subject of a scam, this time a sexual one coming out of South Africa. A 45-year-old Cape Town woman, Helen Cohen Alon, claimed that she had been sexually harassed by Warne over the phone (what else?). It was called 'phone sex'. For those uninitiated in such terminology, this is not a form of bestiality with an inanimate object. It refers to extreme, even lewd, expressions of desire transmitted via a mobile phone. Ms Alon had been busy trying to sell her story around the world for a reported US$250,000 to US$500,000. There were nibbles of reduced offers but no takers.

A few factors made the brunette and her tale appear suspect. For a start, Warne had never been seen with other than a shapely blonde. Nor had he ever shown an interest in older women. The less than alluring Ms Alon didn't realise that these kinds of allegations were common, although she was aware that South African female predators had a history of predetermined schemes to blackmail celebrities. (One recent example was the plan to ensnare Manchester United soccer club's manager, Sir Alex Ferguson.) It's probable that Warne left her a suggestive message. It was his style. And perhaps she lured him into something more. But he did not physically have sex with her. Judging from Ms Alon's demeanour and endeavours, there is much to be said for Warne's discretion. This time, for the first time, the media and press supported him.

David Hookes publicly supported Warne, and called Ms Alon 'a dopey hairy-backed sheila'. This did nothing to raise the debate in the media nor to illuminate the issue. Hookes, who had become a media personality by shooting from the lip, incurred the wrath of federal Sex Discrimination Commissioner Pru Goward, Victorian Premier Steve Bracks and cricket commentator Tony Greig, who two lives ago (before England and Australia) was born and raised in South Africa.

Hookes apologised, explaining that 'hairy-back' was an expression used by English-speaking South Africans to insult Afrikaners. This brought more blokey guffaws but did serve to diffuse the issue for Warne. From then on, Ms Alon was seen as the culprit, and Warne the victim.

Inspired by Ms Alon's try, a 38-year-old Melbourne stripper, blonde and shapely, and therefore far more credible than Ms Alon, rushed to a magazine – *New Idea* – to tell her breathless tale of romance with Warne and his naughty phone calls.

This exotic dancer and mother of two claimed that apart from the usual frenetic phone intercourse, she had actually indulged in some exotic dancing with Warne – and not vertically either.

'My husband and I had been separated for seven months', she said, 'and Shane gave me the attention I'd been craving. It was nice to have someone interested in me – and he had a very overwhelming presence.'

This tawdry episode did nothing for Warne's marriage to the long-suffering Simone.

***

The year's lay-off, during which Warne worked hard on his fitness, was the best thing that could have happened to his career. All the old injuries to shoulder and fingers had more time to heal. Warne gradually became confident enough to try all his bowling repertoire – including the flipper, and even the wrong'un, that put so much pressure on his shoulder. He began to take bags of wickets at a higher rate than before the enforced lay-off.

Now, while nothing had ever gone 'smoothly' in Warne's life or career, the main publicity up until early 2005 appeared favourable as Warne attempted to rehabilitate himself with a solid public relations campaign. Channel 9 sought to help and protect its investment in him with favourable stories on its high-rating Sunday night show *Sixty Minutes*, and in its sister magazine *Woman's Weekly*.

Warne was depicted as the reformed family man, happily enjoying life with Simone and their three kids.

His retirement from one-day international cricket allowed him to start his 2005 season with Hampshire in April, which would be a useful preparation for the much-publicised Ashes in England. His openness about his mild hair-loss problem was aired in TV ads for a hair-replacement company, with a cute segment with former England captain Graham Gooch. His phone rings and he tells Warne it's for him.

It came across as harmless fun. Yet it was soon a case of life imitating advertisements. Warne could not resist temptation, and was a recidivist when it came to a certain style of blonde, busty English lass and leaving messages on mobiles. London has a whole class of these women who float around the West End clubs, bars and party scenes in search of a good time and big spenders. In this respect, nothing much has changed in London since Shakespeare's time.

Warne and other top sportsmen/celebrities had a certain attraction for them. There was always a chance, too, for women to flog lurid stories of innuendo and sleaze to the tabloids. The *Mirror* was a willing party when it came to their long-term target and enemy, Shane Warne. Predictably, another 'hot' story surfaced about sex on car bonnets and other places of quick access.

This was just before Simone arrived at Southampton with their three kids – perfect timing by the antagonists at the *Mirror* with their aim to do maximum harm to Warne's private life, and to disrupt Australia's Ashes plans.

Simone arrived to a barrage of media reports. It was the last straw. She turned around and took the kids back to Melbourne and the Brighton home they had been attempting to sell. Simone now wanted a divorce. Warne was devastated. Yet somehow, through some strong stress management and focus, he was able to overcome his troubles and perform at his peak in the Ashes, taking a magnificent 40 wickets for under 20 runs each. On top of that, he batted better than he had for years. It was another unpredictable twist in the Warne saga. Long before the Ashes were over, Warne's amazing skills and supreme performances were being beamed into a billion homes around the world in a way that would swamp the negative publicity generated by his marital problems and bimbo hunts. He was back in the super-fame 'bubble' he loved so much, where he was insulated from attacks and reality. Warne had quickly regained the admiration of the public, especially sports loving blokes in England and Australia, who cheered him on.

This caused his enemies down at the *Mirror* to gnash their teeth. Not only had Warne almost kept the Ashes for Australia single-handedly; he had become a sentimental favourite with the British public, as popular as the great Andrew Flintoff himself.

Their schemes to bring down the champion had failed. Could they find a retrospective 'beat-up'? The tried and trusted pious angle – that Warne was a serial cheater on his wife – had evaporated since Simone's departure and pronouncements on separation. Reaching for new heights of banal invention, the tabloids – this time the *Sun* joined in – found a woman who claimed that she had cavorted all night with him. The night of blissful debauchery, she alleged, exhausted him. This led to Warne being dismissed for a duck in Australia's first innings of the Fourth Test – caught off a leading edge by Bell in the covers off Jones.

She was proud and pleased to have played her part in winning the Ashes for England, she said. No doubt she was also pleased with the cheque from a grateful tabloid.

In a further TV interview with Tracey Grimshaw, five years after the *Mirror*'s Donna Wright beat-up, I pointed out the silliness of the new attack. I also explained that Warne was often dismissed early in an innings by being caught in the covers off a leading edge. Unless the tabloid was suggesting that women of easy virtue were often doing their bit for England and other opposition this way, the story was a nonsense.

The *Mirror*'s feverish pursuit of Warne would not have helped him if he had any hope of reconciliation with Simone. Yet it would provoke not outrage from the public, but distaste for the tedious tabloid obsessions with him. This kind of story would be largely ignored from then on. Proof of this was the spate of two-paragraph Warnie-accompanied-by-mystery-blonde items in social and sports columns in Australia after the 2005 Ashes. Nevertheless, in England there was another story, this time in the *News of the World*, another assiduous follower of Warne's bimbo hunt and antics. In May 2006 he was pictured cavorting with two blondes, again set up by a tabloid tormentor. Yet he had the temerity to gain a contract to advertise a mobile phone company. Perhaps he was also contemplating the promotion of slimming pills. He did continue the promotion of hair replacement in TV ads and charmed everyone, even experienced director/cinematographer Rob Copping, who has seen prima donnas come and go through many feature and documentary films.

Bold Warnie had never been bolder.

***

The real challenge would be how to end this soapie. A Hollywood ending might be appropriate for a tragi-comedy. Warne goes on chasing blondes. In early 2006, he also 'acts' himself in *Neighbours*, which presents a wonderful symmetry from the days in England when he acted out his own fantasy video. Simone starts a new life as a TV star, including a celebrity job interviewing during Melbourne Cup Week and a spelling competition on Channel 7, pointedly the 9 Network's main rival. She didn't do terribly well to begin with. But who could blame her for spelling phlegm as flem, especially under the lights and in front of cameras reaching a vast TV audience? Perhaps she was thinking of the former Australian fast bowler Damien Fleming, known as 'Flem'. Her several misspellings did her no harm. She is attractive, with a neat figure and pleasant nature, which is just right for the medium that is suspicious of people who have faces creased from the pressures of deep thought. No one really ever loved a smart-ass on TV, except for Barry Jones, who was once Australia's prime-time superstar mainly because he was a comfy, teddy bear of an intellectual, and unthreatening. Channel 7 expanded Simone's profile by putting her on *Dancing with the Stars*. She is now a star who has risen with hardly a trace.

A happy ending and twist for Warne could have him continuing to take bags of wickets and helping to win back the Ashes in Australia in 2006–07, then 2009 in England. Perhaps he takes his 1000th wicket to win the Ashes and then retires.

But hold the phone. It's way too early. If any producer wished to adapt this amazing sportsman's biography to any screen, large or small, they should forget it for the time being. The story of Shane Warne, master spinner and media personality, has plenty of episodes to come.

STEVE WAUGH
AND TWIN
TROUBLES

Twins Steve and Mark Waugh were not like peas in a pod. They were more like one pea split in two. Mark was flamboyant in style and nature. He was the one with the ready hand of friendship with people he didn't know and a jaunty, 'Hi, I'm Mark Waugh'. Steve, as he matured, was the serious one, more closed off and wary of too much public contact. Mark was the single man who preferred race-tracks, beers with mates and gambling – not just on horses, but on the proverbial fly crawling up the wall too. He enjoyed his embar-rassingly fat cricket salary for a single man with no responsibilities. Steve was the opposite, marrying young, squirrelling and investing money as if fearful that any moment he would be dumped and banished from such riches. Mark batted like a cavalier, a swordsman with flair. He cared little for the big scores, and never went beyond 153 in a Test. He was the player for the cameo – a 60 or 70 in less than a session was good enough for him, although he showed excep-tional guts and application on the rare occasions he was needed to stay for a win or a draw. Steve was all guts and application, even if nothing hinged on it. He batted always as if his life depended on staying at the wicket. Steve hated getting out, and mid-career changed his attitude and technique to lessen the chances of being dismissed. Flamboyance of any kind was eliminated. He refused to loft the ball. He even gave away thoughts of the hook or pull with its attendant risk of a mistimed catch. Only late in his career did he

306

introduce the dicey slog-sweep shot. And then only in one-dayers to start with.

Match-day madness

When rumours circulated in the mid-1990s about one of the Waugh brothers being involved in some sort of money deal with a dodgy Indian bookie, no one wondered if it was Steve. Everyone knew it had to be Mark. He haunted casinos where these hail-fellow-well-met criminals would hang out. Shane Warne was one betting mate with the same predilections. They were immature lads with more money than sense looking for adrenalin rushes off the cricket field. While Steve was diligently making more money writing diaries in his hotel room, or changing a baby's nappy, Mark was looking for ways to lose what he had. There was always more coming, as long he stayed in the Australian team. But suddenly, early in 1995, Mark Waugh's hedonist lifestyle – to which he had become accustomed – was in jeopardy.

Just before the Australians took off for the West Indies for a make-or-break series that would decide who was the top dog in cricket, the team captain Mark Taylor called the Waugh brothers, Shane Warne and vice captain Ian Healy to a meeting.

Taylor informed Healy and Steve that Mark and Warne might be dumped from the tour. They had been giving information over the phone to Indian bookies they had met in a Colombo, Sir Lanka hotel casino in the previous year. The detail passed on was restricted to pitch conditions, weather and how they thought the team might go. All innocuous stuff – if that was as far as it went. That was all the Australian Cricket Board had wished to know. Had the two star cricketers been bribed to throw games? The gambling behind cricket was huge, especially in India and Pakistan. Match-fixing and bribes had become more than rumours in the 1990s among top cricketers. Mark and Warne denied vehemently that they had ever taken bribes.

They claimed they would never, ever play badly on purpose to help Australia lose a game of any kind.

At that first meeting of the team's inner circle, the vast differences in the twins were evident. Steve was shocked. He never gambled and would eschew the sleazy demimonde inhabited by what he saw as dead-beats and wheeler-dealers. Yet his shock was in part because he knew that he himself, his brother, Shane Warne and Tim May had been offered US$200,000 by Pakistan's Salim Malik to throw a one-day international in Rawalpindi in 1994.

Then, Steve had advised his brother to tell Malik to 'fuck off', which was what the other three had done. It was stunning to be told six months later that Mark had become mixed up in something akin to Malik's nefarious offer.

But Steve calmed down when his twin explained himself. Steve was well aware of his brother's love of the bet. Mark regarded himself as lucky and a good gambler. If he lost a bit, he'd somehow get it back, he thought. He was vulnerable too, to the grinning, back-slapping illegal bookie, who would tell him he was the best batsman he had ever seen, or that he was his biggest fan.

Naive and open, Mark Waugh and Shane Warne had no idea they could be walking into an ancient and well-worn trap. The rich Indian 'fan' would offer them money – paper bags full of it – for nothing. Just because they were terrific blokes and great cricketers. And because they were actually good blokes, they would not refuse the offers. They were not flattered by the comments and praise. They were immune to it, having heard it from real fans for years. They said they didn't want to offend these donors. Taking the paper bags was a way to get rid of them and not offend them. Mark and Warne liked to be loved. They saw no harm in what happened, not even when the bookies rang them to ask how the weather was at the ground before a Test; not even when asked how they thought their team would be composed, or how it would play.

It was not as if these two were underpaid like their Asian counter-parts and needed the money. Nor was avarice necessarily involved.

They were not greedy guys, just profligate and unthinking. Money, to these sportsmen in their early 20s, was more like monopoly than the real thing.

What they didn't realise was that they were being set up for a sting. Perhaps the bookie would wait until one of them was in debt at a casino. Say it was US$100,000. The bookie would pay it off and maybe pass on a fatter paper bag than at Colombo, with US$50,000 in it. Then the bookie might ask Mark to make a couple of scores under 10 in both innings, just in one Test. Perhaps Warne would be asked to avoid taking a wicket in both innings, just in one Test. That would be the sting. They would be trapped, suborned forever, their personal integrity compromised.

But fortunately for Mark and Warne the sting never had a chance to develop. Australian cricket authorities became aware of the early entanglement and they acted to nip the match report practice in the bud. The two cricketers' stories were believed by the ACB. They were fined what amounted to pocket money for them. The entire cricket team was informed about the whole tawdry business and it was swept under the covers and not made public. Mark and Warne were allowed to tour the West Indies. They and Steve Waugh played important roles in wresting cricket's best-team-in-the-world crown from the West Indies.

In the next few years, stories broke on corruption and match-fixing in India, South Africa and Pakistan. Journalists in every cricket-playing country were alert and looking for any new sensation. They probed officials and players in search of a good rumour, a scoop or even just a new angle about the match-fixing controversy. It was inevitable that the story of the Mark Waugh/Warne transgressions would surface somewhere. It did, late in 1998.

Both men suffered as the first (and only) Australians to be implicated. Until then, Australia seemed the cleanest, most untouchable national team in the world. This was backed by the fact that they rarely lost and were clearly the top cricket nation. If any of its players had been taking bribes then many more games would have been lost.

The timing was bad for these minor culprits. They were lumped in with the players accused of throwing games by playing poorly, when the indiscretions of Mark and Warne were not even close to match-fixing. Steve supported them both without giving the media any insights to his own feelings.

'He [Mark] . . . clearly regretted what had transpired', Steve reported in his autobiography *Out of My Comfort Zone*, 'especially the stigma forced on Mum and Dad and our three grandparents.'

Mark needed all the support he could get. He and Warne were going to be in the public eye for months as match-fixing allegations were investigated by the ICC and individual nations. The Pakistanis were to the fore, or so it seemed, in attempting to clear up the problem. When Mark and Warne refused to go to Pakistan to assist an official enquiry, Pakistani authorities were granted permission to come to Australia in January 1999 to conduct their Judicial Commission Hearing into bribery and corruption. Neither player had to attend, but they felt it prudent to do so, especially as they had proclaimed their innocence. Besides, they had been assured they would be asked to give evidence, and not interrogated. Wisely, they were represented by one of the best barristers in Australia, Michael Shatin QC, who happened, usefully, to be a cricket tragic.

In court, Pakistani-style

It began in a tribunal courtroom in King Street, Melbourne on 8 January. On the wall was a portrait of Mohammad Ali Jinnah, the founder of Pakistan. A small Pakistani flag sat on the bench. The judge in charge of the hearing, Abdul Salam Khawar, began with a short prayer to 'the almighty Allah' for the 50 or so present – most of them media. The two cricketers had demanded that the hearing be public. Warne's father, Keith, wife, Simone and agent, Austin Robertson, were present. Each witness swore an oath and told the court his father's name, in keeping with Pakistani law.

First Waugh, then Warne, was cross-examined at length by the Pakistani lawyer Ali Sibtain Fazli, and his assistant, Ali Sajjad, followed by Salim Malik's counsel, Azmat Saeed. At one point, Azmat made a telling slip and referred to the hearing as a 'trial' and had to correct himself. At times, Waugh's counsel, Shatin, had to step in to stop the Pakistanis pushing into irrelevant areas as they thrashed around trying to find holes in the sworn statements by the cricketers. Waugh looked uncertain and nervous, just as if he were beginning a difficult innings against bouncers, but he showed his faculties were as acute as ever, when he pointed out a major mistake by the Pakistanis. Azmat tried to make much of a statement – a summary of Waugh's evidence presented in Pakistan in September 1998. The Pakistani lawyers had prepared this summary. Waugh said: 'Everything is correct except for two sentences where it appears the language barrier . . . everything is mixed up . . .'

The Pakistani version suggested that Waugh and Salim spoke for an hour and a half at the reception in Rawalpindi on 21 October in 1994 when Salim attempted to bribe him. Waugh denied the length of time they chatted. Salim spoke briefly to Waugh, with Warne in earshot, at the reception and offered him the US$200,000 bribe. An hour and a half later (*not* after an hour and a half's discussion, which would suggest something conspiratorial), a still-shocked Waugh made it clear in another even shorter conversation with Salim that he rejected the offer.

Azmat, who had a disconcerting and sometimes abrupt manner on his feet, went through a few histrionics, approaching Waugh in the witness box and pushing the statement under his nose. But Shatin was alert, pulling out the original transcript covering Waugh's actual testimony in Pakistan. The barrister went one better and produced the tape for the judge from which the full transcript – not the Pakistani summary – was made.

Warne, looking suitably sombre in a dark suit and conservative tie, performed as he had promised before the hearing when he said he looked forward to giving evidence. It was vintage Warne: direct, ingenuous and confident. He pitched his responses at just the right level, neither being disrespectful nor genuflecting towards the occasionally aggressive Pakistan Cricket Board lawyers, who seemed intent on tripping up the Australians rather than accepting evidence and asking for expansions. Fazli and Sajjad were mostly indistinguishable in their approach from Salim's counsel, Azmat. If anything, the hearing appeared to drift into a showdown between two nations as intense as any Test match, with attack and defence from both sides.

The grilling of the players (Waugh about 80 minutes, Warne about 45 minutes) led nowhere, as their responses remained consistent and credible. Neither was near cracking on any point. In fact, they enhanced their positions without dissembling.

Both were asked about the one-day game in Colombo on 7 September 1994, which Australia won, scoring 7 for 179 with Pakistan managing just 9 for 151. The Pakistani lawyers suggested that they had evidence that this match was fixed. Waugh and Warne knew nothing about it.

'We only ever play to win', Warne said with certitude. He pointed out that he won the man-of-the-match award in that game, hardly the performance of someone who had been bribed. The allegation was that a couple of the key Pakistanis deliberately played poorly in the game.

On a couple of occasions, the Pakistani legal contingent went further and alluded to the possibility that the Australians may have thrown the First Test in Karachi, played from 28 September to 2 October 1994 when, at the end of the fourth day, Pakistan was 3 for 157 and the game was on a knife edge. That night, Salim made the first US$200,000 offer – to Warne and May – to throw the game the next day by bowling badly (outside the off-stump). May had a neck injury but Warne bowled at his best and helped reduce Pakistan to 9 for 258. The home team seemed beaten but a last wicket stand between the hard-hitting Inzamam Ul Haq and Mushtaq Ahmed turned the game around. Warne bowled to Inzamam Ul Haq in what became the last over. The batsman lunged and missed the ball.

Healy missed a tough stumping and the ball went for four leg-byes, giving Pakistan a 1 wicket victory in one of the closest, most thrilling Test finishes in history. Harold 'Dickie' Bird umpired the game and said it was the best match he ever saw. Warne took 5 for 89 off 36.1 with 12 maidens, one of his finest performances considering the tightness of the game, and he was awarded man-of the-match. To suggest that the Australians would throw the match, or that they could contrive to lose it with such a good delivery and a tough missed stumping was absurd. Shatin picked up on this and intervened after the question arose a second time.

'It's outrageous to make any allegation of that nature without any warning or notice', the QC railed indignantly. 'Everyone who loves cricket saw that incident and saw the ball beat both the batsman and the keeper, and those of us who were Australians were disappointed and those who were Pakistanis were happy.'

It was not clear where Fazli and Sajjad were heading with this. Were they implying that Salim had actually bribed May and Warne, or even the whole team, seeing that Healy missed the stumping? If this were the case many of the Australians would be better giving away cricket and taking up careers as thespians or at least American professional wrestlers. It appeared that the Pakistani lawyers were intent on casting doubts on as many Australian names as possible without a shred of evidence or plausibility, knowing full well that the media worldwide would pick and run with any name or hint of wrong-doing. It was mischievous and foolish and demonstrated the feeble position the Pakistanis were in when dealing with the inquiry into their fellow countrymen. If ever there was a need for the world cricketing body – the ICC – to have powers in matters such as match-fixing, it was now. There was some hope here. Its member countries' chief representatives were currently assembling in New Zealand to consider how much power the ICC could exercise in this area.

The next day, 9 January, Tim May gave evidence. Fazli struggled to make much of the mention of Steve Waugh's name. May had said he had heard from Warne that he and Warne, and the Waugh brothers, were offered collectively US$200,000 to throw the one-day game between Australia and Pakistan on 22 October 1994 (as mentioned). (Pakistan won this game, scoring 1 for 251 in just 39 overs, after Australia had made 6 for 250. Mark Waugh scored a brilliant 121 not out. Warne took 0 for 47 off nine overs with one maiden and May 0 for 65 off nine.)

Fazli seemed unable to grasp the reason for May assuming that the bribe offers to the four Australians would amount to US$50,000 each. May said he had made the simple long division in his head and assumed the US$200,000 would be offered in equitable parts.

'I am an accountant', May said without bombast as he shifted in his seat. The remark and the fiddling around the non-issue by the Pakistani lawyers caused another amused stir among the mainly Australian media, who were enjoying the theatre. A few of them giggled when Shatin's seven-year-old son, James, who was sitting in the audience during the second morning of the hearing, yawned audibly. Was he bored? Not for long. His father jumped to his feet during a prolonged interrogation of May by the earnest Sajjad.

'If he [Sajjad] wants a job as a junior on the O'Regan Inquiry [into possible bribery in Australia]', Shatin remarked, 'I'm sure something can be arranged . . .'

It was a scathing yet appropriate put-down. May was being treated as if the hearing were an inquisition into his activities, not as a helpful witness to corruption in Pakistani cricket.

The hearing was studded with humour. Azmat asked Warne what Salim's hotel room number was during the First Test in Karachi in September 1994 when the attempted bribe took place. This ridiculous question drew a titter, but Azmat no doubt would have made much of it, had Warne remembered. (I later rang Azmat – an engaging figure when not involved with courtroom theatrics – at his hotel and asked him for his room number. Fortunately for him, he could recall it.)

Azmat asked Warne why he referred to Salim as 'the Rat'.

'Because that's his nickname with the Australians', Warne replied. 'Some of them think he looks like a rat.'

Both Australians admitted liking a bet.

'I own horses', Waugh said, 'and I like to bet on the races, golf and rugby.'

'On cricket?' Azmat asked.

'Never on cricket', Waugh replied.

'You say you took money [from the illegal Indian bookie 'John' for weather and pitch reports]', Azmat said. 'Did you ever give money *to* a bookmaker?'

'Most of the time', Waugh responded, again getting a laugh from the audience.

Azmat tried to make something of Waugh having an account with Centrebet, the legal Darwin-based betting operation, but this also led up another blind alley.

Waugh did revise the number of times he gave 'John', the Indian bookie, weather and pitch information from 'a handful' to 'about 10 times'.

When Waugh's interrogation – for that was what it seemed – was over judge Khawar released him but ordered that he make no contact with Warne, then corrected himself and said 'no immediate contact'.

Shatin, showing humour and a knowledge about cricket, remarked: 'Good, I was beginning to worry about Sunday [10 January 1999, when Warne and Waugh would need to communicate in a one-day international against England].'

Warne admitted liking blackjack and roulette and the occasional bet on Australian Rules football.

'Do you bet on the cricket?' Azmat asked again.

'No, never', Warne replied.

Warne did elaborate on his discussions with 'John', the illegal Indian bookie who had given him US$5000 at his Colombo hotel in September 1994, which Warne claimed had 'no strings attached'. However, he apparently felt obligated to give him some information about later matches. He heard from 'John' again in early December 1994, just before the one-day game in Sydney against England.

'He telephoned me at the hotel', Warne testified. 'He asked me the make-up of the team. I said, "I don't know. That's up to the selectors and the captain but in Sydney we always play two spinners". He asked me what the pitch was like and I said I hadn't seen it. He said, "Good luck, do you think you'll win?" I said, "Bloody oath we will".'

Warne next heard from 'John' just before the Boxing Day Test later in 1994. He phoned him at the team hotel in Melbourne, congratulated him on his form and asked what the pitch was like.

Warne replied: 'Mate, it's a typical MCG pitch. It should be a good batting wicket. It should turn a bit and keep a bit low towards the end of the game'.

'John' asked if it was going to rain. Warne replied that 'you could never tell in Melbourne, but I don't think so'. 'John' wished Warne a merry Christmas.

The third and last time Warne heard from 'John' was in Perth in February 1995. The player informed the bookie that it was hot in Perth and that the wicket was a normal WACA pitch – 'fast and bouncy'.

'Is the pitch going to crack up?' the bookie asked.

'No', Warne responded, 'it's got a good coverage of grass. It should hold together.'

Warne said he had not spoken to 'John' since February 1995, which was the month the Salim bribery allegations became public, and when he was fined in private by the ACB for his dealings with 'John'.

Shatin brought the hearing back into perspective by asking both cricketers at the end of their questioning if Salim Malik had ever challenged them face-to-face about their allegations. There were chances during the Pakistani visit to Australia for three Tests in the 1995–96 season and when the World Cup was played in 1996. Both Waugh and Warne were adamant. He had never confronted them. They had not exchanged a word with him since October 1994, not even when he batted against them. In fact, the whole Australian team refused to speak to him, giving him a frigid reception. This was quite an admission, given their penchant for sledging.

The firm-jawed Alan Crompton, the ACB chairman during the time the illegal bookie payments were made to Warne and Waugh, and later a solicitor with the Supreme Court of NSW, made the most definitive statements yet in defence of the Australian crick-eters. He was the last witness at the hearing and took the stand after May on Saturday morning, 9 January. It was clear in this articulate lawyer's mind that they had done nothing beyond give weather and pitch reports to the Indian bookie. The conduct of Warne and Mark Waugh 'amounted to a breach of the players' contract in that it brought the game of cricket into disrepute'. Crompton stuck to a clear enunciation of the ACB's attitude, punctuating his sentences with 'arhs', which, coming from him, sounded precise. The matter was handled in private, as were all matters relating to a breach of the players' contract in off-the-field incidents. On-the-field incidents were dealt with in public. Crompton would not be budged from this as the Pakistani lawyers variously tried to characterise the ACB's actions as 'sweeping it under the carpet' and amateurish in that it did not keep detailed written notes on the procedures for discipline. The Pakistanis picked on the apparent dictatorial approach of Crompton and Graham Halbish, the then chief executive officer at the ACB. They had taken action against Warne and Waugh, then reported the incident to 12 of the other 14 board directors at a Sydney meeting on 28 February 1995. In effect, Crompton and Halbish presented the board with a fait accompli. Yet none of the 12 expressed any disagreement with the action. Crompton pointed out that this approach – of chief executives making decisions quickly in time-restricted, critical circumstances, and then present-ing them for ratification or otherwise to a board – was the way most businesses operated. While denying a cover-up, the former ACB chairman admitted he had been concerned that if the off-field transgressions of Warne and Waugh were made public at the time they. could be confused with the then (February 1995) public problems facing Salim Malik involving match-fixing and bribery. The blow-up four years later seemed to confirm Crompton's concern. It's probable that had the dealings of Warne and Mark Waugh been made public when discovered in late February 1995, far more drastic action would have been forced on the conservative ACB by the media and the Australian public. It may be that the ACB's approach, whether viewed as appropriate or not, saved the players' careers.

In quizzing Crompton, Sajjad said Warne and Waugh were effectively charged by the ACB with bribery. The witness's jaw extended in the Pakistani lawyer's direction.

'They were not charged with bribery', he said firmly. 'Bribery has nothing to do with this matter . . . Had I thought it had anything to do with bribery, I would have viewed these whole circumstances quite differently and I would have handled them quite differently.'

Warne and Waugh were disappointed that their 'stupidity' in taking money from the bookie for innocent information about the weather had been confused in the public mind, it seemed, with the bribery and match-fixing allegations aimed at several Pakistani players. It had been a diversion – by Malik's counsel in particular – in an effort to get Malik exonerated from wrong-doing. Some sections of the media did nothing to prevent the confusion and seemed to blur the two distinct issues. It annoyed the players. After the hearing, both were incensed with the front-page headline in the Melbourne *Herald Sun* in the afternoon edition of 8 January. It screamed 'MATCH FIX' and featured photos of Warne and Waugh. Both players told the media door-stopping them at the hearing that 'the matter [of the paper's report] was in the hands of their lawyers'. The next morning, the paper's headline was 'INNOCENT' with bigger shots of the two players. The accompanying story was much clearer in its reporting of the players' positions.

The Pakistani enquiry was an ordeal for Mark Waugh and Warne, but it cleared the air, and both were able to resume their careers without the stigma attached to them before it. However, both would be affected by it. The game was never quite as much fun for Mark after the story broke. And for Warne, it was part of an accumulation of bad media and press that almost truncated his career. After their evidence was aired, the cricket world was consumed by far more damaging reports from several countries. Apart from Pakistan's Salim Malik, the involvement in match-fixing of India's gifted Mohammad Azharuddin and South Africa's talented Hansie Cronje were shocks to the cricket world.

Revelations damaging to cricket reached a zenith in 2000 before an interview I had with Steve Waugh at Telstra Dome, formerly Colonial Stadium.

The Steve Waugh interview

'Show me the money!' a cricket fan yelled after the thrilling, hard-fought one-day tie between Australia and South Africa last Friday night at the Colonial Stadium in Melbourne. The cynical joke echoed the doubt concerning cricket following revelations about corruption.

Steve Waugh's answer to the distractions of the past five months is simple enough: 'Go out there and play great cricket'.

He put in personally with a brilliant century in the first game and the teams could do no more than play as competitively as they did after a sluggish start by the Proteas.

The Australian public sees Waugh as the biggest hope for the game. While the sport's image plummeted, his stocks soared. Early in April 2000, he stood as the most admired leader in world cricket – alongside Hansie Cronje. Now Waugh, with his integrity and huge success, stands alone. That's why Australians every-where applauded him whenever he appeared in public. You sensed some relief in the unprompted standing ovation he received when in Melbourne on *The Footy Show*. Here was a guy who the paying sports lovers could trust; at least that is what they hoped.

Again, Waugh's response to that in my August 2000 interview with him was typically pragmatic: 'Mate, I've just played the game the way I always have, as have all the team. We play to win for Australia, every time. I shouldn't be applauded for that'.

There is no doubt Waugh is rejuvenated by his mission. It showed in the way he nearly stole the second (tied) Colonial game with a defiant 30 and the manner in which he compiled his unbeaten 114 in the first. It was only his third century in 296 one-day internationals. His aggression was atypical. Yet here Waugh, 35, reverted to the free flow of his youth. He was out to show the world that Australia at least was fair dinkum about playing outstanding cricket.

It's personal for Waugh. He sees everything he has bled for – literally, if you examine the inside of his baggy green – over 15 years, eroding away because of the corruption. No player in the history of Australian sport – Allan Border and Don Bradman included – has done more to elevate a national team to the top, both by performance and by personal effort. Now in his career twilight years, he is compelled to redouble his efforts.

Waugh claims two brushes with corruption. The first was a one-day match versus Pakistan in 1994.

'I took 3 wickets for 14', he said with a self-deprecatory grin. He felt 'everything wasn't quite right'. It wasn't that Waugh never bowled as well as those figures suggest. It was the lazy manner in which the Pakistani batsmen got themselves out that made him suspicious.

The second game was less obvious. It's mentioned in the O'Regan Inquiry into Australian cricket. It wasn't so much what was done on the field but 'what was said by opposition players to us after the game'.

Waugh didn't believe there was any other occasion in his two decades of international or any other form of cricket when a game had been corrupted. Unfortunately, and this is what he fears, it doesn't matter. Plenty of other encounters not involving Australia have come to light involving bribery and throwing of matches. Waugh is well aware that in our satellite age of instant visual consumption, image – not substance – counts. Cricket in general is on the nose, horribly and depressingly for all honest players and loving fans.

If it weren't for the corruption he would have much to be happy about. He is leading the top one-day and Test teams in the world. Both have established record-winning streaks under him. Waugh has the best Test captaincy record in terms of wins (70.59 per cent of games played under his leadership) of all time. He is now ahead of some of the greatest captains in more than 130 years of international cricket: Don Bradman, Douglas Jardine, Frank Worrell and Lindsay Hassett, who all hover within about 2 per cent of a 60 per cent winning rate. During his captaincy of 17 Tests, he has maintained his batting average – built up in the previous 111 games – at just over 50. This places him in a select group of five Australian batsmen headed by Bradman (99.94) and including Greg Chappell (53.86), Jack Ryder (51.62) and Allan Border (50.56), who have averaged 50 or more from at least 20 Tests.

Heady stuff. Yet not for Waugh. The scandals, and his own personal scars – now a decade old – from defeat, variable form, and a fickle media and public, sober him.

Naturally, Waugh wants his team to get the recognition it deserves after the glory of last season. A combination of free spirit and daring, brilliant psychology and the best planning ever by Waugh and new coach, John Buchanan, have Australia aiming at ever-new heights. Last season it thrashed Pakistan, India and New Zealand in turn. But at the end of it, this unparalleled success passed with hardly a mention in the mainstream media. The biggest ever horror story in the game dominated daily with disclosures on the greed of cricketers and crooks illegally stuffing their secret bank accounts from Calcutta to Cape Town with tens of millions of dollars. Murders – there have been two, and now probably a third, related to the corruption – also grip attention more than a good news cricket story or even a riveting tied game. It won't end for another year at least as several inquiries unearth more skulduggery.

Waugh's time as a top cricketer is running out. He is unlikely to step down unless forced to by injuries. With help from a personal trainer and Dave Misson, the team's fitness man, he is doing everything possible to avoid breaking down. There was more dash in his old legs in the Colonial games, which he put down to his preparation and the long lay-off. He didn't pick up a bat until a week before the first match.

Selectors threatened to dump him from the one-day game last year and critics called for his dumping last season. But Waugh endured and did enough to justify his place. His Colonial form will silence the nay sayers for the moment. Yet he is circumspect about his place.

'If they [the selectors] one day decide to drop me', he says with a shrug, 'well, OK. It's no big deal. It happened before to me and others.' [He was dumped from the one-day team early in 2002, when Ricky Ponting took over as one-day skipper. Two years later, in early 2004, he resigned as Test captain when Ponting again took over.]

Who would blame him for hanging on as long as he felt he could contribute to Australia's success? He thrives on competition and leading a strong combination of cricketers to further glory and – most importantly to Waugh – recognition for the teams' achievements. He still has goals. He is looking beyond a summer of five Tests versus the West Indies, that he says will not be as easy as the pundits are predicting. [This was predictable hype on his part. They won the series with more ease than experts expected.] He wants to equal, then break, the world Test winning record of 11 in succession held by the West Indies. Then there is 2001 in

India. Then England. [This was achieved with a streak of 16 Test wins in succession.]

'In my time we've never beaten India in India in a [Test] series', Waugh says. [He never managed to do this.] 'I'd like to beat England again for the seventh time [in succession].' [This was achieved.]

He enjoyed creating a little history by playing in the enclosed Colonial stadium for the first time. The crowds and TV ratings suggest that the experiment will lead to further games, even perhaps Tests, in the winter under the roof. [The first ever game officially designated as a Test was the Australia versus The World game of October 2005.] An impressive 36,000 turned up for the tied game when the cricket went head-to-head with a close Australian Rules knockout semi-final clash at the MCG across town between Hawthorn and North Melbourne. It attracted 50,000, a figure reduced by the out-of-season flannelled fools. It was a win for cricket and the Australian Cricket Board, whose innovation and daring were rewarded. The original intention of the ACB was to stage the three 'Super-Challenge 2000' matches at Colonial to cash in on the mighty clashes between these two sides during the 1999 World Cup. Inadvertently, the contest (these three one-dayers in August) proved a vital boost for the game after the long run of rotten publicity. Had the matches not been staged, cricket – desperate for some positive media spin – would have had to wait until late November for an international fixture in Australia.

Waugh enjoyed the combat more than anyone, not the least reason being his lack of enjoyment when he first entered the big-time. He is now having serious fun making up for his dreadful early years in the mid-1980s when he was under-prepared and part of a team of easybeats.

Waugh wants to extend his own career at least three years to the 2003 World Cup in South Africa. [As noted, he didn't make it.] He also wishes to be around when the public regards all cricket as 'fair dinkum' again. [This happened more quickly than most observers expected.] At the moment, he laments that 'this era might be known as one of bribery and corruption, rather than that of a great Australian team'.

Waugh knows his history. He fears that the current fiasco could be labelled in a similar way to 'the bodyline and throwing eras', that heard the cry: 'It's not cricket'.

No one would use that phrase now. It has been rendered meaningless by Salim Malik, Mohammad Azharuddin, Hansie Cronje and a host of other bit and large players involved in the grubby demimonde of mafia-controlled betting in India and Pakistan.

Steve Waugh and South African skipper Shaun Pollock – and their teams – made a fair start this week to countering all that. But it is just the beginning of the beginning.

21

BRADMAN'S BEST

Bradman's Best was published in August 2001. Here is an edited version of my speech at the media launch, a post mortem of the reaction to the book, and samples of the public and media responses to it.

***

It has been said that Sir Donald Bradman was to sport what Einstein was to science and Mozart to music. Some sports fans might think that's a bit flattering to Einstein and Mozart. But allowing for the comparisons, Bradman's selection of his 'best ever' cricket team is one of his more creative formulations or compositions.

His thoughts about a 'dream team' first emerged 30 years ago, oddly enough, as an off-shoot from the apartheid issue. In 1970, protest against apartheid was gaining attention worldwide. It had stopped a cricket tour of South Africa by England.

Bradman, aware that it would hit Australia, began to investigate the issue with his trademark thoroughness. He shuttled between South Africa and England, a bit like sport's answer to Henry Kissinger, meeting the prime ministers of both countries.

Bradman also struck up a dialogue through letters with anti-apartheid protestors in Australia. Among them was politician Meredith Burgmann. She sensed Bradman's mind changing as he probed the issue in their correspondence. He went to a rugby union Test between Australia and South Africa in Sydney. Bradman didn't like what he saw. Barbed-wire barricades. Violence. Disruption. This, along with the racist views expressed by South Africa's prime minister John Vorster, caused Bradman to make what he told me was one of the toughest decisions of his life.

Running against public opinion, Bradman stopped that South African cricket tour. 'We will not play them until they choose a team on a non-racist basis', he said.

This helps explain why Nelson Mandela was such an admirer of Don.

That courageous decision by Bradman left Australia without an international series in 1971–72, and the prospect of a big hole in Australian Cricket Board revenue.

The ACB and Bradman decided to invite a world team to tour in place of the South Africans. It was to play Ian Chappell's Australian side.

Bradman had just retired after 36 years as a Test selector. But he rolled up his sleeves and sat once more at a selection table to consider the best available players. He and his co-selectors – Neil Harvey, Sam Loxton and Phil Ridings – came up with a truly international, multiracial team.

It included Garry Sobers (captain), Rohan Kanhai, Clive Lloyd, the Pollock brothers, Tony Greig, Sunil Gavaskar, Farokh Engineer, Beshan Bedi, Zaheer Abbas, Intikhab Alam and others.

These players made up a world-class team in every sense.

So the stage was set for a World XI to play five Tests against the Australians. The tour started with a minor incident when Tony Greig and Hilton Ackerman arrived at Adelaide airport. They were met by a couple of middle-aged gentlemen in open-neck shirts and cardigans.

They introduced themselves as Don and Phil. They could well have been the Everly brothers to young Greig and Ackerman. They in fact thought 'Don' and 'Phil' were from a local association of cricket lovers.

Greig and Ackerman asked Don and Phil to take their bags to the

326

coffee shop while they looked around the airport. They met the two mature gentlemen in the coffee shop.

After a bit of chat, Greig said to Don: 'Do you have anything to do with cricket around here?' – meaning 'around the airport area'.

Without batting an eyelid, 'Don' replied: 'The two of us run the game here'.

Greig assumed he meant the airport area. Moments later, Garry Sobers walked into the coffee shop. He made a fuss over Don.

Greig and Ackerman were stunned. Their willing bag carriers were Sir Donald Bradman and Phil Ridings.

Bradman himself liked that story. He never let Tony Greig forget it. Bradman loved being anonymous although he was anything but that as he worked to make the series a success. The World team won a close contest 2-1.

The fans supported the Tests and Bradman enjoyed them as much as anyone. He had sought excellence and perfection throughout his career. It was most satisfying for him to sit down and view the world's best.

Bradman watched Test cricket for 80 years, beginning in 1921 when, at age 12, he saw an Ashes match at the Sydney Cricket Ground. In that game Charlie Macartney made a magnificent 170. This innings inspired the young Don to become a Test cricketer. Half a century later, in that 1971–72 season, Bradman witnessed what he considered were the best individual bowling and batting performances ever in Australia.

In Perth, Dennis Lillee took 8 for 29 against the World XI. He captured 6 wickets for 0 runs in his last 13 deliveries in one of the most devastating spells of bowling ever. Bradman had seen plenty of ferocious, brilliant performances: Frank Tyson at Sydney and Melbourne in 1954–55; Harold Larwood at Adelaide in 1933 – and many others. But he put Lillee's effort at the top, especially as it was against the best the world could offer in the early 1970s.

In Melbourne, Garry Sobers smashed 254 for the World XI. Bradman said of Sobers: 'With his long grip of the bat, his high back-lift and free swing, Garry Sobers consistently hits the ball harder than anyone I can remember. This helps to make him such an exciting player to watch. The emphasis is on power and aggression rather than technique – the latter being the servant, not the master.

'The uncoiling of those long steely wrists as he flicks the ball wide of mid-on is a joy to watch. It is unique and superbly controlled, while the full-blooded cut is tremendous.'

The key to Don's approach in choosing his batsmen for Bradman's Best is in that line: 'The emphasis is on power and aggression rather than technique'.

That 1971–72 experience stimulated Bradman's thoughts on the make-up of the best ever team in history – if every Test player from every era was available at the peak of his form. It excited his sense of, and search for, excellence. As a player, he always strove for the best – think of his 254 at Lord's in 1930. (He said that innings was the best he ever played.)

Why?

'Because every shot went where it was intended.'

Even the cover drive that saw him brilliantly caught by Percy Chapman was a copybook stroke. Don marched to his own inner drum – his personal assessment of expertise in his craft. No critic could sway him. He was a true master craftsman, monitoring his own brilliance from the inside looking out.

In 1948 in England, Bradman captained the nearest to perfect-performing squad ever to tour. The Invincibles did not lose one game in 34 contests. In 1958, he published *The Art of Cricket*. Still today, there is no better manual on the sport. All this meant that when Bradman watched a cricketer, he saw with clarity all mental and technical skills, and faults.

When he first viewed Greg Chappell, for instance, he saw enormous potential. But there was a problem with Greg's grip that restricted his range of shots. The teenager didn't have a cover drive. He hardly scored on the off-side. Bradman showed Greg a better way

Murdoch takes block: Billy Murdoch was one of Australia's leading captains and batsmen. He led Australia to its historic, thrilling win at the Oval, Kennington, in 1882, which led to the birth of the Ashes.

That lethal right arm: S. F. Barnes demonstrates his bowling action in 1920. He was one of the all-time leading bowlers.

Half-dressed, still best: The fiery Australian speedster Fred R. 'The Demon' Spofforth, who did the most to win the Test at the Oval, Kennington, in 1882.

'Well bowled, Harold': Harold Larwood, England's best exponent of Bodyline bowling. He contained Bradman after the MCC feared the Don would score 1000 runs in a season.

The Master: Bradman's stroke of perfection. Every shot by him brought into play an unmatched technique when playing orthodox and unorthodox strokes. His unique methods helped him become the outstanding cricketer of the 20th century and the best performer in the history of Ashes cricket, where no one has come remotely near his record of 12 fifties, 11 centuries, 6 double centuries and 2 triple centuries.

Bradman the bowler: Bradman demonstrates his bowling style of a different kind. Head steady, body over the ball, balance and concentration – all hallmarks of his batting technique.

Two Australian greats: Keith Miller (left) and Bradman were two truly brilliant Ashes cricketers with different approaches to the game and life. Their common ground was giving everything for their country in competition.

The corkscrew: Keith Miller executes one of his favourite pull shots, where his body ends up coiled. Miller hit sixes like this with his right hand off the bat.

Miller delivers: Keith Miller delivered some of the most devastating bowling spells ever in Ashes cricket. His ability with the ball curtailed his capacity with the bat over time.

Explosive Botham: Ian Botham lets go a fast one. He was England's top all-rounder of the 20th century.

King Arthur: Opening Batsman Arthur Morris hooks for four. Bradman chose him to open his best 'Dream' World and Australian teams.

Brain and brawn: Big Alec Bedser was the best England paceman Bradman ever faced. He was chosen in Bradman's best 'Dream' World and England teams.

Lyrical Lillee: Dennis Lillee was chosen to open the bowling in Bradman's best 'Dream' World and Australian teams.

Best on paper: Bradman's letter to the author naming his best ever England team. When asked whether he had listed (Godfrey) Evans at number seven, Bradman replied: 'He'll bat where his captain tells him to!' The author had not questioned Evans's position in the order; he wanted to be sure of Bradman's writing. The team, in batting order for the best England team 1877 to 2000, was: Hobbs, Hutton, Compton, May, Hammond, Grace, Evans, Trueman, Bedser, Barnes and Verity.

Brightly writes the Don: Bradman was a prolific letter writer, receiving at times more than 600 letters a day. He responded to the 'sensible ones', which amounted to up to 80 a day. He always wrote back to children.

to hold the bat. Greg took the advice, and increased his shot production all around the wicket.

During the 1970–71 season, in which English fast bowler John Snow intimidated Australian batsmen, Bradman took a quiet moment outside the Tests to say to Ian Chappell: 'What happened to your hook? You used to be a good hooker'.

Don knew his man. A bit of praise sowed the seed that was to release Chappell from a batting straightjacket imposed by former coaches. Ian spent the winter with his brother Greg working on the shot. On a concrete pitch, they hurled a baseball at each other until they got it right. The Chappells were both happy hookers by the following season when they had to face Garry Sobers' World XI. They dominated, making more than 1000 runs between them.

In the same season that John Snow was doing damage to Australian batsmen, Dennis Lillee was picked to play for Australia for the first time. The media was pushing him to indulge in a bumper war. Bradman spoke to him at a function before his first Test. 'Keep bowling the way you have been', Bradman said, 'and forget about this bumper war business.' Lillee was most grateful for the advice. He bowled well and took 5 wickets in an innings.

There are endless examples of Bradman dispensing advice, but never dictatorially, and always when asked. His mind was forever on improving a player and therefore the game.

Six years after the 1971 experience of selecting an international team, Bradman was reminded of the potency of a World XI when Kerry Packer's World Series Cricket rocked the traditional game. Suddenly, Don and all cricket fans were watching Super-Tests. Lillee, Walker and Bright were bowling to Viv and Barry Richards, Tony Greig and Clive Lloyd. The Chappell brothers were facing Garner, Roberts, Proctor and Underwood.

Bradman was seconded to entice stars such as Bob Simpson out of retirement to bolster the ranks of official Australian cricket. Most of the big guns had defected. Bradman was acutely aware of the power of Packer's circus. The entertainment was raw at times, but high class – world class, in fact. Don was a key figure in the compromise with Packer, which restored the old order and gave Packer the TV rights that he had been after in the first place.

In short, the concept of a super team – a world-class side – had been demonstrated vividly once more.

In 1995, while interviewing Don for my biography of him, I asked him if he had ever thought about a best ever, no restrictions world team. He gave me that characteristic half-grin and replied, intriguingly: 'Often'.

He enjoyed roaming the eras choosing the finest side: without national boundaries, without horse-trading between the states, without compromise and without inhibitions. It inspired him. It was the most exalted level of thought in an unpaid job with few rewards and decades of criticism. Everyone knew better than the selectors. For every happy player chosen, there were three or four who were disgruntled with the selection panel. And as Don was seen as the game's supremo, he copped the most flak.

I waited a few years before pursuing the question of his dream team. By then, we had discussed scores of the best players. I had a fair idea of what he felt about most of them.

I wanted to know his world team. But Don at first refused.

He wrote to me: 'As regards to the question of a best XI, I am not prepared to do this. From experience it would lead to a massive increase in my mail, which despite my 89 years, is almost driving me insane.'

Don sometimes received thousands of letters a week. He replied diligently to what he called 'the sensible ones'. He was compelled to do this because of his sense of noblesse oblige – his self-imposed obligation to the nation and the world. This meant sitting at his battered portable typewriter up to four hours every day belting out those famous, succinct letters that were often punctuated with his dry wit. He wrote 80 a day on average. Forget Patrick White. Don Bradman was the great communicator.

I doubt there has been a better letter writer, or one more prolific than the Don. I believe his output may one day be seen as a contribution to the nation on a par with his cricketing achievements.

Now, to avoid the problem with the mail, I suggested to him that this book only be published posthumously.

Soon afterwards, I was thrilled to receive a letter which Sydney barrister and cricket tragic Thos Hodgson this week referred to as 'the Magna Carta of cricket'. It was not quite King John's declaration at Runnymede in 1250. Yet it was a powerful declaration from Don Bradman.

The letter contained his dream team.

It is, in batting order:

1. Arthur Morris
2. Barry Richards
3. Don Bradman
4. Sachin Tendulkar
5. Garry Sobers
6. Don Tallon
7. Ray Lindwall
8. Dennis Lillee
9. Alec Bedser
10. Bill O'Reilly
11. Clarrie Grimmett
12th man. Wally Hammond

Congratulations to every player. I'm sure the living players selected, and the families of those who are not, will rank this honour from Sir Donald Bradman high in their illustrious records. A special acknowledgment to Arthur Morris, who is here today [at the launch of *Bradman's Best*].

Don wrote of Arthur: 'I think Arthur, towards the close of the 1948 tour, was playing the finest cricket of any left-hand bat I've seen. He had that wonderful quality so noticeable in good players – plenty of time to play his shots. All strokes came alike – hooks, drives, cuts, glances. [He had] powerful wrists and forearms . . . Great team man; studious and intelligent observer'.

I believe Barry Richards, as much as anyone, comprehends the significance of Don's selection. Bradman indirectly helped to end Richards' Test career. He was a member of the South African team in 1969–70, but played only four Tests in his career, not counting his performances in World Series Cricket and for a world team against England in 1970.

His placement in Bradman's Best will go some way to bolstering his strong claim to being one of the game's greats. Last week I received a fax from Richards. It said:

IT IS INDEED A GREAT HONOUR TO BE SELECTED IN A TEAM BY THE ULTIMATE PEER WITHIN THE CRICKET COMMUNITY.

TO BE MENTIONED AMONGST SO MANY LEGENDARY NAMES HAS FOR ME COMPENSATED IN SOME WAY FOR THE FACT THAT I HAD SUCH A SMALL TASTE OF INTERNATIONAL CRICKET.

IN MANY WAYS IT IS OVERWHELMING, BUT IT GIVES ME A SENSE OF GREAT PRIDE.

Like most members of this team, which is very much in Bradman's image, Richards is a man of grace and humility.

Now, Don made all his choices without fear or favour. Three players selected – Clarrie Grimmett, Bill O'Reilly and Wally Hammond – were not fans of the Don. O'Reilly, in particular, made some pithy remarks about him. In tapes released after his death, O'Reilly said he didn't criticise Don while he [O'Reilly] was alive because he didn't want to 'piss on a national monument'.

Perhaps Bill was more eloquent when he was alive.

I put O'Reilly's remark to Don. Again, there was that little half-grin, and he replied: 'I agree with the principle that you shouldn't desecrate national monuments. And if there were a national monument to Bill, and even if it were on fire, I wouldn't desecrate it.'

That was the best spontaneous response I've had in 36 years of journalism.

Here are some observations about Bradman's Best.

One important factor in Don's selection process was that he didn't just choose a list of 12 outstanding players. The temptation in such an exercise is to pick names that you think ought to be selected, or must be selected. That wasn't Don's way. His approach was simple enough. He went for a winning 'team'. He chose aggressive batsmen who could score fast runs so that a penetrating bowling line-up could dismiss any opposition twice.

Bradman would always choose a left-hand, right-hand opening batting combination if he had outstanding candidates for each spot. Arthur Morris, a left-hander, and Barry Richards, a right-hander, filled the bill.

Bradman took the number three spot (funny, that).

That left one recognised batsman to choose for the number four spot.

He couldn't go past Sachin Tendulkar, whom he admired for his shot production, compact defence and many other qualities.

Bradman chose only four specialist batsmen. Garry Sobers, the all-rounder, really made it five. Sobers averaged around 58 in Tests and was one of the greatest batsmen of all time. And of course, Bradman's Test average of 100 made him worth two of the best of all time. This means the best ever team, in effect, has the standard six batsmen.

Bradman would always choose a brilliant keeper ahead of a batsman who could keep. That's why he opted for Don Tallon. And anyway, Tallon could bat. You have to look well beyond the stats with this selection.

Choosing only four batsmen and an all-rounder allowed him to select a brilliant bowling line-up. But how did he choose from the large number of champion pacemen stretching back to Fred Spofforth in the 1880s?

Ray Lindwall made it a less problematic decision. He could bat. Ray had scored two Test centuries, two more than everyone except Sir Richard Hadlee. But Don regarded Ray as a better bladesman than Hadlee.

Lindwall took the number seven spot.

Bradman went for Dennis Lillee at number eight. Few would argue that Lillee was one of the best – if not *the* best – fast bowler of all time.

Alec Bedser was placed at nine. Bradman already had three pacemen – Lindwall, Lillee and left-armer Sobers. Instead of going for more of the same – think of the outstanding but metronomic West Indies foursomes of the 1980s – he decided on a brilliant swing-bowler. Unlike the others, Bedser preferred bowling into the wind. He could also become the work-horse as a stock bowler when required.

The dream team's speed quartet has variety. It has pace, guile, swing, bounce, right-arm, left-arm and strong elements of intimidation.

The number 10 position was also easy for Bradman. He regarded fast leg-spinner Bill O'Reilly as the best bowler he ever saw or faced.

Number 11 was a tougher choice. He always favoured a left-arm orthodox spinner in any of his teams, if possible. But he already had one in Garry Sobers, who could also bowl wrist spin. This freed up Bradman to select another spinner. It got down to Clarrie Grimmett or Shane Warne. He bracketed them and O'Reilly together as the best three leg-spinners in history. Grimmett got the nod, mainly because he worked so well in combination with O'Reilly.

Bradman also witnessed Grimmett at his brilliant best in England in 1930. Wally Hammond had crushed Australia in 1928–29, making 905 runs at an average of 113.13. In 1930, Grimmett, with an unprecedented bag of deceptive deliveries, carved up and demoralised Hammond. This left the way clear for Bradman to dominate. He scored 974 runs at 139.14.

Against all odds, Australia won the series 2-1. And of course,

Bradman had many personal tussles with Grimmett and knew his exceptional abilities at first-hand.

Bradman's Best then, in effect, has eight top-line bowling options, given that Sobers was three bowlers in one. And if you like Sachin Tendulkar's style of spinning, you have a ninth alternative.

Compare this to the 2001 Australian Test team with its four bowlers – one of the best ever attacks: Brett Lee, McGrath, Gillespie and Warne. Bradman's dream team has twice the bowling options, and therefore, on paper, twice the firepower.

Finally, Wally Hammond was picked as 12th man. Bradman found it tough to separate him and Viv Richards. Whenever Bradman couldn't separate the skills and records of players he would look at something else on which to make a choice. Hammond was a more useful bowler.

***

Mike Selvey, a cricket writer on the *Guardian* newspaper, England, ran a competition to see if anyone could pick the same team as Don before the team was announced. Selvey had a cute tie-breaker should more than one contestant pick the team.

They had to finish the sentence: 'Douglas Jardine should get a posthumous knighthood because . . .'

I couldn't resist responding to this on the email with: 'Douglas Jardine should get a posthumous knighthood because of his services to Australia, which, after the Bodyline series, lifted its rating against England and did not relinquish the Ashes for another 20 years'.

But Mike Selvey need not have bothered with the tie-breaker. I doubt that anyone in the world has picked the same team as Don. And I invite you to ponder why.

Of course, Bradman's Best is a theoretical team. What relevance could it have in the practical world of international competition?

Late last year in one of my last conversations with Don, we discussed this concept. I invite the International Cricket Council and the ACB to consider some thoughts that came from our chat.

What if the best Test team – over say, a four-year period – was to play a World XI in a series of three Super-Tests?

The teams could battle for the Bradman Cup of Excellence, of course with approval from the Bradman Trust. The Trust would get a percentage of proceeds for those naming rights. I would be surprised if a global organisation was not keen to be a sponsor.

In choosing the World side, the selectors would be allowed to pick any player from any country, including players not chosen for the best national cricket team. In other words, say the top team was Australia, as it is now. A player such as Stuart MacGill could be chosen for the World XI.

The ICC selection panel would be from the elite of the game. How about Alan Davidson, Sir Garfield Sobers and Ian Botham? Or Imran Khan, Allan Border and Sir Vivian Richards? Or maybe three of Bradman's Best – Barry Richards, Dennis Lillee and Alec Bedser.

If this all sounds fanciful, think of the lopsided Ashes competition we are currently witnessing (in 2001), or the imbalance we may well see in the three Tests coming up against New Zealand next season.

With no disrespect to England or New Zealand, who would we rather watch playing Waugh's Australians? Those teams, or a World XI containing the best from all the other playing nations. Think of Lara, Tendulkar, Donald, Pollock, Kallis, Laxman, Harbhajan Singh, Wasim Akram and Muralithuran – as long as Darrell Hair wasn't umpiring.

Money, of course, would have to be a big incentive. Players would have to be offered enticing contracts. A month every four years could be set aside for the Tests at a weather-proof venue such as Colonial Stadium.

In one-day cricket, the same approach could apply. The suggestion here is that within a year of winning the World Cup, the number one side would play a best-of-five series against The World.

As we've seen, World Test teams have been selected before to play England in 1970 and Australia in 1971–72. And let us not forget

Kerry Packer's World Series Cricket. It worked well enough. And without cooperation from official cricket.

Anyway, food for thought. It comes out of Bradman's Best.

Author's postscript

Just after the speech (in August 2001) I was in email correspondence and phone discussions with the ICC's Malcolm Speed concerning the World XI idea. The suggestion of the top of the table team (over a four-year period) to play a World XI was taken up four years later by the ICC, with three one-dayers being played in October 2005 at Melbourne's Telstra Dome, then a Test at the SCG. Australia won all four games with ease. This prompted much criticism and did raise the problem of a champion team facing a team of champions from different nations. The Australians, top of the one-day and Test tables for many years, formed a unified, dedicated squad with much to play for, especially after England had narrowly beaten them (2-1) in the 2005 Ashes, which had finished just weeks earlier.

The results did not seem to enthuse the ICC with just one 50 being scored in two innings by the World XI, which was beaten comfortably by Australia by 210 runs. But more thoughtful planning and selections would see a better competition. The selectors picked some players on reputation rather than form, and this showed in the pressure moments. Three Tests may have been better than the one, which tended to make it seem like an exhibition. The problem with three Tests would develop if the national team won the first two Tests easily. This would turn away spectators and TV viewers. Another problem would be in extending the time for this event to make it a more attractive series. The ICC's Speed had said in 2001 that 'fitting in such an event' in the already tough and tight schedules for teams in international cricket was a hurdle.

Yet despite all these obstacles, the search for excellence – a level of cricket one cut above Tests between national XIs – remains a laudable aim. There needs to be an incentive for reaching the top of the international table, and this concept has its merits. It's up to the ICC, if there is a will and imagination, to consolidate the idea, tried once but found wanting in practice.

***

Bradman's Best was published on 12 August 2001, with simultaneous publications in Australia and England, after a commendable effort by the publishers to keep the contents under wraps. It was not quite Harry Potter, but weeks before publication Norman Harris in the London *Observer* noted: 'The books containing the 11 precious names will be guarded like gold bars'.

Bradman's Best stimulated much reaction. Competitions sprang up in both countries with prizes for those who could pick nearest to Bradman's choices. (No one did.) Newspaper columnists in both countries made up simulations of a game between the Don's team and their own.

Even London's venerable magazine, *The Spectator*, became involved when writer Frank Johnson was inspired to choose his own Philosopher's XI, starting with Plato and Aristotle.

'Donald Bradman's posthumous ideal cricket XI of all time was revealed this week', he wrote. 'Few political scoops have inspired so much conversation and argument . . .'

The fact that Bradman had only chosen two English names – Bedser and Hammond – caused Johnson to remark: '. . . another humiliation for English cricket at Australia's hands in this dreadful summer [2001]. But at this point we English should stop conceding that, at this or that, we are not world-class. What is the most important and hardest of man's functions? It is to think. The selection of an international, 'dream' thinking XI would tell a different story about the English'.

Johnson, tongue firmly in cheek, finished his article with: 'So: five English speakers; three Frenchmen; two Greeks; one German. No Australians were selected'.

In response to this, I wrote a letter to *The Spectator* (published 1 September 2001): ' . . . I agree with Frank Johnson's Philosophy First XI, except for a glaring omission which has overtones of vindictiveness. Surely England's most radical, and in my opinion best, modern philosopher, Professor Brian O'Shaughnessy, author of those monumental tomes *The Will* and *Consciousness and the World*, should be in the team, even as 12th man.

'Has Professor O'Shaughnessy been left out for reasons not obvious from your clearly biased selection process? Is this the meaning behind Frank Johnson's rather pointed last line: "No Australians were selected"? Did the good professor's accident of birth in Australia cause him to be overlooked?'

The fun continued.

Predictably, there was much criticism of Bradman's selections. His choice of Tallon batting at number six raised many eyebrows. Yet it was noticeable that no critic seemed to take the time to analyse Bradman's thinking. Some ignored the fact that Bradman had seen more of the great cricketers than anyone else over a long period. So if critics had not seen, for example, Tallon, they tended to avoid the fact that Bradman had been able not only to watch him, but to play with and against him. This in turn was one of the beauties of Bradman's selections. They covered nearly eight decades.

Matthew Engel, an assiduous Bradman detractor, felt he was given a free hit with the Don's selections. He commented in the London *Guardian*: 'The odd thing is, that with the whole of history to go at – and without ever having to worry about Graham Thorpe and Michael Vaughan being out injured – the great man has come up with a side every bit as inadequate as England's [in 2001]. As an all-time World XI, it is surprisingly flawed and decidedly beatable . . . The fact that he played in England and Australia is all too evident'.

Engel then chose his own team – not surprisingly, flawed and decidedly beatable yet still strong: Sunil Gavaskar, Jack Hobbs, Don Bradman, Viv Richards, Denis Compton, Garry Sobers, W. G. Grace,

Les Ames (keeper), Malcolm Marshall, Shane Warne and Michael Holding, with Wilfred Rhodes 12th man.

Engel noted that, because of apartheid, Barry Richards played in only four Tests: 'His ability at the topmost level was never fully tested. For all we know, he was another Graeme Hick'.

This comment smacked of selective amnesia. Richards acquitted himself brilliantly in World Series Cricket, which even Bradman – who disliked the concept even more than Engel did – saw as a cut above official Test standard in the 1970s.

Mark Nicholas in the London *Daily Telegraph* made some thoughtful criticisms, saying: 'Imagine Tallon at six and Lindwall at seven scrambling for their helmets in the face of Andy Roberts, Michael Holding, Joel Garner and Malcolm Marshall'.

That mighty West Indian speed quartet would be hard to combat. But on Bradman's reasoning, his top five – Richards, Morris, Bradman, Tendulkar and Sobers – would have scored enough runs for it not to matter.

Nicholas pointed out that only Bradman and Sobers were chosen in both Bradman's team and *Wisden Almanac*'s five cricketers of the year. Those who missed out (only just) were Warne, Sir Vivian Richards and Sir Jack Hobbs. '. . . the arguments rage', Nicholas added. '. . . Wasim Akram picked his greatest team and could find no place for Sachin Tendulkar. E. W. Swanton might arouse from his deepest sleep if he heard that Wally Hammond had not made it.'

Yet at least Wally got to carry the drinks!

Nicholas also noted that Richie Benaud said that Warne is the greatest spinner he has seen, which reiterated a basic point about the choices. Bradman did see Warne, Grimmett and O'Reilly, and played against the latter two. Benaud did not play against Grimmett or O'Reilly and would have seen very little, if anything, of Grimmett and little of O'Reilly. Any selection, and thoughts, for that matter, would seem to have more credibility if the selector saw and/or played against the nominees.

'A billion Indians and equally vociferous Yorkshire folk might baulk at Barry Richard's four-match Test career being acknowledged before the lifetime achievements of Sunil Gavaskar and Sir Len Hutton', Nicholas added. 'The fact that not one member of the West Indian juggernaut that flattened the rest of the world through the 80s has made the final XI will spill a few rum and cokes across the Caribbean.'

Here Nicholas seemed to drift from a main plank in the Bradman approach. He was not looking to award 'lifetime achievements' but to select the best combination of cricketers in a team. And while no one could disagree with the devastation and brilliance of the awesome foursome from the West Indies, how would their penetration, variety and balance stack up against that of Lillee, Lindwall, Bedser, Sobers, Grimmett and O'Reilly?

Nicholas' nomination of Sunil Gavaskar as the unlucky Indian not to be recognised by Bradman in this team was a sensitive point. Gavaskar had been chosen by Bradman in a real World XI in 1971–72. He was so disappointed that he did not gain a place in the dream team that he claimed it was not authentic.

'I refuse to believe the Bradman dream XI was actually Sir Don's personal selection for the world's greatest-ever combination', Gavaskar told the BBC. 'Even when he was the target of bodyline tactics in 1931–32 [sic] he never uttered a word. I am sure he would not have stuck his neck out for something like this which is bound to give rise to a huge debate.'

Gavaskar added: 'Sir Don was a man who steered away from all controversies in his lifetime'.

Which is correct. That's why *Bradman's Best* was published posthumously.

The BBC also reported: 'Gavaskar's sentiments contrast sharply with those of countryman Sachin Tendulkar'.

Tendulkar commented: 'It is a great honour to be among those names especially when Sir Don himself chose the team and made me bat at number four. After Sir Don bats and before Sobers. What else can you ask for? All I can say is that it is a great honour. There are a lot of great names that missed in that list, and my name was considered. I'm on top of the world.'

It's easy to understand Gavaskar's feelings. Yet he may have had some further reflection when he was called upon by the ICC to be a selector of the World XI that played Australia in October 2005. After the team's drubbing by Australia, he and the other selectors were criticised for their choices, especially the tendency to go for 'name' rather than form players. The Gavaskar case further demonstrated the difficulty of choosing world teams, whether hypothetical or actual. Everyone – Bradman included – has a varying point of view in choosing a side, depending on their bias towards their own country or favourite individuals. They are also limited by the range of players they have seen.

***

Most commentators were preoccupied with picking their own teams to rival Bradman's Best. Several newspapers and media outlets opened up the columns to readers for their opinions. Those in *The Times* were especially entertaining, including the thoughts of Richard Penney: 'As someone whose career peaked with the Dublin Fleas XI, I hesitate to suggest that Sir Donald's judgment could be flawed. However, while I can live with the absence of Compton, Miller and S. F. Barnes, to include the inestimable Barry Richards ahead of the sublime John Berry Hobbs is evidence that Sir Donald needed stronger spectacles'.

Perhaps Mr Penney's respect for the Don's eyesight may have been increased marginally with his selections for his best ever Australian and England teams. They included his favourite Hobbs, along with his expendable Compton, Miller and S. F. Barnes.

Peter Crush would be given the humility/humour/generous and imaginative thinking awards after he wrote: 'Who am I, the cricketing equivalent of pond life, to be even asked to question the opinion of a cricketing god like Don Bradman? He clearly picked a side that he wanted to play in, and that alone should not be dismissed lightly as his happiness would probably ensure a double hundred'.

After Mr Penney questioned the Don's seeing capacity, two emailers to *The Times* went further, attacking his sanity. John Cottrell wrote: 'Two specialist spinners when he has Sobers and Tendulkar? Bradders must have been bonkers'.

Giles W. Smith wrote: 'Not much to quibble about but Tallon at number six with an average of 18? Did the great man lose his marbles? He isn't even close to Evans, Knott, Marsh. What would have happened if Martian seamers produced five unplayable ones at an overcast Headingley and Tallon had appeared at 9 [runs] for 5 [wickets]? Still, the whole debate is a lovely idea'.

Edward Little, showing a certain perspicacity, was less concerned with Bradman's mental stability, and more interested in how his brain worked: 'His selection shows a fascinating insight into his mind. The balance is somewhat old fashioned and shows a degree of arrogance that was his personal trademark. Who else would pick only four first-line batsmen? Obviously he backed himself to make most of the runs.'

One observer's arrogance can be another's self-confidence. Bradman's first five selections – it is misleading to leave out Sobers – were made with the belief that they could do the job enough in a five Test series to win against any other team, perhaps with the exception of Mr Smith's Martian XI. This would apply especially with these five superstars batting together in Don's team and generating a celestial brilliance.

As Bradman remarked: 'If they can't make 500, who can?'

Perhaps the *Guardian*'s editorial of 17 August 2001 on the selections was as good a summary observation as anybody's: 'Matthew Engel, unconcerned that his batting average is 99.94 lower than the Don's, has already criticised the composition of the Bradman team in this paper . . . but no two pundits will ever agree. Bradman allowed his closeness to his team-mates to influence his selection; ask a Yorkshireman and it is a fair bet that the entire "dream" team would be from God's own county; and, as for computers, they will rely on averages, an unreliable arbiter of greatness. Would Spofforth have routed today's England, or Jessop saved the day with a sparkling hundred? We will never know . . .'

BRADMAN'S BEST
ASHES TEAMS

Bradman's Best Ashes Teams *was published in August 2002. These selections were from all players from the first international between England and Australia in March 1877, until the end of 2000. Bradman again did not select the best 11 players for each team. His decisions came from much thought into the combination of players, and with regard to their impact on the opposition team.*

***

Bradman's selections for the Australian and England Ashes teams contained plenty of surprises, and perhaps one selection that he may have changed had he lived a few more years. That was the position of Australia's wicket-keeper. But his cut-off point was the end of 2000. He chose Don Tallon as the best keeper he ever witnessed, and would not have changed his mind on this point. But he did remark in the book *Bradman's Best* that if Adam Gilchrist 'maintained his batting average above 50 and his form behind the stumps, he would be the most valuable keeper-batsman in history'.

Gilchrist did just that. Bradman's observation came in late 1999 after he had been 'enthralled' by Gilchrist's great 149 not out in 163 balls against Pakistan in the Hobart Test. In this game, Australia scored 6 for 369 in the fourth innings of the Test to win – the third highest winning score in the final innings of a Test.

I rang Bradman in the morning, something I usually refrained from doing because it was his letter writing time. Yet I knew he would enjoy Gilchrist's performance. I need not have bothered. Bradman had already set aside his letter output to sit and watch this electric display.

Gilchrist went on at the same pace in scores of Tests, and averaged around 50. This ranked him behind Bradman himself (average 99.94) in a bunch of the game's greats all averaging between 45 and a tickle over 60.

***

'No Greg Chappell, Shane Warne or Victor Trumper.'

That was my first reaction to Bradman's all-time best Australian cricket team, 1877–2000. In Chappell's place at number five in the batting order was the less known Charlie Macartney, whose career spanned 1909 to 1926. Few selectors would have left out Chappell, let alone chosen Macartney. Also, few selectors would have left out Shane Warne, for the combination of O'Reilly and Grimmett. But Bradman did and he had his reasons. Bill Ponsford was chosen instead of Trumper, a decision that would probably receive evenly divided support and disagreement.

The team in batting order was:

Arthur Morris (NSW)
Bill Ponsford (Victoria)
Don Bradman (NSW and South Australia)
Neil Harvey (Victoria and NSW)
Charlie Macartney (NSW)
Keith Miller (Victoria and NSW)
Don Tallon (Queensland)
Ray Lindwall (NSW and Queensland)
Dennis Lillee (Western Australia)
Bill O'Reilly (NSW)
Clarrie Grimmett (Victoria and South Australia)
12th man: Richie Benaud (NSW)

I asked Bradman why Greg Chappell had not been selected.

'Several batsmen of more or less equal merit could have been chosen', Bradman replied. 'Greg Chappell, Stan McCabe, either of the Waugh twins, Allan Border and others would have filled the position admirably. But Macartney was not only a great batsman, he was also a very good slow left-arm bowler. He added strength to the bowling.'

Bradman's significant advantages over any other selector are indisputable. He was the greatest batsman, if not cricketer, of all time. He was a shrewd, knowledgeable captain with incisive tactical and strategic skills, and he was arguably the most accomplished and experienced selector ever. He understood the technical aspects of the game as well as anyone, which he demonstrated in the finest manual on the sport ever written – *The Art of Cricket*.

In this case, he had seen both Macartney and Greg Chappell at their best, an advantage that no other living, experienced observer could claim. His memory was prodigious even in old age and right up until his death in February 2001. Bradman was strong-minded without being stubborn. He did not live in the past. He admired Greg from his early days as a schoolboy cricketer, and did much to assist his rise to pre-eminence in Australian cricket in the mid-1970s. Bradman even advised him when he was 19 and a state player to change his batting grip so that he could play off-side shots. Bradman supported him being given the Test captaincy once his brother Ian resigned from the job. Bradman ranked Greg as one of the finest stylists Australia has produced, in the line of Victor Trumper, Charlie Macartney and Mark Waugh. Yet he only found a place for one of them – Macartney – at number five.

Bradman took the exercise of selection seriously. He would not slot in a player just because he was glamorous or popular. Nor would he leave out someone who was forgotten by most fans because he played nearly a century ago. Bradman selected the best combination, applying the same principles he did during almost four decades as a state and national selector. Players were chosen according to team and skill balances and needs.

This was Bradman's vision. It was unique. No one else could look down the tunnel of the 20th century and expertly choose the right players to blend into the best team. But for a few champions such as Trumper, Warwick Armstrong and Clem Hill, Bradman had viewed the best ever Australians for the entire 20th century.

He again said there was to be 'no argument' with him over his selections. Yet while debate over selection at Bradman's level was impossible, you could attempt to understand his reasons and logic. We discussed his analysis at length.

Some observers will suggest that Bradman left out Greg Chappell for other reasons, such as his support for Kerry Packer's World Series Cricket. Bradman did express his distaste for Chappell's signing with World Series Cricket in 1977 when he was already contracted to the Australian Cricket Board. Bradman had always been a stickler for maintaining a contract and therefore honouring your word. Yet Bradman also acknowledged to me much later (in 1995) that the 1970s were a time of change. Cricketers of the 1970s era were caught in a time warp. They were all-year-round sportsmen who were paid poorly for their work. The pay was certainly not enough to maintain a family. Bradman better appreciated Chappell's actions as top cricket became fully professional by the 1990s.

Bradman was also unhappy about Chappell's instruction to his brother Trevor to bowl underarm on the last ball of a one-day game against New Zealand in 1981. The action prevented New Zealand from the unlikely chance of winning with a six off the last ball. There was a howl of protest, with which Bradman agreed. Greg's action had been against the spirit of the game. Yet Bradman did not hold a grudge against Chappell for it. It was viewed as an unfortunate lapse, a silly momentary mistake.

Another indiscretion by Chappell annoyed Bradman more. When he signed with Packer and resigned from the Australian captaincy after the tour of England in 1977, he was voted off the Queensland selection panel and not selected for the state. The Queensland administration paid out his contract and he was made unwelcome in official state cricket circles.

In an interview with Chappell that appeared in the Sydney *Daily Telegraph* and Adelaide *Advertiser* on 2 November 1977, he attacked the Queensland administration. Chappell repeated critical comments made by Bradman in private to him about the Queensland administration when he (Chappell) was considering changing from South Australia to Queensland in 1973.

Bradman was incensed and sent a blistering letter to Chappell in which he accused him of a breach of trust and of distorting the context of their private discussions. Bradman, even in these heated moments, kept his humour. He concluded by reminding Chappell of an old Chinese proverb: 'He who throws mud, loses ground'.

Chappell apologised in writing. Bradman, still riled, accepted the apology because Chappell had been man enough to make it.

Yet all these incidents were 20 to 25 years before Bradman died. Bradman and Chappell, as correspondence between them in the 1980s and 1990s verifies, had long since patched up their differences after a 40-year connection.

Early in 2000 I asked Bradman if those old rifts had caused him to omit Chappell from his best ever Australian side. He was adamant that they had not.

'Greg's all right', he said in a conciliatory tone. 'He's all right.'

I believe, from Bradman's reaction, that his choice of Macartney over Chappell was purely on cricketing grounds.

The Governor General: Charlie Macartney

Bradman's first impression of Macartney was in the first Test he ever saw – at the Sydney Cricket Ground on 25 and 26 February 1921. It was the Fifth Test of the 1920–21 Ashes series. Macartney played one of his best innings, making 170. His timing for such a show was impeccable. The 12-year-old fan from Bowral would never forget the all-round display of stylish, powerful stroke-play. Five years later during the 1926–27 season, Bradman was selected to play for a NSW Country XI against a City XI at Sydney Cricket Ground No. 1. Macartney, 40, who had just retired from Test cricket, was playing for City. City batted first. Macartney, coming in at three, turned on a Test standard performance with a dashing century featuring leg glances and drives. Bradman rushed around in the covers and in the deep, living a dream. Only a few years earlier, such a first-hand encounter would have been a back-yard fantasy for him.

City scored 8 for 301. Bradman was soon in for the NSW Country team, also at number three. He went for his shots from the first ball.

'Yes, I was inspired by Charlie', Bradman said. 'I wanted to perform well in such company.'

Bradman found a partner in Frank Cummins from the Hunter Valley and they put on 82, Bradman making 60 of them and Cummins 19. Bradman stepped up his rate as wickets fell and raced into the 90s. He was on 94 and the score 7 for 167 when the game was officially over. Macartney, impressed by the country kid's verve, thought he deserved 100. He called for and got a one over extension of the game from the sympathetic umpires. Bradman sliced his ninth four passed point to reach 98. He lunged at the next delivery and was caught in slip. Macartney shook his hand, told him he had batted well and wished him luck. Bradman was buoyed by the gesture and recalled the game as if it were yesterday. It may well have had a minor influence on his attitude in his assessment of Macartney more than seven decades later.

Macartney scored seven Test hundreds in his 35 Test career, including a century before lunch on the first day of the 1926 Leeds Test. He was perhaps the hardest hitting top-drawer batsman to play for Australia, and he had all the strokes. The shortish, square-shouldered right-hander loved to improvise. He refused to let bowlers get on top and would always attempt to dominate early in an innings.

He averaged nearly 42 runs an innings, which was close to the averages of McCabe and Mark Waugh, while well short of Greg Chappell (nearly 54) and Steve Waugh and Allan Border (both 50 plus). Macartney's bowling (45 wickets at the excellent average of 27.55) put him in the genuine all-rounder class, which provided the Bradman team with a strong third spin option of a different variety to support the O'Reilly/Grimmett combination.

At the beginning of his career, Macartney was selected more for his spinners than his batting. On his first tour of England in 1909 he took 64 wickets at 17.85 runs apiece. He took a long run for a slow bowler, and had a deadly quicker ball.

Macartney was one of five new faces in the Australian team along with the seven players Bradman selected in the World team. The others were Bill Ponsford, Neil Harvey, Keith Miller and 12th man, Richie Benaud.

Warne out

Once more, Bradman preferred the spin combination of O'Reilly and Grimmett to Shane Warne, the best leg-spinner in the 60 years since O'Reilly's retirement in 1946.

Many observers implied that Warne was omitted from Bradman's World team because of controversial off-field headline-making activity. None of this sat well with Bradman's creed to which he adhered throughout his life. He wrote it down for Sam Loxton, one of his 1948 Invincibles:

When considering the stature of an athlete or for that matter, any other person, I set great store in certain qualities which I believe are essential in addition to skill.
They are that a person conducts his or her life with dignity, with integrity and, most of all, with modesty. These are totally compatible with pride, ambition and competitiveness.

I love to see people with personality and character, but
I resent utterly the philosophy of those misguided people
who think arrogance is a necessary virtue. It is only endured
by the public, not enjoyed.

Yet despite these standards, which may well be construed by some as ruling out Shane Warne from any Bradman team, I don't believe it did. We spoke often about Warne and the comparisons to O'Reilly and Grimmett. At the time Bradman gave me the World and Australian teams, in October and November 1998, the details of Warne's 1994 dealings with the Indian bookie – 'John' – had not emerged in public. Yet Bradman knew of them. He had a private intelligence network that would put ASIS and MI6 in the shade. Warne's self-confessed 'stupid and naive' taking of money from 'John' for match-day intelligence made the news in December 1998. A month later on 8 and 9 January 1999, I attended the Pakistan Judicial Commission Hearing into bribery and match-fixing. It was held in Melbourne. Bradman was particularly interested in a first-hand account of the hearings. I had long phone chats with him about the performances of Warne, Mark Waugh and Tim May under aggressive interrogation from Pakistani barristers.

At no point did Bradman stand in judgment on Warne about this or any other non-cricket incidents. Bradman only had one encounter with him – on Bradman's 90th birthday. He didn't find him arrogant and he liked his 'character'. While Bradman was a man of high principles – as expressed in his creed – and solid family values, he was also very much a man of the world. Not once in six years did I hear him moralise about the private lives of others. He did not approve of some off-field activities but did not let it affect his attitudes, unless an activity impacted on a cricketer's performances for his country or state.

O'Reilly/Grimmett v Warne

Bradman had positive reasons for selecting O'Reilly and Grimmett as a spin combination rather than negative excuses for leaving Warne out. He thought them the best spin team in cricket history. He regarded O'Reilly as the best bowler he ever saw or faced. He delivered fast leg-breaks with bounce and bite.

In four Ashes series from 1932–33 to 1938 he sent down 1228 overs with 439 maidens and took 102 wickets at 25.64. Bradman also pointed to O'Reilly's outstanding first-class record (see table below) and club performances. In 45 years from 1895 to 1939–40, only seven players in Sydney first grade district cricket had a bowling average of less than 10 runs per wicket, when taking 30 or more wickets in a season. O'Reilly did it seven times. No other player did it more than once.

'This reflected his outstanding ability as much as his Test and first-class record', Bradman said. 'It must be set against the fact that in his era (1927–1940) batting averages improved by sizeable margins.'

O'Reilly was complemented by Grimmett, who preferred to bowl into the wind with his variety of leg-breaks, wrong'uns, top-spinners and flippers.

Bradman ranked Shane Warne with these two but thought they were both marginally more effective performers at Test, first-class and club level – a view supported by the statistics.

The table below compares Test and first-class figures, with Stuart MacGill's figures added for interest:

	Tests	wkts	runs/wkt	wkts/Test	1st class	wkts	runs/wkt	wkts/match
O'Reilly	27	144	22.59	5.33	136	774	16.60	5.69
Grimmett	37	216	24.21	5.84	248	1424	22.28	5.74
Warne	140	685	25.25	4.89	265	1178	25.70	4.44*
MacGill	40	198	27.20	4.96	164	700	29.57	4.26

Strike rates, that is, the number of balls delivered for each wicket taken is also pertinent. MacGill is best in Tests with 51.57, followed by Warne (57.30), Grimmett (67.18) and O'Reilly (69.61).

I received Bradman's Australian team in a letter in November 1998. Late in 2000, he confirmed that the selections stood. Apart from the Macartney, Warne and Trumper surprises, several points distinguished the team:

- Bradman played with or against eight of the selections.
- Bradman saw every player chosen perform in Test cricket.
- Only Charlie Macartney ended his Test career before Bradman began his.
- Only Charlie Macartney played Tests before World War I.
- Six players – Morris, Bradman, Harvey, Miller, Tallon and Lindwall – played in Bradman's all-conquering 1948 side, the Invincibles.
- Two players – Macartney and Grimmett – were born in the 19th century. The rest were born in the 20th century.
- Five players – Bradman, Morris, Harvey, Lindwall and Benaud – captained Australia.
- Only Bradman and O'Reilly played before and after World War II. (O'Reilly played just one Test after World War II, versus New Zealand early in 1946.)
- Four players performed in Test cricket in the 1920s – Macartney, Ponsford, Grimmett and Bradman.
- Four players performed in Test cricket in the 1930s – Ponsford, Grimmett, Bradman and O'Reilly.
- Seven players performed in Test cricket in the 1940s – Bradman, O'Reilly, Morris, Harvey, Tallon, Lindwall and Miller.
- Six players performed in Test cricket in the 1950s – Harvey, Morris, Tallon, Lindwall, Miller and Benaud.
- Three players performed in Test cricket in the 1960s – Harvey, Benaud and Lindwall.

- Only Dennis Lillee performed in the 1970s and 1980s.
- No player who played in Tests in the 1990s was selected.
- All players chosen performed at Test level between 1907 (the year before Bradman was born) and 1984 – a 77-year span.
- Seven of the team played for NSW; four for Victoria; two for South Australia; two for Queensland and one for Western Australia. No Tasmanian was represented.
- Eight players scored centuries in Test cricket; four hit double hundreds and one – Bradman – scored two triple hundreds.

Ponsford v Trumper

Bradman's choice of Bill Ponsford as the right-hand opening bat was predictable. They had forged some of the biggest, most important partnerships in cricket history. Bradman had seen Ponsford's exceptional skills and big-occasion capacities at close range. He considered Victor Trumper for the spot – read everything published about him, listened to experts who saw him and studied the record. But as he did not ever see Trumper bat, Bradman opted for the devil he knew.

'There is no doubt Trumper was a great player', Bradman said, 'and one of the finest stylists of all time. By all accounts he would have been great in any era.'

We discussed Trumper's averages as we did all the choices. In 48 Tests and 89 innings, he scored 3163 runs at 39.04 with a highest score of 214 not out. He hit eight centuries and 13 half-centuries. Against England in Ashes contests, which was the only real yardstick of the era a century ago, he had 74 innings and scored 2263 runs at 32.79, with a highest score of 214 not out.

Ponsford played 29 Tests and scored 2122 runs at 48.22. He hit seven centuries. In 20 Ashes matches, he had 35 innings and scored 1558 runs at 47.21, with a highest score of 266.

Apart from the statistics, the record shows Trumper was the more dashing player, while Ponsford was a more reliable opener and a better performer when a series depended on him lifting his rating. His massive scores of 181 and 266 in the last two Tests of the 1934 series in England, and his 110 at the Oval in 1930, were evidence of his temperament under pressure. Ponsford performed at his best when he had to make a big score to help secure the Ashes in England on both these occasions. He was no slouch when it came to the pace of making his runs either. In his big partnerships with Bradman and others, he blended solid defence with attack. He had a mind to go for his shots when he had set up an innings. Ponsford still holds the record for the most runs made in a day in first-class cricket in Australia – 334 not out against NSW at the MCG during the Christmas match of 1926.

Trumper, as spectacular as he was, often tended to go missing in action in Ashes series when it counted. In his first series of 1899 in England he made a magnificent 135 not out at Lord's in the Second Test, but put together just 145 in the other eight innings. He averaged 35.00 and tended to perform more consistently against the counties. In 1901–02, he had a shocker, scoring 219 runs at 21.90 when Australia under Joe Darling and Hugh Trumble romped in 4-1.

In 1902, Trumper delivered at the critical moment for the first time in his career with a fine 104 at Old Trafford in the Fourth Test. Australia won and took the Ashes 2-1, again under Darling. Trumper was sixth in the averages for the two teams, scoring 247 at 30.88. In 1903–04, he had his best series, amassing 574 at 63.78. But in the series crunch game – the Fourth Test at Sydney – when a match-winning knock was required, he scored 7 and 12. England won the series 3-2.

Trumper had another forgettable Ashes in England in 1905, scoring only 125 at 17.86. In 1907–08, he had a mid-series slump at the top of the order, scoring 4 followed by three successive ducks. The selectors thought about dumping him for the dead rubber last Test. (Australia had an unassailable lead of 3-1.) Instead they opened with Charlie Macartney and dropped Trumper down to seven. He scored 10 and was put back to number three for the second innings from where he walloped 166. His series aggregate was 338 at 33.80.

In 1909, confidence in him as an opener was low. He batted down the order for another ordinary return, considering his outstanding talent. His 211 total was made at 26.38. Trumper, still down the order in Ashes competition, began his final campaign in 1911–12 against England in fine style, scoring 113 at Sydney in the first innings. But it was downhill from there as he hit 14, 13, 2, 26, 1 not out, 17, 28, 5 and 50 for an aggregate of 269 at 29.89. Australia lost the series 1-4.

A dispute stopped Trumper going to England in 1912, then World War I prevented international competition. Trumper died in 1915 of Bright's disease, aged only 37. Had he lived, he would probably have played against a young Ponsford, who first represented Victoria at age 18 in 1918.

First impressions, lasting

First impressions were lasting for Bradman. He missed the thrill of seeing Trumper, but at 19, over Christmas 1927, he travelled by train to Melbourne for his second first-class match for NSW, having scored a century in his first against South Australia in Adelaide. Bill Ponsford was the man of the moment. While Bradman had hit his initial century in a fine knock against the great Clarrie Grimmett, the effort hardly rated a mention in the papers. At the same time in that previous week, Ponsford had hit a world record 437 against Queensland. Melbourne, naturally, was abuzz with the feats of one of their own, Bradman recalled.

'He followed up with 202 against us – the first time anyone had scored successive first-class double hundreds in Australia', Bradman said. 'I remember it well. I did a lot of chasing in the outfield, which I didn't mind so much in my youth. It made an impact on me. I was particularly impressed by his powers of concentration. He played each ball on its merit and never lost control . . . He handled [leg-spinner] Arthur Mailey with aplomb. Bill crouched at the wicket and shuffled his solid frame into position with ease. He always seemed to be at the pitch of the ball.'

Bradman recalled that in 1927–28, when he first played for NSW against Victoria, Ponsford was given 'top billing' in Sydney. Posters would urge fans to 'come and see Ponsford play'.

'He was the big drawcard', Bradman said, 'because of his ability to build big scores and rapidly.'

It made Ponsford the number one target for bowlers in Australia from 1923, when he scored 429 in 477 minutes against Tasmania, until 1929, when it became clear that Bradman himself had an even bigger appetite for runs.

Bradman remembered the 'plots' to get Ponsford with speed.

'I was privy to it from my first season', he noted. 'He wasn't seen as vulnerable, not at all. It was simply that something had to be tried to remove him. Our [NSW] bowlers feared what would happen if he got set. Not everyone fancied chasing around while he accumulated two, three or even four hundred, as he did twice. The only player ever to have done so, I believe.' [The West Indies batsman Brian Lara has since done it.]

England, too, worried about Ponsford's mega-scoring capacities. While Bradman was the number one target during the Bodyline series, Ponsford opened the innings and faced the early onslaught. Larwood had broken Ponsford's finger in the Second Test of the 1928–29 series and this put him out of the Ashes contest. Ponsford had been the master over him in 1930. Larwood aimed his short stuff at him in 1932–33. Ponsford's answer was to turn his back and take the ball on the body rather than risk a catch to the close-packed leg-side field.

'I saw him black and blue in the dressing rooms [during Bodyline]', Bradman said. 'He showed a lot of courage, but he naturally didn't enjoy being hit so often. Bill didn't believe the game should be one where the object of the bowlers was to get the batsman out by any means – physical injury included. That aside, there have been few cricketers in history that could play fast bowlers as well as Bill did.'

Ponsford had a short back-lift, but his strong wrists and heavy bat allowed him to get real power from his shots.

'Bill had excellent timing', Bradman added, 'and preferred to play shots in front of the wicket. He drove extremely well, mostly on the on-side. He had a very, very good square cut, which he would use when the mood struck.'

Bradman concluded that Trumper would have been a better player to watch, but that he could not go past Ponsford for efficiency and results. It was this that swayed his selection. Bradman would always choose an attacking batsman who would give his side a better chance of winning over an attractive player who didn't always achieve results. Bradman wasn't selecting a side for its aesthetics. He was after the best winning combination.

Morris, artist with a blade

Ponsford's partner was the left-handed Arthur Morris. Bradman in 1950 considered him one of the two best Australian batsmen playing (the other being Neil Harvey) and judged him the finest left-hander since Clem Hill. In Bradman's opinion, a half century later no better opener – left-handed or right – had emerged, so Morris was selected at the top of the order in the best-ever Australian side.

Bradman found him a 'flawed genius with the bat, but a genius nonetheless'. He found fault with the way he gripped the bat and how that affected his late cut. He thought he played his off-side shots with stiff forearms and with less wrist than the purists would like. Bradman also noted he wasn't always straight in defence and that he often played the cover drive with his bat well away from his pads. Yet all this was acceptable. Morris was still outstanding. He, too, got results at the beginning of an innings.

'I believe it would have been wrong to consider asking him to change anything, as some of his critics did', Bradman remarked. 'He was simply a superior cricketer with an elegance of his own.'

All shots except the late cut came easily to Morris and he was even on top of that by late in his career. He brought his artistry to the hook, cut, all the drives and glances. Bradman even admired the ease he brought to the lofted drive, a shot Bradman rarely played himself because of its riskiness.

'Other factors blended to make him "great" that nothing could change', Bradman said. 'He had outstanding courage and a fine temperament. He was relaxed and with humour on any big occasion. I recall well his cheeriness and confidence at Leeds in 1948 when we were faced with a huge task. We managed a triple century partnership (which won the Ashes Test and series). His calm determination during it was a feature. There was a certain tension in him before batting, yet this was always preferable to out-and-out nerves or, the other extreme, being unemotional to the point of carelessness.'

Bradman came to most of his conclusions about Morris during his sensational 1948 Ashes tour. It started ordinarily for him. Match by match he improved until mid to late in the tour he was playing as well as anyone Bradman had ever seen on tour. The figures support this. Only Bradman himself did better.

Two for the price of one

Bradman's selection of himself at number three was automatic. With anyone else in his place – for instance, any of the best and most worthy in Australian cricket history such as Greg Chappell, Clem Hill, Trumper or Mark Waugh – Australia would appear vulnerable against the England attack. You imagine that the bowlers in Bradman's all-time England team – Trueman, Barnes, Bedser, Verity, Grace and Hammond – would have fancied themselves against any Australian line-up without Bradman. His killer instinct often choked off the opposition on the first day with a fast hundred or a massive score. No matter what happened to the openers, when Bradman entered any arena over his 20 years in top cricket the opposition braced itself. Their only chance of staying in the competition would hang on the early removal of this one player from the field of battle. No other individual in any team sport in history had Bradman's impact on a contest.

In statistical and actual terms he was worth two of the best of the rest in Australian cricket history. In effect, with a batting line-up of Morris, Ponsford, Bradman, Harvey, Macartney and Miller, Australia had the equivalent of a seventh batsman. In most of the tight Ashes contests over 129 years, that would make the difference between winning and losing a series.

Neil's appeal

Bradman's ideal team on paper consisted of:

- Two recognised opening batsmen of whom one is a left-hander
- Three other batsmen of whom one is a left-hander
- One all-rounder
- One wicket-keeper who is also a good bat
- One fast bowler to open with the wind
- One fast or medium-pace bowler to open into the wind
- One right-hand off-spinner, or a right-hand leg-spinner
- One left-hand orthodox first-finger spinner.

Bradman would place at least one other left-handed batsman in the top six, if the player was superior or equal to right-handers vying for a place. He only ranked four other left-handers with Neil Harvey, his choice for the number four spot. They were Arthur Morris, Garry Sobers, David Gower and Brian Lara. Bradman ranked Harvey with the finest batsmen – left or right – Australia has produced down the ages. These factors were important in deciding who would fill the number four vacancy.

Bradman noted that Harvey was: 'Strongly built in a compact frame. He had no technical faults. He was blessed with supple wrists and was a strong driver and powerful cutter. He could hook extremely well and enjoyed the shot. He appeared to struggle against spin early in his career, but mid-career became one of the best players of spin I ever saw. Neil liked to dance to the ball, and apparently his mastering of spin on tours of Pakistan and India was something special to behold. He was also one of the best outfielders of all time. His work in the covers, even late in his career, was sensational'.

Harvey was very much in the Bradman mould. He liked to get on with the game. He was a naturally attacking cricketer as was Bradman's choice for number five, Charlie Macartney.

More flamboyant, yet just as aggressive on his day or when in the mood, was all-rounder Keith Miller at number six. Miller was selected in front of a fine group of all-rounders including Richie Benaud, Alan Davidson, Monty Noble and Warwick Armstrong.

Bradman saw Miller as a 'dangerous' new ball bowler who could swing it both ways, and was nearly as fast as Ray Lindwall. Bradman also admired his batting and his big-hitting ability, but was critical of his lack of application and concentration at times.

Miller, another member of Bradman's 1948 Invincibles, had remarkable Test figures with both bat and ball. Here are the comparisons with the four other champions in Australia's history, and Garry Sobers, whom Bradman chose ahead of Miller for his best ever World team.

	Tests	Runs	Average	Centuries	Wickets	Runs/wkt
Sobers	93	8032	57.78	26	235	34.03
Miller	55	2958	36.97	7	170	22.97
Noble	42	1997	30.25	1	121	25.00
Armstrong	50	2863	38.68	6	87	33.59
Benaud	63	2201	24.45	3	248	27.03
Davidson	44	1328	24.59	–	186	20.53

The statistics do not tell the full story for any cricketer. Performances under pressure or at key moments, and the strength of the opposition, should carry weight. Yet over time statistics are strong indicators of a player's capacities. Bradman choice of Sobers as the number one all-rounder of all time is hardly disputed by any astute observer or anyone who saw him perform. But Miller was close – perhaps equal – in his overall impact. His batting did not have the sustained brilliance that Sobers attained over 38 more Tests. Miller was more flamboyant and more likely to surrender his wicket attempting a big hit. In his prime, probably during the unofficial 'Victory Tests' in England just after the war, he was a magnificent performer. In a game at Lord's in August 1945, playing for the 'Dominions' against England, he smote seven sixes in a blast of 185.

Miller's bowling returns are far more impressive than Sobers', and because of this some have argued that the Australian was the more valuable player. He could be quick and lethal if in the right frame of mind. He and Lindwall formed one of the best ever opening bowling combinations. Yet as Sobers ranked among the great batsmen of all time, and was effectively three bowlers in one with his fast-medium, orthodox left-hand spinning and wrist spinning, he was Bradman's number one selection.

Monty Noble wasn't far behind Miller's achievements with his right-hand attacking batting and off-spin. Benaud, a hard-hitting right-hand bat, a fine leg-spinner and outstanding leader, could hardly be separated in effectiveness from Davidson, an attacking left-hand bat and brilliant left-arm pace bowler. His returns of 186 wickets at just 20.53 place him at the top of the 20th century's best in statistical terms.

Bradman bracketed him among the elite.

Tallon on top

Bradman placed Don Tallon, the wicket-keeper, at number seven in his Australian team. The selection and placement of him at number six in Bradman's World team brought most criticism, yet it came from those who had never seen him bat or keep. All those who witnessed Tallon's keeping were at one in saying he was the best keeper ever. Without exception, Test players who played for or against him marvelled at his acrobatic skills behind the stumps. His leg-side catching, his stumping off medium-pace and spin were superlative.

His place as a batsman at number six or seven suggests he was in the all-rounder class, and someone who could bat. His Test average of under 18 runs an innings would tend to contradict that. Yet if ever the figures lied, they did with Don Tallon concerning his batting skills. In the 1930s, he was judged as one of the most talented attacking batsmen in first-class cricket. He made the Queensland state team at 17 years, in 1933–34, and two seasons later – in 1935–36 – impressed Bradman with a dashing 88 in a state game. It was just one innings among many in that season (and the next four before war stopped play) that stamped the young Tallon, then still a teenager, as a prodigious all-rounder. Another innings of 193 in 187 minutes against Victoria at the Gabba in 1935–36 ranked as one of the finest innings of the 1930s. Bradman didn't see it, but read about it and was informed of its outstanding class by witnesses.

Having experienced at first hand his ability (both with the bat and behind the stumps) early in the season, Bradman was prepared to consider fast-tracking Tallon into the Test team. Indeed, in the next season – 1936–37 – the way was opened up for him by Bradman and the other Test selectors. Tallon was chosen to play in a trial game between a Bradman XI and Victor Richardson's team that had played a brilliant tour of South Africa. Bradman thought so highly of Tallon's batting that he placed him not at six or seven, but at five in his team's order. Unfortunately Tallon was dismissed for 3, when all but Bradman (212), Leo O'Brien (85) and Alan McGilvray (42) failed.

After the war, when he made the Test team, Tallon's chances were limited by the great batting in front of him. Morris, Barnes, Brown, Bradman, Harvey, Hassett, Miller and Lindwall would variously, and in different combinations, build huge scores that would limit the chances for the rest of the side led by Tallon. Yet there were flashes of his 1930s brilliance. In Melbourne in the Third Test of the 1946–47 Ashes, he managed 35 and a brilliant 92. There were other sporadic reminders of his batting skills.

Lethal Lindwall

Bradman would have chosen Tallon as a keeper even if he had been a bunny with the bat. His selection at seven summed up Bradman's attitude to his batting skills, which he considered even ahead of the bowling all-rounder, Ray Lindwall, who stood at number eight. Lindwall and Lillee (at nine) were chosen ahead of a long list of fine speedsters including Jeff Thomson, Ted McDonald, Alan Davidson, Glenn McGrath and Fred Spofforth. Lindwall, all things being equal with the other candidates, would always be chosen because of his ability with the bat. He hit two terrific Test hundreds and impressed Bradman with his technical skills. Lindwall had started his career as a batsman, and was disabused of carrying on with it as his prime function by Bill O'Reilly at St George, his Sydney club. O'Reilly ordered him to open the innings and bowl as fast as he could. Raymond Russell Lindwall of the poetic, smooth run-up and action, never looked back. His batting technique always suggested he could have done more. But his importance in maintaining Australia's world dominance in Test cricket 1946–1952 was as a great opening bowler of enormous skill.

Bradman regarded Ted McDonald as the best Australian fast bowler he had seen until Lindwall came along.

'McDonald was tall and had a perfect rhythm', Bradman recalled, 'rather like Larwood after him, and Lindwall much later. McDonald had real stamina and pace. Yet he didn't rely entirely on speed. He could swing the ball, cut back to medium pace and even deliver spin. I first saw him in 1921 (in the Fifth Test of the 1920–21 Ashes) and later batted against him in 1930 when he was playing for Lancashire. He was still very quick when he wished to be. He knocked my middle stump out of the ground.'

Bradman made 9 in the first innings of that Lancashire match of mid-May 1930. In a devastating spell, McDonald, then 38, removed Archie Jackson (LBW, 19), Bradman and Vic Richardson (caught, 0) in the space of a few deliveries. Australian captain Bill Woodfull, who normally opened, sent Bradman and Jackson in to open in the second innings. They weathered the McDonald onslaught this time, Jackson making 40 and Bradman 48 not out.

After the 1948 tour, Bradman ranked Lindwall almost in McDonald's class, but thought McDonald, who was much taller, had a better bouncer because he didn't have to dig it in so short to get lift. However, as Lindwall's career progressed through the 1950s, Bradman acknowledged that his ability with the short ball was as good as anyone he had seen.

Bradman admired Lindwall's courage, and was aware of his capacity, learned from his rugby league days, to carry injuries. 'Lindwall had wonderful stamina. He could swing the ball either way, and had a nice, deceptive change of pace. Ray also had great control over line and length.'

By the end of Lindwall's career, Bradman ranked him with McDonald as the best Australian fast man he had seen. He had the advantage of having faced them both. Another factor in the choice of Lindwall was his combination with Miller. They formed one of the best fast-bowling partnerships of all time. Such links coincided with Australian Test superiority. Ted McDonald and Jack Gregory before them were a fearsome coupling in the early 1920s under Warwick Armstrong. Lillee and Jeff Thomson in the sides led by Ian and Greg Chappell in the 1970s were awesome. From 1999 into the 21st century the various combinations of Glenn McGrath, Jason Gillespie and Brett Lee were formidable in teams captained by Steve

Waugh and Ricky Ponting. (McGrath has a record that puts him at least in the same category of Australia's best ever fast bowlers.)

Bradman's Australian best ever team allowed the use of Lindwall and Miller, or Lindwall and Lillee, to open the bowling.

Lillee's emergence

Dennis Lillee emerged a decade after Lindwall. Well before the end of Lillee's career, Bradman rated him with McDonald and Lindwall. Position nine went to Lillee.

'Taking his entire career into account', Bradman said, 'he was the best paceman I ever saw. He showed enormous courage in returning from his serious back injury. Lillee was a dangerous bowler, who could both intimidate and out-think batsmen. He swung the ball both ways and had a magnificent leg-cutter.'

Lillee was one of Bradman's last official selectorial decisions in Ashes cricket. The lanky, raw young West Australian tearaway didn't let him down. Lillee took 5 for 84 in an innings in his first Test in 1970–71, and a year later turned on a performance in Perth that ranked him in Bradman's mind – after just two seasons in Test cricket – as one of the greats in history. In a Test against the World XI, he took 6 wickets for 0 runs in 13 deliveries, and ended with 12 for 92 for the match.

When Lillee made a comeback after breaking his back in 1974, he was less the demon and more the determined intimidator, who out-thought batsmen with guile, accuracy and brilliance. He went on as the world's leading speed man for another decade.

All-rounder, leader in reserve

Places 10 and 11 went to the leg-spin twins, Bill O'Reilly and Clarrie Grimmett, and 12th man went to leg-spinning all-rounder, Richie

Benaud. Bradman preferred an all-rounder as his first reserve. He narrowed the choice down to Richie Benaud and Alan Davidson, who could hardly be separated on the figures or performances over coincident careers. Bradman always looked for a 'breaking point' – an attribute such as a specialist fielding skill that gave one player the advantage over the other. In this case, it was Benaud's leadership abilities. Bradman regarded him as the best post-war captain he had seen.

Yet Benaud was a champion all-rounder in his own right. He rated highly in the line of outstanding Australian leg-break bowlers. They began with H. V. Horden and Arthur Mailey through Clarrie Grimmett and Bill O'Reilly, who all played before World War II. Benaud played in the 1950s and early 1960s, and was followed in the 1990s by Shane Warne and Stuart MacGill. Benaud was often a match-winner with the ball, most notably in England in 1961, but his aggressive batting also had its moments. In 1957–58 in South Africa he was instrumental in winning a series with two dashing centuries.

Bradman chose a strong, well-balanced Australian side with six talented batsmen, arguably the best wicket-keeper of all time, and a bowling line-up with plenty of options. The three pacemen – Lillee, Lindwall and Miller – are nicely complemented by a trio of spinners. Grimmett and O'Reilly provide two different kinds of leg-spinner, while Macartney delivers variety with orthodox left-arm finger-spin.

This team would always be hard to beat, especially with Bradman in the line-up.

England

The selection of W. G. Grace ahead of Ian Botham, named as 12th man, spinner Hedley Verity instead of Jim Laker, and the choice of early 20th century medium-pacer S. F. Barnes, were the most controversial decisions in Sir Donald Bradman's all-time best ever England team, 1877 to 2000.

The team in batting order was:

Jack Hobbs (Surrey)
Len Hutton (Yorkshire)
Denis Compton (Middlesex)
Peter May (Surrey)
Wally Hammond (Gloucestershire)
W. G. Grace (Gloucestershire, London County)
Godfrey Evans (Kent)
Fred Trueman (Yorkshire)
Alec Bedser (Surrey)
S. F. Barnes (Warwickshire, Staffordshire, Lancashire)
Hedley Verity (Yorkshire)
12th man: Ian Botham (Somerset, Worcestershire, Durham)

Bradman, once more, was looking for the best team balance. When asked why he chose Grace as the all-rounder over Botham, he said that he wanted a batting all-rounder at number six. If he had been looking for a bowling all-rounder, he would have chosen Botham over Grace.

'The first five – Hobbs, Hutton, Compton, May and Hammond – are all top-line batsmen', Bradman said, 'and Grace made up the complement of six.'

Bradman judged Grace a more effective batsman and leader than Botham. 'Many observers in England rate Grace the greatest cricketer of all time', he said. 'He was certainly the most outstanding cricketer, character and leader of the 19th century.' Bradman judged him the best captain in the England team, ahead of Hutton and May.

The comparative figures for the Test careers of Grace and Botham are:

	Tests	Runs	Average	100s	Wickets	Runs/wkt	Catches
Grace	22	1098	32.29	2	9	26.22	39
Botham	102	5200	33.54	14	383	28.40	120

These statistics don't reflect the fact that Grace was 32 years of age when he first played Test cricket. Furthermore, batting averages were much lower in the 19th century because of poorer pitches. Grace's average of 32 would be equivalent to at least 50 in the 20th century.

Their career figures in first-class cricket present more instructive comparative analyses:

	Matches	Runs	Average	100s	Wickets	Runs/wkt	Catches
Grace	878	54,896	39.55	126	2876	17.92	875 and 5 stumpings
Botham	402	19,399	33.97	38	1172	27.22	354

Once more, Grace's batting average is deflated by comparison because of the conditions but his bowling figures are also deflated (flattered) by the state of the pitches.

'The other bowlers (Trueman, Bedser, Barnes and Verity) would be selected ahead of Botham, and Grace for that matter, taking into account their speciality and importance to team balance', Bradman noted. He also pointed out that Hammond at times was a 'superb' medium-pacer, which gave England a sixth bowling option. This further off-set the need for Botham in the balance of this particular line-up.

Verity v Laker

Bradman was not inclined to leave out any of his three paceman choices – Trueman, Bedser and Barnes, which meant he could only select one spinner. He reduced his choices to either Verity or Laker.

Bradman batted against both left-arm orthodox spinner Verity and right-arm off-spinner Laker, but took into account that Laker was not at his prime during the 1948 Ashes, when Bradman faced him. Laker played in three 1948 Tests and his series figures of 9 wickets at 52.44 reflect the pasting he received.

'He was inexperienced then', Bradman recalled, 'but developed into the best off-spinner of the post-war period along with [the West Indies'] Lance Gibbs. Laker managed outstanding accuracy and control. He had a nice high arm action and could spin the ball hard.'

Laker is best known for taking a world record 19 wickets for 90 runs at Manchester in the Fourth Test of the 1956 Ashes. Bradman reported on that match where the wicket was described as 'a dustbowl, a sub-standard Test wicket, conducive to prodigious spin'. He recognised the performance as one of sustained brilliance, but ranked Hedley Verity's 15 for 104 at Lord's during the 1934 Ashes as an even more impressive effort, 'given the comparative conditions and batting strengths of the opposition'.

In 1956, Laker bowled to McDonald, Burke, Harvey, Craig, Miller, Mackay, Archer, Benaud, Lindwall, Maddocks and Johnson. This line-up on paper was deep in batting ability – everyone down to number 10, keeper Les Maddocks, and number 11, off-spinner Ian Johnson, could bat. That was on paper. They were a demoralised bunch after England had thrashed them by an innings and 42 runs at Headingley. Laker took 11 for 113. Australia lacked top quality batsmen compared to its 1934 line-up to which Verity delivered. It read: Woodfull, Brown, Bradman, McCabe, Darling, Chipperfield, Bromley, Oldfield, Grimmett, O'Reilly and Wall.

Verity took 7 for 61 and 8 for 43 on a rain-affected pitch, but Bradman concluded that 'while it was testing for a period after lunch on the final day, I played on worse pitches. Hedley bowled superbly, taking advantage of the conditions. He kept a remarkable length, and encouraged by some indifferent batting, made the ball spin and jump awkwardly'.

Bradman's decision to include Verity in his team may well have been influenced by the fact that the Yorkshireman dismissed him eight times in Tests – more often than any other bowler.

Verity took 144 Test wickets at 24.37 in 40 Tests. Laker took 193 at 21.24 in 46 Tests.

Barnes-storming

Bradman had been intrigued with the career of the dark, brooding S. F. Barnes ever since he could remember. The great English medium pacer was very much in the psyche of Australian cricketers and fans in the early part of the 20th century. Bradman was only three years old in 1911–12 in Australia when Barnes had a sensational Test series, taking 34 wickets at 22.88. And he would have been too young to appreciate the bowler's effort in the Triangular Test Series in England in 1912. Then Barnes took 39 Australian and South African wickets at just 10.35 followed by 49 wickets at 10.93 in four Tests in South Africa in 1913–1914. But at the age of seven or eight, Bradman became aware of the name Sydney Francis Barnes.

'When we played scratch "Test" matches in the schoolyard or the street, all the boys wanted to be Trumper when batting and the bowlers all wanted to be S. F. Barnes, even though he was English', Bradman recalled with amusement. 'He was very much the talk among cricketers. His performances in Australia had given him legendary status here. He was the most respected English cricketer of the so-called Golden Era before World War I.'

When Bradman began playing first-class cricket in 1927–28, the conversations he had with bowlers who had seen Barnes and batsmen who had faced him confirmed his genius. Bradman also read widely about Barnes' style, ability and record.

Barnes could deliver swing and cut, and then spin, with such cunning that few batsmen knew what was coming from ball to ball. Like O'Reilly, he was tall, long-limbed and straight-backed, and with a short, springing run-up.

Bradman concluded in 1950 that Barnes and O'Reilly were the two greatest bowlers of all time, and maintained that view for the rest of his life. Yet he could not find a place for Barnes in his best-ever World team. When asked about this Bradman replied: 'My understanding was that they [Barnes and O'Reilly] were similar in style, aggression, intelligence and abilities. Barnes was probably quicker but did not have a wrong'un [googly], which gave O'Reilly the most marginal advantage. There was not much point in having two such similar players in the one team. I could only choose one. Another point for O'Reilly [in the World Team] was his pairing with Grimmett.'

In 1938, when discussing with writer Neville Cardus the comparison between these two giants of the game, Bradman made another point, which was also in O'Reilly's favour: 'I never saw Barnes, so I could not speak of how he bowled the leg-spinner. I only know that O'Reilly bowls it as well as I can imagine anyone bowling it. It couldn't possibly be nastier.'

In Ashes Tests, Barnes had a slightly better record, taking 106 wickets at 21.58, but in an era where the conditions were better for bowlers.

Barnes was one of just two players in the three teams (World, Australia and England) chosen by Bradman whom he never saw play, which was a great compliment to his reputation and record. However, Bradman and Barnes were playing in the same English seasons in 1930, 1934 and 1938. In 1930, when Barnes was 56 and Bradman 21, the press tried to arrange a match where they played against each other. Bradman would have loved the experience, but the long, tight schedule for the Australians on tour, and Barnes in the Lancashire league, didn't allow the confrontation.

I received Bradman's best ever England team in February 1999 and late in 2000 he confirmed it had not changed.

Some features that distinguished the team were:

- Surrey and Yorkshire both produced three selections. Hobbs, May and Bedser were from Surrey. Yorkshire's three were Hutton, Trueman and Verity. Two – Hammond and Grace – played their county cricket at Gloucestershire.
- Bradman played against seven of the players chosen: Hobbs, Hutton, Compton, Hammond, Evans, Bedser and Verity.
- He did not play against the remaining five: May, Grace,

Trueman, Barnes and Botham. Two of them – Grace and Barnes – finished playing before Bradman was a Test player. The other three – May, Trueman and Botham – played after he had retired.

- Bradman never saw Grace or Barnes play. These were the only two selections he made in the three teams (World, Australia and England) that he never saw.
- Hobbs, Grace and Barnes played before World War I.
- Three players – Grace, Barnes and Hobbs – were all born in the 19th century.
- Only Botham played Test cricket during the modern era (1975 to 2000). He played his 102 Tests from 1977 to 1992.
- Grace began playing Tests in 1880 and Botham finished playing in 1992, a spread of 112 years.
- Five players captained England: Hutton, May, Hammond, Grace and Botham.
- Three players – Hutton, Compton and Hammond – performed in Tests before and after World War II.
- One player performed in the 1880s – Grace.
- One player performed in the 1890s – Grace.
- Two players performed from 1900 until 1914 – Barnes and Hobbs.
- Two players performed in the 1920s – Hobbs and Hammond.
- Five players performed in the 1930s – Hobbs, Hutton, Compton, Hammond and Verity.
- Four players performed in the 1940s – Hutton, Compton, Hammond and Evans.
- Six players performed in the 1950s – Hutton, Compton, May, Evans, Trueman and Bedser.
- Two players performed in the 1960s – May and Trueman.
- Only Botham performed after 1970.
- No player performing in the 21st century was chosen.
- Eight players hit Test centuries; five players hit doubles; and two hit triples.

A line-up of class

Jack Hobbs was one of the many fine early 20th century England players Bradman did see, but late in his career. He didn't have the force or stroke range of earlier seasons when Bradman played against him in 1928–29. Yet what Bradman saw was enough to convince him that Hobbs was one of the game's greats. He had emerged as a Test player early in 1908, the year Bradman was born, and nearly a decade after Grace had bowed out at the top. It was a suitable time for someone to wait before challenging Grace's dominance of the game in England. Hobbs, a taciturn, low-key character, was a contrast to the forceful Grace, yet he was to develop as a batsman of greater quality. Bradman, ever the detective looking for clues concerning a player's technical faults, observed Hobbs (then aged 46 to 48) at close quarters in 14 matches, including 10 Tests, in 1928–29 and 1930. He branded him without any deficiencies at all. He ranked him technically the best batsman he ever saw.

Bradman found his choice of the other opener, Len Hutton, similarly faultless with footwork, stroke-play and shot production, yet believed he could have been more aggressive in his approach. Bradman thought less of batsmen who were intent on keeping the ball out of their stumps and not giving a catch than those who had a forceful way whenever they were at the wicket. He always believed it was necessary to take the initiative from bowlers, set a mood and pave the way for team-mates to follow.

The Don scorned 'stodgy' play. It left the bowlers in charge and 'fellow batsmen in the dressing-room with an air of gloom'.

Bradman noted that Hutton eschewed the hook if bowlers tried to tease it out of him, but found him a good hooker when he wanted to use it. Hutton's dour character, lightened by a whimsical sense of humour, was too much in evidence at the crease for Bradman's liking, yet he recognised him as an outstanding cricketer.

Hutton achieved much in his career. In 1938 he made 364 at the Oval against Australia, and surpassed Bradman's record of 334 made in 1930 – two records that still stand in Ashes cricket. Hutton was the first professional to regularly captain England, and the man who won back the Ashes in 1953, and successively defended them in Australia in 1954–55. He was also the first professional to be elected to the Marylebone Cricket Club before his career finished and the second (after Jack Hobbs) to be knighted for his services to cricket.

His main challenge for this position was from an equally dour fellow Yorkshireman, Herbett Sutcliffe, the one-time partner for Hobbs in the actual England team.

'He performed far better than he looked', Bradman remarked. 'He was more at home against pace than spin, but he managed to work his way through against spin with courage. He played one of the finest ever innings on a sticky at Melbourne in 1929.'

Bradman played in that game, which England won by 3 wickets. The opening stand by Hobbs (49) and Sutcliffe (a chanceless 135) of 105 was arguably the best ever partnership in Test cricket on a rain-affected pitch. It set up an unlikely victory when England was set 332 to win.

Sutcliffe was a fine hooker and scored more from the on-side, which was perhaps a consequence of being a batsman brought up on wet wickets in England's north. He wasn't keen on the drive and preferred pushes and edges through slips and gully. It irritated spectators at times, but he could point to the scoreboard, where more often than not he was piling on the runs for his county or England.

In 27 Ashes Tests, Sutcliffe scored 2741 runs at the excellent average of 66.85, the second best average in Ashes history (Bradman averaged 89.78 from 5028 runs in 37 matches) for anyone playing in at least 20 games. Hutton, also in 27 Tests, scored 2428 runs at 56.46, while Hobbs averaged 54.26 from 3636 in 41 encounters against Australia.

Master Compton

Bradman described his choice for the number three spot in the England side – Denis Compton – as a 'glorious natural cricketer' and regarded the Middlesex champion as a master batsman, despite his occasional unorthodoxy.

'His left elbow does not always please the purists', Bradman wrote in *Farewell to Cricket* [Hodder & Stoughton, London, 3rd edition 1952], 'and in some respects his stroke production is not up to the standard of other masters.' Bradman thought he had a good cover drive, although he didn't rank it with that stroked by Wally Hammond. He liked Compton's daring in playing the sweep and his other improvisations, which some incorrectly saw as imperfections. Bradman thought he had a weakness against the short ball after the 1948 series and put it down to indecision over how to play it – either by getting his back foot across in the technical prescribed position to hit it, or by a more 'stand-and-deliver' pull shot. However, that assessment was made when he had to face Lindwall and Miller, who peppered him with head-high bouncers. Then he won some or lost some, mainly because of inexperience in facing such a lethal delivery, at least as sent down by these two intimidators. Bradman considered that later in Compton's career he was more circumspect in playing the shot and more selective in his counter-attacking.

'He had another characteristic capacity common to all the masters', Bradman added. 'He played the ball late and had time to do it.'

Compton was a poor runner between the wickets. Trevor Bailey noted that 'a call from Denis was merely the basis for negotiation'.

Compton, barring injury, was an automatic pick for England from 1938 to 1956, and in the late 1940s was the most attractive of all the country's batsmen. At times Hutton, an almost exact contemporary, and later Peter May, were regarded as more effective batsmen, but Compton's aggressive yet cheerful and carefree demeanour at the crease made him one of the most attractive crowd pleasers of all time. Compton, who was also capped for England in soccer, was the superstar drawcard of his day.

His only rival for the coveted number three spot in England's team was left-hander David Gower, whom Bradman also regarded as one of the great natural talents in the history of the game. Bradman enjoyed watching Gower and ranked several of his innings highly, particularly his 123 at Sydney in 1990–91 and his 157 at the Oval in 1985. Gower scored 8231 Test runs at 44.25 and made 18 centuries.

May be the best

Peter May, the choice at number four in the batting order, super-seded Compton as England's leading batsman by the mid-1950s. His polish and style was accompanied by a temperament that pulled England, Surrey and Cambridge University out of many a predica-ment. Perhaps his best 'hour' in this respect came at Melbourne in the Second Test of the 1958–59 Ashes when he arrived at the crease with the score at 3 wickets for 7. Alan Davidson, swinging the ball prodigiously with his long left arm, had England on the ropes under low cloud. May weathered the conditions and the brilliant bowling and went on to a century.

'May was the finest batsman in arguably the best and most balanced line-up England ever put in the field', Bradman said, refer-ring to England's 1956 team. Its batting order through the Ashes series, which Bradman covered as a journalist, included Peter Richardson, Colin Cowdrey, David Shepherd, May, Tom Graveney, Cyril Washbrook and Denis Compton.

May, at 183 centimetres, was broad-shouldered and had strong forearms. Blessed with excellent timing, he was a superb driver, especially through mid-on.

Hammond's edge

Behind him at number five in the batting order was Wally Hammond, whom Bradman regarded as the best England bat produced from 1928 until World War II. Hammond, according to Bradman, was the most majestic and graceful cover drive of all, whether on the back or front foot. His athletic build allowed him to deliver shots with timing and power. Hammond was balletic in his movements. He used his dainty feet to advantage, learning all the steps back and forward from the great Charlie Macartney on Australia's tour of England in 1926.

'There probably was never a more balanced player than Wally', Bradman said.

Hammond was Bradman's biggest rival over the decade 1928–1938. Hammond, aged 25, on the tour of Australia in 1928–29, out-gunned the Test tyro Bradman, aged 20, in their first Ashes encounter – but Bradman was never 'beaten' again over the next six series. Honours were even during the Bodyline series of 1932–33, although considering England captain Douglas Jardine's tactics, Bradman – with a marginally superior average (56.57 to 55.00) – could claim to have done better, especially when his team was soundly beaten 4-1.

Bradman noted two areas to work on when attempting to deal with Hammond. One was his reluctance to hook or pull when 'bounced' or attacked with short deliveries. The other was no attacking on-drive. But these were minor deficiencies in an otherwise near-perfect technique. Bowlers could only work on them, hoping to force an error. The only factor that could beat such a champion was brilliant bowling. Leg-spinner Clarrie Grimmett delivered this in 1930, and gained a psychological hold on Hammond. Bill O'Reilly, on occasions, also challenged him with his exceptional skills – but that was it. No paceman ever really had his measure.

Bradman also noted that Hammond was, at times, a talented medium-pace bowler. 'He was most dangerous when he failed with the bat', Bradman said. 'He liked to have some success, one way or another, in every game he played. If he had concentrated on his bowling I believe he would have been bracketed with the best medium-pacers in history.'

Hammond took 83 wickets in Tests at 37.80. In first-class cricket he took 732 wickets at 30.58.

Grace and other favourites

Number six in Bradman's all-time line-up was W. G. Grace, himself an attacking bat, who would have stood up as a 'great' in any era. The best known images of him were of a portly man, but his physique was not done justice to by the development of the camera. When he was 20 in 1868, there was no more athletic cricketer than the good doctor, yet there were few photographers around to show future fans his lean, fit figure. He was a sprinter and could throw a cricket ball 120 yards (110 metres), which was further than anyone else in the UK.

Evans above all others

When I received Bradman's handwritten letter containing his all-time England team, I at first had a little trouble deciphering who he had picked at number seven. I rang him, congratulated him on a 'work of art', and said that I wished to check who he had at number seven.

'Is it Godfrey Evans at number seven?' I asked.

Bradman replied sharply: 'He'll bat where his captain tells him to!'

'I'm not questioning his position in the order. It's just that I'm not sure of your handwriting.'

'Yes', Bradman said, 'it's Evans.'

Godfrey Evans, the wicket-keeper, was a stocky extrovert. This man from Kent was a character with flair, who took advantage of his showmanship. He stumped with a flourish and caught with movements that reminded onlookers of a Catherine wheel. Bradman, as ever, chose the keeper for his ability behind the stumps rather than his capacity to keep and bat.

'Evans was both spectacular and safe', Bradman said. 'On occasions when Australia amassed huge scores, he hardly let a bye go through, which demonstrated his skill and concentration. [Alan] Knott and [Les] Ames were better batsmen, but Evans was the superior keeper. I also rank George Duckworth highly as a keeper, despite his raucous appealing!'

Bradman recalled that Duckworth was so deft down the leg-side that Australian batsmen refused to glance in case he caught them. Bradman also spoke of Bert Strudwick, a Surrey and England keeper from 1902 to 1927, but never saw him play. Some English experts ranked him above all others.

Their figures read:

	Tests	Runs	Average	Centuries	Dismissals	Catches	Stumpings
Evans	91	2439	20.49	2	219	173	46
Knott	95	4389	32.75	5	269	250	19
Ames	47	2434	40.56	8	97	74	23
Duckworth	24	234	14.62	–	60	45	15
Strudwick	28	230	7.93	–	72	60	12

The truest paceman

Bradman regarded Yorkshire's Fred Trueman, at number eight, as the best England fast bowler ever. 'Fred Trueman was England's pace bowler with the lot', he remarked, 'fire, courage, guile, pace, line, length, swing and cut. I don't think any batsman I saw was comfortable against him in his prime.'

Trueman began as a blustering tearaway, but when his career settled he emerged as a master bowler who could lift for the big occasion, especially in Ashes contests. In 10 consecutive seasons he took 100 or more first-class wickets, including 175 at 13.98 in 1960. Again at this level, Trueman took four hat-tricks, 10 or more wickets in a match 25 times and 5 wickets or more in a match 126 times. His 307 Test wickets at an outstanding 21.57 took just 67 matches. Trueman was a hard-hitting tail-ender, who usually had a dip at the bowling. His swashbuckling leg-side affronts with the blade got him three centuries, but none in Tests. He was a brilliant natural fielder, specialising at short-leg.

His biggest challenger as England's best paceman came from Frank Tyson, who in 17 Tests had the remarkable figures of 76 wickets at 18.56. He was the fastest bowler England produced. During the second innings of the third Ashes Test at Melbourne in 1954–55, Tyson delivered what Bradman regarded as the quickest spell he ever saw in a Test. Tyson skittled Australia, taking 7 for 27. He took most wickets in the series, won by England – 28 at 20.82. Injury cut him down in his prime.

Another bowler with an impressive record was Bob Willis, who in 90 Tests took 325 wickets at 25.20 and finished his career in 1984.

Bradman was not as impressed with Harold Larwood, the speed demon of the Bodyline series, as many would expect. He pointed to the statistics, that show Larwood took just 31 wickets in Tests at 41.29 apart from the 1932–33 series. Larwood's only other Ashes in Australia (1928–29) yielded 18 wickets at 40.22, when Bradman had no trouble with him in his debut Tests for Australia. In 1930 in England, Bradman particularly – and other Australian bats – put him to the sword. Larwood then took 4 wickets at 73.00. In the 1932–33 Ashes, when he came to prominence armed with bodyline tactics, he managed 33 wickets at 19.52. In all, Larwood bowled in 21 Tests and took 78 wickets at 28.35.

In *Farewell to Cricket* (Hodder & Stoughton, London 1952 edition) Bradman spoke of Larwood's 'notoriety' during the Bodyline series and thought almost any of the leading fast bowlers could have achieved this using similar methods.

In their tussles, Larwood dismissed Bradman four times during Bodyline, and unsettled his normally dominant rhythm against the English attack. Larwood's effort won the Ashes for England. Bradman ranked medium-fast Ken Farnes as a superior bowler because he moved the ball off the wicket better. He took 60 Test wickets at 28.65.

Smart Alec Bedser

Alec Bedser was Bradman's choice at number nine. He also chose him in his World team and placed him ahead of all other medium-pacers, even Maurice Tate. Bradman personally found Bedser a more difficult opponent than Tate in England but added the proviso that he (Bradman) was at his prime as a batsman when he faced Tate, and in his declining years when he faced Bedser.

'Alec had a dangerous leg-cutter, which was really a fast leg-break', Bradman observed. 'He also had a brilliant in-swinger that dipped late. I always had problems with it.'

Bradman was dismissed six times by Bedser. The Surrey star had the world's greatest batsman ever five times in succession from the final Test in Melbourne of the 1946–47 season and the first two Tests of the 1948 season in England. Bedser squeezed four catches from him close on the leg-side when his late-dipping in-swinger was employed.

Bradman admired Bedser's never-say-die attitude, and his physical toughness. Bedser never left the field from injury in his 51 Tests.

S. F. Barnes was slotted in at number 10, and Hedley Verity at number 11 added some spin variety to a formidable six-man attack. Ian Botham, as 12th man, was an outstanding slipper.

He was England's 'warrior' all-rounder, who took on the Australians at their own aggressive game. His medium-fast bowling record ranked him with the best in England's history. Botham could also be formidable with the bat. He would invariably attempt to dominate bowlers from the first deliveries he faced in an innings, and was a key factor in winning big games with adventurous batting that thrilled spectators.

Postscript

It's pure speculation to consider whether or not Bradman would have changed his mind six years after his original selections, which held at the end of 2000.

For Australia, the continued success of Gilchrist as a keeper/batsman would have pressed a claim for the keeper's spot. But I don't believe Bradman would have changed his mind. He regarded Tallon as the best keeper he ever saw. Ponting, Hayden and McGrath would have had increased claims for selection. Warne would have been very tough to resist. It's possible that Bradman would have considered swapping Grimmett for Warne, especially as he bracketed Warne with Grimmett and O'Reilly – meaning he really couldn't separate them – in 1995. A decade on, Warne had become an even better bowler.

For England, only one player, Flintoff, could challenge for a spot. The one place for him was as an all-rounder. Yet it's highly unlikely that Bradman would have considered dumping Grace for Flintoff, especially as he had already left out Botham for Grace.

Bradman was the greatest cricketer to play the game and, coincidentally or otherwise, he had a sharp and brilliant mind to go with his skills. His team choices are unique records of one exceptional individual's view – the perceptions of a genius of the game.

BRADMAN: MAN OF LETTERS

One of the more poignant symbols of the Don's passing (February 2001) is the end of the incredible flow of letters to and from his Kensington Park, Adelaide home over nearly seven decades. By Bradman's own conservative calculation he received five million letters and responded to more than a million of the 'sensible' ones. He grumbled about the mail, yet you always felt he had a passion for his correspondence. Don preferred the crisp letter to the even crisper phone call. He would reply, make his point and move on. There was never a superfluous thought. Humour and observation were frequent and he enjoyed maintaining this dying art of communication.

'I've got a pile of mail you couldn't jump over', he told me on his 90th birthday. Was he pleased or complaining? Probably both. These letters reflected his fame, about which he often scoffed. They also represented his longevity against the odds. Every year was a bonus after he turned 25 when, on the 1934 Ashes tour of England, he was operated on for peritonitis that was expected to finish him. In the end, the life of this diminutive, hard-headed survivor spanned almost the entire 20th century. From an Australian sporting perspective, it will go down as his. Certainly, he attained an almost royal elevation, and was afforded easy access to prime ministers, community and business leaders, the media and members of the public.

Apart from the amazing sporting achievements that set him apart, what was the real Bradman character? Before I started his biography,

I had heard rumours: he could be blunt; he didn't suffer intelligent people gladly, let alone fools. I was warned that he wouldn't cooperate with Dean Golja – the photographer who accompanied me – for more than five minutes on the first day of interviews at his Adelaide home on that hot February day in 1995. Were any of these stories accurate, or just the usual myths about a famous individual? We arranged the interviews through the mail, and had yet to meet.

I hired a car. If Dean were 'dismissed' after a few minutes at Bradman's house he could explore Adelaide while the interview went on. Lady Jessie Bradman, then 85, radiant and courteous, greeted us at the front door with the disconcerting news that 'Don' had a toothache. Dean glanced at me. Would this mean it would be even tougher for him to steal a few shots? Lady Bradman showed us into the famous living room with its emphasis on floral furniture and decorations. Seconds later, Bradman appeared in casual attire.

His physique was taut with sinewy, strong forearms – the limbs that had thumped a cricket ball more often per innings and with more timing and power, pound for pound, than any other cricketer.

'What do you want?' he said in that familiar, nasal voice as he opened his hands to us, indicating he was at our disposal. There was something world-weary about him. Yet that was about the extent of his display of irritation about more 'publicity', which was his term for all media attention. We sat on the lounge suite in front of the imposing portrait of him above the mantlepiece.

There was portent in the story behind that picture. Bradman liked it the moment it was unveiled years ago. Former Test cricketer and friend, Arthur Mailey, also at the unveiling, leaned across to him and whispered that the legs were too long. Bradman agreed. He later had a restorer lop off the offending limbs below the knee. The painter's signature at the bottom of the painting was placed at the top. The message was clear. Better not to be the sensitive artiste when dealing with the Don. I began by speaking about the questions I had sent him in advance. I had kept them innocuous in case I put him off before we were face to face.

'They were corny', Bradman remarked.

Dean proceeded to take around 400 photographs from many angles over the next six hours as the interview proceeded. So much for the warnings about photographers. The Don was oblivious of the ubiquitous camera capturing him in the longest portrait session he ever allowed. Dean secured what was required. I did not want an old man in repose, as interesting as such impressions can be. The aim was to portray him as he approached 90 years – intellectually vigorous, humorous, pensive, thoughtful and with powers of concentration that would put any monk to shame.

Dean later sent 'The Don' some of the shots. He wrote back a polite letter with the comment: '. . . I return herewith what I consider to be the worst four'.

You could take this as bluntness or refreshing directness. Whatever, it sat well with his integrity, for which he said he wanted to be remembered above all. The Don should have no fear. Writer Raymond Chandler said honesty is an art. The Don had it down to a fine art.

English cricket writer Sir Neville Cardus once described a Bradman innings thus: 'It was never uninteresting; he simply abstained from vanity and rhetoric'. Such were his responses to hundreds of questions I put to him on that first day and over the ensuing five months. His answers were buttoned-down, logical and without a misplaced syllable. Allied to his succinct use of the language was an obsession with accuracy, which bordered on eccentricity. Australian Cricket Board staff would often send him written information for comment or approval. The Don would send some letters back. The request would be ignored; instead, there would be grammatical corrections scribbled in the margins.

I was thankful for his humour. For a few seconds here and there his impassive, impenetrable visage would transform into George Burns, sans cigar:

Q: How would you go against the recent crop of great West Indian fast bowlers? What would your average be?

A: About 50.

Q: Fifty? Why 50? That's half your actual average . . .

A: Well, I will be 88 next birthday.

Q: Could you give instances of critical moments where Lady Bradman was a great support to you . . .

A: Critical? She's always critical.

Q: Recent media reports have listed you as being a suitable choice to fill the role of first president of an Australian Republic in 2001. How do you feel about that?

A: I'll be 93 in 2001. I might be getting a bit old to run the country, don't you think?

Q: How did you keep fit as a youngster?

A: I chopped a lot of wood.

Q: Modern top cricketers do a lot of training to keep fit: weights, sprints, distance running, callisthenics, diet and so on. How did you keep fit as a first-class cricketer?

A: I did a lot of running between the wickets.

***

The first interview session went an hour over the allotted time. I decided The Don had been too generous and called a halt.

'I enjoyed that', he said with a grin as he bounced off the sofa. 'Dean, would you like more shots?'

Moments later, The Don lost his balance. He swung his arms trying to right himself. Dean, standing close, hurled himself onto the sofa. Bradman fell backwards but right into Dean's hands.

I couldn't help remarking: 'Well caught, Dean!'

We moved to the front garden with Bradman a little unhappy about this minor show of frailty. Dean tried to get him to smile. He wouldn't. Dean appealed silently to me. I stood behind The Don and tried a joke.

'Just think, Sir Don, you'll be able to tell your grandchildren you were photographed with one of Australia's great writers.'

The Don loosened up enough for Dean to capture him smiling. Lady Bradman joined us on the front porch for the best photos taken of her in her twilight years. They caught her eternal beauty and grace.

***

I completed the Bradman biography in 1995 with countless other interviews, usually over the phone. The Don would send me helpful items – even some of the more bizarre letters he received from around the world, names and addresses withheld.

Journalists would send him his obituaries for approval. Not surprisingly, he hated these reminders of his mortality. People treated him as a mythical figure, more public property than human being.

During the 2000 Olympics, a rumour spread like wildfire through the Olympic village that Bradman had died. The director of the Bradman Museum at Bowral, Richard Mulvaney, had a string of calls asking if it were true. Mulvaney rang Don. His housekeeper answered the phone. 'He bounded down the stairs and out to do some shopping', she told him. 'Seemed fit as a fiddle.'

'When?'

'An hour ago.'

Mulvaney had to sweat over whether something had happened in the streets of Adelaide. I was also rung about the rumour. I phoned Bradman a few hours after Mulvaney had called him. He answered in that familiar nasally tone. I had a legitimate question for him that had nothing to do with his alleged demise. But Bradman knew of the rumours.

'I'm pretty sure I'm still here', he said with a rueful chuckle. 'But the rumours have to be right some day, don't they?'

Bradman wasn't thrilled about this, but his dry humour warded off depressing feelings caused by intermittent reminders of his mortality.

He recalled an eight-year-old writing to him and saying: 'I'm sorry it has taken so long to write to you, but I'd always regret it if it was too late.'

Bradman wrote back: 'Not half as much as I would'.

He remembered a 10-year-old who wrote to him with: 'I've been wanting to write to you for a long time, but my grandfather says you're dead. But recently my father told me you were alive. I'm writing to find out the truth.'

Bradman wrote to me about one obituary writer and remarked: 'His rationale for sending it to me was that he wanted me to know in what high regard I was held BEFORE I died, not afterwards. Strange how the minds of some people work.'

Bradman responded to the writer: 'My death has been reported prematurely on two occasions, once when it was announced in a North Queensland paper that I had succumbed to a bout of dysentery and once when I was hovering near death in a London hospital in 1934 after an operation for appendicitis. Now I'm sure you won't be surprised to know that I received your epistle with little enthusiasm. I had a close call in November [1994] when I had a serious throat operation but, having survived that, I hope your obituary won't be used for quite a while yet . . .'

That said, Bradman reverted to his pedantic form: 'You refer to my "padding a golf ball against the surface of a corrugated iron tank". Not so. I threw the ball against the circular brick tank stand (about 18 inches [46 centimetres] high) on which the tank rested.'

The writer could take heart from the fact that he wasn't alone in this error. The *Encyclopaedia Britannica* has him hitting a 'soft ball against a corrugated metal water tank'.

Bradman's reply to this writer added: 'You then refer to me "bouncing the ball off the twisted palings of a backyard fence". In fact I threw the ball at the rounded rail to which the palings (on the other side) were nailed.'

***

Fame and longevity had developed this extended, macabre 'death-watch'. He did everything to avoid publicity after he retired from cricket in 1948. His pet hate was being recognised and asked for an autograph. Even when he was 90, people would stop their cars when he was walking to shops near his home and ask him to sign something. In their twilight years, he and Lady Bradman would drive out of Adelaide and check in at hotels under an assumed name. It was one of the better times of their married life.

'Once (on a trip to Bowral for the opening of the Bradman Museum) we actually checked in and weren't recognised', he told me with undisguised glee. In 1996 he was picked up in his car by radar doing 72 kmh in a 60 kmh zone. The policeman didn't recognise him until Bradman showed him his licence.

'It's an honour and a privilege to meet you', the policeman said.

Bradman replied: 'Well, I'm very sorry I can't say the same to you.'

The policeman wrote him a ticket for A$173.

Bradman laughed about it and bore no grudge, realising that the officer was only doing his duty. That was Bradman's way if there was nothing personal in an incident.

His unwanted position as the tallest of tall Australian poppies created bitterness from some towards him. Yet I could only recall one individual whom he openly disliked. He would instead say, on the odd occasion, that a person was 'not my favourite' cricketer, politician or journalist. Bradman was well aware of those who had slighted him, but would not be drawn on his deeper attitude to them. He once wrote to me that Michael Parkinson 'hated his guts' for not being interviewed by him on TV, claiming that he wrote pieces about him with the odd 'barb' thrown in. The barbs seemed more like goads to draw Bradman onto the set. It was a pity they never got together. Frank Sinatra and Bradman were the two people Parkinson regretted not interviewing.

All prime ministers – from Billy Hughes in the 1920s on – had glowing things to say about Bradman, and he got on well with most of them. He liked Menzies, supported some aspects of Hawke–Keating fiscal management and appreciated John Howard's approach to running the country. It wasn't just because they were all cricket lovers. Bradman admired good fiscal managers who kept the Australian economy sound. As a successful stockbroker, investment adviser and company director, he knew what he was talking about. Like many of his generation, his attitudes were coloured, too, by his experience of being thrown out of work during the Depression. Bradman often wrote unsolicited advice to Reserve Bank governors. He was concerned about issues such as keeping inflation in check.

***

That world-weariness we encountered at the beginning of our first interview was replaced by keen interest as the research and writing for *The Don* progressed. I spent time poring over the *Wisden* year books at the MCC library at the MCG. Several times Bradman offered to look things up in his own set of *Wisden*. (He had one of only two private sets in the world.) This saved me much labour. I asked him to find the first recorded cricket match where Harold Larwood and Bill Voce applied the full force of bodyline. It occurred in a county game between Nottinghamshire and Northamptonshire in August 1929.

Bradman enjoyed helping me find such incidents. At the end of the project he asked if he could read the book, which was not part of our original arrangement. We had agreed that it was to be 'unauthorised'. No one would interfere with the editorial.

'I only want to check the manuscript for factual errors', The Don explained. I agreed, having come to know him as not precious about fair criticism. I sent the book overnight to him. A day later, I received a phone call. He had read it – all 250,000 words. What's more, he had typed notes – four pages of them – of comments and mistakes. I was stunned. In my experience, no editor had ever been through a sizeable manuscript so fast. Of course, he knew the terrain. It was his life. Yet his attention to information he had never seen before was remarkable. He asked if I could make another trip to Adelaide to discuss it. I arrived a few days later. Anticipating Lady Bradman's hospitality, I brought flowers. Don greeted me at the door at 9.30 am.

'Oh, thanks a lot', he said, reaching for the flowers.

'They're for Jessie.'

'Oh', he said. 'Why doesn't anyone ever bring me flowers? They're always for Jessie.'

The Don led me upstairs, past his favourite portrait of himself executing a cover drive, and into the inner sanctum – the Bradman study. A cricket library featuring those *Wisden* year books dominated it. We sat opposite each other at a card table, each with a copy of the manuscript, and began sifting through his 80 points. I was relieved to find he had mainly picked up literals and typing errors. He made no reference – as anticipated – to the 'editorial' that considered his character and style.

'. . . Now, point 14, you have me going out to bat at Leeds flanked by two bury policemen', he said looking over his glasses at me like a benign schoolmaster. 'You mean burly, don't you?'

The Don loved a malapropism: 'Point 24. You've got here that I "did it for prosperity". You mean posterity, don't you?'

He was reminded of a dinner party he had attended where a barrister was 'pontificating' about how well he cornered witnesses in the box.

'He said he liked to go for the jocular', Bradman said. 'He meant jugular and he wasn't joking.'

We began slicing through the manuscript, stopping for coffee mid-morning and a scotch in the living room at noon. By now The Don's amazing recall was coming into play. He was certain that he had hit his first run ever in his maiden innings at Lord's, in 1930, to mid-off. I had it rolling to mid-on. He asked for my sources. I produced three. He squinted into the distance of 65 years and with unbombastic certitude described the shot, and who ran across from where to field it.

'I remember it particularly', he said. 'It was my first Test run at Lord's.'

There could be no argument.

Bradman's Test average of 99.94 or, rounded off, a century every time he went out to bat, was well known. Unknown was his average from the time he first played competitively at 11 years until his first full season of cricket at 16 years. I checked several sources and came up with 166, an indication for anyone who had cared to check his efforts by 1923 that the Boy from Bowral might just be extraordinary. The Don, point 35, questioned this.

'I think you've given me one too many innings', he said, indicating a particular match for Bowral when he was 14. Again, the question: 'What are your sources?' The Don listened. Unconvinced, he stood up, wandered over to his library and pulled out a tiny 1922–23 scorebook. He was correct, once more. We made our recalculations and arrived at the same figure, which will one day make a trivial pursuit question – 187. A more testing question for sporting buffs would be Bradman's schoolboy average. The answer? He didn't have one. It stood at infinity. He was never dismissed in a school match. (This fact caused other schools to avoid playing Bowral High if Bradman were selected to play against them. He was just too good and made any contest one-sided.)

The Don also queried the position of one hit made in his record as the fastest century maker in any game of cricket anywhere in the world. Bradman had moved from 54 to 154 off 22 balls in just 12 minutes in a 1931 match between a combined Blue Mountains team and the Lithgow Pottery Cricket Club. He noticed that in the three (then eight-ball) overs he took to score the runs, I had one scoring shot in incorrect sequence. The list of shots was 6,6,4,2,4,4,6,1 (first over, 33 runs); 6,4,4,6,6,4,6,4 (second over, 40 runs); and 6,6,1,4,4,6 (third over, 27 runs).

There was method in his exceptional attention to detail. The Don was a perfectionist in everything he did. Cricket just happened to be his first choice of sport. At age 40, when he retired from cricket, he turned his formidable mind to golf. Within weeks he had ironed out the cricket movements that produced the greatest shot range the game has seen, but which made it difficult to hit low golf scores. The result was the rhythm of a professional golfer, still with a few cricketing chinks, breaking par at every course he played.

Bradman's approach was always to apply his mind to any sport's rules and parameters, and to use his physical agility and gifts to play as well as he could. It's not surprising that his book, *The Art of Cricket*, first published in 1957, is still the finest instructional work on the game. Having studied the game as if he were taking a Masters degree, The Don then reduced it to its basics in demonstrating how it should be performed.

This total command of his chosen sport has given him outstanding vision. He showed this early in his career when comparing baseball with cricket in a discussion with American star baseballer, Babe Ruth, in 1931. Ruth wanted to know what impressed The Don about the American game. The reply surprised him. The Don thought the skill levels were comparable. It was the professional presentation of baseball that attracted him. He predicted cricket would have to be better marketed to survive. Forty years later, it was The Don who introduced one-day cricket to Australia when a Melbourne Test match against England was washed out during the 1970–71 Ashes series. The concept alarmed purists, but not him. He saw it as a necessary accessory to keep the game popular and financial. However, he was myopic over the issue of cricket becoming professional. Bradman, of the old amateur school, believed that sportsmen should have real jobs away from their 'games'. But changes and more demands on cricketers meant that it was impossible for players to travel the world representing their country while maintaining their families.

***

As ever, Lady Bradman's great hospitality was evident at lunch on that final day of reviewing *The Don*. She and their housekeeper prepared a three-course lunch, complete with excellent wines.

Bradman enjoyed a drink. In retirement, he had long buried his wowser image of the 1930s. Once, when Jessie left the room during the meal, he told a mildly risque farm joke. I can't recall it exactly. It had something to with servicing a sow. The convivial atmosphere elicited glimpses of Don, the country boy.

During the breaks we relaxed and discussed issues other than cricket. The Bradmans proved to be a well-informed couple on everything from politics to the republican debate. Bradman and I coasted through the remaining points in the manuscript in the afternoon, and discussed many things including Lady Bradman's health. She had suffered for years from chronic leukaemia. The Don's deep love and respect for her courage and character came up, as it had in several previous discussions.

'She'll be telling people how well she feels on the day she dies', he said. There is no doubt that her strength sustained him through thick and thin, and the Bradmans' long relationship saw plenty of the latter, especially in health matters concerning them and their children.

We discussed 'fame' and how it had destroyed others – from sportspeople to entertainers such as Elvis Presley. The Don had held onto his small-town, family values no matter with whom he mixed, which strengthened rather than diminished his character and being. He felt for Boris Becker who would not be able to visit any country without being recognised. Tennis stars, more than cricketers, could hide nowhere.

I asked him if he had his time over again would he want fame.

'No', he said emphatically. 'I hate it.'

Despite The Don's heartfelt disdain for the limelight he could never escape it. Something in the Bradman mystique has lingered over most of the 20th century. Those letters kept pouring in from all over the world after he retired from cricket in 1948. The flow increased through the decades to a peak in the late 1990s. Each recipient of a response would probably place the letter among his or her most treasured documents, creating a strong Bradman constituency in itself.

Add to that perhaps another 20 million items from bats and balls to books and portraits that he signed over 70 years – all held dear by their owners and passed on through generations – and there is a mighty Bradman supporter base that will linger for centuries yet. It helps explain why The Don maintained his fame and affection out there.

***

That memorable day with the Bradmans ended with more scotch and coffee in the evening followed by another three-course meal, and more wine. A taxi arrived. The Don thumped the car's bonnet in a last gesture of farewell. As we drove away, the driver asked: 'Was that who I thought it was?'

I only needed to say 'Yes'.

Discussions over the book didn't end there. I had shown The Don my choice of the front cover photograph. Lady Bradman liked it. He was more circumspect, but didn't object. I had chosen a non-cliched shot of him waiting to bat at age 20 in a Shield game for NSW when he scored a triple century. His casual cross-legged stance and enigmatic gaze spelt both cool determination and pensiveness. It was a look that meant despair and disaster for a thousand bowlers. I judged it out of 1500 photos as the most telling portrait of Bradman, the great competitor.

The Don had other ideas. When the book's editor at Pan Macmillan, Amanda Hemmings, sent him a copy of the cover, he wrote to her complaining that his cricket attire needed a clean-up, he was wearing a NSW jacket and he appeared 'gloomy'. I rang Don and explained my choice, saying his pads could be air-brushed. Further, the fact that he was wearing a NSW blazer was irrelevant. Everyone who knew his name associated it first with representing Australia. I argued that rather than gloomy he looked determined. Having had many discussions with him, I realised when he was unconvinced. The conversation would be punctuated by pregnant silences.

'What's more the editor [Amanda Hemmings] said you look sexy', I said as a last resort.

'She's 50 years too late', he quipped. It was the argument-breaker. The photo was in. That wry wit, which kept him sane through an eternity of adulation and attacks, was always lurking.

Early in November 1995 Jessie's chronic leukaemia worsened. Bradman wrote to me: '. . . the most awful tragedy has occurred in that Jessie is in hospital with terminal cancer. My life is at an end and I just cannot explain my devastation and grief . . . A partnership of over 70 years is ending and really a chapter in Australian life and history. It is so sad and unfair that this wonderful lady should suffer in this way.'

Another letter of further poignancy followed in which Bradman said: 'Life without Jessie would be meaningless for me and I can only pray that medical skill and prayers will do the trick . . .'

I decided not to bother him with news about the book but a week later I realised that Bradman was interested in what kind of publicity it generated. He sent me a note: 'A friend told me he heard your interview with Philip Satchell (ABC radio Adelaide). Regrettably, I missed it. But I am told you handled Satchell with aplomb and put him in his place. I must confess he is not one of my favourite interviewers'.

After that I sent him reviews, good and bad.

Bradman responded: 'I am surprised that the criticism has been so poorly written. In the days of [English critics] Robertson-Glasgow and Cardus one could be carved up with style and panache. They could write.

'At least you haven't yet had my experience with an Indian journalist who converted my refusal to give him an interview into a full-page "exclusive" article in his Indian paper. In varying degrees I have been taking it on the chin for over 60 years. It's not funny.'

There was always the odd miserable hack willing to make a spurious attack on The Don. It would usually get published. After all, he was the tallest poppy Australia ever had. Despite 'taking it on the chin', there were times when Bradman hit back. Business executive Bob Mansfield was once told by Bradman to fire the writer of a pernicious piece. Mansfield agreed that the article was bad and said he would have obliged him if he could. But the writer didn't work for Fairfax anymore.

Around Christmas 1995, Bradman had a stroke. He didn't tell me at first. But his writing was shaky. That definitive signature was barely recognisable. Within two months, he was fighting to come to terms with the physical set-back: 'I am afraid the publicity surrounding the book has brought an avalanche of requests for signatures and other things but I am immune because it has been going on for 50 years. Currently the big problem is of course my stroke which has prevented me attending to mail etc but thankfully I've had good secretarial support.

'Worse than this however is the terrible worry over Jessie. She is standing up to her chemo remarkably but it is cruel and if this is the price she has to pay for keeping alive one wonders if it is worthwhile. Old age is not funny.'

In March 1996 Kerry Packer visited Bradman in an effort to persuade him to be interviewed by the Nine network. Bradman had never granted a commercial TV interview in the 40 years of the medium in Australia. He had rejected approaches by several personalities, including Bob Hawke on *60 Minutes* (when he had TV aspirations after he left politics), Ray Martin on various programs, and Mike Munro on *This is your life*. They had offered record amounts of money, but Bradman said *nyet* to all of them. He couldn't be bought.

But necessity was the mother of opportunity, if not invention. About A$1.2 million was needed to complete the building of the charitable Bradman Museum Trust at Bowral. Mulvaney and Kerry Packer were brought together, and it was decided that the Nine network, courtesy of Packer, would raise the money in exchange for Bradman being interviewed on the show. This would circumvent the need to offer Bradman money to appear. It was a generous offer by Packer, given the differences between him and Bradman, which had arisen during the World Series Cricket crisis. Yet still Bradman had to be persuaded. Packer flew to Adelaide and was entertained at lunch at the Bradman home.

'Who would you like to do the interviewing?' Packer, the experienced salesman, asked. 'You can have anyone you like.'

'Ray Martin', Bradman replied. When he rejected Martin earlier he told him that if ever he did a TV interview, it would be with him.

Bradman wrote to me about the interview: 'I agreed most reluctantly and it was a terrible ordeal for me – especially coming so soon after I had had this wretched stroke, but Ray Martin was wonderful to work with'.

***

I wanted to write a newspaper account of how Packer secured the interview for his Nine network. The meeting and rapprochement between Australia's richest man and the country's most famous individual seemed like a good story. I rang Bradman. He hit the roof.

'That was a private meeting', he 'roared' in that piping voice of his. 'I'm not telling you anything. Packer won't tell you anything, so how are you going to write the story?'

At that moment my mobile phone rang. I excused myself, answered it and then came back to Bradman, with apologies.

'How many phones have you got?' he asked.

His fear was not so much that I would provide detail of the meeting. He worried about the avalanche of mail he would receive after the article appeared. His amazing self-imposed obligation, which bordered on addiction, to respond to what he called the 'sensible' letters, meant he would have much more to do than his usual four hours and 80 letters a day once the article appeared.

Bradman at no point demanded that I didn't publish the article. That wasn't his style. My source was Bob Mansfield, who was present at the meeting with Packer. After that article appeared I didn't write anything else about Bradman except in updated editions of *The Don*. Of course, it didn't matter. The mail – several hundred letters a day – still poured in. Mention of Bradman would occur in papers here or abroad every day. He was, and always will be, a measuring stick for all sporting achievement. A journalistic cliche is that 'so and so' is 'the Bradman' of ping-pong or horse training or two-up.

The man himself never understood why there was constant attention on him. He wished it would all go away, but it never did. As English cricket writer E. W. Swanton wrote, Bradman 'has been, if any man ever has, a victim of his own fame'.

***

Early in 1997 I tried to persuade Bradman to have some of his letters published in book form. But he would have none of it.

In September 1997, Lady Bradman died aged 88 and Don went into his shell. He was shattered. In several phone chats Bradman remarked that 'life wasn't worth living without her', and 'I've nothing to live for'. This was not meant to engender sympathy. Bradman was simply stating the facts as he saw them.

Early in 1998, the Becker Film group and I began discussing a film on Bradman's life. The Museum was supportive, but Don was ambivalent. He worried about the further run of 'publicity' a cinema release would bring. I tried to talk him around and reached the point where he said he would 'think about it'.

I began writing a script. Then I received a note from Bradman about an unrelated issue. At the end of the letter he said: 'I hope you don't go ahead with the film idea. In my brief time remaining on earth I was hoping for a period of rest and privacy'.

When he put it in those terms, I couldn't go on with the project. I rang him, then Becker, to say I was pulling out.

Now Australia has lost one of its greatest sons. It's sad to think there will be no more phone calls and no more mail in that familiar scrawl from a friend of uncommon brilliance. However, like probably 99.94 per cent of all recipients of those million or so letters Bradman wrote, I'll be keeping mine for posterity.

ACKNOWLEDGEMENTS

There are many people to acknowledge and thank for information, interviews and photographs when covering so much Ashes cricket history. They include Martin Ashenden, Colin Beames, Jan Beames, Sir Alec Bedser, Eric Bedser, Tamara Bell, John Bradman, Bev Friend, Diana Georgeff, Jack Grossman, Neil Harvey, Greg Hodgson, Thos Hodgson, Sam Loxton, Lady Pippa O'Brien, Larry Maddison, Tony Maylam, Rod Mater, Norman May, John Miles, Arthur Morris, Richard Mulvaney, Christian Peterson, Peter Philpott, Keith Stackpole, James Sutherland, Max Walker and Ian Woodward.

Thanks on the eighth occasion to publisher Jane Palfreyman, and to editor Brandon VanOver.

Roland Perry
May 2006

PHOTO CREDITS

The author and publisher gratefully acknowledge Newspix for permission to use the pictures captioned *I am Freddie, hear me roar*; *Bad luck, mate*; *Oh, what a feeling (of relief!)*; *You talkin' to me?*; *My ball, Michelle*; *The great cricket fan*; *The revolutionary Mr Packer*; *Happy Hookes*; *'That ball'*; *Warnie the thespian*; *Two Australian greats*; *The corkscrew*; *Mark the Spark*; *Even Steve*; *The Flying MacGilla*; *Trapping the Don*; *Bradman the bowler*; *The corkscrew*; *Miller delivers*; *King Arthur*; *Brain and brawn*; *Lyrical Lillee*.

Thanks to Getty Images for permission to use the pictures captioned *Nice one, Dennis* and *Explosive Botham*.

Thanks to *The Herald & Weekly Times* Photographic Collection for permission to use the pictures captioned *The 19th century's finest*; *Half-dressed, still best*; *Bradman the bowler*; *Murdoch takes block*; *'Well bowled, Harold'*; *Jardine's straight bat*; *The Master*; *Brotherly love*; *Brightly writes the Don*.

INDEX

Boycott, Geoff 148, 263, 264
Boyle, Henry 89, 94, 106, 109
    Ashes 1888 94
    English Test 1882 106, 109–12
    MCC v Australia 1878 89
Bracks, Steve 301
Bradman, Sir Donald 2–4, 14, 30,
    145–71, 201, 260, 320, 325–401
    apartheid issue 217–31, 325–6
    Ashes 1920–21 (spectator) 349
    Ashes 1930 30, 133
    Ashes 1932–33 132–41
    Ashes 1934 155, 371
    Ashes 1936–37 142–3, 165, 166, 256
    Ashes 1938 165, 183
    Ashes 1946–47 209, 215
    Ashes 1948 166, 167, 370
    Ashes 1953 (commentator) 143
    Australian Cricket Board member
      160, 218, 244
    batting record 145–8
    batting technique 156–9, 203
    best-ever Australian team 345–68
    best-ever English team 360, 368–84
    best-ever team 331–44
    Bodyline TV drama 281, 282
    Bodyline used against 132–44, 382–3
    Botham compared 256
    captaincy 45, 165–70, 321
    Centenary Test 1977 227, 231
    character 149–53, 209–16, 385–401
    competitiveness 163
    courage and determination 155–6
    death 143, 385
    death of Jessie 401
    Engel's best-ever team 339
    giants of the *Wisden* century 131
    golf 161–2
    Grace compared 145
    Greig and Ackerman meeting 326–7
    impact on cricket 103, 325
    intelligence 171

    interview with 386–9
    knowledge of cricket 159–60
    leadership 165–70
    letter-writing 330, 385
    Mandela's admiration for 223–4, 326
    Miller compared 209–16
    natural athleticism 160–2
    1926–27 season 350
    1936–37 season 364
    1948 'Invincibles' 354
    other cricketers, opinion on 164
    other sports 161–3
    Packer meeting with 252–3, 399–400
    peritonitis 162
    portrait at Lord's 173
    son John, relationship with 217–24
    South Africa Test 1931–32 134
    stockbroking career 154, 218, 392
    stroke 399
    Test average 394
    Wisden cricketer of the year 340
    World Series Cricket, reaction to 244,
      245, 252–3, 329, 348
    World XI Series 1971 326–7
Bradman, Lady Jessie 135, 163, 214,
    219, 222, 224, 386, 388, 391, 393,
    395–9, 401
Bradman, John 217–24
    anti-apartheid views 217–21
    children 224
    Miller's funeral 174
    name change 222–3
Bradman Museum 151, 216, 389, 391,
    399
Bradman's Best 325, 331–44
Bramall Lane, Sheffield
    Third Test 1902 120
    Victory Test 1945 189–92
Braund, Len 118, 123
Brearley, Mike
    Ashes 1977 263
    Ashes 1978–79 250